Learning to Teach Modern Foreign Languages in the Secondary School

A companion to school experience

Second edition

Norbert Pachler and Kit Field

RoutledgeFalmer
Taylor & Francis Group

LONDON AND NEW YORK

First published 2001
by RoutledgeFalmer
2 Park Square, Milton Park, Abingdon, Oxon OX14 4RN

Simultaneously published in the USA and Canada
by RoutledgeFalmer
270 Madison Ave, New York, NY 1006

Reprinted 2002, 2003 (twice), 2004

RoutledgeFalmer is an imprint of the Taylor & Francis Group

Typeset in Bembo by
HWA Text and Data Management, Tunbridge Wells
Printed and bound in Great Britain by
TJ International, Padstow, Cornwall

British Library Cataloguing in Publication Data
A catalogue record for this book is available from the British Library

Library of Congress Cataloging in Publication Data
Pachler, Norbert
    Learning to teach modern foreign languages in the secondary school :
a companion to school experience / Norbert Pachler and Kit Field.–
2nd ed.
        p. cm. – (Learning to teach subjects in the secondary school series)
    Includes bibliographical references and index.
        1. Languages, Modern–Study and teaching (Secondary) I. Field, Kit.
    II. Series.

PB35 .P13 2001
418′.0071′2–dc21   00-051823

ISBN 0-415-24020-4

Dedication

A la memoria de José Ramon Redondo Gallego (1916–1999), hijo de Montiel, madrugador y amigo de la caza y de insaciable afán de saber, de deshacer agravios y de enderezar entuertos.

Si no eres par, tampoco le has tenido;
Que par pudieras ser entre mil pares;
Ni puede haberle donde tú te hallares
Invicto vencedor, jamás vencido.

Orlando Furioso a D. Quijote

Contents

Introduction to the series

This, the second edition of *Learning to Teach Modern Foreign Languages in the Secondary School*, is one of a series of books entitled Learning to Teach Subjects in the Secondary School covering most subjects in the secondary school curriculum. The books in this series support and complement *Learning to Teach in the Secondary School: A Companion to School Experience* (Capel, Leask and Turner, 1998, 2nd ed.), which addresses issues relevant to all secondary teachers. These books are designed for student teachers learning to teach on different types of initial teacher education courses and in different places. However, it is hoped that they will be equally useful to tutors and mentors in their work with student teachers. In 1997 a complementary book was published entitled *Starting to Teach in the Secondary School: A Companion for the Newly Qualified Teacher* (Capel, Leask and Turner, 1997). That second book was designed to support newly qualified teachers in their first post and covered aspects of teaching which are likely to be of concern in the first year of teaching.

The information in the subject books does not repeat that in *Learning to Teach*; rather the content of that book is adapted and extended to address the needs of student teachers learning to teach a specific subject. In each of the subject books, therefore, reference is made to *Learning to Teach*, where appropriate. It is recommended that you have both books so that you can cross-reference when needed.

The positive feedback on *Learning to Teach*, particularly the way it has supported the learning of student teachers in their development into effective, reflective teachers, has encouraged us to retain the main features of that book in the subject series. Thus, the subject books are designed so that elements of appropriate theory introduce each behaviour or issue. Recent research into teaching and learning is incorporated into this. This material is interwoven with tasks designed to help you identify key features of the behaviour or issue and apply these to your own practice.

Although the basic content of each subject book is similar, each book is designed to address the unique nature of each subject. In this book, for example, the unique contribution of modern foreign languages to the linguistic, social and cultural development of pupils is highlighted, as is the development of communicative competence on the basis of linguistic awareness. The second edition takes account of changes to the National Curriculum and to the way teachers are trained.

We, as editors, have found this project to be exciting. We hope that, whatever the type of initial teacher education course you are following and wherever you may be following that course, you find that this book is useful and supports your development into an effective, reflective modern foreign languages teacher.

Susan Capel, Marilyn Leask and Tony Turner
October 2000

Illustrations

TABLES

FIGURES

ACTIVITIES

Contributors

ABOUT THE AUTHORS

Norbert Pachler is a Senior Lecturer in Education at the Institute of Education, University of London, with responsibility for the Secondary Postgraduate Certificate in Education (PGCE) in Modern Foreign Languages (mfl) and the MA in Modern Languages in Education. His research interests include all aspects of mfl teaching and learning, comparative (teacher) education, as well as the application of new technologies in teaching and learning. He has published widely in these fields. In 1999 he edited *Teaching Modern Foreign Languages at Advanced Level* and co-edited *Learning to Teach Using ICT in the Secondary School*, both published by Routledge. More recently he has contributed to *Issues in mfl teaching* and the *Encyclopedia of Language Teaching and Learning* also published by Routledge. He holds a Dr phil degree, has taught in secondary and further education and has worked for the inspectorate and advisory service of a local education authority on curriculum development and in-service training. Norbert is currently joint editor of the *Language Learning Journal*.

Kit Field works as a Principal Lecturer at Canterbury Christ Church University College, where he is currently Director of Continuing Professional Development. He previously was Lead Professional Tutor on the PGCE Secondary programme and Deputy Director (Curriculum) for the Secondary PGCE programme. Kit qualified as a teacher in 1982 following degree studies at the University of Warwick and a PGCE course at the University of Exeter. In 1995 he gained an MA in Curriculum Studies from Canterbury Christ Church University College. Kit has published in the fields of mfl teaching and learning as well as subject leadership, mentoring and Office for Standards in Education (OfSTED) inspections. He is joint author of *Effective Subject Leadership* and editor of *Issues in Modern Foreign Language Teaching*, both published in 2000 by Routledge.

CONTRIBUTORS

Jo Bond studied at Oxford University, holds a Masters Degree in French and German and has been teaching modern foreign languages to a wide ability range at Key Stages 3 and 4 and to 'A' level in West Midlands secondary schools since 1986. Amongst others

Jo held the post of Modern Languages Co-ordinator. Jo was involved in the development of the Graded Objectives in Modern Languages (GOML) scheme in the West Midlands and produced Key Stage 3 material in French and German including a series of readers. Jo also created cartoons for several Centre for Information on Language Teaching and Research (CILT) Network publications and wrote a chapter on grammar for the CILT title *Aus eigener Erfahrung: von GCSE bis 'A' level*.

Roswitha Guest is Head of German at Whitton School, Twickenham, where she has taught German (and French) since 1991. She also taught English as a Foreign Language (EFL) for a number of years to adolescents and adults. She has a BA (Hons) in Psychology, European Literature and Art, a PGCE in mfl (German and French) from King's College, University of London, as well as an Royal Society of Arts (RSA) qualification for Teaching English as a Foreign Language (TEFL) from International House, London.

Ana Redondo is currently Curriculum Manager for Modern Languages in a London comprehensive school and is interested in a wide range of issues in education and initial teacher education (ITE) in general and the teaching and learning of mfl in particular. Ana has been working as a mentor with various higher education institutes (HEIs) and has been involved in a number of (inter)national projects and in-service education and training (INSET) provision with various local education authorities (LEAs). She has written stories for the teaching of Spanish and she contributed on mixed ability teaching to *Issues in Modern Foreign Language Teaching* published by Routledge in 2000.

Acknowledgements

Our approach to mfl teaching and learning has been influenced by a wide range of people: pupils, colleagues, educators and students as well as trainees with whom we have worked over the years and who have helped us in formulating and testing out our hypotheses. As it is impossible to thank them all individually, we would like to take this opportunity to acknowledge their formative influence on our thinking. We also thank our colleagues who have contributed.

Our particular thanks, however, goes to our families whose forbearance, support and encouragement made this book possible.

Acknowledgement is also due for and to the following:

- three former PGCE students for allowing us to include extracts from their personal logs;
- Jonathan Day for his case study on e-mail use;
- Naomi Fletcher for her task sheet 'Finding out about Fontainebleau';
- Chantal Fourey-Jones, Kate Green and Jan Thomas for their ideas on reflection activities;
- Colin Philpott for permission to include a unit of work from his department;
- Cathy Pomphrey for permission to include her ideas on teaching learning strategies;
- Carmel Fung at the School Curriculum and Assessment Authority for providing useful statistics;
- QCA for permission to reproduce an extract from the non-statutory guidance;
- Guilde-Buchhandlung Carl Kayser for permission to include material by Harald Seeger;
- Editions Gallimard for permission to reproduce Jacques Prévert's poem: *Déjeuner du matin*;
- Michèle Deane for permission to include her diagram 'Downward spiral'; and
- Mechtild Hommelsheim-Bart and colleagues for the multi-skill continuous assessment task.

Abbreviations

A	Advanced
ACCAC	Curriculum and Assessment Authority for Wales
ALL	Association for Language Learning
APL	accreditation of prior learning
AQA	Assessment and Qualifications Alliance
AS	Advanced Subsidiary
ATL	Association for Teachers and Lecturers
ATs	Attainment Targets
CALL	computer-assisted language learning
CEP	Career Entry Profile
CILT	Centre for Information on Language Teaching and Research
CLT	communicative language teaching
CMC	computer-mediated communication
CPD	continuing professional development
DES	Department of Education and Science
DfE	Department of Education
DfEE	Department for Education and Employment
EC	European Community
EFL	English as a Foreign Language
ERA	Education Reform Act
ESOL	English for Speakers of Other Languages
EU	European Union
FL	foreign language
FLA	foreign language assistant
FLTeach	Foreign Language Teaching Forum
GNVQ	General National Vocational Qualification
GOML	Graded Objectives in Modern Languages
GTC	General Teaching Council
HEIs	higher education institutions
HMI	Her Majesty's Inspector

ICT	information and communications technology
IEP	Individual Education Plan
INSET	in-service education and training
IQ	intelligence quotient
ITE	intitial teacher education
ITT	intitial teacher training
LEAs	local education authorities
LLB	Languages Lead Body
LMS	local management of schools
LNTO	Languages National Training Organisation
MARRA	monitoring, assessment, recording, reporting and accountability
mfl	modern foreign languages
NAGC	National Association for Gifted Children
NALA	National Association for Language Advisers
NC	national curriculum
NCC	National Curriculum Council
NFER	National Foundation for Educational Research
NLS	National Literacy Strategy
NLS	National Language Standards
NQTs	newly qualified teachers
OCR	Oxford, Cambridge and RCA Examinations
OfSTED	Office for Standards in Education
OHP	overhead projector
PGCE	Postgraduate Certificate of Education
PoS	Programme of Study
PPP	presentation-practice-production
PSHE	personal, social and health education
QCA	Qualifications and Curriculum Authority
QTS	qualified teacher status
RSA	Royal Society of Arts
SCAA	Schools Curriculum and Assessment Authority
SEN	special educational needs
SENCO	special educational needs coordinator
SMSC	spiritual, moral, social and cultural
TEFL	Teaching English as a Foreign Language
TES	*Times Educational Supplement*
TL	target language
TTA	Teacher Training Agency
TVEI	Technical Vocational Education Initiative

Prologue

CAVEAT MAGISTRA!

Modern foreign languages (mfl) teaching, with the aim of helping pupils achieve some proficiency in a foreign language and enjoy their mfl learning, can be very rewarding. Trying to open the horizons of pupils to how people from foreign countries communicate with each other and live is an exciting challenge. An mfl teacher can be the catalyst for a curiosity in young people for foreign cultures and people, broaden their horizons and help them overcome negative stereotypes they might hold. Through their mfl learning experience pupils may also gain a better understanding and a different perception of themselves.

Amongst many other things, mfl teachers need to be imaginative, creative, patient, outgoing, enthusiastic and very well organised in order to be a successful. Teaching is a highly complex task; teaching mfl even more so. It requires, for example, the management of pupils, the classroom and resources, interpersonal skills, subject and professional knowledge or the ability to empathise with young people. Mfl teachers need to plan well, regularly try out new ideas, cater for the needs of and differences in individual pupils, make learning challenging and enjoyable, assess pupils' learning regularly, evaluate their actions constantly and adapt to an ever-changing educational context.

There are a number of challenges facing mfl teachers that trainees[1] need to be aware of on starting their course of initial teacher education (ITE), as these can have a profound impact on their work, for example:

- the status of mfl in society and the media in the UK;
- the perception of mfl being a difficult subject;
- the importance of memorising as well as the ability to recall a large number of linguistic items;
- the importance of understanding and being able to use new linguistic structures to generate (unique) utterances;
- the comparatively limited opportunities for real-life use of mfl skills in the UK;
- the highly conceptual nature of the subject matter;

- the necessity of good general communication and social interaction skills;
- the use of the target language (TL) as main means of classroom instruction and interaction; or
- the constraints resulting from pupils' invariably limited linguistic means in the TL compared with their conceptual understanding, world knowledge and cognitive development aged 11+.

Becoming an effective mfl teacher requires a commitment to keep up with new developments in the field as well as a willingness to engage in continuing professional development and to challenge sometimes deeply held personal views on what constitutes effective mfl teaching.

ABOUT THIS BOOK

Our perspective on mfl teaching and learning is based on our own experience of teaching pupils, students and trainee teachers, in-service education and training (INSET) and curriculum development work, dialogue with colleagues nationally and internationally as well as reflections on the ideas expressed in the scholarly work of practitioners and researchers. Consequently, the aim of the book is to help the reader progress in her professional development by providing stimuli for discussion, reflection and evaluation of a wide range of good practice.

In this book we aim to address the perceived tension between theory and practice. The book is *not* intended as *a prescriptive set of rules* on how to teach nor as a collection of 'tips for teachers' but instead as *a framework for mfl teaching based on an understanding of pertinent theoretical issues, possible approaches, strategies and examples* to help trainees learn to teach mfl effectively.

The book is primarily aimed at mfl trainees on a programme of ITE and it is under-pinned by one main premise, namely the need for an aspiring mfl teacher to develop a *personal approach to mfl teaching*. Whilst the content of mfl teaching is prescribed in many ways in the form of statutory frameworks and requirements as well as examination specification (formerly syllabuses), the 'art' of mfl teaching lies in choosing the most effective and appropriate methods to develop in pupils the relevant knowledge, skills and understanding about the TL and culture(s) and to maximise their learning. This is why the ability in mfl trainees to make personal professional judgements is so important. Mfl trainees learn a lot from observing and working with mfl teachers in schools and/ or teacher educators during the course of their ITE. This book is aimed to support this learning process.

We hope that the book will also be useful to mentors and tutors who work with mfl trainees and provide an overview for them to some of the most important issues mfl trainees tend to cover during their ITE.

The text is designed to allow the reader to 'pick and choose' chapters and refer to specific topics at any one time rather than read the book from cover to cover.

Each chapter features the following sections:

1   introduction: offers a brief contextualisation of the topic;
2   objectives: identify what the reader should know, understand and/or be able to do having read the chapter and carried out the activities in it;

3   discussion: investigates the most important theoretical and practical issues of a topic, gives examples of classroom application and activities invite the reader to reflect on the content of the chapter and relate it to her work in school are included. Wherever possible trainees should record their work on the reflection activities in a personal 'journal' as these reflections can yield very useful evidence against the standards for newly qualified teachers (NQTs). Wherever practicable trainees should try to discuss findings with peers, their mentor and other colleagues as well as their (HEI) tutor(s); and

4   summary: emphasises the key points in a chapter.

Individual examples in the book are given in one modern foreign language, either in French, German or Spanish, as these are the main mfl taught in secondary schools in the UK. Most of the examples, we hope, are transferable to other languages.

Whilst it is intended that the content of the book applies across the range of mfl taught in secondary schools, this book is primarily concerned with general methodological considerations. No systematic discussion of pertinent, language-specific issues can be provided in the space available, for example how to address the possible difficulties pupils may have with the correlation of the spoken and the written word in French, the inflectional tendencies of the German language and its comparatively flexible word order or differences in scripts/alphabets/writing systems. These issues may occasionally be touched upon in the practical examples given. For language-specific issues, other resources and publications need to be consulted.

Because of the many differences particularly in teaching methods, the issues involved in post-16 mfl teaching are dealt with separately in an Epilogue. Our primary concern in this book is with the teaching of mfl at 11–16. In the Epilogue we examine some of the most important issues concerning mfl teaching at post-16, but do not attempt to cover this complex area in detail. This is done in a separate, complementary book edited by one of the authors of the current title, Norbert Pachler, entitled *Teaching Modern Foreign Languages at Advanced Level* and published by Routledge in 1999. Also, a number of the issues raised in this book are examined in greater detail in another complementary book edited by the other author of the current title, Kit Field, entitled *Issues in Modern Foreign Language Teaching* and published by Routledge in 2000.

In order not to make the style of the book too unwieldy and to avoid formulations such as 's/he' or 'his/her', we use the feminine form generically when referring back to – what could be called – the 'natural' gender of nouns like 'the pupil', 'the teacher' or 'the mentor'. Only the term 'mfl department' is used in this book when referring to teams of mfl teachers although schools may also be organised on a faculty basis etc.

SECOND EDITION

In this second edition of *Learning to Teach Modern Foreign Languages in the Secondary School* we take account of important recent changes to (the statutory) requirements governing the teaching and learning of mfl in the secondary school since it was first published in 1997. These include the publication in 1999 of a new mfl National Curriculum (NC) for England, changes to examination requirements at GCSE and A level, the introduction of the National Literacy Strategy, the findings of the Nuffield Languages Inquiry, the publication of a new framework for initial teacher education (DfEE Circular 4/98) and the introduction of new induction requirements for newly qualified teachers (NQTs).

For ease of reference and space we refer to the statutory framework for England only throughout the book. This should only have a negligible impact for readers training and/or working in other parts of the UK and beyond, as they can easily substitute references to the statutory requirements for England with those applying to their own contexts. References to the statutory requirements for England tend to be used for contextualisation and exemplification purposes of generic principles and frameworks.

We have restructured some of the content of the book in line with constructive suggestions received from trainees, colleagues and reviewers. There are now separate chapters on the teaching of grammar and cultural awareness. Also, a discussion of classroom management has been included. We have updated all chapters and have included references to new insights gained from research, personal professional experience and background reading. In particular, the chapter on the use of information and communications technology (ICT) has been revised considerably in the light of recent developments in the field and the requirements of Annex B of DfEE Circular 4/98.

The book is now accompanied by a comprehensive website and some online tutorial material, written and maintained as well as regularly updated by Norbert Pachler and hosted by the Institute of Education, University of London. The website, which contains all web addresses referred to in this book and many more, can be accessed at *http://www.ioe.ac.uk/lie/pgce/*. Whilst every effort has been made to ensure all internet addresses (URLs), as well as all other information, included in the book are correct at the time of going to press, readers should note that they are liable to change frequently given the provisionality of the internet. We will make every effort to ensure changes and new developments are reflected online.

We would be delighted to hear and receive feedback from our readers about the usefulness of the materials and ideas contained in this book. To this end, we have set up an online message board accessible from the main page of the website accompanying this book in the section 'ICT recourses', where readers can post messages and exchange ideas with other readers. Those readers who would like to contact the authors directly should send an e-mail to *norbert@languages.zzn.com* with their comments.

NOTE

1   The term 'trainee' rather than 'student teacher' is used in this book to describe teachers in training in recognition of the multiplicity of routes into teaching.

1   Introduction

In recent decades the teaching and learning of modern foreign languages (mfl) in secondary schools in the UK has witnessed a number of important developments. Teaching and learning methods have gone in and out of fashion and there have been considerable innovations in the field of educational technologies. In addition, many changes have occurred in the wider educational context. All of these impact on pupils' learning experiences.

In this chapter we consider the rationale behind teaching and learning mfl in the secondary school, examine which mfl should be studied as part of secondary education and give an overview of the statutory framework governing mfl teaching and learning.[1]

OBJECTIVES

By the end of this chapter you should:

- be aware of the rationale and purposes of mfl teaching and learning in the secondary school curriculum today;
- be able to appreciate the benefits of offering a diversity of mfl as part of the secondary school curriculum;
- be aware of the findings of the Nuffield Languages Inquiry and the implications of the National Literacy Strategy; and
- have gained a basic understanding of the statutory framework for England as well as the GCSE criteria for mfl.

MFL IN THE SECONDARY SCHOOL CURRICULUM – RATIONALE AND PURPOSES

The rationale and aims for the study of mfl in the secondary school curriculum are very similar throughout the UK and beyond.

One important *reason* for the study of mfl as part of the secondary school curriculum is the recognition that it has an important role to play in terms of contributing to the personal, social, cultural and general linguistic development of pupils in preparation for their adult lives, both for work and leisure. This is explicitly reflected in the 1999 mfl NC Orders:

> For example, MFL provides opportunities to promote:
>
> - *spiritual development,* through stimulating pupils' interest and fascination in the phenomenon of language and the meanings and feelings it can transmit
> - *moral development,* through helping pupils formulate and express opinions in the target language about issues of right and wrong
> - *social development,* through exploring different social conventions, such as forms of address, through developing pupils' ability to communicate with others, particularly speakers of foreign languages, in an appropriate, sympathetic and tolerant manner, and through fostering the spirit of cooperation when using a foreign language to communicate with other people, whether other learners or native speakers
> - *cultural development,* through providing pupils with insights into cultural differences and opportunities to relate these to their own experience and to consider different cultural and linguistic traditions, attitudes and behaviours.
>
> (DfEE/QCA 1999a: 8)

Very important in our view is the provision of what Eric Hawkins calls an 'apprenticeship in foreign language learning' (Hawkins 1987: 282), the development of a foundation in pupils for future mfl learning by arousing in them a curiosity for and an interest in learning (about) foreign languages and cultures. As such, the study of mfl 'exposes learners to new experiences and enables them to make connections in a way which would not otherwise be possible, and this in itself deepens their understanding of their mother tongue' (DES/Welsh Office 1990: 3).

In addition, mfl learning, like other subjects of the secondary curriculum, is very valuable in teaching young people important transferable skills such as working with reference material, e.g. dictionaries, and other skills such as (inter)personal skills, study skills or problem solving, equipping them for their working lives and providing them with the skills base required by employers. Indeed, the 1999 mfl NC Orders list a number of opportunities for promoting so-called key skills through mfl:

> For example, MFL provides opportunities for pupils to develop the key skills of:
> - *communication,* through developing their awareness of the way language is structured and how it can be manipulated to meet a range of needs, and through reinforcing learning in specific areas such as listening, reading for gist and detail, and using grammar correctly
> - *application of number,* through talking and writing about the time and measures in the target language, and carrying out conversions about distances and currency

- *IT,* through using audio, video, satellite television and the internet to access and communicate information, and through selecting and using a range of ICT resources to create presentations for different audiences and purposes
- *working with others,* through developing their ability to participate in group conversations and discussions
- *improving own learning and performance,* through developing their ability to rehearse and redraft work to improve accuracy and presentation, and through developing learning strategies such as memorising, dealing with the unpredictable, and using reference materials
- *problem solving,* through developing their ability to apply and adapt their knowledge of the target language for specific communication purposes.

(DfEE/QCA 1999a: 8)

Mfl learning can be seen to be instrumental in preparing pupils for life in present-day multi-cultural Britain and Europe. Mfl have a valuable contribution to make to the wider school curriculum in terms of cross-curricular themes but also as a focus for extra-curricular activities. The former is exemplified in the 1999 mfl NC Orders, the latter is examined in detail in Chapter 8:

For example, MFL provides opportunities to promote:

- *thinking skills,* through developing pupils' ability to draw inferences from unfamiliar language and unexpected responses, through enabling pupils to reflect on the links between languages, and through developing pupils' creative use of language and expression of their own ideas, attitudes and opinions
- *financial capability,* through knowledge of different currencies and exchange rates
- *work-related learning,* through opportunities to cover work-related contexts within the topic of the world of work.

(DfEE/QCA 1999a: 9)

From a national economic point of view the argument has repeatedly been put forward that – in the current context of competitive international economic activity – the UK, as a trading nation, urgently needs a work force with competence in mfl (see e.g. DES/Welsh Office 1990: 4). When wanting to sell goods to customers abroad the fact that English is the international lingua franca is insufficient. The business world is in the process of globalisation both in terms of national businesses increasingly operating in an international context and in terms of multi-national companies establishing themselves firmly on the national scene. Pupils might well find themselves one day in a work situation requiring them to operate in a modern foreign language in the UK. It could, indeed, be argued that it is this national economic concern that has become more important than any other in justifying the place of mfl in the secondary school curriculum. Whereas in 1988 a DES/Welsh Office policy document for England and Wales talks about the fact that 'the study of foreign languages can help to serve both individual needs and the needs of the country' (DES/Welsh Office 1988: 2), the 1993 Dearing Report on slimming down the NC makes specific reference to the economic argument:

> We must assume that today's school children may need to pursue part of their career in any part of the world. Britain's economic prosperity will also depend increasingly on our relationships with our trading partners in both Europe and the wider world.
>
> (Dearing 1993: 3)

Equally, the fact that revenue from tourism makes a major contribution to the country's gross national product, should be an important incentive to study mfl.

A 1987 HMI discussion paper proved to be very influential in laying the foundations for the current rationale for mfl teaching and learning for England. It influenced the so-called Harris Report (DES/Welsh Office 1990), which still provides a useful point of reference and delineates the following *purposes* for mfl teaching in the secondary school:

- to develop the ability to use the language effectively for purposes of practical communication;
- to form a sound base of the skills, language and attitudes required for further study, work and leisure;
- to offer insights into the culture and civilisation of the countries where the target language is spoken;
- to develop an awareness of the nature of language and language learning;
- to provide enjoyment and intellectual stimulation;
- to encourage positive attitudes to foreign language learning and to speakers of foreign languages and a sympathetic approach to other cultures and civilisations;
- to promote learning of skills of more general application (e.g. analysis, memorising, drawing of inferences);
- to develop pupils' understanding of themselves and their own culture.

(DES/Welsh Office 1990: 3)

These purposes for mfl teaching and learning in the secondary school build largely on *the tenets of communicative language teaching* (CLT), which has been the prevailing approach to mfl teaching since the 1970s. Its most important characteristics are briefly summarised by Johnstone (1988: 12):

- an increase in the amount of foreign language used for everyday classroom and personal purposes;
- the introduction of functions (asking for, offering, refusing etc.) and general notions (food, hobbies, time, travel etc.) as constituents of a language syllabus, in addition to grammar, vocabulary and situations;
- a gradual move beyond course-books as sole or even principal determiners of the language syllabus and towards the use of authentic texts and other personalized inputs selected by teachers and pupils themselves;
- an extension of group, paired and individual activity, to complement whole-class work;
- the gradual introduction of information-exchange, based on role-play and simulation, and to a lesser extent of practical skills activities ... and of communication games;

- the introduction of assessment, in many cases related to graded objectives, for purposes of 'diagnosis' and of 'formative evaluation'.

A detailed discussion of CLT and its implications for mfl teaching methods can be found in Chapter 3.

The emergence of CLT to some extent went hand in hand with the inclusion of mfl, predominately French, in the curriculum of many comprehensive schools, which were established in the wake of the reform of secondary schooling from the mid-1960s onwards. The move away from grammar translation towards communication skills is a reflection of the wider range of ability and motivation of pupils studying mfl: 'None of the foreign language teachers down the ages ... ever had to face the challenge that we face: they never met, in their classes, more than a select minority of quite able learners' (Hawkins 1994: 109).

As a consequence of the widening in the ability and motivational range of learners in the 1980s a large number of mfl teachers began to focus in their work on graded objectives, i.e. short-term, achievable learning targets that were assessed at regular intervals with a view to enhancing learners' motivation and their sense of achievement. These objectives mainly centred around language skills required for communicating in seemingly authentic situations.

Prior to the introduction of the GCSE a sizeable number of pupils studying mfl from the age of 11 tended to opt out at 14 leaving in the main the more able and better motivated pupils to continue their study of mfl to 16. Tables 1.1 and 1.2 show how the number of pupils entering for GCSE examinations and achieving grades A*–C has risen steadily since the introduction of the GCSE. Implicit in this growth is a widening of the ability range of pupils studying mfl.

Table 1.1 Percentage gaining grades A*–C in GCSE French, German, Spanish and Italian from 1988–1995 (Grade A* was introduced in 1994)

Year	French % grade (A*–C)	French Number of candidates	German % grade (A*–C)	German Number of candidates	Spanish % grade (A*–C)	Spanish Number of candidates	Italian % grade (A*–C)	Italian Number of candidates
1988	49.82	269033	54.67	76320	56.80	19125	76.02	2890
1989	53.25	256737	56.92	80456	59.38	21091	74.82	2991
1990	49.27	280890	59.48	84306	61.17	24870	77.62	3901
1991	45.99	304587	58.38	91277	61.02	27406	75.44	4369
1992	46.92	322653	56.28	101388	60.03	29468	74.78	4937
1993	48.53	319642	57.13	108398	59.63	32145	74.83	5978
1994	49.44	328306	58.53	118985	58.37	36335	75.16	5479
1995	50.00	350027	54.99	129386	58.51	40366	77.99	5610

Source: SCAA

Table 1.2 Percentage gaining grades A*–C in GCSE French, German, Spanish and other mfl 1997 and 1998

Year	French % grade (A–C)	French Number graded (A*–U)	German % grade (A*–C)	German Number graded (A*–U)	Spanish % grade (A*–C)	Spanish Number graded (A*–U)	Other mfl % grade (A*–C)	Other mfl Number graded (A*–U)
1997	51.2	335997	56.4	134604	59.2	43468	77.9	27733
1998	50.4	337577	56.1	131286	57.5	47406	75.4	18357
1999	52.6	342227	56.9	137011	59.2	49329	76.3	18846

Source: http://www.qca.org.uk/gcse-results/

Despite these very encouraging statistics, the 1999 NC Orders make it possible for those pupils to be disapplied from mfl:

- who make significantly less progress than their peers: they are able to study fewer NC subjects in order to consolidate their learning across the curriculum;
- who have particular strengths and talents: they are allowed to emphasise a particular curriculum area by exchanging a statutory subject for a further course in that curriculum area;
- for whom wider work-related learning is deemed desirable than is possible alongside the full statutory requirements: they are able to carry out extended periods of work experience etc.

This invariably devalues the status of mfl. Given the (perceived) difficulties inherent in mfl teaching and learning outlined in the Prologue, it can only be hoped that school managers take account of the fact that the spirit of the original NC Orders, which first entitled pupils to the study of mfl between ages 11 and 16, is upheld in the 1999 Orders, that disapplication, therefore, will involve only a very small number of pupils, that mfl remains an essential part of the curricular entitlement for all pupils and that Shirley Lawes' (2000: 18) fears are unfounded:

> The real irony is that in recent years there has been considerable emphasis placed on making modern languages more accessible to the full range of learners at Key Stage 4. Some commentators have argued that in so doing, mfl learning has lost some of its intellectual challenge and become more of a skill-based, functional activity. GCSE has undergone changes to reflect the functional emphasis and to enable more learners to aspire to examination success. Now, it is arguable that the very learners whose needs the Key Stage 4 curriculum has striven to meet, may no longer be there. Will Curriculum 2000 succeed in inspiring the rest?

The decision – in response to a resolution passed in 1988 by the European Community as was – to include a *European dimension* in the school curriculum provides a set of *guiding principles* in this context deserving of the attention of mfl trainees (see also Capel and Pachler 1997: 263–7). Mfl play an important role in delivering the objectives identified in this resolution:

- to strengthen in young people a sense of European identity by emphasising the value of European civilisation and the foundations on which the European peoples intend to base their development today, that is in particular the safeguarding of the principles of democracy, social justice and respect for human rights;
- to prepare young people to take part in the economic and social development of the Community and in making concrete progress towards European Union, as stipulated in the Single European Act;
- to make them aware of the advantages which the Community presents but also of the challenges it involves in opening up an enlarged economic and social area;
- to improve their knowledge of the Community and its Member States in their historical, cultural, economic and social aspects and to emphasise

the importance of cooperation between EC Member States and with the rest of the world e.g. initial and in-service teacher training/exchanges.

(Central Bureau 1993: 4)

Reflection
Activity 1.1 Producing a
display for an open evening

Imagine your placement school is in the process of organising an open evening for prospective pupils and their parents. The head of mfl wishes to produce a display for pupils and parents pointing out the benefits that can be gained from the study of mfl. What arguments would you include in the display that could appeal to pupils and parents?

'WHICH LANGUAGE?'

When at one time the study of a (modern) foreign language was considered to be an integral part of a rounded education and a prerequisite for access to church, state and the judiciary or literary, philosophical and other writing (see e.g. Hawkins 1994: 110 and Reeves 1986: 2–3), today a much more *pragmatic rationale* prevails focussing on the benefits derived from the ability to communicate directly with speakers of other languages for work, e.g. conducting business transactions, or leisure purposes, e.g. on holiday.

This shift in emphasis has not only brought about an increasing focus on listening and speaking skills rather than on translating, reading and writing, but has also necessitated considerable changes in the knowledge, skills and understanding covered by the study of mfl as part of the school curriculum.

In the same way the reasons for learning languages have been developing over time, the question of which language to learn – French, German, Spanish, Italian, Russian, Welsh, Irish ... or instead Greek or Latin? – has attracted different answers according to changing cultural, economic, political, educational and societal contexts.

As a number of observers note, there are numerous valid reasons to support a *diversity of mfl* as part of the school curriculum (see e.g. Kenning 1993: 10). The choice of which language(s) to offer and which to learn is determined by a number of factors such as:

- the importance of the language in terms of trade and industry;
- the number of native and non-native speakers of the language;
- its usefulness for leisure purposes;
- its (perceived) level of difficulty;
- the attitudes of learners towards it;
- the availability of specialist teachers;
- the influence of the target culture(s) on the learner or the society she lives in;
- its use as a medium for scientific discourse; or
- its significance in terms of output of works of a literary or philosophical nature.

There is *no one* language that outperforms all the others on these criteria. The relative importance of the various criteria can vary. It is on the basis of these factors that governments decide which languages should be included in the national frameworks, schools decide which languages to offer and, given the opportunity, pupils decide which language to opt for.

Reflection
Activity 1.2 Choice of language

- What were the reasons for choosing your foreign language(s)? Which of the factors listed above applied to you? Were there any other considerations?
- Discuss with your mentor, a class teacher you work with closely or a peer what implications the reasons for choosing a particular language may have on its teaching.

Marie-Madeleine Kenning argues that there is a case for diversification of mfl provision in the school curriculum and that there is justification for a number of different mfl to be taught. According to her, published research data shows that: 'whatever the language, the majority of pupils think it is useful, enjoyable and not difficult and want contact with the foreign community; at the same time the degree of positiveness varies' (Kenning 1993: 12).

At the time of starting to study mfl it is impossible to pre-determine which particular language an individual pupil will find most useful in later life (see e.g. DES/Welsh Office 1988: 8; Kenning, 1993: 11).

Yet, despite these reasons for a diversity of mfl provision, since the 1970s when mfl became part of the curriculum in a large number of secondary schools, French has been by far the most commonly taught language in the UK.

In 1988 the DES/Welsh Office recognised that this predominance of French is 'clearly inappropriate' (DES/Welsh Office 1988: 8) and suggested:

> larger schools now offering only French as a first foreign language should offer two alternative first foreign languages; and smaller schools might break altogether with the tradition of French as a first foreign language, offering some other language in its place, with French normally offered as a second foreign language.
>
> (DES/Welsh Office 1988: 9)

To facilitate these changes the Department of Education and Science (DES) funded pilot diversification projects in ten Local Education Authorities (LEAs) in England between 1988 and 1990 which showed considerable success measurable, for instance, in a significant increase in GCSE entries in German and Spanish (see Tables 1.1 and 1.2 and Passmore 1996: 11).

A survey carried out jointly by the *Times Educational Supplement* (TES) and the Centre for Information on Language Teaching and Research (CILT) (see McLagan 1996) revealed, however, that the diversification of mfl provision in secondary schools is proving to be rather difficult. There are a number of reasons for this:

- lack of teachers qualified in languages other than French;
- increasing introduction of French in primary schools on a non-statutory basis;
- the predominance of French in middle schools;
- reduction in LEA mfl support in the wake of the delegation of funds directly to schools under the local management of schools (LMS);
- time constraints in the curriculum;
- time-tabling problems;
- cost implications of smaller second language groups;
- the relative limitation of teaching and learning resources available for languages other than French; as well as
- the 'compartmentalisation of subjects which is perpetuated through the school system into university and then through teacher training' (Evans 1996: 24).

Since the late 1980s and seemingly in recognition of the distinct advantages of a broad mfl skills base in personal, social and cultural terms for individual pupils as well as in economic terms for the nation as a whole, secondary schools and their mfl departments would appear to be doing their best to tackle these challenges. According to the TES/CILT survey, 80 per cent of secondary schools offer a second foreign language.

> Of those that do, 60 per cent offer German; 25.7 per cent Spanish; 25.3 per cent French; 4 per cent Italian and 2.4 per cent Russian. Most introduce the second foreign language in Years 8 or 9 but only a small percentage of pupils take it up to GCSE.
>
> (O'Malley 1996: 10)

Newly qualified mfl teachers play a vital part in the diversification of mfl provision in secondary schools. The more mfl they can teach, the better the chances for pupils to experience a variety of mfl during their schooling. When advertising posts, mfl departments often look for people with more than one language in order to sustain a diversified mfl curriculum and to give some flexibility in time tabling. For guidance on how to find a teaching post see Chapter 13.

The TES/CILT research shows that schools are experiencing considerable difficulties in finding staff with two mfl (see O'Malley 1996: 10). This has clear implications for intending teachers of mfl: in the light of this survey the ability to offer two mfl would seem to afford distinct advantages in terms of employment prospects.

THE NUFFIELD LANGUAGES INQUIRY

The Nuffield Languages Inquiry (see Nuffield Languages Inquiry 2000 and *http:// www.nuffield.org/language/*), was set up to investigate what foreign language capability the UK needs, to what extent present policies and arrangements meet these needs and what strategic planning and initiatives will be required in the light of the present position. The final report of the inquiry, which draws on evidence received from a wide range of individuals, organisations and specialist consultants, notes that '(capability) in other languages – a much broader range than hitherto and in greater depth – is crucially important for a flourishing UK' (Nuffield Languages Inquiry 2000: 5). Sir Trevor McDonald and Sir John Boyd, the joint chairmen, point out that:

> The UK has no automatic monopoly on political or economic success. In a world of alliances and partnerships we need to understand where others are coming from. In a competitive world we cannot afford to be without strong and complete skills: no skills – no jobs. The need to strengthen our children's literacy, numeracy and technology skills is clear and we support it. Side by side with these should go the ability to communicate across cultures. It too is a key skill.
>
> (Nuffield Languages Inquiry 2000: 4)

The main findings and proposals of the inquiry include the suggestions that languages be designated as a key skill, that there should be a national languages strategy and that a languages 'supremo', who works with government at raising the profile of languages, be appointed. Other suggestions concern early language learning – about which non-statutory guidance is included in the 1999 NC mfl Orders – a foreign language require-ment for university entry and certain designated vocational qualifications and the establishment of a national standards framework for describing and accrediting language competence.

In Section 4.2 of the final report (see Nuffield Languages Inquiry 2000: 44–9), challenges and obstacles in relation to languages in secondary schools are identified and respective recommendations are made.

Challenges and obstacles:

- the range of languages is unbalanced;
- qualifications are inflexible;
- continuity is at risk;
- there are defects in curriculum organisation;
- courses provide a poor foundation for future learning;
- public examination results are below average;
- boys achieve far less well than girls;
- new technologies are not used effectively;
- good opportunities are being wasted;
- a more positive climate is needed; and
- a more coordinated approach to teachers' professional development is needed.

Recommendations:

- create a new balance and diversity of languages;
- keep language learning for all up to 16;
- recognise progress through graded awards;
- introduce modular accreditation;
- review curriculum content and examination syllabuses;
- all schools should maintain active international links;
- review and reinvigorate the Foreign Language Assistant Scheme;
- offer incentives for schools which create bilingual sections;
- boost the use of technology; and
- government and business should promote languages as key life skills.

The report comes to the conclusion that the UK is doing badly:

We talk about communication but don't always communicate. There is enthusiasm for languages but it is patchy. Educational provision is fragmented, achievement poorly measured, continuity not very evident. In the language of our time, there is a lack of joined-up thinking.

(Nuffield Languages Inquiry 2000: 5)

Whether or not any of these suggestions will be acted upon, and if so to what extent, remains to be seen.

Our reasons for making reference to these problems in this book are simple: clearly, we don't do so in order to put the reader off from choosing mfl teaching as a career. Indeed, candidates for initial teacher education are increasingly in short supply. Nevertheless, we believe new entrants into the profession need to be aware of the challenges facing them. Only then, we feel, will they be able to make their commitment count fully. However, viewed from another perspective, the current systemic weaknesses in mfl teaching and learning provide ample scope for ambitious graduates to make a difference and enjoy a rewarding professional life.

THE NATIONAL LITERACY STRATEGY

In 1998 the Department for Education and Employment published a framework for teaching literacy in primary schools, entitled the National Literacy Strategy, with the aim of raising mother tongue literacy standards. Whilst the National Literacy Strategy does currently not apply directly to mfl teachers – the extension of the initiative into secondary education is, however, underway at the time of writing – it potentially has a considerable impact on mfl teaching and learning in secondary education. Whilst in the past it often fell to mfl teachers to introduce pupils to grammar and its terminology, the National Literacy Strategy specifies long lists of language items to be covered each term for pupils aged 5 to 11, focussing on language at word (sounds, spelling and vocabulary), sentence (grammatical knowledge and pronunciation) and text (comprehension and composition) level. Learners starting to study a foreign language in Year 7 can, therefore, be expected to have a basic knowledge of metalanguage, i.e. language allowing them to talk about language. This might make the teaching of new grammatical and linguistic concepts in a modern foreign language and a dialogue between mother tongue and foreign language teachers easier.

THE 1999 MFL NATIONAL CURRICULUM ORDERS FOR ENGLAND

In the remainder of this chapter we discuss the statutory framework governing mfl teaching in England. We are only able to provide a brief overview here and trainees are encouraged to consult the Orders, also available online at *http://www.nc.uk.net/*, for more details. Approaches to mfl teaching in other parts of the UK are similar (see note 1).

Schools in England are obliged to offer one or more of the official working languages of the European Union (EU): Danish, Dutch, Finnish, French, German, Modern Greek, Italian, Portuguese, Spanish or Swedish. In addition schools may offer any other modern foreign language. Non-EU languages can only be offered as a NC language alongside the *possibility* of studying an official working language of the EU (see DfEE/QCA 1999: 17).

In the main pupils study one EU language and can often – typically from Year 8 or 9 onwards – opt for one, or exceptionally more, additional language(s) provided their school has a diversified mfl curriculum. In theory the statutory requirements apply only to pupils' first, that is their NC language, but in practice schools tend to deliver all mfl in the curriculum on this basis.

The Graded Objectives in Modern Language (GOML) National Coordinating Committee submitted a paper to the mfl working group advising the government on the design of the NC, mfl Orders, which featured the following objectives for mfl learners:

> ... secondary school foreign language learners ... should be able to operate at their own level of intellect and maturity as:
> 1   a person abroad
> 2   a host to, or interpreter for, a foreign national in the UK in everyday situations in work and leisure
> 3   a consumer of publications and broadcasts from abroad
> 4   an active participant in collaborative work in a multilingual environment.
>
> (Page 1989: 75)

The fact that these objectives, by and large, were included gives some indication of how deeply current thinking is rooted in CLT (see also Chapter 3).

The NC mfl Orders consist of a Programme of Study (PoS) as well as four Attainment Targets (ATs).

The PoS comprises two sections, the first delineating requisite knowledge skills and understanding and the second giving details about the breadth of study. The first section is subdivided into four different aspects:

Acquiring knowledge and understanding of the target language

1   Pupils should be taught:
    (a) the principles and interrelationship of sounds and writing in the target language
    (b) the grammar of the target language and how to apply it
    (c) how to express themselves using a range of vocabulary and structures.

Developing language skills

2   Pupils should be taught:
    (a) how to listen carefully for gist and detail
    (b) correct pronunciation and intonation
    (c) how to ask and answer questions
    (d) how to initiate and develop conversations
    (e) how to vary the target language to suit context, audience and purpose
    (f) how to adapt language they already know for different contexts
    (g) strategies for dealing with the unpredictable [for example, unfamiliar language, unexpected responses]
    (h) techniques for skimming and for scanning written texts for information, including those from ICT-based sources

(i) how to summarise and report the main points of spoken or written texts, using notes where appropriate

(j) how to redraft their writing to improve its accuracy and presentation, including the use of ICT.

Developing language-learning skills

3   Pupils should be taught:

(a) techniques for memorising words, phrases and short extracts

(b) how to use context and other clues to interpret meaning [for example, by identifying the grammatical function of unfamiliar words or similarities with words they know]

(c) to use their knowledge of English or another language when learning the target language

(d) how to use dictionaries and other reference materials appropriately and effectively

(e) how to develop their independence in learning and using the target language.

Developing cultural awareness

4   Pupils should be taught about different countries and cultures by:

(a) working with authentic materials in the target language, including some from ICT-based sources [for example, handwritten texts, newspapers, magazines, books, video, satellite television, texts from the internet]

(b) communicating with native speakers [for example, in person, by correspondence]

(c) considering their own culture and comparing it with the cultures of the countries and communities where the target language is spoken

(d) considering the experiences and perspectives of people in these countries and communities.

(DfEE/QCA 1999: 16–7)

The section on the breadth of study lists the following:

5   During key stages 3 and 4, pupils should be taught the knowledge, skills and understanding through:

(a) communicating in the target language in pairs and groups, and with their teacher

(b) using everyday classroom events as an opportunity for spontaneous speech

(c) expressing and discussing personal feelings and opinions

(d) producing and responding to different types of spoken and written language, including texts produced using ICT

(e) using a range of resources, including ICT, for accessing and communicating information

(f) using the target language creatively and imaginatively

(g) listening, reading or viewing for personal interest and enjoyment, as well as for information

(h) using the target language for real purposes [for example, by sending and receiving messages by telephone, letter, fax or e-mail]

(i) working in a variety of contexts, including everyday activities, personal and social life, the world around us, the world of work and the international world.

(DfEE/QCA 1999: 17)

By way of a brief summary, the NC can be said to promote the development of an ability in pupils to use the target language (TL) in a variety of real-life contexts on the basis of some knowledge and an understanding of linguistic and cultural aspects using authentic materials and information and communications technology (ICT). However, given the very limited amount of time – rarely more than 12.5% of curriculum time in Key Stage 3 and 10% in Key Stage 4 – and the often adverse conditions of mfl learning, expectations of what can be achieved need to be realistic:

> Learners at beginners level should be able to take part in simple transactions and conversations, often featuring simple and familiar language and contexts; their pronunciation will be intelligible, their knowledge of language forms limited and largely implicit; whilst able to communicate meaning, their ability to produce grammatically correct language will vary.
>
> (Pachler 2000b: 537)

The list of statements contained in the PoS can be seen as an assortment of good practice and shares wide endorsement by mfl professionals. Their loose structure does, however, mean the NC is very much a framework for teaching rather than learning, requiring from mfl teachers considerable skill and professional judgement in ensuring grading, sequencing and progression. Also, in comparison with curriculum frameworks in many other countries there is very little guidance on content. To compensate, the NC is supplemented at Key Stage 3 by non-statutory schemes of work, available at *http://www.standards.dfee.gov.uk/schemes/*, and optional tests and tasks (see SCAA 1996 and 1997), which – if followed by departments 'as is' – could be highly prescriptive. The lack of content specified in the NC can be seen to lead to GCSE specifications (formerly syllabuses) overshadowing the NC PoS at Key Stage 4 and, as a consequence, to a considerable amount of teaching to the test.

In addition to the PoS, the NC features four Attainment Targets, namely

- listening and responding;
- speaking;

Reflection
Activity 1.3 Carrying out lesson observations relating to the NC Orders for England

Observe a number of mfl lessons of a class of your choice focussing on the coverage of the PoS. Choose a number of the PoS statements and observe through which activities they are covered. Table 1.3 gives some examples.

Table1.3 Carrying out NC-related lesson observations

No.	PoS statement	Activity
5.a	communicating in the target language in pairs and groups,	• practice of new vocabulary through identification of cards in a game of 'pairs'; • structured role play for buying food; instructions provided on cards in diagrammatic form; • survey to identify most popular food; • open-ended drama – pupil 'A' tried to sell as much food as possible to pupil 'B', who had a limited money supply
	and with their teacher	• pupils gave excuses for being late to the lesson and for not having correct equipment; • pupils asked to take blazer off
5.h	using the target language for real purposes	• excuses for being late; • requests to take blazer off; • requests for equipment; • greetings and goodbyes; • asking page numbers; • asking for vocabulary.

- reading and responding; and
- writing.

The Attainment Targets, which each consist of eight levels of increasing difficulty plus a description for exceptional achievement, set out the 'knowledge, skills and understanding that pupils are expected to have by the end of each Key Stage'.

> Each level description describes the types and range of performance that pupils working at that level should characteristically demonstrate. The level descriptions provide the basis for making judgements about pupils' performance at the end of key stage 3. At key stage 4, national qualifications are the main means of assessing attainment in modern foreign languages.
>
> (DfEE/QCA 1999: 38)

During Key Stage 3, the great majority of pupils is expected to work within level 3 to 7 and at age 14, i.e. at the end of Key Stage 3, the majority of pupils is expected to attain at levels 5/6. The GCSE Criteria for mfl published in 2000 set out the following grade description for Grade C (QCA 2000: 4):

> Candidates identify and note main points and extract details and points of view from language spoken at normal speed. The spoken texts include past and future events. They are drawn from a variety of topics which include familiar language in unfamiliar contexts.
>
> Candidates develop conversations and simple discussions which include past, present and future events, involving the use of different tenses. They express personal opinions and show an ability to deal with some unpredictable elements. Although there may be some errors, they convey a clear message, and their pronunciation and intonation are generally accurate.
>
> Candidates identify and extract details and points of view from authentic and simulated texts, drawn from a variety of topics and which include past, present and future events. They show an ability to understand unfamiliar language.

> Candidates express personal opinions and write about a variety of topics, both factually and imaginatively, including past, present and future events and involving the use of different tenses. They use an appropriate register. The style is basic but despite some errors the writing conveys a clear message.

Grade descriptions for Grades A and F are also available.

The GCSE Criteria form the basis upon which specifications are drawn up. They require the content of specifications to be consistent with the NC Orders.

There are the following four, equally weighted assessment objectives:

> AO1 understand and respond to spoken language
> AO2 communicate in speech, showing knowledge of and applying accurately the grammar and structures prescribed in the specification
> AO3 understand and respond to written language
> AO4 communicate in writing, showing knowledge of and applying accurately the grammar and structures prescribed in the specification

At least 10 per cent of the total marks for AO2 and AO4 must be allocated to knowledge and accurate application of the grammar and structures set out in the criteria.

Instructions should normally be in the language in which the candidate is expected to respond, 'except where the nature of the task would make the instructions difficult to understand' (QCA 2000: 3) and there is a requirement for candidates to express themselves in the TL when speaking and writing.

> In listening and reading, where a response is spoken or written, it must be in the modern foreign language, except where a response in another language is a necessary part of the task (for example, in an interpreting exercise) or where a non-linguistic response is a natural and appropriate alternative to a response in the modern foreign language. A maximum of 10 per cent of the total marks for the subject may be awarded for answers in English, Welsh or Irish. No more than half of this maximum allocation may be assigned to any particular assessment objective.
>
> (QCA 2000:3)

However, pupils do not have to follow a GCSE course. They can also take the General National Vocational Qualification (GNVQ) Key Stage 4 language units or the Certificate of Achievement, provided it is offered by a Qualifications and Curriculum Authority (QCA at *http://www.qca.org.uk*) accredited provider. Within the 1999 NC pupils will also be able to take locally designed accreditation. For details about assessment contact the appropriate accreditation body (see Endnote 1).

SUMMARY

In this introduction we have shown that there are a number of diverse educational, economic, vocational and linguistic reasons for including the study of mfl in the secondary school curriculum.

The aims and objectives governing the study of mfl have changed over the years as has the composition of the pupils learning mfl. These developments go hand in hand

Reflection
Activity 1.4 Familiarising yourself
with the GCSE Criteria and GCSE
Specifications for mfl

Obtain a copy of the GCSE specification used by your placement school. In your opinion, how well does it test the requirements in the NC PoS?

with changes in society and are a reflection of changes in national educational policy.

The advantages of a broad national mfl skills base have been outlined.

A brief examination of the statutory requirements for England (together with some related documents) as well as of the National Literacy Strategy and the Nuffield Languages Inquiry, has introduced the framework and the context governing current mfl curriculum planning, delivery and assessment in the secondary school curriculum.

NOTE

1   Due to lack of space the National Curriculum Orders discussed in this chapter, and used as point of reference throughout the book, apply to England only. Wales, Scotland and Northern Ireland have (statutory) requirements of their own. For details contact the Curriculum and Qualifications Authority for Wales (ACCAC at *http://www.accac.org.uk/*), the Department of Education for Northern Ireland (DENI at *http://www.deni.gov.uk/*) or Learning and Teaching Scotland (LT Scotland at *http://www.ltscotland.com*).

2 On Becoming a Modern Foreign Languages Teacher

This chapter sets the scene for the work of modern foreign languages (mfl) trainees during their initial teacher education (ITE) course both at higher education institutions (HEIs) and in placement schools.

In recent years the work of trainee teachers in the UK has been subject to a number of fundamental changes. At the time of writing it is governed by DfEE Circular 4/98 (see DfEE 1998; also available online at *http: //www.dfee.gov.uk/circulars/4_98/summary.htm*)[1]. The increase in the amount of time trainees spend working with pupils and teachers in schools rather than with tutors in HEIs has been widely welcomed. Nevertheless, the gain in practical experience has created and/or reinforced certain tensions and has

---

OBJECTIVES

By the end of this chapter you should:

- understand the nature of the competence- and standards-based approach to ITE;
- recognise the importance of subject knowledge and application;
- recognise the importance of a symbiotic relationship between theory and reflective practice;
- appreciate differences in mfl learning styles and have started to consider your preferences in terms of mfl teaching styles;
- be aware of possible stages of your development as a trainee teacher; and
- appreciate the nature of your work in schools from two perspectives, your own as well as that of your mentor.

necessitated a redefinition of the roles of the key players involved. Although by now reasonably well established, the concept of partnership in ITE continues to evolve (see also Pachler and Field 2001).

TOWARDS A MULTI-DISCIPLINARY APPROACH TO MFL TEACHING

The main aim of mfl teaching is to enable pupils to communicate in the target language (TL). To be an effective mfl teacher requires a range of skills and knowledge. We posit that there is no single way of mfl teaching and that, therefore, it is important for mfl trainees to develop a personal approach to mfl teaching against the background of the respective statutory requirements by which they are bound and of what we know about mfl teaching and learning from research. In recent years an increasing number of commentators and policy makers has expressed the need to establish a theoretical framework for mfl teaching. This perceived need relates to the fact that there are many different source disciplines that potentially inform mfl teaching.

> As an applied discipline, language learning obviously needs to be informed by a 'conceptual framework': i.e. by a body of knowledge, drawn from various areas, which both helps to render the teaching experience coherent and provides a basis for evaluating its effectiveness. Without such a body of knowledge, refined into principles for classroom practice, there simply exists no criteria – beyond the weight of custom or fashion – for deciding what is or is not pedagogically effective.
>
> (Roberts 1992: 6)

This observation identifies two key concerns for mfl trainees: that mfl teaching is an applied discipline and as such inextricably linked to a number of source disciplines; and that these disciplines provide a wealth of knowledge, which allows a better understanding of the teaching process. This body of background knowledge is important but is not sufficient to ensure effective mfl teaching.

Gerhard Neuner and Hans Hunfeld draw attention to a number of disciplines and factors, which can yield important information for mfl trainees (translated here loosely from German; see 1993: 9):

- findings from the field of psychology;
- pedagogical knowledge and research into teaching;
- findings from the field of (applied) linguistics;
- conceptions about the foreign country;
- individual differences of learners;
- previous experience of modern foreign languages (mfl) learning;
- conceptions about work with (literary) texts;
- specific objectives of learners;
- traditions of teaching methodology; as well as
- methods of mother tongue teaching.

To become knowledgeable about and keep abreast with this wide range of considerations requires commitment and enthusiasm on the part of the mfl trainees.

THE IMPORTANCE OF SUBJECT KNOWLEDGE

A document compiled by the National Foundation for Educational Research (NFER) re-affirms as one of the central ingredients of effective teaching the importance of *higher* subject knowledge (see Tabberer 1996: 3–4).

In the case of mfl, subject knowledge can be seen as a high level of proficiency in and good structural knowledge, as well as the ability to make effective use of, the TL, wide-ranging awareness of the culture(s) of the countries where the TL is spoken, some knowledge of the linguistic theories underpinning the language learning/acquisition process as well as a familiarity with the respective statutory framework and related documents. More recently it also comprises knowledge and the ability to make effective use of information and communications technology (ICT).

Subject knowledge is an important consideration for all mfl trainees. Even for a native speaker there are issues that need to be considered. The adaptation of the use of the TL in terms of complexity, speed of delivery, register and tone must be addressed if pupils are to understand and respond appropriately. Although a key competence of every ITE course, there is often only little time to develop personal proficiency in the TL or cultural awareness. Also, there is often only little time to engage with theories of language learning and acquisition. As is the case throughout a teaching career, the onus is on the individual to maintain a high level of subject knowledge, including up-to-date linguistic competence and cultural understanding.

In a recent study Jim Coleman (1996) highlights a lack of national standards of linguistic proficiency for mfl graduates. Some observers are concerned about the impact of a perceived decrease in standards of linguistic proficiency on mfl teaching methodology, particularly the focus on communicative competence. Too little emphasis on structural aspects of the language, they argue, could have detrimental effects on the future of the nation's linguistic potential:

> If these issues were not raised prior to or during A-level, and now have to be postponed indefinitely during the undergraduate course, only to be taken for granted during the PGCE [Postgraduate Certificate in Education] year, then we must assume that a generation of teachers will be coming forward that has never been exposed to or learned certain aspects of German grammar and syntax.
>
> (McCulloch 1996: 15)

Reflection
Activity 2.1 Subject knowledge

Obtain a copy of examination specification (formerly syllabus) at GCSE and, where appropriate, A/AS level used by the mfl department at your placement school for your main modern foreign language(s). Reflect on how well you feel your first degree course or equivalent has prepared you for meeting the requirements of the specifications in terms of your subject knowledge. Use Table 2.1 to record your reflections.

Table 2.1 Mapping personal subject knowledge against examination requirements

Requirement	Degree course content	GCSE requirement	A/AS level/ requirement
Cultural awareness			
Structural knowledge of language			
Non-literary topics			
Literary topics			
Key skills			
Other (specify)			

In Chapter 7 and the Epilogue the recent shift at GCSE and A/AS level towards a detailed prescription of grammatical content is discussed. This shift in emphasis affects the type of mfl education prospective mfl teachers experience but it also demands of trainee teachers working with advanced mfl learners a high degree of subject knowledge and makes the ability to transmit knowledge about linguistic structures all the more important.

SUBJECT APPLICATION

We have already noted that subject knowledge is essential but not enough to being an effective teacher. Mfl trainees need to be able to teach pupils subject knowledge and relevant skills in *appropriate* ways. They need to acquire knowledge in a wide range of fields to be able to do so effectively.

Lee Shulman's (1987 quoted in Bennett 1993: 7) seven categories of knowledge clearly underline the complexity of the teaching process. They are adapted in Figure 2.1 and related to the process of learning to teach mfl.

There is much to be learnt in the course of ITE and often only little time is available to focus on subject knowledge. As Shulman's categories indicate, the onus is on subject application and the ability of trainees to develop in pupils mfl-related knowledge, skills and understanding.

COURSE EXPECTATIONS: THE STUDENTS' POINT OF VIEW

In this chapter, with permission of the writers, we present two authentic case studies of mfl trainees. They are drawn from accounts written during a PGCE course. The views expressed are invariably personal and specific to individual circumstances but, nevertheless, illustrate a number of general issues about the process of trainees' development. The case studies are divided into two sections: an initial statement giving reasons for wanting to become a teacher written before the start of the PGCE course, which are included in this section, and a concluding statement on completion of the course, which can be found at the end of this chapter.

Other interesting case study material can, for instance, be found in Grenfell 1998.

No.	Category	Mfl relevance
1	**Content knowledge**: referring to the amount and organisation of knowledge in the mind of the teacher. This includes both substantive and syntactic structure of a subject, ie the variety of ways in which the basic concepts and principles of the discipline are organised, and the ways in which truth or falsehood, validity or invalidity, are established.	need to update linguistic competence, cultural awareness/intercultural (communicative) competence and ICT competence on a regular basis
2	**General pedagogical knowledge**: with a special reference to both broad principles and strategies of classroom management and organisation that appear to transcend subject matter.	need for an understanding of adolescent development and the relationship between language and learning in general
3	**Curriculum knowledge**: with particular grasp of the materials and programmes that serve as 'tools of the trade' for teachers.	growing familiarity with the content and application of the statutory framework, specifications as well as commonly used resources including ICT
4	**Pedagogical/content knowledge:** that form of content knowledge that embodies the aspect of content most germane to its teachability. It includes, for any given subject area, the most useful forms of the presentation of those ideas, the most powerful analogies, illustrations, examples, explanations and demonstrations. In other words, the ways of representing and formulating the subject that make it comprehensible to others.	knowledge of and a willingness to experiment with and evaluate different approaches to foreign language teaching including ICT; awareness of relevant background reading and research
5	**Knowledge of learners and their characteristics**.	awareness of the existing language skills of learners and of what motivates the individuals within a class; awareness of how current approaches to mfl teaching and learning relate to learning theories
6	**Knowledge of educational contexts**: ranging from the workings of the group or classroom, the governance and financing of schools, to the character to communities and cultures.	knowledge of the institutional, local and national context of mfl teaching including policy matters and inspection findings
7	**Knowledge of educational ends, purposes and values, and philosophical and historical background.**	knowledge of how current approaches to mfl teaching and learning have evolved; awareness of the rationale and purposes of mfl teaching and learning how they relate to the wider secondary school curriculum

Figure 2.1   Lee Shulman's seven categories of teacher knowledge

CASE STUDY ONE

Initial statement

From the age of thirteen pupils are encouraged to investigate career choices, or rather that was the case in my educational experience. At this time no other career option appealed to me in the same way as teaching and the situation has not changed in ten years. When I ask myself what I wanted from a successful and satisfying career, teaching fulfils most of my requirements. Teaching allows me to continue to work with my subject interests. I want to work in a team but also with the public, a combination which demands good communication and diplomacy skills. I see teaching as an immense challenge because the potential for rewards, satisfaction and excellence is infinite, but on the other hand failure is unacceptable.

I want to be able to bring or even drag out the best in my future pupils and I am fully aware that that does not mean expecting them all to achieve grade A.

My desire to be a teacher has been reinforced by teaching both English and French (to small groups and individuals) and by the satisfaction that these experiences have brought me. I discovered that I have confidence, discipline and organisational skills which enabled me to teach a language and to engage my pupils' interest. I feel I am able to relate to the educational, personal and social needs of young people and to deal with them within the teaching environment.

I am aware of the conflict between teaching a modern foreign language to enable pupils to pass an exam and teaching it to prepare pupils for using a specific language in and outside of the countries it is spoken.

I am also concerned about the behaviour of today's pupils and the lack of respect they seem to have for each other and for adults. Any improvement, however small, I can make to this situation during my career will give me great satisfaction.

CASE STUDY TWO

Initial statement

Unlike a lot of people on this course who seem to have wanted to teach all their lives, the one thing I knew that I was not going to do when I graduated was teach. This was mainly due to my father recommending that teaching was not a profession to go into. As he is himself a teacher, I figured he must know what he was talking about, so I took his advice. I went on to work in a variety of mainly personal assistant (PA), research and sales and marketing roles, none of which ever seemed particularly satisfying or rewarding. I finally decided I had to re-examine what I was after in a career. The result pointed to the fact that I had been avoiding a profession which I secretly thought I might enjoy.

I have not forgotten my own experiences in secondary school, sometimes sitting in a (language) classroom feeling incredibly stupid and panicking because I had not understood what the teacher had been explaining and was too scared to ask. Of course this is a very naive thing to say, but I would like to think that I could persuade pupils in my class not to be afraid to make clear that they have not understood what I have tried to explain. I believe this to be a crucial point in beginning to build a sound working relationship with a class. I am of the opinion that as long as a pupil is making an effort to understand, that pupil deserves the best effort that I can make to help her. I also believe that if that pupil is not making the effort, it is my job to give her a reason to make that effort.

As far as teaching my particular subject is concerned, I am convinced that my enthusiasm for what I have to teach is of prime importance in helping me do my job well. I want to be able to impart this enthusiasm to my pupils, but I can see that this is where the difficulties are most likely to occur. The reason for this is because I have for the majority of my life been taught using very conservative and academic methods. It is all I know and it is what I am most comfortable with at present. To complicate matters further, I am naturally a quite reserved character. So when I see videos of teachers using 'radical' communicative methods, I think 'brilliant!' and then I think 'but I can't do that'. I believe the methods are effective, I can see how they would work, but I am not sure that I am capable of applying them myself. Ideas on how to teach mfl have changed drastically since I was at school, and although it is a change which I approve of it is also one which I will have to make an effort to adapt to successfully.

On a more general level, classroom management is my greatest worry at the moment, particularly after having seen some classes during my induction week in school. I am aware that with the best lesson plan in the world, if the class is not managed correctly the pupils are not going to learn as effectively as they could.

Planning my work I do not as yet see as a big problem. I am fairly confident of being able to get straight in my own mind the objectives of a lesson and being able to get from there in terms of suitable activities to meet these objectives.

**Reflection
Activity 2.2 Comparing personal and
course expectations**

The discussion in this chapter so far has highlighted the complexity of mfl teaching and has shown how much there is to be learnt by a trainee teacher. This activity aims to help you decide priorities for your professional development.

• Reflect on and note down how the discussion so far in this chapter relates to your personal expectations concerning the ITE course. In your opinion, what knowledge and skills does an effective mfl teacher need? Also, what characterises a good mfl teacher? What types of behaviour do you think are best avoided by an mfl teacher?
• What expectations did the two trainee teachers have initially about teaching? How do their expectations relate to your own?
• Then, carefully study your course documentation. What expectations are stated in the documents? How do they compare to your expectations?
• What issues arise from this comparison? What will your priorities be?

**Reflection
Activity 2.3 Pupil expectations**

Carry out a survey amongst pupils at your placement school asking them what characteristics they wish to see in an mfl teacher. Note down positive and negative responses. Are there any differences in your own and the pupils' perceptions?

THE COMPETENCE-/STANDARDS-BASED APPROACH TO INITIAL (MFL) TEACHER EDUCATION

In the early 1990s a competence-based approach was introduced to ITE in England and Wales, 'a set of observable and assessable behaviours, a sort of National Curriculum for intending teachers' (Norman 1995: 5). In the late 1990s this was replaced by a standards-based approach. Trainees are now required to meet all the standards set out in DfEE Circular 4/98 by the end of their thrity-six-week course (of which at least twenty-four weeks need to be spent in schools) to be eligible for qualified teacher status (QTS). Subsequently, trainees have to successfully complete a period of induction in their first teaching post in order to be entered on the register of the General Teaching Council (GTC) and to be entitled to teach as fully qualified teachers in maintained schools. The standards in DfEE Circular 4/98 are grouped in four broad categories:

• knowledge and understanding;
• planning, teaching and class management;
• monitoring, assessment, recording, reporting and accountability; and
• other professional requirements.

In addition, trainees are required to meet all the standards set out in Annex B of DfEE Circular 4/98, the initial teach training (ITT) NC for the use of ICT in subject teaching. For a detailed discussion see Chapter 12.

Evidence from the first round of inspections of ITE providers in the late 1990s across all subjects suggests that trainees are finding the standards relating to monitoring, assessment, recording, reporting and accountability (MARRA) most challenging of all. They are:

a   assess how well learning objectives have been achieved and use this assessment to improve specific aspects of teaching;

b   mark and monitor pupils' assigned classwork and homework, providing constructive oral and written feedback, and setting targets for pupils' progress;

c   assess and record each pupil's progress systematically, including through focused observation, questioning, testing and marking, and use these records to:

i   check that pupils have understood and completed the work set;

ii   monitor strengths and weaknesses and use the information gained as a basis for purposeful intervention in pupils' learning;

iii inform planning;

iv   check that pupils continue to make demonstrable progress in their acquisition of the knowledge, skills and understanding of the subject;

d   are familiar with the statutory assessment and reporting requirements and know how to prepare and present informative reports to parents;

e   where applicable, understand the expected demands of pupils in relation to each relevant level description or end of key stage description, and, in addition, for those on 11–16 or 18 and 14–19 courses, the demands of the syllabuses and course requirements for GCSE, other KS4 courses, and, where applicable, post-16 courses;

f   where applicable, understand and know how to implement the assessment requirements of current qualifications for pupils aged 14–19;

g   recognise the level at which a pupil is achieving, and assess pupils consistently against attainment targets, where applicable, if necessary with guidance from an experienced teacher;

h   understand and know how national, local, comparative and school data, including National Curriculum test data, where applicable, can be used to set clear targets for pupils' achievement;

i   use different kinds of assessment appropriately for different purposes, including National Curriculum and other standardised tests, and baseline assessment where relevant.

(DfEE 1998: 11)

The full list of standards can be accessed at and downloaded from *http://www.dfee.gov.uk/circulars/4_98/summary.htm*.

From 2000–1 all trainees are required to successfully complete tests in numeracy, literacy and ICT in order to gain QTS. These changes have been introduced in a bid to ensure newly qualified teachers (NQTs) are able to implement the various governmental strategies for raising standards. For more details on the skills tests see the Teacher Training Agency website (TTA at *http://www.canteach.gov.uk/info/skillstests/*), where some support material can be found.

THEORY *AND* PRACTICE IN (MFL) ITE

The previous section showed that ITE courses are required to assess mfl trainees in terms of standards, that is trainees' ability to display certain observable types of behaviour. In order to be able to show these types of behaviour and to ensure pupils learn, mfl trainees need to develop professional judgement and an ability to reflect, amongst other things, on their own behaviour, and the effectiveness of their teaching as well as on the quality of pupils' learning. This requires practical as well as theoretical knowledge. The relationship between theory and practice is, therefore, an important issue.

Reflection and theorising are increasingly seen as central features underpinning trainees' development and as catalysts in moving trainees from dependency to autonomy (see e.g. Furlong et al. 1996: 32 and Roberts 1998: 47–60).

Given the number of source disciplines, the perceived level of difficulty of mfl and the wide-ranging literature on its methodology, mfl teaching has substantial theoretical underpinning. The ability to analyse the processes of their classrooms is central to the work of trainee teachers.

> 'Theory as intellectual process' ... is inadequate; what should be offered is theoretical knowledge which may be tentative and to be questioned, but which is also specifically believed 'to be of practical value' and usefully assimilated into the professional development of student teachers.
>
> (Dunne 1993: 105)

The existence of a standards-based model in ITE must, in our view, not be seen as bringing theory and practice in conflict with each other.

> The most useful role of theory for the practitioner is to offer a strong construc- tivist foundation for their activity, and to provide a basis upon which to question the leading fads and rhetoric of the field. ... The role of researchers, then, is to provide comprehensible input for practitioners, and the role of practitioners is to provide rational interpretation of those ideas for researchers to ponder. Both are locked into a symbiotic relationship that eventually propels the field and advances knowledge.
>
> (Bialystok and Hakuta 1995: 218)

Mfl teaching, we believe, requires practical knowledge including – but going beyond – reflection on what can be observed. That is, practical knowledge, which is predicated on theoretical understanding enabling teachers to make deliberate choices at various stages of the teaching process.

Jon Roberts (1998: 54–8) distinguishes eleven different purposes for, or types of, reflection:

- to raise awareness of personal images of teaching;
- to raise awareness of one's personal theories, values and beliefs;

- to reflect on one's own language learning style;
- to raise awareness of one's current performance as a learner;
- to develop the ability to analyse teaching situations;
- to recall and analyse new and recent learning experiences;
- to review and access one's own actions in class;
- to raise awareness of one's routines and their rationale;
- to test the consistency between classroom events and educational theories;
- to become able to reframe interpretations of one's practice; and
- to become aware of the social and political significance of one's work.

Reflection can be seen to offer a very useful means of integrating theory and practice and of enabling trainees to deepen their understanding of their own personal and professional development. However, awareness of the multi-faceted nature of the term and the concept is important to ensure the appropriate type of reflection is used for a specific purpose.

Reflection
Activity 2.4 Reflecting on practice

When reflecting on your work on the course, refer to Roberts' types of reflection.
What type of reflection do you tend to engage in? Why?

For Bevis Yaxley (1994: 26) the process of reflection consists in the first instance of the description of good practice, leading on to the articulating of the principles that underpin this practice. This, in turn, leads to the sharing of ideas through open discussion, whether orally or in written form, followed by a process of challenging and justifying professional decisions. The final phase of reflective practice in this model is the close scrutiny and questioning of practice as an independent professional.

At certain stages of their course, trainees might find it difficult to relate what they are taught at university to what they observe in school. For Michael Grenfell this potential tension in subject methodology between placement school and HEI is important in so far as it requires trainees 'to decide *for themselves*' (1998: 171) and respond practically, intellectually and emotionally. Teachers 'who are simply told what to do and what not to do' are less likely to develop the 'multitude of senses, knowledges and ways of acting … required in schools and in classrooms' (1998: 178).

Grenfell (1998: 131–44) outlines the following thirteen problem areas or dichotomies that some of his trainees experienced:

- the incongruity between personal views of teaching and those presented on the course;
- past experience that has proved to be successful versus a new approach that has not;
- the choice to be made between trusting what I know about teaching and learning from and trusting what others tell me to do;

- the need to respond personally to the pedagogic approach versus the need to fulfil the course requirement;
- the ability to criticise versus the ability to do better oneself;
- to teach by technique versus to teach through individual personality;
- the need to attend to personal security versus the need to attend to the pedagogic needs of the pupils;
- how can I be a teacher versus how can I be myself?;
- 'I want everything planned so that I know what I am doing' versus 'I want flexibility to take pupils' response into account';
- how far to bring the approach to the particular class versus how far to bring the particular class to the approach;
- do I use the target language or English?;
- to teach grammar versus to teach through the target language; and
- who do I turn to with problems?

Reflection
Activity 2.5 Tensions frequently experienced by trainees

Consider Grenfell's thirteen dichotomies. To what extent are they representative of problem areas you have encountered and are facing? Have you been able to resolve them? What strategies did you use?

Grenfell also emphasises the importance of the personal theories of school-based mentors. Rather than viewing their practice as behaviours to be modelled and copied, regarding what teachers say and how they teach as being in some ways theoretical 'allows trainees to be explicit about what they think, and in so doing, objectifying it' (1998: 148). This, Grenfell argues, allows trainees to change and discuss change as well as 'to develop ways of thinking and acting which allow them to become competent as a teacher in a range of contexts' (1998: 148).

Different levels of theorising, to be addressed at different stages of (trainee) teachers' development and by different partners in the training process, can thus be identified.

STAGES IN THE DEVELOPMENT OF TRAINEES

In the course of ITE, learning takes place at different rates. Mfl trainees undergo a developmental process, which is governed by individual personal differences. One change most mfl trainees undergo is the gradual shift from a concern with themselves as teachers, as lesson planners and deliverers of subject matter, towards an increasing concern for pupils as individuals and of the necessity to cater for the needs of the full range of pupils in their care.

Based on their work with primary PGCE students, John Furlong and Tricia Maynard (see 1995: 73–97) suggest that there are a number of different broad stages of development. These stages are summarised in Table 2.3.

Table 2.2   Stages in the development of trainee teachers

No.	Stage	Summary
1	Early idealism	Trainee teachers often come to the course with an educational philosophy based on good or bad examples from their own 'careers' as pupils
2	Personal survival	Trainee teachers can feel quite overwhelmed by their first experience of teaching, they tend to feel insecure and want the pupils to accept them as teachers; they use strategies such as copying the mentor, appraising their initial idealistic view of themselves as teachers and working at gaining and maintaining classroom control
3	Dealing with difficulties	Trainee teachers start to appreciate the complexities of teaching and gain a basic understanding of certain aspects of the job; many look to pupils for feedback and judge their own effectiveness by how well pupils like them; teaching strategies and classroom organisation become increasingly important and trainee teachers often try to assimilate the teaching style and methods used by their mentor
4	Hitting a plateau	Whilst having gained certain basic competences many trainees can lack real understanding; they can often act like teachers but not really think like teachers at this stage
5	Moving on	Trainees start to think of themselves as professional educators

DEVELOPING A PERSONAL APPROACH TO MFL TEACHING

Gradually, as mfl trainee teachers become more familiar with the processes of classroom organisation and more confident in interacting with pupils, they begin to develop their own personal teaching style. Mfl trainees need to determine their personal approach to mfl teaching on the basis of:

- the statutory requirements for mfl and their methodological implications;
- the learning styles and individual differences and needs of pupils;
- personal preferences concerning teaching styles;
- the policies and practice prevalent in placement schools; and
- good practice described in relevant literature/lectures or observed in mfl classrooms.

The last few decades have witnessed a wide range of approaches to mfl teaching, none of which provided a panacea. In an appendix to his book *Designing tasks for the communicative classroom* David Nunan (see 1989: 194–6) provides an interesting overview of important language teaching methods. His matrix provides a useful tool for analysing personal preferences concerning mfl teaching and learning.

Table 2.3 Questionnaire

		Questions	Score
1		**Do you believe that language is essentially**	
	a	a set of rule-governed structures?	
	b	a system which has developed to convey meaning?	
	c	composed of a unique rhythm and spirit based around the culture of the country where the language is spoken?	
	d	built around correct, grammatical concepts?	
2		**A modern foreign language is best learnt by**	
	a	memorisation and forming of good language habits	
	b	listening, reading and then practising	
	c	undertaking realistic tasks, achievable only by use of the TL	
	d	acquisition through constant exposure to and immersion in the TL and culture	
3		**The primary aim of learning a modern foreign language is**	
	a	to achieve a practical command of speaking, listening, reading, writing	
	b	to achieve functional and linguistic objectives	
	c	to provide basic communicative skills as well as essential academic learning skills.	
	d	to provide enjoyment and stimulation through access to a foreign culture.	
4		**An mfl course should be structured so that the language presented**	
	a	is graded in forms of ever-increasing levels of difficulty	
	b	is determined by the learner's individual needs	
	c	is based around grammatical items and associated vocabulary	
	d	consists of excerpts from cultural texts	
5		**The purpose of classroom activities is**	
	a	to practise and reinforce correct forms of language	
	b	to engage the learner in communicative tasks	
	c	to allow the learner to respond to commands, questions and clues in her own way	
	d	to build upon structures and language forms learnt previously	
6		**The learner's chief responsibility is**	
	a	to listen, repeat and to respond	
	b	to negotiate objectives and to respond accordingly	
	c	to move towards independence, autonomy and responsibility	
	d	to remain passive and to allow the materials and activities to determine the nature of learning	
7		**The teacher's place in the teaching/learning process is**	
	a	to act as a model of good TL use and to orchestrate drill practice	
	b	to facilitate through presentation, advice and the provision of authentic, realistic tasks	
	c	to provide comprehensible input and orchestrate a variety of related activities	
	d	to teach, test and to reinforce accurate language forms	
8		**In the main the following materials should be used by the teacher:**	
	a	a course book and visual aides	
	b	audio tapes and transcripts	
	c	authentic, realistic materials	
	d	structured examples and related exercises	

Reflection

Many trainees tend to start to teach in a way they have been or would like to be taught. Below are two activities intended to broaden your perspective and to encourage you to consider other strategies to meet the needs and preferences of pupils in your classroom.

Activity 2.6 features a questionnaire (Table 2.3), which is based on Nunan's matrix. It also builds on Kolb, Rubin and McIntyre's (1974) learning styles inventory. The purpose of this activity is to guide you towards an understanding of your own preferred learning style and at the same time to make you aware of the principle features of other styles. In Activity 2.7 you can then apply the understanding of learning styles gained in Activity 2.6 and start to develop your own approach to mfl teaching.

Activity 2.6 Identifying preferred learning styles

- Read through the questions and statements in Table 2.3. For each question/statement there are four contrasting views. There are no 'right' or 'wrong' responses. You are asked to respond to each question/statement in terms of how it best corresponds to your own personal views. Do not think too hard before responding. Allocate 2 points to the response closest to your views, 1 point to the one ranked second; give −1 point to your third favourite response and −2 points to the response you agree with the least.
- Transfer your points into Table 2.4. For the time being disregard the acronyms at the top of each column.
- Then, plot your scores on the grid in Figure 2.2 and join them to a geometrical form. You should end up with a drawing in the shape of a kite. Your preferred learning style is represented by the quadrant in which the majority of your kite shape can be found. It is defined by combining two of the descriptions in Table 2.5, which account for the two axes. The graph shows your preferences and strength of feeling.

Table 2.4 Scoring table

No.	OBH	LMPU	ERP	SGA
1	a =	b =	c =	d =
2	a =	c =	d =	b =
3	a =	b =	d =	c =
4	a =	b =	d =	c =
5	a =	b =	c =	d =
6	a =	b =	d =	c =
7	a =	c =	b =	d =
8	a =	c =	b =	d =
Total				

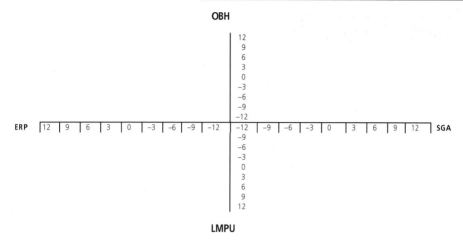

Figure 2.2 Plotting grid

Table 2.5 Description of learning styles

Off-by-heart language learning (OBH)	Learning to manipulate language for personal use (LMPU)	Exposure, repetition and practice (ERP)	Structured grammar approach (SGA)
The content of a course is defined within strict topic areas. Set phrases and key vocabulary are learnt irrespective of their grammatical complexity in order to meet perceived needs and corresponding usefulness in given situations. Learning 'parrot fashion' enables a task to be completed.	Language is learnt through the personalisation and manipulation of language forms presented. Motivation is achieved through realistic and successful communication. The learner is personally involved and takes considerable responsibility for her own learning.	The process of learning is through immersion in the language. Unstructured practice is reinforced through the reactions of others. The learner learns which parts of language work in which situations, thereby identifying and developing positive linguistic habits for herself.	The explanation of grammatical concepts in a logical sequence and the structured application of this knowledge lead to a sound understanding of language structures. This understanding facilitates a sound mastery of linguistic systems.

Reflection
Activity 2.7 Developing your personal
approach to mfl learning

- Having identified a preferred learning style, reflect upon the types of learning activities associated with it. What are the implications for your mfl teaching?
- Then consider activities that will suit other learning styles, for instance by talking to other trainees. What are the implications for your mfl teaching?

When planning mfl lessons, try to account for the full range of learning styles!

SCHOOLS' EXPECTATIONS AND THE MENTOR'S POINT OF VIEW

Ana Redondo

The role of the mentor as an agent in the development of mfl trainees, in helping them to progress through the stages in Figure 2.3, is very important. In order to maximise the effectiveness of the mentor's experience and advice, mfl trainee teachers need to establish a good working relationship with their mentors and staff at the placement school. In order to be able to do so it is important for mfl trainee teachers to gain some awareness of schools' expectations. This section offers advice and guidance from the point of view of the mentor. Mentors are those experienced mfl teachers who are responsible for trainees during their time at a placement school. This includes induction, support in organisational matters, observation of practical teaching, the giving of advice, guidance and diagnostic feedback, the provision of input on methodology and appropriate approaches as well as, importantly, assessment of practical teaching and target setting.

Why schools and mentors work with trainees

Schools and departmental teams agree to take trainee teachers for a whole host of reasons. A study carried out by researchers at the University of Warwick (Barker et al 1996: 57) for the Association for Teachers and Lecturers (ATL), amongst a representative sample of ITE courses, found that subject mentors saw a number of benefits arising from participation in a partnership scheme and receiving trainee teachers (see Table 2.6).

You need to realise, though, that these *benefits to mentors come at a certain cost*, for instance an increased demand on time, workload and administration, as often work with trainee teachers is carried out without receiving any financial rewards or time off in lieu (see Barker et al 1996: i). Having an additional person in the team has a number of implications for the work of a department. This you need to be aware of whilst on a school placement.

Table 2.6   Perception of the level of benefit in percentages (non-mfl specific)

Benefits	Subject mentors
Professional development	90
Job satisfaction	81
Management skills	76
Curriculum innovation	64
Morale	54
New teaching methods	45
Addition of new resources	42
Support with extracurricular activities	36
Career prospects	26
Pupil motivation	20
School status	12

The role of your mentor

It is important for you to appreciate that *established channels of communication need to be observed*. These vary from course to course and school to school. Your course handbook, as well as the staff and departmental handbooks provided by your placement schools, should contain all the relevant information with which you need to familiarise yourself.

At the same time there tends to be a school ITE coordinator/professional tutor (usually a senior teacher or deputy head) with overall responsibility for trainee teachers, who works in tandem with subject mentors.

In each department there usually is a named individual, the so-called subject mentor, who often has undergone a training programme with the respective HEI and who is your main point of contact during your stay at the placement school.

The responsibilities of subject mentors vary from one ITE course to another. However, they typically include liaison with the HEI, giving regular advice and feedback to trainees regarding their progress and performance against the standards as well as contributing to their assessment. Subject mentors tend to carry out their duties in consultation with all members of staff in the mfl department, who work with the trainee as well as the ITE coordinator/professional tutor at the school.

It is important for you to *be clear* from the very beginning *what you can realistically expect from your mentor*, for instance how often and when you will be able to meet with her. At the same time you *need to be fully aware of your responsibilities*. For instance, in terms of personal organisation you need to appreciate that any necessary equipment and resources in the school or department required for teaching, for example the TV and video, need to be booked well in advance. Failure to do so might result in you being unable to proceed with a lesson according to plan and cause disruption.

Building a professional relationship with members of staff at your placement school

Usually you will be asked to observe and work with a number of experienced teachers. The aim is for you to gain as wide a range of experiences of teaching styles and pupils' responses to them as possible. This is an important part of your learning experience during your ITE. It is important that you *establish a good working relationship with all members of staff*, not just with your mentor.

Working closely with more than one mfl teacher can, on occasion, create certain tensions: you might experience uncertainty as to what teaching styles and strategies to adopt or reject and sometimes advice given by different teachers might seem inconsistent or even irreconcilable to you. You should follow up specific observations made in lessons that trigger questions and seek clarification, as the reasons for employing particular teaching strategies are not always obvious to an observer. In many instances there is more than meets the eye to the way teachers manage their lessons and relate to pupils who they know well. If any doubt still persists, issues can be raised with your mentor and/or HEI tutor without necessarily personalising them. When seeking clarification in this way you engage in the important process of reflection on practice. This can provide you with an increased understanding of individual pupils and their behaviour as well as teachers' approaches to dealing with them. However, you *need to display a professional attitude* throughout this process. You need to be acutely aware that some questions you may want to ask might be sensitive.

Any worries or *problems need to be resolved in a mature and professional manner by following the correct procedures* normally outlined in the course handbook. Remember that *not all professional relationships necessarily turn into personal friendships*.

In the event of a personality clash, which can occur occasionally, mediation through a third party can help to resolve possible tensions.

Learning from members of staff

You need to understand that *you will normally be expected to model your practice on the agreed policies of both the department* you work in *and the placement school* more generally. Where asked to do so, you need to follow the routines set by members of staff for different groups as pupils can benefit from experiencing continuity of practice and consistency. Often certain variations to set routines are possible but they need to be discussed with and approved by the member of staff responsible for a given class. Innovation and exploration of new approaches to teaching are exciting, desirable and commendable in a trainee teacher and, as can be seen in Table 2.6 above, perceived as a benefit by mentors. They must, however, not upset pupils' well-established routines, which can serve them well in maximising their learning.

Appreciating the range of responsibilities of members of staff at your placement school

To ensure high quality in collaborative teaching, there is a need for frequent information exchange and discussions between the trainee teacher and the relevant member of staff.

You will soon become aware that, beside teaching lessons, a typical day of an mfl teacher may include: tidying up the classroom and getting ready in between lessons, doing break and gate duties, attending meetings (at lunch time or after school sometimes on several days in the week), invigilating detentions (at break time or after school), meeting visitors, discussing work with pupils outside lesson time, running lunch-time or after-school clubs, photocopying, covering lessons for colleagues, dealing with and responding to post or making and receiving phone calls. Importantly, they also need time for a break, their lunch and socialising with colleagues! Subject mentors often have other responsibilities apart from those for trainee teachers. You *need to respect the busy schedule of (mfl) teachers and observe arranged meeting times*.

In the light of these demands and in order to obtain an accurate picture from the beginning of what teaching entails, trainee teachers need to *play a full part in school life*. This will probably include you staying on after school for staff and departmental meetings, being attached to a form group for registrations, pastoral and guidance time, attending assemblies, attending parents' evenings, performing break duties, contributing to extra-curricular activities or assisting in fund-raising activities.

**Reflection
Activity 2.8 Finding out about
your mentor's daily routine**

Ask your subject mentor whether you can shadow her for a whole teaching day (including break, lunchtime and any free periods) and after school to become familiar with her daily responsibilities and duties.
- In the course of the day list all her duties and responsibilities, note the time of occurrence and their duration.
- Then discuss with your mentor how representative the day was and which other responsibilities and duties she has on a regular basis.

The trainee teacher as a role model

From the very start you *need to see yourself as an educator not merely as a subject specialist*. Your need to take on the wider brief of teachers, which includes concern for your pupils' spiritual, moral, social and cultural (SMSC) development. One way of taking on the full role of a teacher is by displaying a responsible and caring attitude towards pupils. You will often be perceived as a (role) model by pupils just as members of staff are and need to gain pupils' trust and respect both inside and, importantly also, outside the classroom. You *need to be acutely aware that pupils observe the behaviour and conduct of those around them carefully* and can be duly influenced in their behaviour and/or attitudes towards the subject. When working with pupils, you must never underestimate the formative influence you might have on them!

Visits from the HEI tutor

Schools are used to visits by a whole host of people such as advisers, inspectors, parents or governors, who come for a range of purposes. Departments welcome this but it

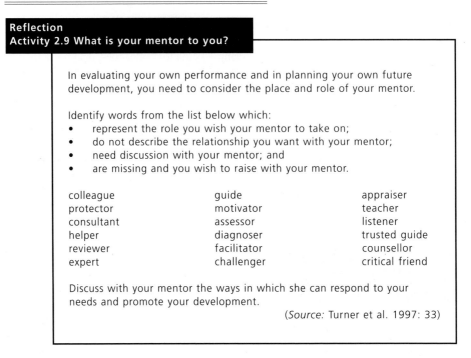

Reflection
Activity 2.9 What is your mentor to you?

In evaluating your own performance and in planning your own future development, you need to consider the place and role of your mentor.

Identify words from the list below which:
- represent the role you wish your mentor to take on;
- do not describe the relationship you want with your mentor;
- need discussion with your mentor; and
- are missing and you wish to raise with your mentor.

colleague	guide	appraiser
protector	motivator	teacher
consultant	assessor	listener
helper	diagnoser	trusted guide
reviewer	facilitator	counsellor
expert	challenger	critical friend

Discuss with your mentor the ways in which she can respond to your needs and promote your development.

(*Source:* Turner et al. 1997: 33)

inevitably adds to their workload. Given that hosting visitors needs to be fitted into an often already tight schedule, visits need to be arranged in advance. Often, your HEI tutor will arrange a visit through your mentor. Should she want to arrange a visit through you, it is very important that you liaise with the relevant members of staff, such as the head of department, your mentor and/or the respective teacher whose class is being observed. You need to observe established procedures such as, for instance, collecting the HEI tutor from reception and where visitors are expected to report to be issued with a visitor's pass.

Accepting and acting upon advice

There is a lot to be learnt from the experience and knowledge of (mfl) teachers at your placement school. Part of their role is to share their practice with you and to advise you on your development as a trainee teacher and set targets. It is your responsibility to take this advice on board and act upon it. You *need to learn from members of staff* at your placement school as well as *learn to work with them. In all your interactions with pupils, colleagues and the school, personal and professional integrity are essential.* When something goes wrong, you need to try, together with your mentor, to identify contributory factors and devise possible strategies for improvement.

Invariably, many things will not work out the first time round during your course of ITE. Qualified practitioners strive every day to improve their teaching. No less is expected from those new to the profession. A genuine desire to contribute to a positive learning experience about the ways people from other cultures communicate and live is what is required.

BECOMING AN MFL TEACHER: THE TRAINEE TEACHERS' POINT OF VIEW

CASE STUDY ONE

Concluding statement

Being a teacher turned out to be much different than I expected or rather much more than I expected. I find being a teacher over-whelming as well as being very challenging. Over this year I have developed not only many skills but also as a person. My previous experiences of teaching really did not prepare me for the 'whole school experience'.

After the time spent at my first placement school I felt that I was ready to be a 'real' teacher and that the rest of the course was simply a formality but beginning again at the second placement brought me back down to earth. For the first few days I felt that I was back at the start of the course again which was rather unnerv-ing. The factor which struck me the most was the different ethos between the schools of my first and second placements. The 'feel' of the two schools is amazingly different. In my second school placement I experienced a pastoral system based on 'Houses' rather than 'Years'.

Throughout this year I have developed in all the competence areas. I have built up a wide range of resources from my first place-ment for all years which I use to supplement the course books and to add an element of fun to my lessons. My planning and prepara-tion overall have become more efficient and I am more aware of how to approach teaching points and more able to pinpoint areas of teaching which need more attention. My record keeping has become more organised and consistent.

I have now developed my own classroom routines which I intend to improve on when I have my own classes and classrooms. I have drawn these routines and practices from observations made at both placement schools. Throughout my practices I have built up my use of pair and group work which has helped me to forge better rela-tionships within my groups. My relationships with both pupils and staff have developed well in both placements.

I have chosen five personal targets as an NQT (newly qualified teacher): displays, authentic materials, special needs, differentiation and extra-curricular activities. Not having my own classroom as a trainee teacher I am unable to provide my pupils with adequate and appropriate visual aids around the room. Next year I intend to make my classroom educationally stimulating as well as attractive and inviting. I am looking forward to developing in all of these areas next September.

CASE STUDY TWO

Concluding statement:
Like most people on the course, I suspect, I feel this year has gone surprisingly quickly. The overall impression I am left with, as the end approaches, is not simply of how much progress I have made, but rather of the realisation of how much more there is to teaching than just 'teaching'! This impression has rollercoasted as I started my practice at my second school, was offered a job there and shown what opportunities are available.

I found combining deadlines for college assignments and teaching quite taxing, partly due to the amount of time which has elapsed since doing my degree, allowing me to get out of practice where essays etc. are concerned. This did get easier as I became more familiar with the criteria and got used to writing again. More specifically to do with teaching, looking back at my initial statement, I see that certain of my fears did not materialise, whilst others did in a slightly different shape from that which I had imagined.

My concerns over planning and preparation, for example, proved to be unfounded. Similarly, where classroom management and discipline were concerned, I found I had very few problems, and was if anything occasionally too strict - and this in turn brought about a problem which I had not foreseen, that of being so strict (wanting to keep too much control) that I was very distant from the pupils I was teaching, even to my tutor group. After Christmas, and even more so after Easter I found that my own self-confidence allowed me to relax and concentrate more on how much pupils were learning, rather than how well they were behaving.

Being aware of pupils' academic abilities not only allowed me to plan more effectively, it also helped me to avoid problems with pupils who would find certain tasks either too easy or too difficult.

**Reflection
Activity 2.10 Mfl trainee teacher's
point of view**

Having read the two case studies, consider the following: did the trainees' perception about teaching change in the course of their ITE? Can these changes be accounted for by the stages of development described in Table 2.6?

SUMMARY

This chapter has shown that ITE has witnessed a number of important changes in the recent past. Certain issues, such as the perceived dichotomy between theory and practice and the importance of subject knowledge in the ITE process, continue to evolve in the light of changing contexts.

Mfl teaching is a highly complex profession requiring an understanding of a number of related disciplines. Learning to teach mfl in the secondary school often features a steep initial learning curve followed by a long process of discovery going beyond the period of ITE into continuing professional development. Teaching mfl is very complex but it can be a very rewarding career.

NOTE

1   At the time of writing the Teacher Training Agency (TTA) is carrying out a monitoring and consultation exercise in relation to the requirements set out in DfEE Circular 4/98. A new, streamlined set of requirements will come into effect in September 2002. Deatils can be found on the TTA website at *http:// wwwcanteach.gov.uk/*.

3 Teaching Methods and Learning Strategies in Modern Foreign Languages

The currently prevailing perspective on modern foreign languages (mfl) teaching, communicative language teaching (CLT), can be seen as an eclectic assortment of traditional and novel approaches based on the tenet of the development in pupils of an ability to communicate in the target language (TL) rather than as a prescriptive method of how to teach mfl (see Mitchell 1994: 33).

Traditional about CLT is the adherence to the model of presentation-practice-production (PPP). This common, but not universally accepted, framework for mfl teaching (see Pachler 2000a) presupposes the need to provide pupils with essential language forms, followed by work on exercises, activities and tasks to enable them to develop effective language habits. The process can be said to be complete when the pupils are able to use and manipulate these language forms to satisfy perceived needs. According to Nunan and Lamb (1996: 46), the PPP model is based on a view of learning as a linear process of understanding, internalising and activating knowledge and that the three stages are characterised by 'a gradual movement from high- to relative low-structure interactions (although many production tasks give the illusion of student control)'. At the different stages of the model, the teacher and learners have different roles (e.g. model, facilitator, monitor; listener, performer, interactor) and they feature different activity types (e.g. exposition, information gap, role play) and interaction modes (e.g. whole-class, pair, small group). Nunan and Lamb (1996: 46-7) conclude that the PPP model, whilst simple, is effective and useful for meeting *discrete* language objectives. For more contextualised and integrated objectives, however, more sophisticated models are required. Given the prevailing emphasis on narrowly transactional skills and memorisation of lexical items in the current interpretation of CLT in Britain, the PPP model can be said to possess fitness for purpose (see also Pachler 2000a).

The change in syllabus design away from a focus on the structural aspects of the TL to topics supposedly relevant to pupils is novel about CLT. These topics tend to centre, on the one hand, around the communicative needs of visitors to a country where the TL is spoken. On the other hand, specifications (formerly syllabuses) are constructed around so-called functions and speech acts, such as telling the time, how to express likes and dislikes or asking for the way (for a detailed list see Neuner and Hunfeld 1993: 140–5). CLT, of which language practice through simulation and role play is an integral part, focuses on meaning and the conveyance of personal needs through language.

Most recently the UK variant of CLT has been characterised by a 'methodological imperative' of maximum use of the TL for instruction and interaction, which is discussed in detail in Chapter 5.

The introduction of CLT to mfl teaching in secondary schools can, amongst other things, be linked to theories and findings of (applied) linguistics as well as the comprehensivisation of the secondary sector and the considerable change in target audiences associated with it.

OBJECTIVES

By the end of this chapter you should have:

- developed some understanding of the methodological underpinnings of current mfl practice;
- gained some awareness of weaknesses of CLT as well as some current and possible future methodological developments;
- familiarised yourself with a framework for developing the main tenet of CLT, communicative competence; and
- become familiar with some aspects of the field of learning strategies.

SOME ASPECTS OF CLT

Current mfl teaching methodology is characterised by an emphasis on communicative competence. This represents a redefinition and broadening of what is deemed to constitute proficiency in mfl learning away from the ability to translate, read and write texts towards an ability to respond, often by way of the spoken word, to aural and oral stimuli. 'Authenticity' of texts and tasks has become increasingly important, as has using the TL in 'real' contexts for communicative purposes. The focus is on the ability to use the TL to communicate personal meaning rather than on knowledge about the TL and there is an emphasis on active participation of learners and language use outside the classroom (see Mitchell 1994 and Pachler 2000a).

In a bid to increase the ability of pupils to communicate in the TL, emphasis has increasingly been placed on the use of the TL for instruction and interaction. As contact with mfl for secondary school pupils invariably comes through language learning, the structured and limited exposure to the TL in a classroom environment, rather than acquisition, subconscious development of language skills devoid of formal explanation, the emphasis on TL use and the focus on 'authentic' material can be seen as an attempt to counterbalance the 'context-reduced' (Roberts 1992: 21) nature of the mfl learning process.

The distinction between language acquisition and language learning is important in the context of mfl teaching and learning in the secondary school as most pupils are in the main, and for a host of reasons, unable to immerse themselves in the TL and the target culture(s). Eric Hawkins (1987: 99) describes the mfl experience of British pupils with the metaphor of 'gardening in a gale'. The limited time available in the school curriculum and the limited exposure to the TL make it difficult for pupils to retain what they have learnt in the classroom when re-entering the world of English outside, as what happens there does not, in the main, reinforce the learning that has taken place in the classroom.

On the one hand this fact puts the onus on mfl teachers, amongst other things, to:

- structure the language pupils are exposed to;
- select relevant, varied and appropriate material for them;
- provide them with ample opportunities to practise and develop, amongst others, the skills of listening, speaking, reading and writing;
- facilitate the development of confidence in their own ability; and
- develop their cultural and structural understanding.

On the other hand the limitations imposed on pupils by their learning environment, e.g.

- the limited amount of curriculum time,
- the limited access to undivided attention by the teacher,
- the lack of exposure to the TL or
- the geographical and affectional distance from the countries and cultures where the TL is spoken,

make it necessary for mfl teachers to aim to equip pupils with the necessary skills and strategies to learn the TL independently.

For pupils to develop linguistic and communicative competence the teacher needs to structure the learning environment in a way the pupils perceive to be purposeful. It was with this in mind that local groups of teachers developed clear objectives and defined syllabuses as part of the graded objectives movement in mfl teaching and learning during the 1970s and 1980s (see e.g. King 1991 or Page and Hewett 1987).

CLT builds on the understanding that the purpose of language is to communicate and that communication is (see Halliday 1975 as summarised in Richards and Rodgers 1986: 70–1):

- instrumental (to get things);
- regulatory (to control others);
- interactional (to engage with others);
- personal (to express personal meaning);
- heuristic (to learn and discover);
- imaginative (to create a world of imagination); and
- representational (to communicate information).

Pupils need to value the purposes of mfl learning and, at the same time, be aware of what they must do to achieve the relevant objectives. Peter Bimmel (see 1993: 5–6) identifies the following characteristics of strategic learning:

- setting of a goal/an objective;
- devising a plan how to achieve the goal/objective;
- putting the plan into action; and
- evaluating whether the goal/objective has been achieved.

These general features of learning are an integral part of the development of competence in the TL. As they are exposed to more and more language, pupils increasingly have to manage the process of learning for themselves. Each pupil is different, will favour different teaching and learning styles and will employ different strategies to manage her own mfl learning.

CLT places the pupil at the centre of the mfl learning process. David Nunan sees the role of the learner in CLT as that of 'a negotiator, interactor, giving as well as taking' (Nunan 1989: 195). One key feature of CLT is its principal aim to provide pupils with the necessary language and communication skills to use the TL effectively and in a purposeful way. This involves communicating to satisfy personal needs as well as the structuring and sequencing of the learning experience.

William Littlewood (see 1981: 85–95) places CLT into a methodological framework consisting of pre-communicative activities, which he subdivides into 'structural' and 'quasi-communicative' activities, and communicative activities, where he differentiates between 'functional communication' and 'social interaction' activities. Littlewood points out that there are no clear dividing lines between stages of learning. According to him, the learner should be guided from dependence on the teacher and opportunities to use the language in the classroom, to using language alone and in real authentic situations. Pre-communicative activities can involve teacher-centred classroom activities. The teacher selects the content of a unit of work, negotiates learning objectives and organises the presentation of material in a structured way. The quasi-communicative activities are intended to offer opportunities to practise the newly learnt language in situations that can easily be related to real life. Functional communication activities take this progression one step further and are based on the premise that TL use is positively reinforced if it can be seen to work. If the speaker uses language to good effect and she achieves the intended purpose for personal gain, the forms of language used stand more chance of being personalised and internalised. To this end information gap exercises can be devised for use in the classroom. They involve the transfer of information which is known only to one user through linguistic means. Social interaction activities require the refinement of language use involving more than simply conveying a message, but doing so in a way which is appropriate to the cultural context.

In the UK context, CLT is frequently characterised by a marginalisation of grammar in the learning process and a diminishing focus on accuracy. This, however, need not be the case. Mitchell (1994: 38–9) summarises CLT in six key descriptions:

1   Classroom activities should maximise opportunities for learners to use the target language for meaningful purposes, with their attention on the messages they are creating and the task they are completing, rather than on correctness of language form and language structure;

2   Learners trying their best to use the target language creatively and unpredictably are bound to make errors; this is a normal part of language learning, and constant correction is unnecessary, and even counter-productive;

3   Language analysis and grammar explanation may help some learners, but extensive experience of target language use helps everyone! ...
4   Effective language teaching is responsive to the needs and interests of the individual learner;
5.   Effective language learning is an active process, in which the learner takes increasing responsibility for his or her progress;
6.   The effective teacher aims to facilitate, not control, the language learning process.

A CRITICAL EXAMINATION OF CLT

Whilst CLT has been and continues to be very influential in mfl teaching and learning in the UK, 'it is not *the* panacea of FL teaching' (Pachler 2000: 38). This section lists some of its shortcomings; for a detailed critical examination of CLT see Pachler 2000.

In the UK

> developments have led, by-and-large, to a narrow transactional-functional orientation in which pupils are prepared for the linguistic (and non-linguistic) needs of tourists ... with the emphasis on "getting by". On the one hand, this approach is characterised by a heavy emphasis on recall of often random lexical items and phrases derived from narrowly defined, idealised interactions and exchanges at the cost of transfer of knowledge and skills across topics. On the other hand, it tends to ignore the teenage learner's communicative needs and does not allow her to engage in meaningful and realistic interaction, both supposedly central tenets of communicative methodology.
>
> (Pachler 2000a: 30)

The realignments to CLT that follow warrant consideration.

Developing grammatical and discourse competence as subsets of communicative competence

For Tony Roberts (1992: 27) the main deficiency of CLT is that, contrary to some of its proponents' assumptions, there is a difference between learning a language *for* communication and learning it *as* communication. He proposes a process starting from 'structure' leading via controlled practice to 'function'. In other words, Roberts views the teaching of grammatical forms as a pre-requisite for meaningful language use by re-iterating that 'doing is subservient to knowing'. He is concerned that in the mfl context, pupils tend not to perceive the need to communicate in the TL and thinks that this poses a real problem as the 'intention to mean' is a fundamental principle of CLT.

Whilst we do not argue for a return to the grammar-translation paradigm here, we advocate an increased focus on grammatical competence and discourse competence, i.e. the inclusion of longer utterances and texts, as subsets of communicative competence. Indeed, the 1999 mfl National Curriculum Orders include an increased emphasis on grammar compared with earlier versions (see Chapter 7 for a detailed discussion of the role of grammar in mfl teaching and learning).

Re-appraising the aims of mfl teaching

CLT, with its transactional orientation, reflects the current functional and vocational rationale for mfl teaching and learning. A re-appraisal of the aims of mfl teaching and learning towards an educational orientation has been suggested by some commentators:

> (the) primary aim should be, like the primary aim of literacy, to enhance the learner's semiotic system, to help him/her to abstract his/her thought from the contextual prison of spontaneous concepts in order to make language a more autonomous object, of which the learner is more fully aware and over which greater control can be exercised.
>
> (Bauckham 1995: 31)

This would require an increased methodological focus on intellectually and cognitively challenging activities, tasks, texts and contexts (see Pachler 2000: 35–6).

Re-defining of the notion of authenticity

We have already noted that CLT can be characterised by syllabus design taking account of topics that are relevant, namely ones that centre around the vocabulary and situations encountered by people when visiting a country where the TL is spoken. Whilst adult learners often draw (part of) their motivation from the goal of visiting a foreign country, this is less true for pupils studying the TL at secondary school. Some of the situations presumed relevant for visitors to countries where the TL is spoken, such as making arrangements for train travel, booking hotel rooms, drinking in bars, eating in restaurants, buying petrol etc. are of limited relevance for pupils, for instance because of their different experiences of the world. This raises questions about the 'authenticity' of topics, tasks and material.

Alan Hornsey (1994: 7) suggest that 'plausibility (might be) a more useful guiding principle than authenticity and that for a teacher there are other -ity words that demand attention'. These, in his view, are:

- learnability,
- repeatability,
- tangibility,
- useability and
- pronounceability.

Mfl teachers working with low achieving and poorly motivated pupils in particular have started to experiment with tasks their pupils can encounter more easily in their everyday lives such as registering foreign visitors at a local hotel (see Alison 1995). The change in the notion of 'authenticity', that is away from situations and material focussing on (the) culture(s) of the TL towards those with more immediate relevance to pupils, i.e. situations and material focussing on using the TL in the UK as part of pupils' everyday experience of life, underpins to some extent the inclusion of vocational contexts into mfl teaching and learning.

Towards 'optimal use' of the TL

The requirement to maximise the use of the TL by teachers and pupils in the 1992 and 1995 NC mfl Orders can be seen to be at least partly based on the misguided notion that mfl learning is comparable to mother tongue learning (see Pachler 2000: 33–4). Amongst many other things, this emphasis on maximum TL use can be seen to lead to interactional classroom dynamics, which are heavily dominated by teachers:

> (whereas) teachers of any subject may tend to tell their pupils "when to talk, what to talk about, when to stop talking and how well they talked" …, FL teachers appear also to prescribe for pupils the very words, even features of words, with which to talk.
>
> (Westgate et al. 1985: 276)

Indeed, the 1999 NC mfl Orders move towards what Ernesto Macaro (2000) calls the 'optimal use' position from a 'total exclusion' or 'maximal use' position in earlier versions. For a detailed discussion of TL-related issues see Chapter 5.

Developing intercultural (communicative) competence

Gerhard Neuner and Hans Hunfeld (see 1993: 87) note that one of the deficiencies of CLT is its failure to take sufficient account of the specificity of different target audiences. In order to address this imbalance they argue the case for an intercultural approach as an extension to CLT (see 1993: 106–27). As a specific characteristic feature of this intercultural approach they see a didactic concept, which fosters comparisons of life and reality in the pupils' own world with that of the countries where the TL is spoken. They warn, though, that this process is characterised by a danger of misunderstanding, threat and incomprehension, which needs careful handling by the teacher. For a more detailed discussion of target culture learning and teaching see Chapter 8.

Intercultural competence and intercultural communicative competence need to be distinguished here. The former describes the ability to know about and empathise with TL speakers and understand the cultural context out of which they live, work and speak, albeit if necessary in their mother tongue or a *lingua franca*, the latter includes in addition the ability to interact in the TL (see e.g. Byram 1997).

Integrating information and communications technology (ICT) in mfl teaching and learning

Noss and Pachler (1999), in their analysis of the impact of ICT on pedagogy, argue cogently that ICT has considerable potential and that it makes new things possible in new ways. Effective ICT use, they argue, has considerable implications for the role of the teacher and requires fundamental changes to teaching methodology. (Some of these issues are discussed in Chapter 12; see also Leask and Pachler 1999.)

A FRAMEWORK FOR SEQUENCING

On the basis of the discussion of aspects of CLT above we suggest a structured approach to mfl teaching leading to the development of pupil independence. This framework for sequencing, summarised in Figure 3.1, builds on the traditional PPP paradigm. It is important to note that the practical examples given for illustration do not refer to the same topic throughout. Also, they are not aimed at the same level of linguistic proficiency.

INTRODUCING THE TOPIC

A sense of ownership in and responsibility for the learning process is a first step to autonomy and personalisation. The introduction of a topic can involve the negotiation of appropriate objectives in order to meet individual pupils' needs but should involve the making explicit of objectives, where possible in the TL, to give pupils a sense of where they are going and why they are asked to carry out certain activities. Pupils should be aware of the value of a topic and, on occasion, they can be asked to identify key language for themselves. This process of negotiation and discussion enables the teacher to establish her role as a facilitator of the learning process and helps the pupil in adopting an active, participatory role.

One possible strategy the teacher can adopt when introducing a new topic is what Jochen and Monika Grell (1985: 105–6 and 117–33) call 'to send positive reciprocal emotions'. In order to foster an atmosphere conducive to learning and to motivate pupils to learn, Grell and Grell suggest the teacher might, for instance, try to relate a given topic to personal experiences, tell the pupils something funny or express positive expectations about, show personal enthusiasm for and use a visual stimulus relating to the topic for pupils to comment upon or respond to. Careful consideration needs to be given to whether and how this be done in the TL.

One strategy, based here around the topic of education, which enables pupils to draw on their existing knowledge of the TL and culture and which can be applied to a number of different contexts, is brainstorming. Though we do not suggest the use of brainstorming every time a new topic is introduced, we feel it is a good example of a strategy that allows for future learning to build on existing knowledge. Again, careful consideration needs to be given to whether and how this should be done in the TL.

		Five stages of sequencing	
Continuous assessment		Introducing the topic	Evaluation
		Presenting a new language focus	
		Practising language forms	
		Exploiting the language	
		Summative assessment and evaluation	

Figure 3.1 A framework for sequencing

First of all, pupils are asked to brainstorm words they associate with the topic in small groups. A nominated scribe notes down all words group members can come up with. Asking pupils to work within a given time limit can add pace and a sense of urgency.

In a second step, pupils group their list of lexical items into categories, for instance buildings, subjects, qualifications, people. Pupils should be encouraged to use the TL and explain contributions to one another.

In a next step, pupils can be asked to produce an illustrated guide in the TL on what they feel they ought to know about the topic 'education' for display.

Public display of the various guides allows for critical analysis of the pupils' work by the teacher through comparison of outcomes of different groups. The emerging gaps in knowledge can be formulated into learning objectives. The teacher's role is to place the content of displays and the learning objectives into a communicative context. This way, through a consolidation of existing knowledge and skills, pupils should be able to experience some sense of ownership of and interest in the topic.

Reflection
Activity 3.1 Communicating lesson objectives

- On the basis of lesson observation, how can the objectives of a lesson and a unit of work be communicated to pupils without resorting to the use of English?
- Survey a group of pupils to find out what they think the objectives of a particular lesson or unit of work are.

PRESENTING A NEW LANGUAGE FOCUS

Having identified objectives and particular linguistic and learning needs, the teacher needs to expose pupils to the language content required. The teacher is the principal (linguistic) resource in the classroom and it is her responsibility to select and organise the content into manageable chunks, encouraging the development of the skills of listening, speaking, reading and writing equally. This should be done within a communicative context as pupils need to recognise the short- and long-term value of these skills. Whilst the teacher needs to ensure she gives pupils enough time to allow them to familiarise themselves with as well as assimilate and accommodate new linguistic items, given the need to progress to higher National Curriculum levels, she also needs to ensure new words, phrases and structures are used in context and to produce more complicated utterances as quickly as possible.

The presentation phase should include the teaching and learning of vocabulary, phrases and structures. These linguistic and structural elements should not be taught in isolation from the culture and potential communicative contexts. Visual aids, such as flashcards, the overhead projector (OHP) or mime and gesture, enable pupils to assimilate words and phrases. Not every item relevant to the topic needs to be taught.

Independence in mfl learning requires pupils to use dictionaries, reference material and (contextual) clues to interpret meaning. As a consequence, the teacher needs to ensure that pupils have the skills to carry out related tasks. The aim at this stage is to begin the process of mastering the linguistic forms so that, at a later stage, pupils can draw on these in real communicative situations for themselves. The pupil needs to be aware of the communicative potential of language forms.

In their resource pack *Steps towards achievement* Nick Pugh and Barbara Murphy (1993: 2) give the following advice about introducing vocabulary using flashcards:

a)   Show the flashcard.

b)   Say the key word/phrase e.g. tennis – je joue au tennis.

c)   Repeat the key word/phrase several times.

d)   Encourage pupils to repeat: as a whole group, as rows/sub-groups and as confidence grows, individually.

e)   Encourage pupils to mime the activity while repeating the key word/ phrase.

f)   Show a new flashcard and repeat the procedure as above.

g)   Once a small group of flashcards has been introduced, use the 'hierarchy of questions' to help pupils learn the vocabulary in three phases:
   – Ask a series of yes/no or true/false questions
      e.g. show a flashcard or mime an action and make a statement.
         Je joue au tennis – oui ou non?
         Je joue au golf – oui ou non?
   – Ask a series of questions which offer an alternative
      e.g. show a flashcard or mime an activity and offer two statements
         Je joue au tennis ou je joue au golf?
   – Ask a series of goal questions
      e.g. show a flashcard or mime an activity and ask
         Que fais-tu?

Question-and-answer work is a very important teacher-led strategy in presenting new language. Mark Oliver (1994: 16) notes that

> a major advantage of question-and-answer work is precisely that the teacher, by the careful choice of questions asked, can ensure that learners are helped to move from supported to unsupported use of given linguistic items in a gradual way.

Oliver (see 1994: 16) proposes a similar approach to Pugh and Murphy but offers a different terminology:

• yes/no questions: requiring the pupil to associate a TL word or phrase with meaning;

• alternative questions: requiring the pupil to repeat a word or phrase, to reproduce language using known material;

• negative questions: providing a bridge from reproductive to productive use of language;

• target questions: requiring the pupil to generate (whole-sentence) answers.

Pugh and Murphy (1993: 2–3) also show how flashcards and mime games can be used effectively to reinforce new vocabulary:

a   Teacher/Pupil chooses one flashcard and spins it quickly in front of class. Class try to identify flashcard.

b   Teacher/Pupil displays group of flashcards. Pupils look away and one flashcard is removed. Class identify missing one.

c   Teacher/Pupil displays group of flashcards. Teacher/Pupil names all but one of the flashcards. Class identify the missing one.

d   Flashcards are displayed. Teacher/Pupil names a flashcard and another pupil must point to the appropriate flashcard. This can be played in teams, with winning pupil identifying/removing the appropriate picture.

e   Flashcards are displayed and numbered. Teacher/pupil names a flashcard and class note the appropriate number. Alternatively, teacher/pupil says a number and class must identify the flashcard.

f   Teacher/Pupil chooses one flashcard without the class seeing. Class must ask questions to try to identify the flashcard chosen. Teacher/pupil reply 'non' until flashcard is correctly guessed.

g   Teacher/Pupil displays one flashcard and makes one statement. If the statement matches the flashcard, class repeats it. If the statement is false, the class stays silent. Class members who make an error are out. Winner is the last person out.

h   Divide the class into teams. Each team has two chairs labelled: true/false. Teacher/Pupil displays one flashcard and makes one statement. If the statement matches the flashcard, a team member sits on the 'true' chair and vice versa. Points are awarded for sitting on the right chair.

i   Divide the class into teams. Place a flashcard face down in front of each team member. Against the clock, each team member in turn looks at their flashcard and identifies it. The fastest team is the winner.

The OHP is an alternative to flashcards for presenting and reinforcing new language. It can also serve as a stimulus for language games and as visual support for the use of the TL. For a more detailed discussion of the potential of the OHP see e.g. Tierney and Humphreys 1992.

Another possible activity in the context of presenting new language focuses on places in a town. Flashcards are placed around the room. A pupil is blindfolded and spun around. The teacher points to individual flashcards and pupils ask in the TL where individual places in town are, e.g. '¿Dónde está el banco?' ('Where is the bank?'). The pupil who was spun around has to reply by pointing at the correct flashcard and by responding, for instance at a basic level, with 'El banco está allí' ('The bank is over there'). Then, symbols for directions can be presented on an overhead transparency. Pupils repeat and listen carefully. Once pupils are familiar with the new words, short conversations can be presented on a tape. Pupils listen for places sought and directions given. Eliciting non-verbal responses from pupils, such as marking simple plans with the appropriate places, ensures that the vocabulary presented has been recognised in context.

Reflection
Activity 3.2 Presenting new language forms

- During lesson observations, note the different resources and methods used by different mfl teachers to introduce new language.
- Discuss with pupils to what extent gestures, colours, size, position, voice modulation or movement can help them memorise new language language.

PRACTISING LANGUAGE FORMS

There is no clear dividing line between the presentation and practice of language forms but, instead, there is a gradual change of emphasis. Practice is one stage in the continuous process of internalising selected language. A behaviourist, habit-forming approach is not necessarily out of place if the pupil is aware of its purpose. Repetition exercises can be effective and are necessary. It is possible for them to be directed by pupils provided they realise the value of the exercises and can see the ultimate goal. Although the skills of listening, speaking, reading and writing can be developed independently of each other this is not advisable as pupils must understand the need to integrate skills in order to be able to communicate effectively. Not to work towards the integration of skills poses the risk of producing 'walking phrase book' incapable of using language spontaneously and of generating their own language in response to stimuli. Course books often provide effective exercises to allow pupils to practise and to experiment with language. Written exercises must relate to the pupils' need to write, listening exercises must contain the type of language which is comprehensible to them. 'Authentic' texts, or texts made to look 'authentic', provide a link between the classroom and the outside world, mfl learning and its use. The traditional, grammar-based approach fell short in this respect:

> One of the major reasons for questioning the adequacy of grammatical sylla-buses lies in the fact that even when we have described the grammatical (and lexical) meaning of a sentence, we have not accounted for the way it is used as an utterance.

> (Wilkins 1976: 10–11)

Just as the TL should be practised in the context of potential 'authentic' use, it should also be relevant to individual pupils' needs. There is no greater frustration for pupils than practising until the skill, word, phrase, structure etc. has been perfected and then not enjoying the opportunity of putting it to good use. The teacher needs to provide opportunities for progression beyond what Littlewood calls 'quasi-communicative' activities. Once again, the emphasis and focus should gradually shift to allow for a smooth transition to the exploitation of language.

Useful in the context of choosing effective tasks for practising the TL is, we feel, Michael Heafford's typology of tasks (1990: 88) despite the fact that the 'value' attributed to activities appears to be determined by unstructured observation of pupils' attitudes to tasks undertaken in the classroom rather than by empirical research and remains, therefore, open to interpretation.

PUPIL ACTIVITIES OF LOW VALUE

1   Choral/individual repetition.
2   Reading aloud from the textbook.
3   Reading out dialogues/role-plays.
4   Translating.
5   Copying from board/book.
6   Word-searches.

PUPIL ACTIVITIES OF MIXED VALUE

1   Doing drill-like activities.
2   Pupil–pupil dialogue.
3   Receiving grammatical explanations.

PUPIL ACTIVITIES OF HIGH VALUE

1   Listening to the target language.
2   Replying to questions in the FL.
3   Asking questions in the FL.
4   Engaging in dramatic activities.
5   Increasing active/passive vocabulary.
6   Reading silently.
7   Relating language to social/cultural context.
8   Doing written work of an error-avoiding nature.

Surveys allow for the repetition of simple questions avoiding the possible boredom arising from having to say the same thing to the same person repeatedly. Half the pupils can be seated in a circle. The remaining pupils are asked to stand opposite those seated. In the context of the topic of education, the pupils standing up could be asked to find out in the TL from those sitting down what their favourite school subject is: '¿Qué asignatura prefieres?' The pupils sitting down reply. When one exchange of information is completed the pupils standing up move one space to the left. They pose the same question to the next pupil and write down the response. Once the circle is completed the two groups swap roles. The process of asking for the favourite school subject is repeated. Pupils will have had a number of exchanges and the information gathered can be used as focus for future work.

Pupils often know numbers, but cannot use them at speed. The following activity was devised as part of a bank of active learning strategies by mfl teachers in the New Mills and Buxton Technical Vocational Education Initiative (TVEI) consortium. The purpose of the activity is to practise numbers. Pupils are placed in groups of four. One is the spokesperson, one an accountant, one an inspector and one a researcher.

The teacher explains that she is an auctioneer. She will sell scrabble letters in lots to the highest bidder. The activity usually works best if letters are sold in groups of five or six. The groups of pupils need to consider how much each set of letters might be worth. Points will be awarded for the group that can produce the longest word or the most words in the TL at the end of the game from the letters purchased. Points are awarded for the number of letters purchased and also for money not spent. Each group has 500 units of the foreign currency. The inspector checks that other groups do not overspend, the accountant organises budgets and the researcher helps the spokesperson. After a while roles within the groups are swapped. To prevent bids of 500 units in one go, groups need to be told that they may only bid in units of three, which can be changed to seven or nine etc. later in the game.

This activity tends to be rather noisy and involves pupils shouting numbers out at great speed. The activity is popular and effective, but does rely on the teacher ensuring appropriate behaviour throughout. Pupils with difficulties in number work might benefit from the use of calculators or other aids.

Reflection
Activity 3.3 Practising language forms

- Observe a number of mfl lessons and note the frequency of use of the types of activities listed by Heafford.
- Also, find out from pupils how valuable they found the different activities. How do pupil responses compare with Haefford's categories?

EXPLOITING THE LANGUAGE

Language should be used in a meaningful way. Opportunities for 'authentic' language use in the classroom are limited. 'Real' communication in the classroom comprises mainly 'classroom talk' and tends to be transactional in nature. This is a valuable part of the process as well as the desired outcome of mfl learning. Pupils need to borrow pens, share books, interact with the teacher. To conduct these transactions and interactions in English represents a wasted opportunity and devalues the potential of the TL. Trainee teachers should aim to devise situations where the goal is not achieved unless the TL is used.

Individual pupils should be able to use the TL in a way that suits their own needs and personalise it. So called 'information gap' activities are often used to stimulate communication. Given that pupils progress at different rates and in different ways the teacher needs to tailor activities to suit the individual pupil. Differentiation can facilitate this process and is discussed in Chapter 9.

Personalisation can be seen to have taken place when linguistic competence is no longer the focus: 'In communicative activities, the production of linguistic forms becomes subordinate to higher level decisions, related to the communication of meanings. ... The criterion for success is whether the meaning is conveyed effectively' (Littlewood 1981: 89).

Evidently, an approach like this presupposes the adoption of specific roles by both pupils and the teacher. Pupils need to assume responsibility for their own learning through active participation. They are unlikely to display this desirable behaviour trait

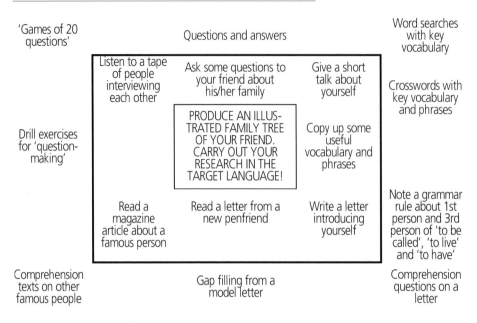

Figure 3.2   An independent study unit

automatically and will have to be accustomed to working in such a way. In the process of working independently a pupil interprets and generates language 'in terms of what s/he already and uniquely knows' (Dam 1990: 22). The teacher is no longer merely the source for information, but an advisor, facilitator, consultant and fellow communicator. In addition, the teacher is an assessor, recorder and reporter of pupils' progress.

The diagram in Figure 3.2 represents the planning of an independent study unit, but also serves as an example for project-based classroom work.

The first stage of planning is the identification of an end-of-unit goal. In this case the goal is to produce an illustrated family tree on behalf of a friend, who must be interviewed to provide the necessary information. The interview and the presentation will be conducted independently of the teacher. This stage is represented by the centre of the diagram. To qualify for this stage, pupils have to prove their ability by completing some tasks. These are represented by tasks inside the second frame. Obviously the tasks are relevant to working independently. If, however, pupils are unable to complete the core tasks, they receive support by being able to attempt simpler tasks, represented on the outside of the diagram. If, for example, a pupil is unable to copy relevant vocabulary and phrases free from spelling errors, she should be encouraged to develop those skills by attempting the wordsearches and crosswords. Clearly, activities are related to each other and pupils have access to exercises and materials to guide their own development. They may, for instance, choose to focus on particular skill areas. This should give the teacher the opportunity to monitor individuals' progress.

Some pupils will be able to enter the scheme at core task level, others will attempt to do so, but quickly realise the need to step back a stage. Others will choose, or be guided, to enter the process at the initial stage. If accustomed to using dictionaries and reference material, pupils can be given the responsibility to direct their own learning. Those pupils who are not able to complete the core task in the allocated time can do so as part of their homework.

In an activity presented by Wendy Bromidge and James Burch (1993: 10–11) the need to focus on the process as well as on the outcomes of learning becomes evident. Over a period of three weeks, pupils are taught and practise the vocabulary and phrases required to produce a magazine. Pupils learn, for instance, to negotiate with each other, delegate tasks, borrow pens or issue instructions. Only when pupils are confident with the language required can they move on to work on producing a magazine. The teacher is less concerned with the outcome, that is the language used in the magazine produced by the pupils, than the process of using the TL when carrying out the task.

For a more detailed discussion of independent learning see Pachler and Field 1999.

ASSESSMENT OF PUPILS

Assessment, which needs to cover the skills of listening, speaking, reading and writing equally, should not only be seen as coming at the end of the learning process but as an integral part; it should, therefore, be continuous and summative. Pupils do not progress at the same rate in all four skills and they need to be aware of the progress they make. Diagnostic feedback, i.e. the teacher telling pupils what they need to do to improve, is an important part of the learning process. Assessment should serve to motivate and inform pupils, but also inform the teaching process and feed into planning and the evaluation of learning opportunities. Assessment and feedback are central aspects of mfl teaching and learning and are discussed in detail in Chapter 10.

EVALUATION OF TEACHING

In addition to assessing pupils' achievement, performance and attainment, there is a need for the mfl teacher to evaluate the approaches employed and the tasks and materials used on an ongoing basis, i.e. lesson by lesson. For lesson evaluation see also Chapter 4.

David Nunan provides a useful checklist for evaluation purposes, which is summarised in Table 3.2 (adapted from Nunan 1989: 135–8).

LEARNING STRATEGIES

One aspect of mfl teaching that has received increased attention in recent years is learner training, i.e. teaching pupils how to learn. Commonly communication strategies and learning strategies are distinguished. Communication strategies allow the learner to overcome a limited linguistic repertoire to ensure communication of meaning takes place. They appear to be more difficult to teach. Learning strategies have been categorised into 'metacognitive' strategies (concerned with managing learning), 'affective' strategies (preparing oneself emotionally and attitudinally for the learning process) and 'social' strategies (pertaining to the interaction with other pupils or language users) (see e.g. Harris 1997: 5–6, Ellis and Sinclair 1989: 151–4 and Oxford 1987: 16–21).

Table 3.2 Evaluation of teaching

Stage	Evaluation criteria
Goals and rationale	Objectives should be realistic, relevant and made explicit to pupils.
Input	Language output must be preceded by input. In order to communicate effectively, pupils must be made aware of the vocabulary, structures and cultural context.
Activities	Activities must be appropriate and devised to facilitate learning rather than to occupy or entertain pupils.
Roles and settings	Pupils must be able to draw on existing knowledge. At the same time they need to appreciate the cultural context of their communication. It is unrealistic to expect pupils to simulate a situation unless they are already conceptually familiar with that context.
Implementation	For real communication to take place, there has to be a transmitter of information and a receiver. Pupils need to use each other to carry out conversations and therefore need training in these roles.
Grading and integration	Tasks should be open-ended so that pupils can operate at their own level. Some require reinforcement, some need to be extended. If the aim is to meet individual needs, tasks must be flexible.
Assessment	There should be a balance between correction of accuracy and the encouragement of communication of meaning.

The overt teaching – probably initially in English and gradually in the TL – of relevant learning strategies, communication strategies and study skills is advisable and Vee Harris' strategy training cycle seems useful in this context (see 1997: 13–15). It comprises the following:

- awareness raising;
- modelling;
- action planning/goal setting;
- extensive practice;
- fading out the reminders;

Below we consider four areas:

- dictionary use;
- developing the skills of listening, speaking, reading, writing and memorising new vocabulary;
- specific activity/task types; and
- study skills.

Dictionary use

Pupils can be encouraged to carry out a wide variety of activities in order to develop dictionary skills. A publication on dictionary skills by Cambridgeshire LEA (1994) implicitly suggests five aspects for the development of dictionary skills. The publication arranges the contents according to the following categories:

- pre-dictionary activities;
- familiarisation with dictionaries;
- using the dictionary to check for accuracy;
- finding the English meaning of words in the TL; and
- finding the TL for English words.

Possible activities for developing dictionary skills include:

- identifying the alphabetical order in a list of words;
- familiarisation with the abbreviations used in dictionaries and their meaning/ significance;
- word manipulation and derivation work;
- matching exercises;
- word correction tasks;
- identifying the correct meaning;
- prediction of meaning; or
- categorisation of words in semantic fields or by grammatical criteria.

For a wide range of useful dictionary activities see e.g. Berwick and Horsfall 1996, Cambridgeshire LEA 1994, Horsfall and Evans 1995 or Pillette 1996.

Developing listening, speaking, reading, writing and memorising new vocabulary

One workable classroom-based approach is to break down strategies on a skills basis, that is identifying strategies that help with the skill areas of listening, speaking, reading and writing as well as other skill areas such as memorising new vocabulary.

Cathy Pomphrey suggests improving pupils' listening skills by raising their awareness of the different factors contributing to successful listening. She does this by administering to her pupils a worksheet/OHT in which she asks them which of the following factors they think could, as well as those which would probably not, help them improve their listening skills:

- shut out other thoughts;
- think in English;
- keep going, even if they miss some words/phrases;
- listen out for important words and phrases;
- talk while the tape is on;
- guess meanings if they are not sure;
- use clues such as noises, pictures etc.; or
- give up if they miss a word/phrase.

She engages pupils in a discussion on these issues and asks them for any other approaches that have (not) worked for them. Similar lists can be drawn up for other skill areas. For useful examples see Harris 1997, Rampillon 1989 or Wilkinson 1994. Harris (1997: 7), for example, lists the following strategies for reading:

1   Recognising the type of text; poem, newspaper article, brochure?
2   Examining pictures, the title, etc. for clues.
3   Going for gist, skipping inessential words.
4   Saying the text out loud and identifying 'chunk boundaries'; how a sentence breaks down and which parts of it to work on at one time.
5   Using knowledge of the world to make sensible guesses.
6   Picking out cognates.
7   Substituting English words, e.g. 'she something on his head'.
8   Analysing unknown words, breaking a word/phrase down and associating parts of it to familiar words, e.g. 'hochgewachsen'.
9   Identifying the grammatical categories of words.
10   Using punctuation or clues; question marks, capital letters, etc.

Reflection
Activity 3.4 Teaching pupils how to learn

Devise a list of strategies for a specific group of pupils you have observed or taught with the aim of getting them to think about the following three aspects of language learning by following the examples by Cathy Pomphrey and Vee Harris (1997):
- speaking;
- writing; and
- memorising new vocabulary.

Discuss with the pupils whether they deliberately use any strategies.
   Work through specific tasks with the pupils and get them to reflect on how they approach these tasks.

Specific activity/task types

In view of the difficulties a large number of pupils have in completing tasks independently in the classroom as well as when being formally assessed, we also recommend a task-based breakdown of strategies, that is analysing with pupils the precise requirements of individual types of tasks – such as gap-filling or matching answers to questions or selecting words/phrases from a list. This seems particularly relevant in the context of teaching as well as testing and assessment in the TL, which demands increasing familiarity of pupils with how to approach certain types of tasks in order to compensate for difficulties they might have in understanding instructions.

For an excellent resource pack on learning about learning see Watkins et al. 2000.

Study skills

Also, pupils will benefit from input on strategies concerned more with how to manage and monitor their learning, for instance setting themselves short-term, achievable targets, keeping vocabulary diaries and revision notes, focussing their learning on areas of perceived weakness, how to go about finding and identifying relevant resources or evaluating the success of their learning. Regular opportunities for reflection on these issues should help pupils become more successful and effective mfl learners. In an account of her experience, Leni Dam (see 1990: 16–37) discusses the use of a student journal featuring description, analysis and evaluation of their learning as a useful strategy. Vee Harris (1997: 9) suggests the following four strategies for monitoring language use:

1   Auditory monitoring: 'does it sound right?'
2   Visual monitoring: 'does it look right?'
3   Grammatical monitoring: 'is that the right tense, adjectival agreement?', etc.
4   Style monitoring: e.g. 'is that the right tone for a formal letter?'

SUMMARY

CLT encompasses a number of different mfl teaching methods. These ideas and strategies ultimately aim to develop independent communication by the pupil. Outcomes differ according to the interests of pupils, their backgrounds, their motivation, their perception of themselves and, of course, their abilities. CLT is a methodological framework and each individual mfl trainee needs to determine her own teaching style within it according to personal and contextual factors. Independent language use can be fostered by active participation of the pupil and it is within the professional judgement of the trainee to decide at what rate to 'let go' (see Page 1992), that is to allow the pupil to be less dependent and reliant on the teacher.

4 Observing, Planning and Evaluating Modern Foreign Languages Lessons

This chapter looks at two central aspects of learning to teach modern foreign languages (mfl): lesson observation and collaboration with experienced teachers as well as planning and evaluation.

Lesson observation and collaboration with experienced teachers provide unique opportunities to gain valuable insights into the teaching process as a basis for learning about teaching. They are essential parts of the learning process for mfl trainees. Our first concern in this chapter is with demonstrating how observation and collaboration can be used to help the mfl trainee develop a personal teaching style.

Our other concern lies with the careful planning and evaluation of lessons and units of work. Planning and evaluation are integral parts of effective teaching and form the foundation for successful pupil learning. Colin Wringe points out that only through planning 'is it possible to see present work in its due perspective and appropriately adjust the emphasis of one's work in the light of what has gone before and what is to follow' (Wringe 1989: 25–6).

OBJECTIVES

By the end of this chapter you should:

- recognise the importance of observation and collaborative teaching in learning to teach mfl and be able to carry out lesson observations effectively;
- understand the importance of planning and evaluation for effective mfl teaching and maximising pupil learning; and
- be able to plan mfl lessons as well as construct outline medium-term, i.e. unit of work, plans.

There are many different proformas for observation and planning in use, which include similar features. Many higher education institutions (HEIs) and schools have their own proformas. In order to illustrate the comments made in this chapter we include exemplar proformas, photocopiable blank versions of which can be found in the Appendix. They are not meant to be prescriptive nor do they purport to be the only appropriate or possible way of recording observation, planning and evaluation. They are intended as a starting point for mfl trainees and need to be tailored to personal needs and preferences. The proformas attempt to bring together the most important features of what we perceive to be good practice in these respects.

FAMILIARISATION WITH DEPARTMENTAL POLICIES AND DOCUMENTATION

On starting to work as a member of an mfl department, it is important to become familiar with prevailing policies and documentation.

The departmental handbook tends to contain policies on all relevant aspects of the work of an mfl teacher in a given school, such as the use of the target language (TL), assessment and marking, homework, discipline procedures, staffing and resourcing of the department, organisation of the mfl curriculum, accommodation, teaching methods used, the departmental development plan, extra-curricular activities available to pupils through the department, job-descriptions of individual team members and any other information useful to outsiders or colleagues arriving new to the department such as newly qualified teachers (NQTs), inspectors and/or trainees.

Familiarisation with departmental policies can provide important background information for trainees. It allows reflection on and learning from the classroom practice observed. Observation of and reflection on why an mfl teacher, for instance, uses certain strategies when giving instructions in the TL might become easier when set against the background of the departmental TL policy. Departmental policies should also inform the planning carried out by trainees. It is, for instance, important to know that certain procedures for the setting and returning of homework are in place when planning lessons.

Reflection
Activity 4.1 Departmental handbook

Ask your mentor for a copy of the departmental handbook.
  Read the handbook carefully. What has the department set out to achieve? What important general processes and procedures for the conduct of mfl lessons are stated? What policies are in place?

OBSERVING AND WORKING COLLABORATIVELY WITH MFL TEACHERS

Lesson observation

In her book on observation tasks for the language classroom, Ruth Wajnryb (1992: 19) makes a very important point:

> Observers need to maintain a sensitive awareness of the potential for vulnerability that inevitably accompanies any observation of teaching. When a teacher opens the classroom door and extends a welcome to a visitor, a basic trust in motive and professional ethic accompanies that welcome. This must be respected.

Mfl trainees need to bear this in mind when they engage in lesson observation. Lack of sensitivity to the potential vulnerability of even the most experienced teacher might lead to tensions. The objective of the exercise is not to evaluate critically the practice of experienced mfl teachers against performance indicators; this is the responsibility of their senior colleagues internally or externally from the Local Education Authority (LEA) or the Office for Standards in Education (OfSTED). The objective for trainees is to learn about the complexity of the teaching process and possible approaches/strategies to maximise pupil learning. Data obtained from lesson observations by trainees should, therefore, be treated confidentially.

In this chapter we describe a systematic approach to lesson observation, which focuses on the gathering of mainly qualitative data, that is verbal descriptions of certain occurrences during the lesson linked to a small number of observation foci per lesson. The foci for observation change regularly. Brian Parkinson (1992: 20) notes: 'It is a common beginner's mistake to try to capture everything, but you will soon find it impossible to look for more than one or two things in any one observation'.

It is important, though, that observation foci relate to the development needs of the mfl trainee. Three types of development needs are distinguished here:

- those perceived by the mfl trainee herself;
- those linked to target setting with the mentor; and
- those triggered by (subject) input (at the HEI).

The approach is systematic in that it is based on the completion of a generic proforma per lesson observed (see Figure 4.1. and Figure A.1 in the Appendix). Before the lesson, the observer decides on one or two foci (rubric: 'observation foci') and notes why she has done so (column: 'comments'). During the lesson, the observer completes the columns 'time' and 'description of action'.

This approach does not make use of fixed observation categories but, instead, allows the observer the freedom and flexibility to concentrate on changing foci. To some extent the lesson observation foci depend on particular lesson objectives. For instance, a Spanish lesson in the computer room, where pupils compose e-mail messages to their e-pals, invariably offers different opportunities for observation than a classroom-based lesson taught in collaboration with the foreign language assistant (FLA) focussing on the oral practice of transactional language relating, for example, to the topic 'clothes'. It is,

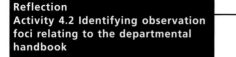

Reflection
Activity 4.2 Identifying observation foci relating to the departmental handbook

Compile a list of possible observation foci based on your study of the departmental handbook. What aspects of departmental practice described in the documentation would you like to find out more about through lesson observation?
Then observe a number of lessons with these foci in mind.

therefore, important to find out from the teacher prior to the lesson what the objectives and the content of the lesson are.

Table 4.1 lists a number of possible observation foci. This list is not exhaustive; importantly it does not feature certain foci which are particularly relevant in the context of ICT use. Given their importance, particularly at the initial stages of ITE, classroom organisation/management issues are listed not under teacher behaviour here but as a separate category.

It might be possible to use the discussion of observation notes as evidence of meeting certain standards. Structured observation notes can not only be useful in facilitating the reflection process but can also be used as evidence of having met certain standards.

Lesson observation is, of course, also carried out by mentors. The foci identified in Table 4.1 can equally be used by teachers observing (parts of) lessons taught by mfl trainees.

The approach to lesson observation suggested above is suitable for a wide range of observation foci and does not require any specific preparation on the part of the observer such as the design of specific observation instruments.

On the basis of targets set, trainees might, however, want to design specific observation proformas or recording sheets for colleagues observing their lessons, such as, for example, a tally sheet to record how often they support TL instructions with gestures or how often they elicit answers from specific pupils.

In Figure 4.2 the lesson observation is not structured in a linear way according to the time of occurrences, but in columns, one column per learning objective identified

Reflection
Activity 4.3 Carrying out lesson observations

Using the lesson observation in Figure 4.1 as an example, carry out a number of lesson observations of your own. A blank proforma (Figure A.1) is included in the Appendix. Choose one or two observation foci per lesson from those identified in Activity 4.2 or those listed in Table 4.1.
After the lessons, complete the 'reflection' column.
NB: Remember to keep your evaluative comments to yourself.

Table 4.1 Possible mfl lesson observation foci

Category	Possible observation foci
Teacher behaviour	• use of the TL for instructions and interaction • use of body language, gesture, mime • use of advance organisers • development and revision of previous learning outcomes • choice of activities in relation to objectives • ways of communicating objectives to pupils • ways of presenting and/or revising new language • amount and characteristics of teacher talk and pupil talk • use of questioning techniques: question and answer exchanges; use of open-ended versus closed questions etc. • use of differentiation • (variation of) pace • use of strategies to motivate pupils • use of teacher-led activity, group work, pair work, individual work • role of the teacher in group work, pair work and individual work • teacher movement around the classroom • strategies for teaching linguistic structures • balance of teacher-centred and pupil-centred approaches • strategies for continuous assessment and feedback to pupils • administration and correction of homework • strategies for error correction
Classroom management/ organisation	• settling pupils down • arrangement of seating and classroom layout • issuing books and equipment • establishing a code of conduct • strategies for reminding pupils of rules • grouping arrangements for specific tasks • use of the TL for classroom management/organisation • use of praise and sanctions • use of the TL for dealing with discipline matters • strategies for dealing with disruptive behaviour
Pupil behaviour	• contexts and type of TL use by pupils • amount of productive language use by pupils per lesson • amount of receptive language use by pupils per lesson • nature of pupil participation in teacher-led activities • nature of pupil involvement in pair and group work • independent pupil learning, e.g. use of dictionaries and glossaries • pupil time spent on-task • types of off-task behaviour, e.g. talking, inattentiveness • reasons for off-task behaviour, e.g. distraction by other pupils • pupil achievement of lesson objectives

Lesson observation sheet			
Class: *9L*	Time: *2.10–3.20*	Date: *08.10.*	Teacher: *M Beauchamp*

Observation foci:	Comments
Target language use: teacher–pupil	*I wanted to see how a unit of work can be introduced and to collect ideas on how to give instructions and explanations, how to organise the classroom and how to conclude a lesson in the target language.*

Time	Description of action	Reflection
2.10	Pupils enter the room individually returning the teacher's greetings: T: **'Bonjour ...' 'P: 'Bonjour, Monsieur. Comment ça va?' T: 'Ça va bien, Merci. Et toi??' P: 'Ça va +/~/-'**	*Pupils used to routine and responded automatically.*
2.15	Oral introduction of topic 'school life'. **'Aujourd'hui nous étudions le système d'enseignement, l'éducation en France. Qu'est-ce que c'est 'l'enseignement' en anglais?... Oui c'est ça.'**	*Used able pupils to translate to ensure comprehension*
2.18	Activity introduced by using able pupils to demonstrate how to brainstorm vocabulary relevant to school life. **'Peter. Donne-moi du vocabulaire associé avec l'éducation. Tu parles et moi, j' écris.'** Gestures and teacher writes answers on board.	*Pupil followed instructions without hesitation.*
2.24	Pupils put into groups of four: **'Vous allez travailler en groupes de 4'.** Teacher uses gestures and counts 1-4 to clarify. Teacher repeats the demonstration. **'Peter, encore une fois. Tu parles et j'écris. Du vocabulaire associé avec l'éducation, s'il te plaît.'** Number 'ones' in group asked to identify themselves. They are then told that they are scribes. **'Numéro un ... lève la main ... numéro un, tu écris. Joanne, tu es numéro un, oui, alors tu écris. Voilà le stylo, tu écris. Marie ... tu écris ... OK? Numéro un ... lève la main ... Tout le monde comprend? ... Vous écrivez.**	*Why were pupils put into groups after the demonstration?* *Giving pupils a number helped; by asking pupils to identify themselves there was no confusion.*
2.28	Ground rules of the brainstorm explained in English. Card clock used to ask time and to set a ten-minute time limit for group work. Teacher issues instructions and time scale using card clock. **'OK. Il est deux heures et demie. Regardez! Il est quelle heure? Oui, deux heures et demie. Vous avez dix minutes. Dix minutes. Combien de minutes Sharon? ... Oui, dix minutes. Tracey, vous finissez à quelle heure? Tout le monde répète: "Nous finissons à deux heures quarante."'**	*Why was the TL not used here?* *Process of setting a time limit seems a useful device.* *Pupils all on task. I guess they are used to brainstorming.*
2.40	Brainstorm of known vocabulary brought to a close. **'OK. Il est deux heures quarante. Posez le stylo. C'est fini. Regardez moi. ... Regardez moi. Wayne ... c'est fini ... regarde moi.'** Teacher asks each group: **'Vous avez combien de mots?'**	*Would the element of competition have added motivation?*

Figure 4.1 Sample lesson observation   *(continued...)*

2.45	Teacher revises key words – les matières, le personnel, les bâtiments – with the use of flashcards and graded questioning.	According to plan these words would serve as headings to allow pupils to put words into categories. Purpose of this activity not entirely clear.
2.47	Distracted pupil shuffles and talks to partner. **'Tais-toi, Wayne'** and gestures used.	Some pupils seemed unsettled. The fact that the teacher knew the pupil's name was very useful.
2.55	Teacher writes category headings on board. Asks for some words from the whole class. **'Voilà des catégories ... les bâtiments, le personnel et les matières. Donne moi un exemple d'un bâtiment ... l'école ... très bien, le bureau, oui. Et le personnel? ... le professeur, merci, le directeur, très bien. Et une matière? ... l'anglais. OK. Voilà vous comprenez.'** As they shout out teacher asks which category to put the word in, repeats the words and writes them on the board. **'L'université, c'est une matière. Tout le monde, oui ou non? Non ... et alors ... Martin? Oui, c'est un bâtiment. Et le directeur ... un bâtiment aussi, non? Excellent c'est une personne.'**	Did there need to be more examples? The teacher assured that all pupils understood what he was doing. Questions targeted: more able first then less able pupils.
3.00	Pupils asked to work in groups to categorise words. **'Allez-y, continuez en groupes.'** Teacher walked around targeting groups which needed help. **'Vous comprenez? Les maths, c'est une matière? Oui, très bien. Donnez-moi d'autres matières. Regardez la liste. La géo? ... oui la géographie. OK. Ecrivez la géographie ici. Bien. Une personne? Le surveillant, bien ... ici. Très bien vous comprenez. Continuez. ...'**	No one had to translate the instructions. Most pupils used English when deciding which categories words from brainstorm should go in. Could some sort of forfeit have been used to make pupils aware that use of English is not desirable?
3.10	Teacher interrupts pupils still in full flow, although some off-task. Teacher targets individuals with questions. **'Donnez-moi trois exemples des matières, du personnel etc..'**	Teacher asked pupils who seemed to have been off-task.
3.15	Homework set: pupils have to copy the instructions into their homework diary. **'Les devoirs. Ecrivez trois phrases à sujet des matières à l'école ... ça commence avec "J'étudie ...". Ecrivez trois phrases pour les bâtiments: par exemple "Le college se trouve à une distance de ...". "Il y a trois salles de français ...". Et écrivez trois phrases au sujet du personnel: "Mon professeur de français s'appelle M. Beauchamp ..."'** Able pupil translates.	Might it have been easier for all in the class and quicker to use English to set the homework?
3.20	Bell rings. Pupils dismissed in twos saying **'Au revoir'** to the teacher on exit.	Lesson running over. Do pupils think about what they are saying when they go through the routine?

Figure 4.1   Sample lesson observation (*continued*)

Reflection
Activity 4.4 Linking learning
objectives to teaching activities

Following the example in Figure 4.3, carry out some lesson observations of your own linking lesson objectives and learning activities.

Ask the respective teacher before the lesson what the learning objectives are and note them in different columns. When observing the lesson, categorise the teaching activities according to these columns. Do all the activities relate to one of the lesson objectives?

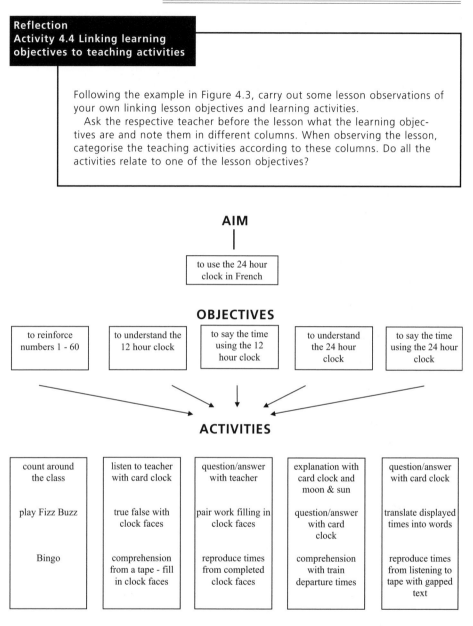

AIM

to use the 24 hour
clock in French

OBJECTIVES

| to reinforce numbers 1 - 60 | to understand the 12 hour clock | to say the time using the 12 hour clock | to understand the 24 hour clock | to say the time using the 24 hour clock |

ACTIVITIES

count around the class	listen to teacher with card clock	question/answer with teacher	explanation with card clock and moon & sun	question/answer with card clock
play Fizz Buzz	true false with clock faces	pair work filling in clock faces	question/answer with card clock	translate displayed times into words
Bingo	comprehension from a tape - fill in clock faces	reproduce times from completed clock faces	comprehension with train departure times	reproduce times from listening to tape with gapped text

ASSESSMENT AND MONITORING

| level of participation | check answers of listening comprehension | level of participation; teacher listens to pairs | check listening comprehension marks | target individuals in question & answer |

Figure 4.2   Lesson observation: linking learning objectives to teaching activities

for the lesson. The observer notes how individual learning activities relate to the various lesson objectives.

Collaborative planning and teaching

The typical progression route for mfl trainees is one from lesson observation via small-group and collaborative teaching to 'solo' whole-class teaching. During collaborative planning and teaching, trainees gradually assume responsibility for planning and teaching (parts of) lessons with support from the class teacher. By our definition collaborative teaching is different from team-teaching, which involves the cooperation of two experienced teachers.

Working with another adult in the class can be beneficial for learners as it significantly improves the pupil-teacher ratio and, therefore, the amount of attention individual pupils can receive.

As could be seen, lesson observations by the mfl trainee should, where possible, be preceded by, as well as followed up with, discussions with the class teacher. It is through these discussions that the class teacher becomes aware of the mfl trainee's level of understanding regarding the processes, which are necessary to plan and teach a lesson and enable the trainee to maximise the benefits of lesson observations.

The mfl trainee working collaboratively with the class teacher is in a unique position. She occupies the place of the learner, yet – at the same time – can increasingly empathise with the teacher. Being able to gradually assume responsibility for what goes on in the classroom allows the mfl trainee to develop an understanding of the skills required for 'solo' teaching. Moving from observation to collaborative planning and teaching involves discussions about, for example, how learning objectives are to be achieved, the teaching strategies and activities to be used and how these relate to the learning objectives identified.

In collaborative teaching the class teacher retains overall control and authority and allows the trainee to participate in aspects of teaching, which she is ready to develop. The level of trainee involvement gradually increases. Invariably, careful planning features prominently in this process. Both the mfl trainee and the class teacher need to be clear at every stage of the lesson who is responsible for what. For an excellent analysis of collaborative teaching with examples of effective practice see Arthur, Davison and Moss (1998: 123–5).

Table 4.2 illustrates the gradual shift in responsibility from the class teacher to the

Reflection
Activity 4.5 Collaborative teaching

With reference to Table 4.2, assess which stage you are currently working at. Then discuss with your mentor and other members of the department you regularly work with what you need to do to consolidate and/or move on to the next stage.

Table 4.2   From observation via collaborative teaching towards 'solo' teaching

Stage	Trainee	Class teacher	Responsibility
1	Observes	assists trainee in choosing observation foci and evaluating observations	class teacher plans and carries out lesson
2	Takes small group	shares lesson plan and provides diagnostic feedback, i.e. identifies strengths and weaknesses so that the trainee can gain a better understanding and improve	class teacher plans lesson and discusses it with trainee; class teacher is responsible for classroom organisation and management – trainee is responsible for group only
3	Takes class for parts of lesson	discusses with trainee skills to be focussed upon, discusses lesson plan, observes and provides diagnostic feedback	class teacher plans and carries out lesson except for parts, that it is agreed trainee should take
4	Collaborative teaching	increasingly less involved in the planning of lessons; observes and evaluates lesson and provides diagnostic feedback	trainee gradually assumes responsibility for planning and teaches lesson with support from the class teacher
5	Plans and teaches with class teacher support	advises on trainee's lesson plan, observes and provides diagnostic feedback	trainee plans and teaches lesson with support from the class teacher
6	Plans and teaches 'solo'	advises on trainee's lesson plan, observes and provides diagnostic feedback	trainee plans and teaches the lesson; class teacher advises on planning, observes and provides diagnostic feedback

trainee. In order to make the graphical representation of this process easier it is divided it into six stages here.

Figure 4.3 is an example of a collaboratively planned lesson, which relates to Stage 3 of Table 4.2. It uses a modified version of the lesson planning proforma suggested later in the chapter.

PLANNING AND EVALUATION

Lesson planning

Lesson plans need to be seen in the context of medium-term planning, the so-called units of work. These normally cover individual topics of study. Ultimately, lesson plans relate via units of work to the scheme of work, which outlines the work to be covered over a period of time such as an academic year or a period of study defined by examination specifications (formerly syllabuses).

Lesson plan			
Class: *8H*	Time: *9.20–10.30*	Date: *31.10.*	Language: *French*

Lesson objectives	
Core	Extension
• to familiarise pupils with the vocabulary and basic phrases related to places in a town • to introduce simple directions enabling pupils to recognise and give instructions to a stranger	• to understand and respond to questions when asking for directions • to ask the way to key places in town

Previous learning outcomes
• concept of masculine and feminine (with 'le' and 'la') • 'il y a' and 'il n'y a pas de' as lexical items • 'où est le/la ...' • 'c'est un/une ...'

Resources required
• flashcards of places – church, school, swimming pool, town hall, cinema, stadium, café, park, library • overhead transparency of a town plan showing these places • tape of 5 brief dialogues asking the way to places in town • worksheet for reinforcement

Time	Activities and strategies	Led by	Comments
9.20	usher pupils in room, take register, check equipment in TL	trainee	opportunity to build on previous experience
9.23	introduce objectives and state expectations in TL and English	class teacher	class teacher retains responsibility for the management of pupil behaviour throughout the lesson
9.29	flascard work: listen, repeat; closed and open questions	class teacher	trainee observes technique
9.45	cassette: listen for gist, detail, focus on language	trainee	class teacher circulates to check all pupils are on task; trainee practises working with a cassette player; focus is on giving clear instructions
10.00	go through pupils' answers and rebuild dialogues	class teacher	trainee assists less able pupils, gauges and monitors outcomes
10.10	use OHP to practise linguistic items; whole-class and pair work	class teacher	trainee provides model answers and circulates to assist and monitor pupils
10.25	set homework in the TL and dismiss class	trainee	class teacher circulates to check, pupils note instructions correctly

Homework
worksheet for reinforcement of places in town and directions

Action to be taken
• prepare flashcard routine to build on what the teacher did in this lesson as a quick revision for next lesson • make up pair cards with the same symbols as on the flashcards • design linguistic support sheets for less able pupils to facilitate pair work in next lesson • define the roles of the class teacher and trainee during the pair work activity

Figure 4.3 Lesson planning: collaborative teaching

Lesson plans outline how a particular aspect of a unit of work is to be covered. Individual lessons need to be linked in terms of content as well as in the development of language skills. Chapters 3 and 6 provide guidance on how to ensure continuity and progression. Strategies such as recapping through 'question-and-answer' techniques, consistency in the use of visual aids, the use of homework to bridge the gap from one lesson to the next, the use of self- and peer-assessment, target setting and, of course, regular marking can all help to achieve a smooth transition from one lesson to the next.

Initially, mfl trainees will be concerned with planning at a micro-level, that is with (parts of) individual lessons, rather than at a macro-level, the unit of work level. Nevertheless, these (parts of) lesson plans need to be firmly rooted in unit of work planning.

> In planning our lessons the all important question becomes not 'How can I occupy them in tomorrow's lesson?' but 'What is now the most pressing thing for them to learn in order to be able to perform the final activity satisfactorily?', 'What is the most effective and economical way of doing it?' and above all 'If they are to do that successfully, is there anything I must do first?' It is no longer a matter of generating activities that are sufficiently novel, stimulating or innocuous to be included but the more finite and easily manageable problem solving one of finding the most efficient means to ends.
>
> (Wringe 1994: 13)

When planning an mfl lesson the trainee needs to consider a number of important issues, which are discussed below. They are exemplified in Figure 4.4, a sample lesson plan.

It is very important to have *clear objectives* for individual lessons. It is considered to be good practice to spell out the objectives to pupils at the beginning of a lesson. There might, however, be some lessons where an element of surprise or discovery militates against such an approach. The objectives need to be identified and made explicit because they remind the trainee of and indicate to pupils what should be achieved by the end of the lesson. They help pupils realise where they are going, what is asked of them and what potential (future) application it may have. To articulate learning objectives in terms of 'By the end of the lesson, you will be able to ...' statements can assist pupils in recognising the value of the work in hand beyond the immediate lesson context. Adopting this language and approach is likely to assist trainees in making the necessary link between lesson objectives and activities. The approach can be seen to make it easier for pupils to understand why they are working on certain activities, what they will be able to do when they have finished the activities, what knowledge, skills and/or understanding they will have gained and how the work in class helps them towards achieving the overall objectives and to do well in the examination.

The choice of objectives has to be firmly rooted in the context of the overall unit of work. 'One-off' lessons by-and-large represent a weakness and should be avoided (see also Wringe 1994: 13).

Importantly, lesson objectives should be multi-dimensional, embracing, amongst others, the following:

- lexical,
- structural/grammatical,
- functional (e.g. expressing likes and dislikes),

Lesson plan			
Class: *8E*	Time: *1.30–2.40*	Date: *25.11.*	Language: *French*

Learning objectives	
Core	Extension
• to ask the way to places in town using 'pour aller au, à la, à l'…' • grammar point: au, à la, à l' • to give directions using 'prenez la première, deuxième, à gauche, à droite' etc.	• to follow directions on a grid/plan and to reproduce dialogues without verbal support • to use a wider range of phrases, such as 'passez …, continuez…' in further dialogues

Previous learning outcomes

Vocabulary for key places already introduced. Pupils have labelled a map.
Pupils have learnt the song 'La première rue à droite'.

Resources required

Flashcards of places, pair cards of places, cassette of short questions and answers asking the way and giving directions, gapped text of transcript, grid/town plan

Time	Activities	PoS and ATs
1.30	Flashcards to remind pupils of key places: teacher-led repetition, graded questioning: **'C'est …? C'est … ou c'est …? Qu'est-ce que c'est?'**	1a 1b AT2 L1,2
1.35	Use same flashcards to introduce 'Pour aller …?'; teacher-led: Place cards on wall; blindfold pupil; elicit 'Pour aller …?' from others; blindfolded pupil points to card from memory **'Peter, où tu veux aller?'** … le cinéma … **'OK. Pour aller … oui … au cinéma? Alors, Peter. Répète: Pour aller au cinéma?'**	2a 2b 2c AT2 L1,2
1.50	Pair work: pair cards, colour coded by gender, face down; one pupil asks 'Pour aller …?' other points out flashcard from memory; gender serves as a clue **'OK. Travaillez avec un partenaire. Vous êtes 'A' et 'B'. 'A', tu poses la question: 'Pour aller à la ou au'. 'B', tu reponds la-bas et tu indiques la carte. Vous avez beaucoup de cartes. Vous devez vous souvenir de la bonne carte.'**	2d 2e 3e AT2 L3,4
2.05	Group work: pupils devise a rule for au, à la, à l'…	1a
2.15	Teacher-led listening activity: asking the way to places; pupils use the pair cards to locate the places mentioned on a grid/town plan **'Voici un texte à trous. Le texte sans mots importants. Ecrivez le texte, mais il faut remplir des trous. Utilisez les cartes pour vous aider.'**	3b 5g 5h AT1 L3
2.30	Individual work: gapped transcript to reproduce the listening text using the pair cards as guide; able pupils asked to reproduce text without the gapped transcript	2j AT4 L3,4
2.38	**'Les devoirs. Sortez le journal de devoirs. Copiez les instructions.'** Write up homework in homework diary in English.	
2.40	Dismiss class **'Levez-vous la classe. Derrière les chaises. Ramassez des papiers. Silence. Au revoir la classe.'**	

ICT	
Flashcards using clip-art	
Homework	
Complete writing up the dialogue.	AT4 L3,4

Action to be taken for next lesson

OHT of the grid/town plan to check through homework.

Evaluation	
re pupil learning	re own teaching
Too many cheated in the pair work and used English. Was the pair work too demanding or badly explained? Written work showed poor spelling: do I need to expose pupils to reading comprehension before getting them to write?	*I need to continue to work on my use of the target language to explain activities. I was too stilted and did not make objectives clear: pupils did not see the point of all activities. Slow change-over of activities: did I stick too rigidly to my lesson plan?*

Figure 4.4   Sample lesson plan

- 'communicative' (e.g. objectives concerning discourse and strategic competence),
- (socio-)cultural and
- transferable skills (e.g. use of reference material).

Objectives of a lesson should also be differentiated. The majority of pupils should achieve core objectives but some will be able to carry out extension work. Some pupils might, for instance, only be expected to remember five new items of vocabulary in a lesson whereas others can realistically be expected to remember eight as well as use them in conjunction with what they learnt in previous lessons such as expressing like and dislike. For a detailed discussion of differentiation see Chapter 9.

When choosing lesson objectives contextual factors, such as the day of the week and the time of day, also need to be borne in mind. When did pupils have their last mfl lesson? Do pupils come straight from PE? Is it the first or last lesson in the day? These and other questions need to be asked as pupils' concentration spans and physical and mental readiness for certain types of activity depend on such factors. Is it a thirty-five-minutes single or seventy-five-minutes double period? This has ramifications, for instance, for the choice and sequencing of activities, the variety of tasks or the amount of work to be covered.

Lesson objectives need to be defined on the basis of previous learning outcomes. They need to build on what has come before by either consolidating it, extending it or applying it to different contexts. When planning a lesson the mfl trainee needs to ask herself questions like: what can pupils realistically be expected to know already? Do certain words/phrases/concepts need to be revised or do they need to be introduced first? Are there any issues arising from previous lessons such as unfinished activities or homework to be collected in and marked? The sample lesson plan in Figure 4.4 includes a rubric on previous learning outcomes where mfl trainees can note relevant points.

Once learning outcomes have been identified, suitable activities can be selected in order to achieve the objectives. Important questions at this stage include: Are the activities chosen sufficiently challenging? Do they move learners on? The description of activities to be carried out in a lesson is a prominent feature of a lesson plan. Activities can be described in terms of teacher action (Figure 4.4) and/or pupil action (see Figure A.2 in the Appendix).

The lesson plan proforma in Figure A.2 in the Appendix implies that all lessons should be started by making objectives explicit and be finished by summarising in a plenary what was learnt. We deem this to constitute good practice.

As part of the planning process mfl trainees need to give some thought to what strategies they will use to set up and explain the various activities. For example, what TL instructions are appropriate or what type of interaction mode is best: teacher-led, group, pair and/or independent work?

Trainees also need to try to anticipate potential problems/disruptions that may arise. For instance, do seating arrangements have to be changed between a teacher-led activity and the following group work activity? Such changes are best kept to a minimum. Where they are required, they need to be well managed.

The sequencing of activities is very important. The paradigm of 'introduction–presentation–practice–exploitation–assessment' applies to lesson as well as unit of work planning (see Chapters 3 and 6 for details). Content should be broken down into manageable steps and input come towards the beginning of the lesson when the receptiveness of pupils is highest (see Harris 1994: 34). Often, revision of work carried out in the previous lesson is necessary prior to new input.

The timing of activities is another essential consideration. Anticipating the length of a particular activity helps to make sure that a realistic amount of work has been prepared.

Pupil responses to classroom tasks vary, yet all types provide some feedback for the mfl trainee about pupils' readiness to move on. Pupils' facial expressions, the number of hands going up, the tone of voice and body language can all be signs of enthusiasm and confidence or boredom and inattentiveness. Pupils' willingness to engage in pupil-pupil and pupil-teacher TL activities gives the mfl trainee an opportunity to monitor the progress of individual pupils.

Timing activities precisely also helps to pace a lesson appropriately, that is to ensure that the change from one activity to the next happens at the right time.

As exact timing is not always possible it is advisable to have a number of end-of-lesson 'fillers' ready in case there are a few minutes left at the end of a lesson to reinforce what has been taught. These 'fillers' might be in the form of a quick game, which should be linked to the learning objectives of the lesson/unit of work providing opportunities for pupils to practise known vocabulary and/or linguistic structures, for instance, noughts and crosses, blockbusters, hangman or lotto, number drills or songs. For useful ideas see e.g. Rumley and Sharpe 1993. There is nothing more frustrating for pupils than having to wait for the bell without work to get on with.

The availability of equipment, facilities and resources clearly also needs to be considered when planning and checked before teaching a lesson. Have I got the correct tape and is it in the right place? What are the procedures for booking the TV and video recorder? How can I get the equipment into the classroom in time for the beginning of the lesson? On the sample lesson plan proforma there is a rubric 'resources required'.

Lesson plans provide an opportunity to demonstrate how the programme of work meets the statutory framework. In England this needs be done in terms of which statements of the Programme of Study, Attainment Targets and level descriptions are covered. For details see sample lesson plan in Figure 4.4.

Detailed planning helps mfl trainees become familiar with the statutory framework. It heightens awareness of the variety of tasks and skill areas covered by the lessons they plan over a period of time, whether or not work is pitched consistently and whether progression is built into consecutive lessons.

The sample lesson plan in Figure 4.4 also features a rubric for homework. Homework needs to be planned in advance in relation to the learning objectives identified for a particular lesson. Is a learning homework most suitable, followed by a short test at the beginning of the next lesson? Should a worksheet be administered asking pupils to match up the newly encountered words and phrases with pictures or symbols? Should pupils be asked to write a short dialogue using the new language? In Chapter 6 the rationale for homework is discussed in detail.

LESSON EVALUATION

As a basis for planning subsequent lessons and in order to develop reflective skills, mfl trainees need to evaluate how lessons went. As the sample lesson plan in Figure 4.4

shows, this can be done in terms of whether or not pupils have achieved the lesson objectives of say, drafting and re-drafting a short text and whether or not the activities and methods chosen were effective in bringing about pupil learning, for example, taking a class of twenty-five pupils to the computer room with two pupils working together on one computer. For a discussion of evaluation see also Chapter 3.

Table 4.3 provides a list of twenty-one questions, which can be used as a checklist to facilitate mfl lesson evaluation. Asking these questions about (parts of) individual lessons can also help foster links and continuity between a series of lessons.

Reflection
Activity 4.6 Lesson planning and evaluation

- In consultation with (the) respective class teacher(s), prepare a number of lesson plans using the proforma in Figure A.2 in the Appendix for a specific class, which you have observed on a number of occasions already.
- Discuss the lesson plans with the respective class teacher, teach the lessons and evaluate them against the quality of pupil learning and the quality of personal teaching. The twenty-one questions in Table 4.3 are intended to help you with this.

As part of the evaluation process, the mfl trainee should also note whether any action needs to be taken before the next lesson (see the respective rubric in Figure 4.4). For instance, was there sufficient time to cover the whole lesson plan? Could certain activities not be finished? Have all objectives have been achieved? Do any aspects need to be revised in the next lesson?

PLANNING A SEQUENCE OF LESSONS/UNIT OF WORK

Planning a unit of work is more than simply ensuring the coverage of the content specified in examination specifications or a chapter of a coursebook. Marilyn Leask and Jon Davison point out that medium-term plans ensure that learning is planned over a period of time and occurs step by step (see Leask and Davison 2000: 66–77). Unit of work planning enables the trainee to think carefully about the exact nature of learning intended to take place over time and can help ensure progression, which needs to be built in by teachers in a multi-faceted manner, from:

- pre-communicative → communicative activities
- simple → complex language
- short → longer spoken and written texts
- implicit → explicit knowledge of grammar
- scripted/didactically prepared (more salient) → authentic (less salient) language

Table 4.3   Sample lesson evaluation

No.	Question	Examples of responses
1	Were my objectives for the lesson clear to me and did I achieve them?	*To me yes, but not to all the pupils. Pupils did not see the point of the listening activity.*
2	Did pupils know what they were trying to achieve at any given moment?	*Mostly, but pupils didn't value all of it. I should relate more to their expectations.*
3	Were my instructions clear?	*No, I thought so but did not always check if pupils understood; frequent pupil questions broke the flow of the lesson.*
4	Were the material and lesson content appropriate for the group?	*Yes, pupils seemed to enjoy the lesson.*
5	Did I cater for the range of abilities in the group? How?	*Yes, through differentiated objectives and activities.*
6	Do I need to re-think the order and structure of my lesson?	*No, but I need to think about the way I give instructions and how I record progress.*
7	Did I cope effectively with disruptions?	*Yes, there were no discipline problems but I did have to keep on at it.*
8	Did I use the target language appropriately?	*Partly. I did not always check comprehension and I should use more examples rather than launching pupils into the activities too quickly.*
9	Did everyone get the opportunity to participate?	*Yes. I targeted questions deliberately using names.*
10	Did I help the more reluctant and less able to join in?	*Yes. I worked with less able pupils during the pair work.*
11	Did I ensure that everyone was on task consistently and monitor their work?	*I tried, but often I heard English being spoken.*
12	Were pupils alert, confident, enthusiastic or apathetic, uncertain, obstructive?	*Pupils were mostly positive.*
13	Do I know what individual pupils' strengths and weaknesses are?	*I think so; better assessment and recording will help.*
14	Did I diagnose and assess pupils' difficulties? Did I respond to them?	*Assessment needs formalising; pupils might see more value in activities if they self- and peer-assess more.*
15	Did I comment on work, praising effort, achievement and accuracy and give encouragement?	*Yes. I tried to follow my mentor's advice on error correction.*
16	Do I know if the pupils learnt anything?	*Yes, but I have no 'hard' evidence of all the skills covered.*
17	Did I include pair/group work?	*Yes. I asked pupils to carry out a survey.*
18	Did I make good use of resources?	*Yes, I think so. The reading activity based on authentic brochures went well.*
19	Do I know all the pupils' names?	*Yes*
20	Did I cover cultural awareness adequately?	*Yes, I had brought in coins from different French speaking countries.*
21	Did I and the pupils enjoy the lesson?	*Yes, pupils were on task most of the time and many put their hands up during the lesson.*

- known/familiar (e.g. classroom, self) → unknown/unfamiliar (world knowledge, target country) words and topics
- teacher-led/aided (e.g. graded questions, examples) → independent (e.g. use of glossary, dictionary and other reference sources; pair-work, group-work) interaction and working modes
- concrete → abstract ideas
- factual → non-factual/fictional spoken and written texts
- predictable → unpredictable situations
- less controversial → more controversial issues.

(Pachler 2000b: 537)

The process of planning a series of lessons raises a whole host of issues related to providing appropriate learning opportunities. Teachers need to ensure medium-term plans feature variety, breadth and balance. Implications for classroom organisation and management, resources, continuity and progression also warrant consideration (see e.g. Hurren 1992: 2).

> From (an initial overview of the forthcoming year's work) it may become apparent that some units are more interesting and have more potential than others. Some may be more difficult and may contain more material and so need extra time or are best not begun near the end of term. Equally, one may become aware in good time of units of work that seem thin and may need supplementing and one may therefore be on the outlook for suitable additional materials or ideas for exploitation. ... One becomes aware that certain pieces of language, certain skills, classroom activities and procedures will occur again and again throughout the year. They are therefore worth spending extra time and trouble on first time round to ensure that they are efficiently mastered from the start. Other, rather complicated activities or unduly time-consuming pieces of material may be isolated or marginal, and may therefore be either omitted or dealt with fairly perfunctorily.
>
> (Wringe 1989: 26)

Importantly, learning opportunities must fit into the statutory framework. If certain learning opportunities are not contained within one unit of work but required by the statutory framework, they need to be included in one of the following units. The level descriptions for each of the four skills of listening, speaking, reading and writing enable the mfl trainee to devise activities of differing levels of difficulty, thereby catering for the respective stage of learning of pupils and ensuring progression.

Illustrative, non-statutory schemes of work for Key Stage 3 are available in French, German and Spanish on the internet (see *http://www.standards.dfee.gov.uk/schemes*) as, indeed, is the NC (*http://www.nc.uk.net*). Amongst other things, they contain examples of grammar items, which should be included at different stages of the learning process. The non-statutory schemes of work also indicate topics that might be selected to provide relevant contexts and content for mfl learning in the NC.

The coursebook can also offer support. Many coursebook writers suggest the level of performance demanded by particular tasks. The mfl trainee needs to relate these notional levels of task difficulty to the pupils' levels of attainment. Discrepancy between the task difficulty and pupils' attainment levels signals the need to adapt the material. It is clearly not appropriate to set pupils certain tasks just because they are in the course-book. Coursebooks do contain many suitable and appropriate tasks and much useful material. However, the mfl trainee needs to evaluate all the tasks and material carefully in relation to the learning outcomes identified in the scheme of work. She also needs to evaluate their appropriacy in terms of difficulty and in relation to the statutory framework and/or examination specifications.

The coursebook can provide a useful basis for planning. It often needs supplementing and the activities in it structuring and sequencing. Equally, frequently certain material has to be omitted. In our view there is no such a thing as the ideal coursebook as certain skills and topics tend to be handled differently and more to the liking of the teacher by different coursebooks. Also, the amount of material provided by a coursebook does not necessarily coincide with the time available or the examination specifications followed.

Reflection
Activity 4.7 Exploring the relationship between individual lessons and the unit of work

Ask your mentor for a copy of the department's scheme of work. See how some of the lessons you have observed in Activity 4.2 fit in with the department's unit of work planning: how do the lesson objectives relate to the unit of work objectives?

Having a coursebook is a useful resource for learners as it visibly structures the teaching and learning material they encounter.

Some departments still pursue what could be described as a 'pick-and-mix' approach, writing their own worksheets, having sets of certain coursebooks, which they use for different topics. Such an approach can work very well but tends to be more demanding in terms of planning time.

For advantages and pitfalls associated with the use of coursebooks see also Chapter 11.

It is important to note that mfl trainees should not plan units of work in isolation from colleagues. Schemes of work and departmental handbooks need to be seen as collaborative efforts. As Clive Hurren (1992: 11) points out, the scheme of work acts as:

- a tool for developing coherent ideas on policy, methodology, priorities, subject matter, etc.;
- a basis for pooling expertise, sharing work loads and apportioning responsibility;
- a means of ensuring a cohesion of approach, objectives, teaching methods and standards amongst colleagues;
- a device for monitoring the effectiveness of current practice;
- a means of expressing the department's work to other departments, to newly- appointed colleagues, to headteachers and curriculum managers, parents, governors, advisers and inspectors;

- a device for interpreting into practice the guidelines of local policies, national criteria, National Curriculum, desirable methodology, etc.

A blank photocopiable proforma for scheme of work planning can be found in the Appendix, Figure A.4. The following section discusses how this proforma can be used. The issues discussed here are not dissimilar from those covered in the section on lesson planning.

Many mfl trainees fear that they will fall behind more experienced colleagues by taking too long over particular aspects of units of work. The identification in advance of the number and length of lessons available for teaching a unit of work can help pace pupils' progress. This gives mfl trainees, and of course pupils, a time-frame to work to.

The section on objectives in the unit of work plan in Figure A.4 indicates what pupils should achieve by the end of the unit. As in lesson plans, they should be multidimensional and differentiated into core and extension outcomes.

Main language items/structures refer to the vocabulary, phrases and structures to be covered. Although much is accounted for by examination specifications at Key Stage 4, there do remain important decisions for the teacher even there. These include the identification of a core, which applies to all pupils in the group, and an extension for those who can carry out additional work. Also, the mfl trainee needs to think about

---

Reflection
Activity 4.8 Auditing teaching and learning activities

How often do you employ the following teaching and learning methods in your teaching? Feel free to add to the list.
5 indicates 'very often' and 1 means 'never'.

investigation	5 4 3 2 1	Example
problem solving	5 4 3 2 1	Example
hypothesising	5 4 3 2 1	Example
trialling	5 4 3 2 1	Example
testing	5 4 3 2 1	Example
explaining	5 4 3 2 1	Example
exploring	5 4 3 2 1	Example
communicating	5 4 3 2 1	Example
memorising	5 4 3 2 1	Example
repetition	5 4 3 2 1	Example
drilling	5 4 3 2 1	Example
improvising	5 4 3 2 1	Example
inventing	5 4 3 2 1	Example
designing	5 4 3 2 1	Example
brainstorming	5 4 3 2 1	Example
role playing	5 4 3 2 1	Example
evaluating	5 4 3 2 1	Example

Does this information help you identify how mfl teaching may contribute to the fulfilment of the aims and objectives of a unit of work for all pupils in the class?
Source: Field, Holden and Lawlor (2000: 27)

how individuals can be supported in acquiring the core. In addition, mfl trainees need to consider which phrases need to be explained with reference to metalanguage and which can/should be taught as lexical items.

Methodology is as important as the content. By varying the types of learning activities, the teacher can make a judgement as to whether pupils of all learning styles and abilities have been catered for equally well. Periodical audits might be useful to monitor the extent to which teaching and learning are varied (see Activity 4.7).

The unit of work plan also features a rubric on 'main material and resources'.

Once the objectives are clear and the material and resources have been selected, core, reinforcement and extension activities can be identified. These activities should cover the language skills of listening, speaking, reading and writing and should be pitched at appropriate levels.

The main activities listed in a unit of work are likely to be those in which pupils can apply the newly acquired knowledge, skills and understanding.

The sections on core, reinforcement and extension activities do not require a condensed version of everything covered in the whole unit of work. The main activities should act as markers or benchmarks signalling a readiness to move on. It is, therefore, important that these activities are, where appropriate, cross-referenced to the statutory requirements or other relevant criteria. Careful monitoring of the activities through continuous and/or summative teacher assessment helps to ensure progression and continuity.

The section of the proforma entitled 'main homework' allows mfl trainees to list the main homework tasks. Homework can, for instance, reinforce work covered in class, prepare pupils for future learning or involve them in creative activities. It is important that homework is carefully planned and contributes to the fulfilment of the stated objectives. For a detailed discussion of homework see Chapter 6.

Importantly, unit of work plans also need to give an overview of the opportunities provided to assess and monitor pupils' progress.

Activities need to be cross-referenced to the statutory framework in order for the mfl teacher to be able to monitor effectively whether pupils have achieved certain levels across the various skills and whether they progress in all aspects of their work. Core and non-core activities can serve to provide meaningful assessment information as can vocabulary tests, revision exercises etc. In addition, mfl trainees should prepare

Reflection
Activity 4.9 Unit of work planning

Observe a sequence of lessons with the same class taught by an experienced colleague.
- Identify what you think the key objectives are and identify the activities planned to prepare the pupils to achieve these. For an example see Figure 4.2.
- How is the learning monitored and what action is taken by the teacher to compensate when successful learning has not taken place?

summative assessment tasks, such as end of unit tests and end of unit goals, in line with the practices at the placement school.

Unit plans require considerable thought and can be time-consuming to prepare. However, they facilitate the process of individual lesson planning and help to ensure progression and continuity and the inclusion of variety and differentiation.

Lastly, unit planning should also take into account the need to provide pupils with the opportunity to become more independent in their approach to mfl learning. Ute Rampillon (1994: 456–9) suggests that there is a need for activities that promote an enjoyment of the subject and enable pupils to become aware of factors potentially impeding their learning. Pupils should have opportunities to combine what they already know with new knowledge. This inevitably requires some guidance on the organisation of learning and the identification of individual needs. By presenting pupils with a range of learning strategies, Rampillon believes that pupils will develop a repertoire of learning techniques upon which they can draw in the future. Evaluation should include a review of whether such learning opportunities have, or have not, been provided. This information, should of course, be used to inform future planning. For a discussion of learning strategies also see Chapter 3.

SUMMARY

Lesson observation constitutes an effective way to learn about mfl teaching and can represent an invaluable tool in the development and formation of a personal approach to mfl teaching.

Effective short- and medium-term planning are key characteristics of successful teaching. They help mfl trainees in mediating and pupils in acquiring the necessary knowledge, understanding and skills in the course of their study of mfl.

Evaluation is an important integral part of an effective planning process.

5 Teaching in the Target Language: A Critical Appraisal

Roswitha Guest and
Norbert Pachler

The use of the target language (TL) for `instruction and interaction is a key methodological question for modern foreign languages (mfl) teachers. Rather than discussing the issues associated with TL use as a recurring theme in various places in the book, we cover them in one single chapter in order to provide a coherent overview of relevant issues. Therefore, the examples given need to be seen in the context of the respective chapters they are linked to, for instance examples of how to teach grammar in the TL need to be related to the overall approach to teaching and learning grammar outlined in detail in Chapter 7.

The various versions of the National Curriculum (NC) Orders in the 1990s established the expectation of TL use as the 'normal means of communication' (DES/Welsh Office 1990: 6) in the classroom. This has resulted in empirical research (see e.g. Dickson 1996, Macaro 1996 and 1997 or Neil 1997) as well as a considerable body of pedagogical literature (see e.g. Macdonald 1993 or NCC 1992a) about whether this policy does in fact lead to the learning gains it promises *prima facie* and how TL use can best be implemented. In this chapter we briefly examine the theoretical arguments and discuss practical suggestions for effective TL use in the light of the 1999 NC Orders. In addition, issues of TL teaching with particular relevance for trainee teachers are included.

Issues relating to TL use are ostensibly twofold: on the one hand they concern TL use by teachers, be it for basic routine or more complex procedural instructions; on the other hand they relate to TL use by pupils, be it with the teacher or peers.

As far as teachers are concerned, TL use is an important issue for native speakers of English or other non-native TL speakers as well as native speakers of the TL. Native speakers of English face challenges such as developing the requisite subject knowledge and confidence of TL use for sustained periods of time. Native speakers of the TL need to take care to ensure their use of the TL is pitched correctly according to the linguistic proficiency of their pupils. Being a native speaker of the TL doesn't necessarily make TL use easier. For example, Macaro (1996: 6) reports:

> In general, teachers saw exclusive or near-exclusive use of TL as being unattainable with all but the most motivated classes. Many felt that the task was certainly harder than the NC statements would lead one to believe. Some had felt guilty at first about lapsing into English but, because they were continually redoubling their efforts, had become reconciled to not being able to attain exclusive use.

It is widely acknowledged that the artificiality of the classroom frequently militates against maximum TL use by pupils and teachers. Maximum TL use requires a suspension of disbelief both on the part of pupils and teachers, i.e. the willingness to pretend neither party speaks English and that the transactions and interactions of the classroom are 'authentic', which is often difficult and, one might argue, sometimes undesirable to sustain. The effort required both by learners and by teachers to maintain maximum TL use can lead to reduced levels of performance on the part of teachers and alienation from the learning process on the part of pupils. The developing of good social relationships between teachers and learners, it can be argued, requires non-curriculum-specific TL, which learners do not have at their disposal. There are, in short, practical difficulties associated with maximum use of the TL.

The amount of TL used by teachers can be seen to depend on many factors such as:

- ability and size of the group;
- motivation;
- group dynamics;
- receptiveness of the pupils;
- environmental factors;
- incidents during previous lesson or break;
- topic area;
- tasks to be attempted;
- discipline problems;
- interruptions from outside etc.

These factors have an even greater influence on the amount of TL used by the pupils to respond to or initiate exchanges with the teacher and/or peers. Established classroom routines, adequate preparation and a feeling of confidence and security are vitally important in this respect.

Whilst maximum exposure to the TL can be seen to be beneficial to the pupils' linguistic confidence and competence, *teaching* in the TL does not automatically lead to *learning* the TL. Simulation of the goal, i.e. independent TL use by pupils in 'authentic', real-life situations, is not necessarily the best means. Clearly, in the acquisition-poor environment of the mfl classroom, exposure to the TL by the teacher as well as the TL material can be seen to be vital in supporting the learning process. However, an important methodological question concerns the extent to which teachers should make the structure of a language explicit or how much they should try to mimic natural processes of language acquisition. The NC requirements can be seen to be underpinned by a belief in the latter. Nevertheless, 'the case for learning the L2 'naturally', like babies acquire their L1, is not proven' (Macaro 2000: 178). Despite the fact that mother-tongue use deprives learners of exposure to TL models, teaching in the TL needs to be systematic in order to be effective. There are occasions when TL use can become a barrier to understanding and, therefore, to learning. There are certain circumstances when it is not appropriate and there are some when it is simply impossible. Importantly also, it needs to be remembered that teacher talk is different from native speaker talk (see e.g. Pachler 1999 or Macaro 2000) and that, therefore, classroom-based exposure to TL is different to that in the real world. In his review of research literature, Macaro (2000: 179) stresses that the mother tongue is the language of thought for all but the most advanced learners and that, therefore, it warrants careful consideration as a learning tool. Codeswitching is described by Macaro as a natural and legitimate operation despite the possibility of interference from the mother tongue. He questions whether inter-ference from the mother tongue is sufficient 'to counter-balance any beneficial cognitive processes that making links between L1 and L2 might bring about' (2000: 179). Macaro hypothesises that beginners use the mother tongue to help them decode texts and that beginners and more advanced learners use it to help them write texts. Also, he suggests that progression from formulaic expression to more 'creative'/independent use of the TL may well require some recourse to the mother tongue as the language of thought.

In his own empirical work into TL use, Macaro (1996: 6) found that mfl teachers listed the following arguments for and against the use of the TL:

positive
- the amount of language that is acquired subconsciously by pupils
- the improvement in listening skills
- exploitation of the medium itself leads to new teaching and learning strategies
- demonstrating to the pupils the importance of learning a foreign language
- demonstrating to the pupils how the language can be used to do things

negative
- TL for instructions can be time consuming
- reaching a point when remaining in the TL becomes counter-productive
- teaching in the TL is tiring and an exhausted teacher stops to be effective

The study also reports that challenging behaviour and/or poor motivation particularly influenced the judgement made by teachers about whether or not to use the TL.

Whilst the NC Orders implemented in the early and mid-1990s promoted the so-called maximalist position on TL use, which assumes that 'there is probably no pedagogical value in learner use of L1 and almost certainly none in teacher use of L1' (Macaro 2000: 184), the publication of a revised NC at the end of the 1990s has seen a shift towards the so-called optimal use position, which sees 'some value in teacher use of L1 and some value in learner use of L1.' (Macaro 2000: 184). Although the NC document contains no explicit references to the medium in which teachers should teach, expectations concerning pupil use of the TL are clear:

> The target language is the modern foreign language that pupils are learning. Pupils are expected to use and respond to the target language, and to use English only when necessary (for example, when discussing a grammar point or when comparing English and the target language).
>
> (DfEE/QCA 1999: 16)

Similarly, the new GCSE criteria (QCA 2000: 3), which define the subject-specific aspects of the GCSE, state that:

> A specification must require candidates to express themselves in the modern foreign language when speaking and writing. In listening and reading, where a response is spoken or written, it must be in the modern foreign language, except where a response in another language is a necessary part of the task (for example, in an interpreting exercise) or where a non-linguistic response is a natural and appropriate alternative to a response in the modern foreign language. A maximum of 10% of the total marks for the subject may be awarded for answers in English, Welsh or Irish. No more than half of this maximum allocation may be assigned to any particular assessment objective.

From this clear inferences can be made about teacher use of the TL.

OBJECTIVES

By the end of this chapter you should:

* consider the practice of teaching in the TL on the basis of a basic understanding of theoretical issues and recent policy developments;
* examine desirability and aims of teaching in the TL;
* assess practicability of teaching in the TL in everyday mfl lessons;
* identify the advantages of using the TL and how to exploit them;
* assess the disadvantages of using the TL and how to overcome them; and
* understand strategies for maximising TL use.

TYPOLOGY OF TL USE

It seems unnatural to be against teaching in the TL, yet if it is such a natural thing to do why does it cause such a debate amongst mfl teachers?

The National Curriculum Council non-statutory guidance offers the diagrammatical representation of TL use in Figure 5.1: the teacher and pupils interacting with each other inside the classroom as a preparation for TL use beyond the classroom.

The following three types of interaction can be differentiated:

* teacher–pupil,
* pupil–teacher and
* pupil–pupil.

Often departments identify key lexical items and phrases for each of these categories as *aide-mémoires* for members of the team in order to encourage appropriateness of TL use in relation to the level of proficiency of pupils as well as to foster standardisation across the department. For pupils these lists become part of the passive and/or active vocabulary they are expected to know (see e.g. Macdonald 1993).

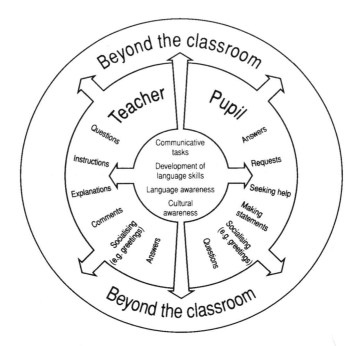

Figure 5.1 Using the TL
Source: NCC 1992 ©

Reflection
Activity 5.1 Departmental policy on teaching in the TL

Obtain a copy of the departmental policy on the use of the TL. What methods and strategies of introducing transactional TL does it suggest? What key words and expressions does it contain?

Experience and OfSTED inspection evidence suggest that, whilst a structured and well-planned approach can facilitate the coherent use of the TL by the teacher when interacting with pupils and – to a lesser extent – pupils responding to or even initiating interaction in the TL with the teacher, TL use between pupils is most difficult to achieve.

Transactional language, i.e. the language of classroom objects, classroom interaction and classroom communication, needs to be taught just like other topic-related language. Possible strategies in this context are, for instance:

- the use of visuals (acetates or flashcards) depicting key words and phrases;
- classroom displays, which are regularly referred to in the course of teaching;
- building up a list of useful phrases and expressions in the back of pupils' exercise books;

- the encouragement of TL utterances by pupils when entering and leaving the classroom or when the register is called;
- the use of pupils as 'translators' to verify meaning in English;
- variation in voice and intonation as an incentive to pupils to repeat words or phrases many times, e.g. *'leise', 'ganz leise', 'schnell', 'ganz schnell'*; or
- the so-called 'sandwich' method of 'wrapping' mother tongue instructions into two 'layers' of TL, e.g. *'Stellt euch leise hintereinander auf'* – 'Line up quietly' – *'Stellt euch leise hintereinander auf'*.

**Reflection
Activity 5.2 Teaching transactional TL**

Design some visuals (OHTs or flashcards) or other material for the teaching and practice of transactional TL phrases for pupils in their first year of study of the foreign language.

THE DECONTEXTUALISED NATURE OF TL LEARNING IN THE CLASSROOM

As has been noted above, the case for TL use is loosely based on the assumption that pupils will acquire the modern foreign language by immersion in a similar way to how they acquire their own. However, the main conditions necessary for this process, that is a 'real' need to communicate in the TL and the constant and varied exposure to (new) target language and the opportunity to try out and practise newly learnt words, phrases and structures, are invariably contrived and/or often absent in the mfl classroom. Mother-tongue learning is highly contextualised, learning the TL in a classroom environment highly decontextualised.

There is no doubt that pupils *acquire* many words, phrases and structures and can consequently use them passively and some even actively. These tend to be the most frequently used items of classroom language such as greetings, instructions, labelled items of furniture and equipment as well as the linguistic habits of the teacher. For real acquisition to take place, there needs to be the opportunity for constant reinforcement. This is one of the reasons why TL teaching tends to work well in the teaching of English as a Foreign Language (EFL) and of English for Speakers of Other Languages (ESOL): learners can often be sent out to practise what they have learnt in lessons and try it out in a variety of real situations when it is appropriate and they feel confident to do so. In mfl teaching and learning this is not really an option.

Other factors, such as class size, curriculum time and timetabling, make language *acquisition* unlikely, even if the teacher does use the TL throughout lessons. In a class of twenty-five or thirty pupils the opportunities for individual pupils to try out new words and phrases and to use the TL meaningfully are invariably limited and usually restricted to perfunctory standard responses. It is difficult for pupils to retain what they have learnt in a lesson without any further reinforcement until the next lesson, often some days later. There is, after all, little need and therefore little motivation to use the TL outside the classroom.

TRANSMITTING INFORMATION VERSUS REAL COMMUNICATION

According to one point of view the focus on active work with the TL by pupils rather than passive learning elevates TL use to communication. A closer examination of the communicative tasks of the classroom would suggest that very often pupils engage in little more than transactions devoid of an important criterion for communication, namely the desire to pass on personally meaningful and valued information: buying railway tickets, making dental appointments or giving directions to a cathedral in some foreign city do not normally fulfil this criterion. The fact that these tasks are conducted in the TL often makes very little difference to the pupils' perception of a 'real' conversation topic and rarely makes the topics more appealing. The issues pupils generally consider worth communicating are usually not suitable for lessons because they are personal and often not related to the task or topic in hand. Many of the situations pupils are expected to communicate in seem contrived as they are not commonly conducted by pupils in English, let alone in the TL.

In terms of classroom transactions and interactions there are, however, a number of opportunities for real communication such as *'Ich habe mein Heft vergessen.'* ('I forgot my exercise book'), *'Kann ich einen Kuli haben?'* ('Can I borrow a pen?'), *'Kann ich aufs Klo gehen?'* ('Can I go to the toilet?'). In subsequent years this list needs to be expanded and built upon to ensure progression; whereas in Year 7 *'Entschuldigung, ich habe mein Heft vergessen.'* ('Sorry, I have forgotten my exercise book') is acceptable, in Year 10 one might expect an explanation as well *'Entschuldigung, ich habe mein Heft vergessen, weil … .'* Not to encourage pupils to use the TL in these contexts is wasting valuable opportunities for TL use.

A great number of pupils can convey and transmit information, which is, indeed, a success criterion at GCSE. What most of them cannot do, however, is to communicate their own ideas, deeply felt emotions, strongly held opinions and all those abstract thoughts many pupils find challenging to communicate in their own language.

AUTHENTICITY OF TASKS

There is another problem with 'real' communication: the 'authenticity' of the tasks. How can 'real' communication take place in such an unreal setting? However hard we try to turn mfl classrooms into a 'foreign' environment, it is still, at best, only a simulation and perceived as such at most times by our pupils. It requires a great deal of goodwill and humour from the pupils to make it work. And even the use of 'authentic' material can work against the teacher. Authentic material for young native speakers, such as magazines and videos, are usually too ambitious for the mfl skills of pupils. The discrepancy between the chronological age and the linguistic age of pupils makes it very difficult if not frustrating to address their specific interests. Yet, material produced specifically for the young mfl learner (especially at Key Stage 4) are often perceived as boring, childish and patronising by pupils.

This problem is even greater when it comes to communicating ideas and thoughts in a discussion. Pupils simply do not have the linguistic 'equipment' and sophistication to express themselves appropriately. Their level of language invariably stifles 'proper' and immediate expression often leading to frustration, embarrassment and, ultimately, opting out. It is very difficult in such situations to insist on 'TL only' rules: if we are interested in pupils' thoughts and opinions we need to allow them to express them. Exclusive use of the TL can make the building up of a good rapport with pupils a challenge.

SOME FACTORS LIMITING THE EFFECTIVENESS OF TL USE

There are certain limits to how much TL can be used effectively in lessons.

Teaching in the TL can be tiring for teacher and pupils. A lot of thought has to be given not only to the lesson plan but also to the wording of instructions and the level of the 'incidental' language ensuring that pupils do not get left behind. It takes great concentration and perseverance not to do the 'natural thing', that is to answer the questions in the language they are asked. There is often the temptation to answer a pupil's question 'What page are we on?' with 'Top of page 48'. One possible strategy is to 'appoint' language guardians, who call the teacher to order in such circumstances, e.g. with '*Auf Deutsch bitte, Frau/Herr ...!*' ('In German, please Ms/Mr ... !').

Pupils' limited attention span can cause a considerable problem. A whole lesson is a long time for pupils to concentrate and few can do it. Indeed, research by Macaro (2000: 187) suggests that long lessons of more than fifty minutes had less average pupil use of the TL in teacher-centred activities than short lessons of approximately thirty-five minutes. And not only pupils: members of staff (non-linguists) who support weaker groups have been heard expressing their discomfort at being exposed non-stop to the TL and experiencing considerable unease that they might be asked a question. It is easy to forget how challenging constant TL teaching can be. From time to time it can be hugely beneficial to remind oneself just how it feels to be in the learners' position. Often during PGCE courses trainees are taught a lesson in a foreign language they don't speak, where the teacher performs standard flashcard routines etc. Many trainees dread being asked questions and realise how often they need to hear the phrases before they can repeat them. Teacher exposure to an unknown language can reinforce the awareness that pupils need plenty of individual/choral practice before being asked to produce new words, phrases or structures in context.

For those pupils who think that mfl are beyond them, unstructured teaching in the TL can confirm their feeling of inadequacy, potentially leading to demotivation and frustration and all the associated discipline problems. As mfl teachers, we need to guard against alienating pupils and try to avoid reinforcing their sense of failure to understand. This can be seen to be particularly important when teaching lower ability groups who need frequent reassurance in the form of repetition and comprehension checks, including in English.

This problem can be overcome by careful lesson planning: if the pace of the lesson is brisk, if the activities are varied, if all four skills are being practised and if there is a balance of 'stirrers' and 'settlers' (see Halliwell 1991: 26), then unacceptably long spells of continuous TL should not normally occur.

Using the TL language should be a challenge to pupils and the teacher, not a threat!

Reflection
Activity 5.3 Focussed lesson observation

Observe some mfl lessons and focus on how the teacher:
- uses the TL to begin and end lessons;
- supports instructions and explanations with mimes and gestures to aid understanding; and
- uses the classroom environment to support the use of the TL.

Also, what aspects of classroom management and discipline are dealt with in the TL?

TL USE FOR THE MANAGEMENT OF PUPIL BEHAVIOUR

The use of the TL for pupil management can be very effective. For instance, when pupils break a classroom or whole school rule, they are usually well aware of their misdemeanour. They are also familiar with the sanctions commonly used in their school and the expectations of their mfl teacher. The teacher can safely admonish the pupils in the TL. Even if the pupils do not understand the words, the situation has made the meaning quite clear.

Supported with gestures and near cognates such as '*Du sollst nicht auf deinem Stuhl schwingen!*' the message usually gets across, occasionally with the help of another pupil: 'She says you must not swing on your chair.' The tone of voice in which the reprimand is delivered, as well as the context, make comprehension possible. This approach does, however, assume that pupils know the rules of the mfl classroom. These should be made very clear in the first few weeks of Year 7 in English and subsequently reinforced and added to.

However, there are obvious exceptions to disciplining and admonishing in the TL, for example, when evacuating pupils from the classroom during a fire drill. Even policy makers recognise that 'In situations where, for reasons of safety, it is essential that instructions should be fully understood, they should be given in the language which is the normal medium of instruction in the school' (DES/Welsh Office 1990: 6). One wonders how many teachers have fulfilled the second part of this advice: 'When the teacher is satisfied that the instructions have been fully understood they should be repeated in the target language.'!

THE TEACHING OF GRAMMAR AND TL USE

Grammar is often perceived to be a difficult – if not the most difficult – part of the subject to be taught in the TL (see e.g. Dickson 1996, Macaro 1997 or Neil 1997). However, quite a number of grammar points can be taught in the TL, particularly if there is an element of physical demonstration and visualisation. A playful approach as well as the continuous use of certain 'stock' types of activities, which can be used for a range of different topics, can help to minimise the need for complex instructions and explanations in English and make it easier to teach grammar in the TL.

Many pupils have difficulties with the German word order when a sentence starts with an adverbial of time. The following activity works well with Year 8. Having taught the activities, e.g. *'Ich gehe ins Kino'* ('I go to the cinema'), days of the week, e.g. *'am Montag'* ('on Monday') and the question word *'wann'* ('when') the teacher writes the words [*ich*] [*gehe*] [*ins Kino*] and [*am Montag*] on individual A4 cards. A bigger sign is made for [*wann?*]. The class is divided into groups of five. The first three pupils go to the front and hold their words up in the correct sequence to form and speak the sentence. Pupil 4 holds up the [*wann?*] sign and asks the question. Pupil 5 – [*am Montag*] – joins them and four pupils re-form physically to make the correct sentence: [*Am Montag*] [*gehe*] [*ich*] [*ins Kino*]. Pupils then make their own sentences (on cards) and perform them.

Poems are an excellent way to teach grammar through rhythm and repetition. The poem *Meine Woche* (My week) teaches the same grammar point as described above. The class is taught the relevant daily activities accompanied by a mime; the pupils decide the mime. When pupils are familiar with the activities in the poem they are shown the poem on an OHT (see Figure 5.2). They read the poem aloud and as they recite they mime the activities. Then they are shown another OHT with a number of words blanked out (see Figure 5.3). Pupils are asked to recite the poem. When they have become proficient at that level they are shown yet another OHT with more words missing (see Figure 5.4). Reciting the poem can become a team or individual competition.

Word order, in particular in the past tense, can be practised with cut-up sentences (auxiliary verb and past participle in different colours) mixed up in small envelopes. This task is almost always performed in the TL using familiar phrases such as *'Ist das richtig?'* ('Is this correct?'), *'Nein, das ist falsch!'* ('No, this is wrong'). It works particularly well if the same colours are used when the past tense is first introduced (on an OHT, for example).

Pupils' speaking skills are often restricted by the number of verbs they know, which limits their communication. Verb endings are a frequent source of error. Pupils can revise and practise verbs and verb endings in the form of two hexagons drawn on the board (side by side). Each corner of the hexagon represents a personal pronoun (see Figure 5.5).

Am **Montag** fahr' ich Fahrrad.
Am **Dienstag** seh' ich fern.
Am **Mittwoch** spiel' ich Fußball.
Das mach' ich sehr, sehr gern.
Am **Donnerstag**, da schwimmen wir.
Am **Freitag** spiele ich Klavier.
Am **Samstag** kommt Frau Stange.
Am **Sonntag** schlaf' ich lange.
Und schon hör' ich die Mama:
"Komm, Peter! Steh auf! Schule!"
Ja, dann ist der **Montag** da.

Figure 5.2 *Am Montag fahr' ich Fahrrad*
Source: Harald Seeger, *Die 'Wer? Wie? Was?' Schatzkiste 1*, © by Gilde-Buchhandlung und Verlag, D-Bonn.

Am ... fahr' ich Fahrrad.	Am ... fahr' ich ... .
Am **Dienstag** seh' ich	Am **Dienstag** ... ich ... .
Am ... spiel' ich Fußball.	Am ... spiel' ich ... .
Das ... ich sehr, sehr gern.	Das ... ich sehr, ... gern.
Am **Donnerstag**, da ... wir.	Am ..., da ... wir.
Am ... spiele ich Klavier.	Am ... spiele ich ... .
Am **Samstag** kommt ... Stange.	Am **Samstag** ... ... Stange.
Am **Sonntag** ... ich lange.	Am **Sonntag** ... ich ... .
Und schon hör' ich die ... :	Und ... hör' ich die ... :
"... , Peter! Steh auf! Schule!"	"... , Peter! ... auf! Schule!"
Ja, dann ist der **Montag**	Ja, ... ist der **Montag** ...

Figure 5.3 *Am ... fahr' ich Fahrrad* **Figure 5.4** *Am ... fahr' ich ...*
Source: Harald Seeger, *Die 'Wer? Wie? Was?' Schatzkiste 1*, © by Gilde-Buchhandlung und Verlag, D-Bonn.

Elicit two verbs (regular verbs to begin with, then irregular and modal verbs much later) from the pupils and write them inside the hexagons (see Figure 5.6). The class is divided into two teams, the members of each team are numbered, the numbers written on pieces of paper and put in a box. A pupil picks a number and the two corresponding pupils from each team go up to the board. At the command *'Auf die Plätze, fertig, los!'* ('On your marks, get set, go!'). Pupils write the relevant verb forms at each corner of their hexagon (see Figure 5.7). Conferring with their team is permitted. The first pupil to finish gets ten points. One point is deducted for each mistake. The second pupil gets one point per correct verb form. This ensures that the fast and careless pupils do not always win.

Question forms are also difficult to learn for pupils. They can be learnt playing the battleship game. From a grid (see Tables 5.1 and 5.2) each pupil has to select one square per row and per column without showing it to their partner. By asking relevant questions, e.g. *'Kommst du mit dem Auto zur Schule?'* (see Table 5.1) or *'Saugst du manchmal Staub?'* (see Table 5.2), they then try to find out what choices their partner has made. If they guess correctly, they can ask again; if not, their partner asks a question. The winner is the pupil who has found out all of her partner's answers first.

This works particularly well in the TL if the questions are quite cumbersome to translate into English. Provided the questions have been well practised before the game starts, most pupils tend to use the TL rather than switch back to English. Pupils would be familiar with the game from Year 7 where the language items used are much less complex.

Successful language games can usually be said to:

- be based on known games;
- not be too long;
- not need lengthy explanations;
- have clear objectives; and
- produce a winner.

Information gap exercises, such as finding out about somebody's timetable, work well if pupils are properly prepared: *'Was hast du montags in der ersten Stunde?'* is no more complicated than 'What subject do you have on Monday in the first period?'

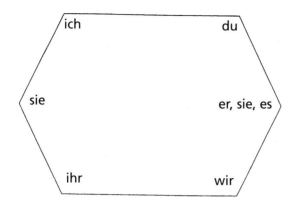

Figure 5.5   Hexagon 1

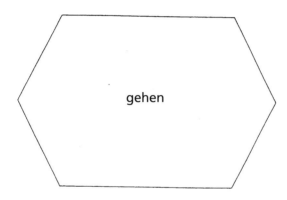

Figure 5.6   Hexagon 2

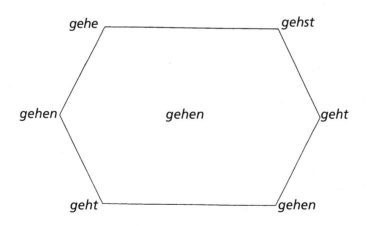

Figure 5.7   Hexagon 3

Table 5.1   *Wie kommst du ... ?*

	ins Schwimmbad	*in die Stadt*	*nach Amerika*	*nach London*	*zur Schule*	*zum Bahnhof*	*zum Golfplatz*
mit dem Zug							
mit dem Bus							
mit dem Rad							
zu Fuß							
mit dem Flugzeug							
mit der U-Bahn							
mit dem Auto							

Table 5.2   *Hilfst du im Haushalt?*

	Spülst du ab?	*Mähst du den Rasen?*	*Wäschst du das Auto?*	*Führst du den Hund aus?*	*Räumst du dein Zimmer auf?*	*Kochst du?*	*Saugst du Staub?*
oft							
manch-mal							
nie							
ab-und-zu							
einmal in der Woche							
zweimal am Tag							
nur für Geld							

Kofferpacken (packing a suitcase) is another excellent activity for practising word order in the past tense as well as vocabulary; it also increases fluency.

In the *Kaufhaus* (department store) variation each pupil writes an item to be bought in a department store on a piece of paper. The class is then divided into groups (between six and ten pupils). The first group lines up at the front of the class (getting them to pick a number from one to six etc. out of a hat will prevent the scramble to avoid being the last in the line!) The first pupil starts the sentence: '*Ich war im Kaufhaus und habe ...* (mentions his or her item or items) *gekauft*'. ('I went to the department store and bought ...') and puts the piece of paper into a(n authentic) shopping bag. The second pupil starts again: '*Ich war im Kaufhaus und habe ein* … (previous pupil's item) *und einen* … (own item) *gekauft*' – and so on to the last person in the line, who has, of course, the most difficult task of remembering all the items. Strangely enough, pupils tend to forget the '*gekauft*' (past participle), but remember all the shopping items. The *Kofferpacken* version (packing your suitcase) works very well with a real suitcase and real items.

CONVERSATIONS

One of the aims, if not the ultimate aim, of mfl teaching is to enable pupils to conduct conversations in the TL. They need to be well-prepared for this and given the skills and confidence to use the TL in a carefully nurtured atmosphere.

Conversations in language learning usually grow from learnt phrases and role plays: For a discussion of how to develop speaking skills in pupils including the use of role plays see Chapter 6. Role plays do have their limitations, though, as this example of a keen and very able pupil's frustration at the lack of conversational skills during an exchange visit demonstrates: 'I can ask for the butter at the breakfast table and what time we have to leave for school because we've done that. But I can't have a proper conversation and it makes me mad!' A purely transactional approach, therefore, seems too narrow. In order to go beyond the scripted, pupils need to be taught conversation strategies such as opening gambits, hesitating, agreeing, disagreeing, asking for help and support, expressing surprise and disbelief and many more.

Adding an element of unpredictability such as a lost granny, boiled eggs or their memory can make a routine role play such as *Im Fundbüro* (at the lost property office) much more interesting and entertaining for pupils. Introducing realia into role plays can liven things up considerably. Most pupils like bringing in unusual clothes, food (real or plastic) or toys – or pictures of these items, either cut out of magazines or drawn (by hand or retrieved from the computer).

Apart from conversation strategies there are other ways of organising role plays so as to encourage spontaneity. Instead of asking pupils to prepare a role play together with their partner, e.g. the shopkeeper together with the shopper, they can be grouped with peers in the same role, e.g. shopkeepers and shoppers in different groups. This way, when shopkeepers and shoppers come together, communication is more realistic and spontaneous because, whilst shopkeepers and shoppers do prepare possible answers in advance, they have to listen very carefully to each other in order to be able to respond meaningfully.

Another way to help pupils make the transition from learnt response to genuine manipulation of the TL is to record the general conversations of groups and discuss with pupils how they can be improved to sound less like a GCSE oral examination and more like a real conversation.

Often, despite the best endeavours of the teacher, pupils remain reluctant to 'spontaneously adopt the FL as their own language of self-expression in the FL classroom, even where the teachers have done so to a considerable extent' (Mitchell 1988: 164). In order to address the issue of spontaneous TL use, the latest NC Orders require for pupils to be taught through 'using everyday classroom events as an opportunity for spontaneous speech' (DfEE/QCA 1999: 17). There is no guidance on how this best be done, however. Recent OfSTED inspections clearly point to the fact TL use by pupils remains a real challenge for mfl teachers (see e.g. Dobson 1998: 2)

ASSESSMENT AND TESTING AND TL USE

Marking in the TL is a good way of increasing pupils' comprehension of the TL. Pupils are mostly interested in the teacher's comments and grades on their work.

Pupils can be given a TL mark scheme and comment list as part of the classroom vocabulary in Year 7. Once they are familiar with the scheme, peer-marking can be introduced. It is a popular activity with pupils, they love the instruction '*Hefte tauschen und korrigieren!*' ('Exchange exercise books and mark each other's work!'). They are usually very fair and try hard to find the appropriate comment. They often do this 'in role', i.e. playing the teacher using teacher language.

Also, pupils can be paired to count and tick off on a profile sheet how often their partner uses the TL.

The GCSE criteria stipulate that 'instructions to candidates (other than general instructions) should normally be in the language in which the candidate is expected to respond, except where the nature of the task would make the instructions too difficult to understand' (QCA 2000: 3). This policy of testing in the TL requires pupils to learn rubrics and instructions in the TL. This alone does not lead to increased spontaneous use of the TL by pupils as these rubrics are part of standard classroom vocabulary and pupils are expected to learn them like other transactional phrases. (For a detailed discussion of assessment issues see Chapter 10.)

WORKING TOWARDS COMPETENCE IN TL USE

As can be seen in this chapter, the TL can be used meaningfully and effectively for a number of types of interaction in the mfl classroom (see Table 5.3).

Some possible strategies for TL use

- Contextualisation increases comprehension. Always ensure pupils know what is going on. Pictures, demonstrations and examples must be carefully selected to avoid ambiguity.
- Use of cognates or near cognates, particularly in German, does not only increase the chances of comprehension, it makes pupils feel more confident and less apprehensive.
- Simplification of language, not only for teacher input but also for pupil production – a single well-chosen word can go a long way. A pupil's '*Entschuldigung, Amir*' ('Sorry, Amir') – he had interrupted Amir – can make the point quite adequately.
  Pupil access to language – this can take the form of 'clouds' with the most useful phrases and key words prominently displayed or lists in pupils' exercise books.

Table 5.3 Using the TL for classroom instruction and interactions

Everyday routines, classroom management and maintaining discipline	Instructions and explanations by the teacher	Pupil interactions with the teacher	Pupil interactions with other pupils
Taking the register	Presenting new language	Asking for clarification	Asking for material/equipment
Getting ready for the lesson	Setting up activities	Expressing problems and apologies	Carrying out pair and group-work activities
Tidying up at the end of the lesson	Making oral comments	Requesting explanations	Initiating information exchange
Dismissing the class	Checking comprehension	Giving excuses	Playing games
Offering praise and rewards	Asking questions	Asking for material/equipment	Expressing agreement and disagreement
Reprimanding and sanctioning pupils	Making written comments in exercise books	Making evaluative comments	Assessing the work of peers
Friendly asides, humorous remarks	Writing on board (*Tafelbild*)	Asking for confirmation	Using fillers
		Requesting permission	
		Answering questions	
		Giving information	
		Humorous remarks	
		Linguistic experiments	

Reflection
Activity 5.4 Useful teacher phrases

With reference to Table 5.1, draw up lists of useful *teacher* phrases in your first and second foreign language for:
• everyday routines, classroom management and maintaining discipline, and
• giving instructions and explanations
for a class of your choice in Key Stage 3 and one for a class in Key Stage 4.
How different are the lists for Key Stages 3 and 4? Is there an element of progression?

Reflection
Activity 5.5 Useful pupil phrases

With reference to Table 5.3, draw up a list of lexical items *pupils* should – in your opinion – have mastered by the end of their first year study of the modern foreign language:
- to interact with the teacher, and
- to communicate with peers.
Then consider how these lexical items could be taught.

- Teaching of key phrases – such as *'Wie heißt das auf Deutsch?'* ('What is the German word/phrase for … ?'*e.g. 'Wie sagt man … auf Deutsch?'* ('How do you say … in German?'), *'Darf ich bitte English sprechen?'* ('May I please speak in English?'), *'Ich habe ein Problem, Herr / Frau ....'* ('Sir/Miss, I have a problem?'), *'Können Sie mir bitte helfen?'* ('Can you help me, please?'), *'Ich bin fertig'* ('I have finished').
- Rewarding pupils' spontaneous use of the TL – words and phrases remembered from previous lessons, an ambitious attempt (successful or not) at a new construction or a combination of words etc. deserve to be praised by the teacher and their efforts recorded (in a separate column) in the mark book.
- Screening out unwanted English contributions – this usually just means ignoring them.
- TL-only sessions: during a designated (previously announced and cleared with parents) period of fiteen minutes of a lesson only the TL may be spoken. Everyone who speaks English (including the teacher) suffers a forfeit. Initially these sessions tend to produce silent minutes. As pupils get used to them they get braver and more adventurous in their use of the TL.
- Request box: pupils write phrases they need on a card and put them into the box. The TL phrases are compiled on an OHT and taught to the whole class.

Competence in TL use, as so many aspects of good practice, is difficult to achieve and requires a lot of practice. Trainee teachers can benefit from considering all aspects of TL use and should develop strategies to address them. Here are some targets a trainee teacher at the Institute of Education recently set herself for her induction year (see Chapter 13):

Be supportive: when a pupil wants to use the TL, I need to offer help and support. The nature of the support given may vary according to the age and the ability of the pupil.

Be consistent: I need to try hard to use the TL as often as possible to be a good role model. Sometimes it might mean to claim not to understand what they are saying just because they speak English.

Be realistic: I need to remember that the use of the TL is meant to enhance classroom teaching, and not to become an intolerable burden. It is sometimes a good idea to have a set period in the lesson when pupils know that they can speak to me in English and when problems can be dealt with.

Be non-critical: I must greet any attempt at using the TL positively or the pupil might not try again. The most important thing is communication, and any understanding of the message should be rewarded.

Be challenging: while asking for the impossible is demotivating, equally demotivating is asking for that which is banal and far below a pupil's capabilities. I need to build progression into both my use of the TL and theirs, using, teaching and expecting more complex phrases with older and more able pupils.

Be flexible: if I want to encourage the use of the TL, I must be sufficiently flexible to respond to what happens in the classroom and to what pupils have to say.

Make it worthwhile: I must reward and acknowledge any efforts, be aware of what pupils are doing in the classroom and listen to two or three pupils each lesson so I can keep a record of their individual achievement as regards TL use.

Involve the pupils: pupils are much more likely to be motivated if they are involved. I can ask them to note and tick useful phrases or expressions in their exercise books each time they use them in the lesson.

Promote a positive attitude: the most important thing is that pupils do not feel threatened and it is up to me that they don't. I must present the TL as something I am going to do with them and in which all have a part to play and not as something that I am imposing upon them.

Reflection
Activity 5.6 Thoughts on TL use

How relevant are the above targets for your own practice?

SUMMARY

There is no doubt in our minds that optimum, i.e. sensitive and appropriate, use of the TL can make a very beneficial contribution to the learning process of most pupils.

Whilst for reasons such as time constraints and the lack of reinforcement outside the classroom it might seem unrealistic to expect any but the most able to be proficient and confident enough to chat spontaneously in the TL at the end of Key Stage 4, pupils can be expected to communicate meaning competently in a finite number of situations within the prevailing statutory framework. Optimum exposure to the TL has a clear contribution to make to achieving this aim.

Teaching in the TL alone is not enough to guarantee successful learning outcomes for *all* pupils. Whilst the more enthusiastic and able pupils can be expected to respond consistently to the challenge given the right environment and levels of support, there will be pupils who will find it at best contrived and at worst alien. The trainee teacher's challenge is to prevent and/or overcome these potential difficulties.

6 Teaching Listening, Speaking, Reading and Writing

In the past, writing for instance in the form of translations, dictations and essay writing as well as reading tended to predominate in modern foreign languages (mfl) teaching. For some time now, though, the full value of speaking and listening has been recognised. Consequently, a multi-skill approach prevails, in which no one skill is taught discretely. The use of terminology such as 'respond', 'react', 'summarise' in the statutory framework encourages the integration of skills.

Progression within each and across the four skills is an important issue.

In this chapter we start from the premise that an important aim of mfl teaching in the secondary school is the development of an ability in pupils to use and learn mfl independently of the teacher. To this end we suggest a structured learning process here based on clear objectives ranging from recognising, memorising and reproducing key linguistic items and structures to using them creatively as building blocks for personalised and meaningful mfl generation.

Because of its importance in helping pupils achieve this objective by extending and consolidating the work carried out in the classroom, homework is also discussed in this chapter.

THE IMPORTANCE OF SEQUENCING AND THE INTEGRATION OF MFL SKILLS

As has been noted in previous chapters, the development of communicative competence in pupils is an important aim of mfl teaching in secondary schools. Real communication consists of more than drawing on a bank of statements and questions suited to a given topic area. It requires language to be tailored to fulfil specific objectives by drawing on situational language and lexical phrases. It is, therefore, essential that pupils memorise, and learn how to memorise, vocabulary.

OBJECTIVES

By the end of this chapter you should:

- appreciate how listening, speaking, reading and writing can be taught;
- be aware of the need for the integration of these four skills;
- realise the importance of pupils taking control of input such as vocabulary, structures and functions and use them creatively, generating their own, personalised language;
- be aware of important criteria for selecting learning activities as well as the need for the sequencing of activities;
- recognise what constitutes meaningful homework in order to extend and consolidate work carried out in class; and
- appreciate the importance of tailoring teaching to the needs of specific classes and the individual differences of the pupils within them.

For William Littlewood (1981) successful 'social interaction' is an important outcome of language use, which requires a certain level of linguistic and communicative competence and is reached via a number of phases of development. It can be very difficult to develop social interaction skills, particularly in a classroom setting. Therefore, we see it as one of the aims of mfl teaching to make pupils aware of the components that comprise successful communication.

One of the challenges for mfl teachers is to devise a programme of learning that progresses from a reliance of pupils on the teacher towards their independence, developing in pupils the ability to generate language of their own within a communicative framework. Both the teacher and pupils must be aware of the importance of the role of the teacher as an agent of learning throughout Key Stages 3 and 4.

Another challenge is the appropriate sequencing of teaching and learning activities. Individual mfl skills, we argue here, should not be taught independently of one another. Their development needs to be fitted within a coherent approach which involves careful monitoring of learning and the selection of appropriate activities.

Although 'meaningfulness' of tasks and activities, e.g. 'authenticity' and the meeting of perceived needs, is important to further the development of language skills in pupils, the 'pre-communicative' phase is equally important in which 'context-reduced', i.e. less than communicative, activities occupy a valid place.

In this chapter we identify various stages of development per skill area. These stages should not be viewed as a simple formula, which can be repeated lesson after lesson, unit of work after unit of work. The nature of the task or given learning objective(s) might not make it possible and/or desirable to cover all stages per skill. In particular, progression does not only take place within an isolated mfl skill but across a number of skill areas. Therefore, successful mfl lessons integrate a number of activities and exercises, developing different (mfl) skills which are carefully chosen to build on previous knowledge and understanding.

The examples given in this chapter by no means represent an exhaustive list.

Essentially, the skills of listening and reading can be grouped together under the label of 'receptive mfl skills'.[1] Similarly, speaking and writing can be categorised as 'productive mfl skills'. It is this categorisation that we use in this chapter for the grouping of listening, speaking, reading and writing.

MEMORISING, AND LEARNING HOW TO MEMORISE, VOCABULARY

Walter Grauberg (1997: 5–33) presents a process for vocabulary acquisition that is similar to the paradigm for language learning presented in Chapter 3 of this book. He distinguishes four stages – discrimination, understanding meaning, remembering and consolidation as well as extension – all of which require active intervention on the part of the teacher, yet which serve to guide the learner towards a greater degree of independent language use. These stages offer a medium- and long-term perspective.

We feel it is important to present a range of vocabulary learning strategies in order that pupils can adopt strategies to suit their own learning styles.

Discrimination

Teachers are guided in their presentation of new vocabulary, in particular key lexical items, by the department's long term plans. By using visual aids (flashcards, the OHP, posters, video stills, photographs etc.) vocabulary can be placed into a broader (cultural) context. Teachers should place new vocabulary in a functional/communicative context. This can be achieved through the demonstration of potential use and/or by exposing pupils to spoken or written texts. Presentation by the teacher should not be purely a passive activity for pupils. Exposure to new lexical items and phrases can include the practice of pronunciation, the association with gestures and movement, the association with previously taught language and the answering of simple closed questions.

Understanding meaning

Teachers should present key vocabulary related to a new unit within a broader (cultural) context. GCSE specifications provide defined lists in relation to given topics, as do many coursebooks. For pupils to understand meaning in a multi-dimensional way, e.g. functional, grammatical etc., there is a need for explanation by the teacher. Explanation is usually accompanied by pupils recording vocabulary for future learning. We would advise against a simple translation from the TL into English. Instead, we would encourage pupils to note down a meaningful example of use in context as well as the TL and mother-tongue meanings of the new lexical item or phrase. In our experience, the rendering of new lexical items and phrases in semantic fields ensures better understanding and recall.

Grauberg (1997: 8) suggests that where inflected forms of words are contained in vocabulary lists, it may save time and effort to explain the infinitive form. Subsequently, pupils should be encouraged to note similarities and grammatical relationships with similar words encountered to assist with 'educated guessing' of meaning. The categorisation of vocabulary can be undertaken in several ways – grammatically, by topic, in the form of mind maps or in the context of stories, songs, rhymes and poems. A varied approach seems advisable.

Remembering and consolidation

A criticism of repeated classroom vocabulary testing is that pupils learn new lexical items for a specific, short-term and de-contextualised purpose. However, this can be seen as a necessary prerequisite to consigning the vocabulary to the long-term memory. Kit Field (1999: 55) suggests a range of ways of learning vocabulary: alphabetical listing, listing according to grammatical concepts (verbs, nouns, adjectives etc.), semantic field mind-mapping, repeated use in context, recital, colour coding or preference ranking. To these can be added: covering the English and testing oneself, covering the TL word and testing oneself, getting a friend or family member to test, matching synonyms, matching opposites, matching words to symbols, gapped texts and dictionary activities. Pupils should be encouraged to experiment with all these methods from early on in their learning process. By making vocabulary learning strategies explicit, teachers can help to ensure effective vocabulary learning takes place. Certainly teachers should draw on a range of strategies which mirror the different 'intelligences' identified by Howard Gardner (1983) in his seminal work *Frames of mind*.

Suzanne Graham (1997) notes that pupils feel vocabulary learning is more successful and enjoyable if it forms part of a game. Puzzles, word-searches, quizzes and challenges can all be usefully deployed.

Extension

By extension we mean the stage at which learners transfer vocabulary from the short-term to the long-term memory. It involves active use for personal communicative reasons. Teachers need to devise activities, which require pupils to use key vocabulary for communicative purposes. This involves the use of the TL for speaking and writing, but may also involve listening and reading, the answering of focussed comprehension questions, the completion of puzzles, the writing of short texts containing a set number of key words/phrases or word association activities. The use of synonyms and exercises demanding the use of opposites serve to extend the construct associated with the newly established meaning.

RECEPTIVE MFL SKILLS

Initially pupils have to recognise and identify key vocabulary, phrases and structures. Activities need to be devised in order to allow pupils to recognise both the spoken and written word and to apply meaning to new language forms. As can be seen in Table 6.1, the pupil needs to proceed from the recognition of new forms via practice to using

Table 6.1 Progression in receptive mfl skills

from:	to:
identification	rebuilding and personalising

Reflection
Activity 6.1 Matching vocabulary learning strategies to multiple intelligences

Howard Gardner's different types of intelligence are:
* logical intelligence
* linguistic intelligence
* bodily kinaesthetic intelligence
* spatial intelligence
* musical intelligence
* inter-personal intelligence
* intra-personal intelligence

With reference to these types of intelligence:
* Can you categorise the vocabulary learning strategies below by the type of intelligence they may appeal to? (NB: any one activity can fall into more than one category.)
* Place the activities under each category into a sequence following the stages discussed above.
* Where are there gaps? Consider additional activities, which can be placed into the model.

Some vocabulary learning strategies:
Repetition, recital, categorising by grammar, categorising by topic, colour coding, testing oneself, being tested, placing in communicative context, matching to symbols, developing puzzles, completing puzzles, formal teacher-led tests, word searches, finding synonyms, finding opposites, dictionary work, rote learning, mnemonics, identifying key words in extended texts etc.

---

them in an individualised and personal way, rebuilding language within 'authentic' and realistic contexts.

LISTENING (AND RESPONDING)

The continuum of examples in Table 6.2 aims to show how mfl learning can be sequenced to encourage a development from identification and recognition of key linguistic items and structures to the use of selected language forms to express personal views. The approach outlined here, we feel, allows for continuity and progression over a period of time.

Table 6.2   Listening (and responding): an overview

from
pre-listening activities
listening for gist/detail (content)
focussing on linguistic structures and forms
rebuilding
to

Pre-listening activities

Listening to a(n extended) passage without preparation can be an extremely difficult task. To understand the location and context of a text facilitates comprehension. This can be achieved/worked towards by way of pre-listening activities. The exact nature of a pre-listening activity is, of course, dependent upon the level of proficiency of the pupils.

Pupils can be set a number of lead-in tasks such as input and practice of key linguistic items through word associations or work with sentence cards taken from the text.

To analyse a listening text in terms of general features is a very worthy first step.

(For a wide range of pre-listening and listening activities see e.g. Dahlhaus 1994 or Turner 1995.)

Listening for gist/detail with a focus on content

It is a particular skill to extract meaning from spoken stimulus material. To record details verbally and/or non-verbally whilst listening to a 'text' can be demanding. And to retain details as well as to respond to a 'text' after listening can also be a challenge to pupils.

Listening activities are best broken down into manageable chunks to suit the particular learning objectives of the lesson and/or the unit of work.

During the first listening pupils can, for instance, be asked to find out how many speakers are participating and guess the mood of speakers. They can count how many questions are asked. Also, they can tally how many known words are used or ascertain the location of a dialogue. Such activities help to contextualise the stimulus material.

During the second listening pupils can be set activities to which they are asked to respond verbally and/or non-verbally. These responses can be used at a later stage as stimuli for follow-up work. Examples of non-verbal responses include the ticking of boxes within a grid, identifying statements as true or false, answering simple multiple-choice questions, completing pictures and diagrams and matching simplified text to pictures and symbols. Possible verbal responses are listed in Table 6.6.

Pupils can also be asked to focus on specific details by having to answer 'closed questions' to which there is a specific answer and which can be found in the stimulus material, such as prices, times, directions, ages, descriptions. For these activities to be successful pupils should be familiar with the key language the stimulus material contains.

SOME PRACTICAL HINTS AND CONSIDERATIONS

by Jo Bond

- Be aware of the level of the group – is it set or mixed ability? Only then select the listening material.
- Listen to the tape yourself first: a transcript does not indicate the speed at which language is spoken, nor the clarity of speech.
- The length of texts will depend on the ability level of the group. Bear in mind that more able pupils tend to have a longer concentration span. With mixed ability or lower ability groups it is advisable to do a series of short aural activities during the course of a lesson with other activities in between. This could be a long dialogue played in sections or several shorter exchanges broken down into clusters of two or three rather than all being played at once. This strategy also gives pupils the opportunity to improve on their last score within the same lesson, thus boosting their confidence in their listening ability.
- Play the tape at least twice but don't forget to explain *exactly* how you are going to do this. For instance, will you play the whole passage through with pauses for answers and then repeat it? Or, will you play it in sections and repeat each section? Pupils find listening particularly difficult as it demands considerable concentration. Careful explanation at the outset can prevent unnecessary anxiety or constant interruptions during the exercise. If the quality of the tape is not so good, do not be afraid to repeat certain phrases or words yourself or to play the tape again. Those who could understand will have already completed the task by then, while those struggling will receive extra help discretely and not feel that they have failed.
- Do pupils need to be familiar with all the language in the text in advance? In most cases this is essential in order to build up their confidence in what can for many be a difficult and demanding exercise. However, in short extracts where many words are recognisable, e.g. hobbies, pupils will enjoy the fact that they can easily identify the new vocabulary with little effort.
- The use of answer forms: a quick table on the board or on a worksheet can be an effective way to elicit answers and useful for oral or written work afterwards. Gauge carefully the amount of information pupils have to give according to their ability. Also, stopping the tape and asking pupils to write down the last word they have heard can be fun and pupils will succeed provided that the speech is not too fast or indistinct.

A third playing of the tape might allow some of the pupils, who have not managed to do so already, to complete the activity.

Focussing on linguistic structures and forms

In order to stretch pupils the teacher can devise activities focussing on the linguistic structures and forms contained in the stimulus material. Pupils could, for instance, be asked to verbalise the non-verbal responses made initially.

One of the ultimate goals of listening activities is the ability of pupils to communicate and express themselves by transferring the language contained in the stimulus material from their passive to their active vocabulary.

Devising a gap-filling activity or providing a transcript out of order requiring pupils to find the correct sequence, asking them to match beginnings and ends of sentences can all be used to make them more familiar with the language forms as can replacing key vocabulary with synonyms or correcting inaccurate sentences.

Consideration needs to be given to the extent of preparatory work on key vocabulary and essential linguistic structures.

Rebuilding

Once pupils have a very clear understanding of the content of the stimulus material and also of how these details have been expressed, the focus can shift towards rebuilding the text. Notes taken in previous activities can be used for this purpose. The teacher can facilitate this process by providing a framework of targeted questions, moving from the expression of factual details to the expression of personal opinion.

READING (AND RESPONDING)

As a receptive skill the process of reading is not dissimilar to that of listening. Through reading pupils can be exposed to new language forms and structures. Activities are different in that the stimulus material is more varied and, crucially, visible to pupils. Access to source material is, therefore, more permanent.

The notion of 'reading for pleasure' permeates these stages.

Table 6.3   Reading (and responding): an overview

from
preparatory activities
reading for gist/detail (content)
focussing on linguistic structures and forms
rebuilding
to

Preparatory activities

As with listening, pupils can benefit from being exposed to written texts after some prior preparation.

At this early stage the teacher can guide the pupil through the text: the content of the passage could be predicted with the help of visual clues or headlines. Also, word associations can be used to reactivate key lexical items.

It is important to encourage pupils to look out for clues. It may be that a particular text contains few clues or, indeed, an abundance of them. Newspaper articles contain headlines, subtitles and pictures. Cartoon strips tell the story in pictures supported by text. Texts containing 'direct speech' indicate the number of speakers. Advertisements consist of slogans and visual clues. All of these can be extrapolated from the main body of the text and serve as material in their own right. (For examples of the use of clues see e.g. Brandi and Strauss 1985.)

Reading for gist/detail with a focus on content

Once pupils have activated relevant linguistic items and structures and are familiar with the context of the text, they are ready to carry out a closer examination. The extraction of key facts and figures is an easier proposition once the context is clear. The teacher can provide tables, diagrams, true/false exercises or multiple-choice activities to elicit non-verbal responses or single word/phrase answers, which serve to summarise the content of the text.

Both individual and pair-work activities can encourage a closer examination of the text.

Questions should be graded and structured, from closed to open, to maximise pupils' opportunities to answer correctly and gradually encourage longer verbal responses.

Focussing on linguistic structures and forms

Texts contain language forms relevant to particular contexts; referral to the language forms used in the text serves to reinforce those structures. The teacher can devise activities requiring pupils to reproduce the specific structures introduced by a text. Gap filling exercises focussing on particular grammatical forms, for instance, can serve this purpose. The teacher could reproduce the text with verb/adjective endings missing, requiring pupils to complete certain sections from memory. Texts can be rewritten by substituting certain lexical items. Also, sections of the text can be reproduced in a jumbled form again requiring pupils to reconstruct the passage in a meaningful way. Clearly, work on activities of this nature also serves to develop pupils' writing skills.

Rebuilding

By this stage pupils should be fairly familiar with the text. 'Open-ended' tasks allowing for a variety of different answers can stimulate original responses. Pupils can be asked to talk or write about their favourite character and what distinguishes her from others.

Figure 6.1 *Ach nein!*

La Mort du Crocodile

Le pauvre crocodile est mort
et tout le monde regarde son corps.
Il flotte dans la rivière –
Son nez , son ventre , ses pattes en l'air.
La grenouille et l'hippopotame
sont tout en pleurs devant ce drame.
La pieuvre , penchée sur une roche ,
sort un mouchoir de sa poche ;
elle cache sa tête dans ses bras
et s'écrie : "Oh , là , là ! là , la !"
Et même le poisson lève la tête
et dit : " Dis donc ! la pauvre bête !"
L'oiseau ouvre tout grand ses yeux ;
le serpent siffle son adieu .
Sur l'autre rive les deux lapins
se donnent tristement la main ,
et monsieur Hibou sage et vieux
dit : "Quel malheur ! oh mon dieu !"
Et l'éléphant invisible
barrit : "Mais non ! c'est pas possible !"
Et quelqu'un caché dans un trou
dit : "Oh , il est mort ! bou - hou - hou !"
Le renard et l'écureuil
près de l'arbre , sont en deuil .
Seule la fourmi qui dort
ne sait pas qu'il est mort .
Quelle scène si triste à la rivière ;
même la feuille tombe par terre ,
car c'était le crocodile préféré
de tous les animaux de la forêt.

Vocabulaire

patte(f) .– paw	bête(f) – creature	quelqu'un – someone
pencher – to lean	siffler – to hiss	en deuil – in mourning
mouchoir(m) – hanky	rive(f) – bank	feuille(f) – leaf
poche(f) – pocket	sage – wise	tomber – to fall
cacher – to hide	barrir – to trumpet	par terre – to the groun

Figure 6.2 *La mort du crocodile*

They can be asked to continue a story, provide an explanation of the events portrayed or produce an alternative account. A response to a text of this nature is individual and personal. Reference material needs to be made accessible to facilitate the expression of opinions and interpretations.

Reading for pleasure: examples from and reflections on classroom practice

It is difficult to build reading for pleasure into the weekly diet of mfl teaching. For a variety of reasons, pupils can be reluctant to carry out independent reading or it can be difficult to find appropriate material, particularly in less widely taught mfl. It would appear that quite a number of pupils do not read for relaxation or as a hobby – there are, after all, so many alternatives available in the form of TV, videos and computer games etc. Without frequent practice the act of reading can appear more difficult and be perceived to take a lot of effort in relation to its 'competitors' and the 'pleasure factor' can disappear. And if the material to be read is in a foreign language … .

Therefore, what is required, it seems, is to enable pupils to discover the pleasure in reading. Below are some ideas and tried-and-tested sample materials largely relating to Key Stage 3, which have been designed to encourage pupils to read.

Ach nein! (Year 7): The cartoon in Figure 6.1 allows pupils to practise the phrases and vocabulary taught in the initial stages of their study of German.

La mort du crocodile (Year 8): The poem about a dead crocodile in Figure 6.2 can be read out with great drama by the teacher – and subsequently by the pupils onto tapes – and exploited at different levels, from simply labelling the creatures to translating the entire poem. The main purpose is to make pupils more aware of nuances of pronunciation. After having read the poem they can write their own couplets or short poem.

PRODUCTIVE MFL SKILLS

Imitation of 'foreign' sounds and the reproduction of accurate written forms comprise the earliest stages of developing productive language skills. Repetition and copying rely heavily on examples provided by the teacher. Eventually, the aim is the generation of personalised language by the pupil in order to satisfy a perceived communicative need (see Table 6.6).

SPEAKING

The speaking activities discussed in this section span the continuum from repetition to free expression.

Repetition

Repetition exercises are a first step towards the development in pupils of speaking skills.

Reflection
Activity 6.2 Receptive skills:
listening and reading

- Build up a bank of activities and strategies enabling pupils to become familiar with the key vocabulary and structures introduced through listening and reading.

  Work collaboratively with your mentor or a class teacher whose classes you teach using some of them. Together with her evaluate the effectiveness of your activities and strategies and decide which work well for different learner types.

- Table 6.4 shows an alphabetical list of *non-verbal* response types. Rank them in order of difficulty. Then, test your hypotheses in the classroom.

  Also, rank the set of *verbal* response types in Table 6.5 Add to the lists, if you wish.

Table 6.4 Non-verbal response types

Response type	Ranking
completing diagrams	
drawing	
gap filling	
labelling	
mixing-and-matching	
multiple choice	
physical movement	
ticking boxes	
true/false	

Table 6.5 Verbal response types

Response type	Ranking
agreeing/disagreeing	
answering in full sentences	
correcting	
gap filling	
interpreting	
mixing and matching half sentences	
one-word answers	
paraphrasing	
rebuilding text	
sequencing	
summarising	
translating	
unjumbling text/scripts	

Table 6.6 Progression in productive mfl skills

from:	to:
repetition and copying	generation of own language

Table 6.7 Speaking: an overview

from
repetition
structured pair work
open-ended role-play
to

Use of visual aids

As can be seen in Chapters 3 and 11, the use of visual aids allows pupils to follow the process of labelling concepts, which can render the translation of words unnecessary. Many items of key vocabulary can be introduced and presented effectively in a visually recognisable form such as through flashcards, real objects, images on acetates or posters.

First of all, pupils should listen to the teacher. Once an item has been presented, pupils can be asked to repeat what they have heard. Often, teenagers prefer not to repeat in front of their peers because of being embarrassed or finding the task difficult. This can be overcome by the teacher encouraging the pupils to shout, whisper, sing and imitate. Longer words and phrases often cause problems. Chanting and clapping to a rhythm can be useful strategies.

The teacher should not simply go through the list of lexical items, assuming that, once covered, learning has taken place. Images already shown need to be returned to and pupils asked to recall the relevant vocabulary. This can increase the pace of the lesson and keep the pupils attentive.

Pantomime competitions

Also, the class can be divided into smaller groups to carry out 'pantomime competitions' where pupils act out – through mime and gesture – what is depicted on individual visual aids. When pupils recognise what peers act out they say the word or phrase in question. All pupils should be encouraged to participate and the last rendition of a word or phrase should be pronounced correctly so that the correct pronunciation is reinforced.

Building up phrases backwards

Building up phrases backwards can also be of help, e.g. *'Je regrette, je n'en ai pas'* becomes *'pas, ... n'en ai pas, ... je n'en ai pas, ... je regrette je n'en ai pas'*.

Repeating a word or phrase if it is correct

In this activity the teacher presents a visual image to the whole group and makes either a correct or an incorrect utterance. Pupils are asked to repeat after the teacher, only if what she has said is correct. If what she has said is incorrect, pupils should remain silent. The activity works best if most of what the teacher says is true (adapted from Buckby 1980: 7).

A more able pupil may be nominated to lead the activity or the class can be divided into smaller groups with more able pupils as group leaders.

Pupils are required to think, to demonstrate what they know and also to participate as group members. The skills of identifying and memorising language are beginning to be developed in this way. Support by the teacher is evident through providing choices.

Guessing

If the teacher conceals the visual aids and asks pupils to shout out the corresponding word or phrase in the target language (TL) pupils are encouraged to use the TL even if they invariably make some mistakes. An element of competition can be introduced, for instance, by counting attempts.

In activities of this kind pupils are required to use their memory and to listen to peers. Correct articulation is rewarded and pupils practise the initial stages of communication.

Distributing visual aids

A natural progression towards communication is to use the same visual aids within a communicative context. There, the teacher encourages pupils within a whole class situation to ask for the items represented on the visual aid in the TL. The 'reward' for an accurate request is for the pupil to receive the visual aid. The pupil hides it from the rest of the class. Once all the items have been distributed the class is asked to find out from individual pupils what their particular visual aid depicts. If the request is correct, the visual aid is revealed; if the guess is wrong or the utterance is incorrect, an appropriate response should be made, e.g. '*Lo siento, no tengo ...*' ('Sorry, I haven't got it.') or '*Lo siento, no es correcto.*' ('Sorry, this is not correct.'). The activity continues until all the items have been revealed.

In this activity communication does take place, albeit within a supported environment.

Structured pair work

The next step towards the development of speaking skills in this framework is structured pair work.

Card games

A natural sequel to the activities above is, for instance, to provide cue cards for pairs to perform similar communicative acts in pairs. Reduced-size copies of the visual aids can be produced. Pupils work in pairs and successful communication is rewarded by the pupil making a correct utterance retaining the card. The game is over when one pupil has gathered all the available cards. This game can be played a number of times in succession.

Information gap activities

Information gap activities are another way of getting pupils to use the newly encountered linguistic items and structures in a communicative context.

Scripting and acting out role plays

On the basis of such preparatory speaking activities, but also listening and reading tasks, pupils can use the new language to script and act out role plays.

These structured pair-work activities encourage repetition of set linguistic items and structures. Pupils neither respond nor communicate spontaneously, yet they do use functional language for a particular purpose.

Open-ended role plays

From structured pair work pupils can move on to open-ended role plays. To make classroom communication of pupils more like 'real' communication, pupils need to be given opportunities to define and express their own needs. In open-ended role plays the language to be used for communication is not restricted to what has been introduced in a given unit of work but pupils have an opportunity to transfer linguistic items and structures from previous units and/or use new ones found in glossaries, dictionaries or other resource material.

In one possible activity pupils write their own 'shopping list' and purchase these articles from an imaginary store. This store can be 'staffed' by pupils, who have a defined list of articles available. As a consequence pupils cannot predict what their peers will say. As dialogues progress, needs and requests will inevitably change, requiring original use of language. This might allow for a sense of ownership of the language used.

The introduction of an element of fun or unpredictability can help to make certain topics more immediately interesting to pupils. Rather than script a standard role play in a restaurant pupils can, for instance, be encouraged to invent a scene featuring a confused or reluctant waiter mixing up things and bringing the wrong orders.

Pupils can make recordings of their role plays under the supervision of the foreign language assistant (FLA). When all groups have had their turn, some of the recordings are played in class. This way pupils can practise their pronunciation, improve their accent and intonation and use their imagination.

WRITING

Whilst writing should be introduced after new lexical items and phrases have been heard and seen, the written word should not be withheld as there is the danger of pupils beginning to imagine their own spellings (see also Hornsey 1993).

The simplest form of writing is copying. At the other end of the continuum is the free expression of ideas within the constraints of the vocabulary and active knowledge of the grammatical forms available.

Copying

Copying is not as simple a task as it might at first seem. Pupils need to copy accurately as a first step towards developing writing skills in the TL but also as a means of recording language forms for future use. Pupils cannot simply be expected to be able to copy without instruction and practice.

Many pupils find it difficult to concentrate and copy accurately. This difficulty can be overcome by providing activities requiring more focussed attention than 'simply' copying. 'Mixing and matching' activities require pupils to select a meaning for a particular word. Pupils might be asked to complete a sentence by filling gaps, choosing words from a jumbled list or unjumble letters to make a meaningful word or phrase out of them, e.g. locogie = 'colegio'. Computer programmes such as ordinary word processor packages or 'Fun with Texts' can be used effectively for this purpose.

The teacher clearly has a key role in identifying and/or correcting misspellings.

Targeted practice

From copying pupils can progress to targeted practice such as:

Table 6.8 Writing: an overview

from
copying
targeted practice
free expression through writing
to

Substitution

The replacement of words by alternatives using appropriate reference material is a valuable skill and possible next step. Similarly, unjumbling sentences can also be used to encourage accuracy. The teacher should insist on accuracy and demonstrate the value of correct spelling. Re-drafting is, for instance, one of the language skills specified in the Programme of Study of the National Curriculum. Pupils might occasionally be given the opportunity to design crossword puzzles and wordsearches containing key vocabulary, as this requires them not only to know the vocabulary/phrases in question but also to reproduce these accurately.

Repetition exercises

Writing is traditionally the form used to practise grammatical structures. Repetition exercises can reinforce correct forms of language. At the same time, work on grammatical exercises out of context can inhibit the aim of free expression. Grading activities in terms of difficulty can help to overcome this risk. The teacher can provide alternative answers for, say, verb endings followed by pupils having to apply rules without such support. Such activities only tend to be perceived as meaningful by pupils if the teacher uses them in preparation for communicative tasks such as, for instance, the writing of letters, memos, faxes and messages requiring the use of information and linguistic structures in a meaningful way.

Reflection
Activity 6.3 Productive language skills: speaking and writing

- Observe a range of mfl teachers at your placement school. How do they encourage pupils to repeat new words and phrases? Use the grid in Table 6.9 to help you record your findings. Which strategy works with which learner types?
- Pupils need a lot of confidence to speak to each other in the TL. With reference to Table 6.10, what forms of support are provided in pair and group work? Which work best with which learner types?
- The table in Table 6.11 consists of three columns: learner types, activity types and support. Which activities are most suitable for which learner type and what support is required? Match up the items in the three columns. Base your choice on the classroom observations you have already carried out.
- Follow-up this activity by including different activity types in your planning; then evaluate them.
- For a range of classes devise differentiated writing tasks and discuss them with your mentor or the respective class teacher.

Table 6.9 Strategies for repetition

Strategy	Year 7			Year 8			Year 9			Year 10			Year 11		
Teacher initials															
Whole group															
Individuals															
Small groups															
Competition															
Teacher changes voice															
Teacher changes pace															
Teacher changes pitch															
Use of gestures															
Use of visual aids															
Others ...															

Table 6.10 Support strategies for oral language production

Support	Comment
Visual stimulus	
Written stimulus (English)	
Written stimulus (TL)	
Props	
Model examples	
'Structure' tables	
Scripts (complete or incomplete)	

Table 6.11 Matching learner types, activity types and support strategies

Learner types	Activity types	Support strategies
	Reporting facts	Fishing lines*
	Substitution	Alternative answers
	Selection of correct forms	Model answers
	Joining halves of sentences	Rules and structures
Beginners	Gap filling	Switchboards
Weak intermediates	Labelling	Closed questions
Strong intermediates	Answering in sentences	Open questions
Advanced learners	Drill exercises	Tables of facts and figures
Others – please list	Scripting	Pictures
	Free expression	Symbols
	Discursive writing	Flow charts
	Others – please list	Others – please list

* Fishing lines are drawn onto a sheet to join two ideas; these may be presented as a tangled web, forming a puzzle.

Responding through writing

Some activities outlined in the sections on listening and reading clearly require pupils to respond in writing in the TL. Support comes in the form of the text provided as a stimulus.

Free expression through writing

A common frustration in mfl learning is the inability to express oneself freely without resorting to translation. Pupils should be encouraged to 'experiment' with and exploit known language by prompting them to write short poems, jokes and slogans within most topic areas. Short stories and the production of texts based on 'my ideal ...' allow pupils to use their imagination. The teacher needs to gauge the extent to which work of this nature is corrected: accurate language production needs to be reinforced, yet at the same time individual and personal use of the TL should not be discouraged.

CREATIVITY AND IMAGINATION

Imagination and creativity can be seen to permeate all mfl work. Indeed, the National Curriculum Programme of Study of the 1999 NC mfl Orders requires that pupils should be taught through 'using the target language creatively and imaginatively' (DfEE/QCA 1999: 17). This notion hardly comes as a surprise as, in Ann Miller's words: 'in the modern languages classroom ... teachers are required, day after day, to involve their pupils in a collective suspension of disbelief' (Miller 1995: 1). And the National Curriculum Council non-statutory guidance notes that 'the interest and motivation of young learners can be stimulated by themes which relate to play and leisure – themes of fantasy, fiction and fun' (NCC 1992: B9).

Traditionally teachers require verbal responses. However, they might also occasionally, and where appropriate, consider other communicative tools such as:

- drawing,
- modelling,
- composing music,
- dance,
- movement and/or
- poetry.

Allowing such a range of responses over a period of time enables the expression of new ideas to be generated in ways which mirror the human means of perception, i.e. through various senses.

Creativity involves addressing different intelligences (see Gardner 1983), including appealing to pupils' emotional intelligence. Goleman (1996) stresses the need to assist pupils in the development of their emotional intelligence, which means that opportunities need to be built into the learning process to allow pupils to respond and therefore to understand, express and use feelings and intuition.

One of the challenges for mfl teachers lies in incorporating into lessons suitable material and activities at appropriate moments. By far, not all language use is purely transactional and much is to be gained from the building of personalised patterns and structures. A multi-sensory approach allows for learning to be channelled in ways other than through verbal presentations. Songs, poems, puzzles, games, the creating of cartoons, artefacts and models can all enhance the learning process, appealing to pupils by adding variety and by catering for the diversity of their preferred learning styles.

The process of learning is not and should not be mechanistic. Language offers the opportunity for play, experimentation and even expression through means other than language. The stimulus for comprehension is often the context, and the incentive for communication may be different from the need to communicate for transactional purposes.

Poetry allows for the close analysis of language. Jacques Prévert's poem *Déjeuner du matin* deals with the sad break-up of a relationship.

Il a mis le café
Dans la tasse
Il a mis le lait
Dans la tasse de café
Il a mis le sucre
Dans le café au lait
Avec la petite cuiller
Il a tourné
Il a bu le café au lait
Et il a reposé la tasse
Sans me parler
Il a allumé
Une cigarette
Il a fait des ronds
Avec la fumée
Il a mis les cendres
Dans le cendrier
Sans me parler
Sans me regarder
Il s'est levé
Il a mis
Son manteau de pluie
Parce qu'il pleuvait
Et il est parti
Sous la pluie
Sans une parole
Sans me regarder
Et moi j'ai pris
Ma tête dans ma main
Et j'ai pleuré

(Jacques Prévert, *Paroles*, © Editions Gallimard)

The poem consists of simple language and records a sequence of activities, which occurred over a period of time. Pupils can easily produce a similar poem designed to account for a happy event in the past, following Prévert's approach.

Some published tape material such as *Un kilo de chansons* (Kay 1978) contains the continuous rhythmic repetition of simple phrases, set to music. Rap music can provide similar opportunities. To allow pupils to record their own songs to a simple rhythm and to add basic musical accompaniment can be an effective way to link in with youth culture and pupils' interests.

It takes a long time to produce puzzles in the form of wordsearches, crosswords or word snakes. Pupils themselves can occasionally be asked to develop such activities and challenge peers to complete them. The production of personalised language forms which actually serve a purpose can lead to a feeling of ownership and achievement.

Television advertisements often make minimal use of language, yet communicate messages through imagery and symbolism. To develop advertisements of their own allows pupils to put limited language skills to good use within a sophisticated context.

Language is often the means by which instructions and explanations are communicated. Success can be measured in terms of how well such instructions have been understood and acted upon. To ask pupils to deliver instructions in the process of making a product such as a meal, model or artefact is a demanding exercise, yet it can be motivating in that TL use can be seen to have an impact on the listener as well as a concrete outcome.

For a detailed discussion of creativity in mfl and more examples of using creativity in mfl teaching and learning see e.g. Jones 1992, Kavanagh and Upton 1994 or Miller 1995.

HOMEWORK

Homework can play a crucial role in the development of relevant (linguistic) skills in pupils. Given the fact that the mfl teacher, though vital in her role as agent in the learning process, cannot do the learning for her pupils, the extension of the limited exposure to the subject matter in lesson time through homework can be beneficial.

Homework can fulfil a number of different functions: it can supplement, extend and/or differentiate what happens in the mfl classroom; it can reinforce or consolidate linguistic items and structures; it allows pupils to work at their own pace and make use of reference material such as dictionaries. On occasion, tasks partially completed in class can be finished off at home. Homework can also yield valuable evidence for assessment purposes.

It is very important to note that homework need not be confined to the skill of writing:

* listening can be fostered by pupils listening to relevant role plays or other texts on short tapes on their personal stereos;
* speaking can be encouraged by pupils having personal tapes onto which they can record pronunciation exercises, role plays or themselves reading aloud;
* reading skills can be developed through reading for pleasure outside the classroom; and
* writing is often developed by way of completion of worksheets or exercises following on from oral or aural classroom work or scripting role plays. Drafting

and re-drafting with the help of the wordprocessor can also be meaningfully encouraged if pupils have access to a computer at home or at the school outside lesson time.

In addition to skill-specific tasks and activities other areas such as cultural awareness, learning strategies and (inter)personal and research skills can be developed through homework. Prompted by some pictures with brief captions in the coursebook, pupils can be asked, individually or in small groups, to produce a leaflet on a region/country where the TL is spoken for a specific audience, e.g. a display for the school's open evening. The teacher can either provide authentic resources such as leaflets for the task or pupils can be introduced to library resources including material on an electronic encyclopaedia. Pupils can be asked to extract relevant information from source material in English or the TL, simplify and, where necessary, translate it.

From time to time the learning or revision of key linguistic items or structures might be an appropriate homework task. In order to enable pupils to gain the most from such homework, they need to be taught some strategies in how to learn new linguistic items and structures as well as revision techniques. Regular revision of some ten minutes or so a day, for instance, can be more effective than isolated longer revision sessions; simply reading words or texts again and again might be less effective than saying words aloud or using underlining or highlighting techniques; revision plans can help to prioritise and avoid omitting important information; mixing topics that are more appealing with ones that are (perceived to be) more challenging might avoid reluctance to revise; making revision notes may help as may making up mnemonics, acronyms such as 'UE': *Unión Europea* or word associations such as *tiempo: hacer calor, hacer frío, mal tiempo* … .

For a range of useful homework ideas see Buckland and Short 1993. See also the online homework guidance available on the DfEE website at *http://www.dfee.gov.uk/homework/*. For other homework recourses see the website accompanying this book.

As can be seen in Chapter 4, in order to maximise its benefits, homework needs to be planned into units of work and lessons, i.e. thought about carefully in advance. Care

---

Reflection
Activity 6.4 Giving written feedback to pupils

- Draw up two lists of comments in the TL you think are appropriate in giving written feedback to pupils about their homework, one list for each Key Stage. These might, for instance, include praise for content, effort or accuracy, encouragement to take more care, be tidier or put more effort into homework.
- Next, ask your mentor or the class teacher for permission to collect in a set of books for each Key Stage and note the comments your colleagues have made about pupils' work.
- Then, compare your lists with the comments found in the exercise book and study the departmental marking policy.
- Finally, discuss the findings with the teacher in question.

needs to be taken that the departmental and school policies on homework are adhered to, for instance in terms of homework days. Appropriateness and manageability are other important considerations when deciding on the quantity and nature of homework.

Instructions need to be clear and unambiguous and the use of the TL for setting homework needs to be thought through carefully. It is important to feed back to pupils regularly and preferably in the following lesson how well they have done and in class to go over some of the areas which caused problems to them. In providing feedback the teacher needs to adhere to the departmental and school marking policies, which will often specify a system of grades as well as the nature of TL to be used for feedback. The policy could, for instance, specify that pupils are given a list of grades in English and the TL on a handout, which they stick into their exercise books for reference and which are used consistently across the department and/or school. For assessment, recording and reporting see also Chapter 10.

Reflection
Activity 6.5 Designing a guide for parents

Devise a guide for parents with suggestions how they can support their child's independent study and homework. Activities might include vocabulary testing, providing opportunities for listening to and reading the TL and researching holiday destinations.

SUMMARY

Both mfl trainees and pupils should recognise the importance of sequencing activities and integrating mfl skills within a communicative framework. Each mfl skill must be developed equally in order to allow pupils to generate language in 'authentic' situations and in an independent way.

Creativity is an important and integral part of mfl work.

Homework can be used meaningfully to extend and consolidate work carried out in class.

NOTE

1   We are, of course, aware that the terms 'receptive' and 'productive' in relation to language skills are not universally accepted. It is, therefore, important to note here that we do not deem listening and reading to be 'passive' skills. On the contrary, we very much acknowledge the importance of pupils engaging actively with what is 'received', hence our focus on 'responding'. We merely use the distinction for purposes of convenience and categorisation.

7 Teaching and Learning Grammar

The ability to use language grammatically correctly is a key component and an integral part of effective communication in the target language (TL). This chapter is based upon the premise that the development of communicative competence is a key goal for modern foreign languages (mfl) teaching and learning in the secondary school. Importantly, however, communicative competence is used here to encompass grammatical competence, socio-cultural competence, discourse competence and strategic competence (see Pachler 2000a). In particular, this chapter deals with grammatical competence as a subset of communicative competence.

Mfl methodology is characterised by considerable changes in the importance afforded to grammar over time.

Until the late 1970s and early 1980s, the so-called grammar translation method prevailed, which came about in the wake of mfl teachers' eagerness to assert equality of status with classical languages. In the grammar translation method, TL structures are typically arranged according to perceived usefulness and in increasing order of supposed complexity with new grammar rules being introduced and explained in the mother tongue, exemplified in the TL and practised through translation out of and into the TL (see Allford 1999: 232). The grammar-translation method can be seen as an expression of mfl teachers' perceived need to justify the position of their subject on the curriculum by stressing the potential for analytical thinking and the training of the mind mfl learning affords. Focus on language forms in grammar-translation often came at the expense of learners' ability to communicate effectively in speaking.

Examinations and their syllabuses (now specifications), i.e. the General Certificate in Education O-level and the Certificate in Secondary Education, reflected the emphasis on grammar and accuracy.

The nature of this approach and of the examination system accompanying it is widely judged to have contributed to a lack of pupil motivation to study mfl at secondary level.

In the late 1980s the General Certificate of Secondary Education (GCSE) was introduced. It emphasised communication in a narrowly defined number of topics with clearly specified linguistic items/phrases, functions and structures at the expense of accuracy. The pendulum swing from great emphasis on form to great emphasis on meaning led to the publication of two consecutive National Curriculum documents in the 1990s, which put little emphasis on and made no explicit mention of grammar.

In recent years grammar has seen something of a renaissance. Pressure from the grass-roots has led to changes in the Subject Criteria, the national criteria published by the Qualifications and Curriculum Authority (QCA), which govern the General Certificate of Secondary Education (see QCA 2000a). Whilst the national criteria continue to consider structural aspects of the TL in the main as a means to an end, they do now feature explicit reference to grammar. For example, all GCSE specifications must, amongst other things, require candidates to:

iv)   express themselves in writing using a range of vocabulary, syntax and structures;

v)   understand and apply the grammar of the modern foreign language, as detailed in the specification for Foundation tier.

(QCA 2000a: 1)

Similarly, the assessment objectives of the Subject Criteria (QCA 2000a: 2) list the following:

AO2 communicate in speech, showing knowledge of and applying accurately the grammar and structures prescribed in the specification

AO4 communicate in writing, showing knowledge of and applying accurately the grammar and structures prescribed in the specification

This trend must be seen also as a consequence of developments earlier at advanced level and as an attempt to avoid a further increase in the gap between GCSE and A level. The most recent Subject Criteria (see QCA et al. 1999) feature a detailed and differentiated list of structures to be covered at advanced subsidiary (AS) and at advanced (A) level (see Epilogue). Of course it must also be seen as an attempt to build on the National Literacy Strategy (NLS) at primary level (see DfEE 1998a and Introduction).

The re-focussing on grammar follows a heated debate in the recent past about whether the requirements of examination specifications and associated approaches to mfl teaching pre-higher education were appropriate in their demands regarding awareness, knowledge and understanding of grammar and whether they furthered the development of transferable and independently expandable mfl learning skills.

As of late the question is no longer whether or not grammar should be taught, but instead how, why and when (see also Jones 2000: 146).

In private many mfl teachers have always held the view that 'there comes a time when pupils must learn some grammar of the TL' (Rivers 1975: 105) irrespective of prevailing methodological trends. Susan Halliwell (1993: 17), for example, points out the value of learning grammar as opposed to acquiring the language. She sees learning as a conscious process and it seems quicker to her than acquisition through immersion. Whilst not conclusive, there is increasingly research evidence pointing to the importance of form-focussed instruction, i.e. explicit grammar teaching (see e.g. Ellis 1997). However, building language forms around grammatical rules independently of communicative needs can be argued to serve no real purpose. Bertrand Russell, for example, put forward the view that:

> The purpose of words, though philosophers seem to forget this simple fact, is to deal with matters other than words. If I go to a restaurant and order my dinner, I do not want my words to fit into a system of other words, but to bring about the presence of food.
>
> (in Page and Hewett 1987: 6)

Clearly, the communicative context determines the form of the message conveyed by a speaker or writer. Grammatical accuracy can be argued to be secondary if the message is understood. Nevertheless, pupils need a grammatical base in order to be able to generate language of their own as opposed to merely reproduce set phrases of others. Communicative competence and linguistic competence should, therefore, not be seen as separate entities.

Learners should not be inhibited in terms of communicative competence due to an adherence to a strictly linear approach to learning grammar, i.e. from simple to complex. Lightbown and Spada (1993: 114) note, for example, that 'it is neither necessary nor desirable to restrict learners' exposure to certain linguistic structures which are perceived as being "simple"'. As Walter Grauberg (1997: 99) rightly points out, even the simplest exchanges require complex language. To empower learners to operate in the present tense only, for example, can be seen to 'strand them linguistically' (see Jones 2000: 149). Yet sequencing of grammar learning can be seen to be necessary to enable learners to build up patterns and structures incrementally.

To teach learners certain grammatical features as set phrases can be seen to be legitimate in so far as it can stand pupils in good stead, for example, in preparation for their public examinations, which feature transactional exchanges in narrowly defined contexts. However, this should not be done at the expense of the development in pupils of an understanding of language and of an ability to generate language of their own. A more beneficial long-term strategy seems to us to be to pay specific attention to language with transferable value, such as the key verbs, lexical items, pronouns, adjectives, adverbs or gender markers.

This chapter focuses on the need for mfl trainees to address the development of grammatical awareness, knowledge and understanding in pupils in a well-planned and structured way within the context of communicative processes. We suggest that grammar should not be presented in isolation but in a coherent framework and that it should not be left to pupils to absorb grammar by osmosis.

OBJECTIVES

By the end of this chapter you should:
- understand some of the important issues concerning the teaching and learning of grammar in the secondary mfl curriculum;
- appreciate the need for a structured approach to the teaching and learning of grammar; and
- be aware of one possible framework for and be able to make informed choices about the teaching and learning of grammar in support of the development of communicative competence.

PEDAGOGICAL GRAMMAR

Definitions of the word 'grammar' are manifold: they range from a 'theory of language' to a description of the (syntactic) structure of a particular language'. Of these grammars, work by applied linguists on what they call 'pedagogical grammar', which focuses on language teaching, syllabus design and the production of teaching material, is of particular interest to mfl teachers.

At ages 11 to 16 it is particularly difficult for the mfl teacher to strike the right balance between accuracy and meaning. To what extent should mfl teachers tolerate errors when encouraging communication? Brian Page (1990: 103–4) is unequivocal about the role of grammar: 'Correct grammar, like pronunciation, serves a social function. It tells the world something about what sort of person we are in the same way as our clothes, our lifestyle, and the newspaper we read.'

Whilst perfect grammatical accuracy is not necessary for communication to take place, it can be argued that to operate effectively as a TL speaker or writer, we have to understand – to some extent – the possibilities that grammar affords us. The ability to recognise linguistic patterns and to make use of and apply grammatical rules aids communication rather than inhibits it. This is recognised by the 1999 NC mfl Orders, which require pupils to be taught 'the grammar of the target language and how to apply it' (DfEE/QCA 1999: 16). This constitutes a marked departure from previous NC mfl Orders, in which there was no explicit and little implicit mention of grammar.

Success at GCSE increasingly requires awareness, knowledge and understanding of grammatical features. Careful preparation of pupils in examination techniques and familiarisation with past examination papers as well as standard 'grammatical' paradigms and standard role plays and letters to be adapted by pupils according to context continue to be useful strategies for gaining good examination results. However, there is a growing need for applied grammatical knowledge, which is reflected in the 2000 GCSE Grade descriptions (see QCA 2000a: 3–4 and Table 7.1).

Furthermore, the GCSE Criteria (QCA 2000a: 3) state that 'at least 10% of the total marks for the subject must be allocated to knowledge and accurate application of the grammar and structures of the modern foreign language prescribed in the specification'.

Grammar is no longer merely implicit and the GCSE Criteria contain lists of grammar items specified for Foundation and Higher Tier (see QCA 2000a: 5–10). Trainee mfl teachers must make themselves aware of these specifications in relation to their teaching language(s). The lists provide examples and also indicate elements where only receptive knowledge is required.

To some extent grammatical understanding can be seen to provide foreign language learners in classroom-based settings with a shortcut. The limited curriculum time available, usually around 10–12.5 per cent, and the acquisition-poor nature of classroom-based learning do not tend to allow for natural acquisition. Grammar can be seen as a tool enabling TL use, and the use of specific and technical terminology, i.e. metalanguage, offers learners access to reference material. The teaching and learning of grammar at 11 to 16 is neither undesirable nor inappropriate. In order to be beneficial, it does, however, need to be structured carefully and a range of issues need to be taken on board during the planning process as, for example, Jane Jones (2000: 151–3) notes (see Table 7.2). Both under- and overemphasis on grammatical structures can lead to

Table 7.1   Extracts from the GSCE Grade descriptions

	Speaking	**Writing**
Grade F	Candidates take part in simple conversations showing some ability to substitute words and phrases. Their pronunciation is generally accurate, and although there may be grammatical inaccuracies, the main points are communicated.	Candidates write short sentences, and respond to written texts by substituting words and set phrases. Although there may be mistakes in spelling and grammar the main points are communicated.
Grade C	Candidates develop conversation and simple discussions which include past, present and future events, involving the use of different tenses.	Candidates express personal opinions and write about a variety of topics, both factually and imaginatively, including past, present and future events and involving the use of different tenses.
Grade A	(Candidates) express and justify points of view, and produce longer sequences of speech using a variety of vocabulary, structures and verb tenses.	(Candidates) produce longer sequences using a range of vocabulary, structure and verb tenses. Their spelling and grammar are generally accurate.

frustration and can militate against free expression. The exact nature of the teacher's methods will depend on, amongst other factors, her personal teaching style, pupils' individual needs and differences, the coursebook followed or the general approach adopted by the whole school in terms of language work.

FOUR STAGES OF DEVELOPING GRAMMATICAL AWARENESS

The four stages of developing grammatical awareness delineated below (see Table 7.3) are intended to link the teaching of grammar to the 'presentation-practice-production' paradigm introduced in Chapter 3.

Stages 1–4 are not meant to promote curriculum planning based on grammar-oriented objectives alone. Instead, a structured and graded approach of developing linguistic understanding is advanced, which is closely linked to other objectives, such as semantic knowledge across different contexts or functions (e.g. expressing likes and dislikes, asking for, refusing etc.).

> Research findings ... challenged the traditional grammar-based course by suggesting that learners acquired particular structures in an order which was psychologically determined but not susceptible to explicit instruction. Acquisition took place in stages and the notion that a learner had fully acquired a structure after a period of instruction was naive. Learning did not occur in linear and progressive fashion but was an organic process characterised by back-sliding, leaps in competence, interaction between grammatical elements, etc.
> (Heafford 1990: 10)

Table 7.2 Some issues associated with teaching and learning grammar

---

1 Selection

Within the overall schematic picture of a typical five-year learning programme, the teacher needs to select structures that will be useful in terms of transfer value as regards other structures and other contexts in order to maximise their generative capacity for the learners. In other words, it is useful to teach structures, which can be used elsewhere, in different combinations, in conjunction with other structures and as springboards for independent language use. ...

2 Sequencing

... It is the role of the teacher to help the learners to make the connections through a mixture of inductive and deductive approaches, with extensive exposure and opportunities to practise making the link. ...

3 Recycling

Whilst the constraints and needs of classroom learning necessitate some drilling of discrete items as an aid to internalisation, it is helpful to the learners to be shown how a structure learnt in one context may be recycled in another one. ...

4 Moving from 'form' to function

... This involves a shift from 'skill-getting' to 'skill-using' and envisages the learner moving from a stage of very conscious attention to the language form to a more unconscious use for real communication purposes. ...

5 Grading of input

It is sometimes useful to restate a very obvious principle such as this assertion that, as well as a sufficient quantity of examples, teachers need to present appropriately graded examples to the pupils. In this way, the first examples will be easier, straightforward and contradiction-free and thus susceptible to helping the learners to infer the pattern(s) and thus to be able to test their hypotheses. ...

6 Use of terminology

Unfortunately, the issue of grammatical terminology has become ... something considered so abstract as to be beyond pupils' comprehension. This (can be seen as) a little condescending. It is the quality and timing of a presentation and explanation of a grammatical structure that is important and not the terminology *per se*. As Carter cogently argues: 'It is not taught for its own sake but to provide an economic and precise way of discussing particular functions and purposes' (Carter 1997: 24).

Source: Jones 2000.

This notion of an 'organic' nature of language development has implications for teaching and learning. Karen Turner, for example, advances the view that a purely thematic, topic-based approach to planning and syllabus design with an unsystematic and disorganised presentation of the grammatical system (e.g. categories of words, the notion of tense, syntactical considerations including cases, the gender of nouns and the notion of agreement, the mood of verbs etc.) is unhelpful to pupils. She proposes a graded, spiralling approach based on grammatical aspects of a language in conjunction with semantic aspects (the meaning of words and sentences) underpinned by the

Table 7.3   Four stages of grammar teaching and learning

No.	Stage
1	input
2	explanation
3	habit-forming
4	communicative application

criterion of 'usefulness to the pupil' (e.g. What does the pupil need to do well in the standardised examination?) with a view to providing a 'tool for learning' (e.g. What helps the pupil in becoming an effective language learner?) (see Turner 1996: 17–18). 'Organising the grammatical core in conjunction with the topic areas means that structures are always contextualised and related to language use.' (Turner 1996: 18) For example, the topic of 'directions' could be seen to lend itself well to the teaching of imperatives (the command form).

The role of grammar in foreign language teaching and learning is complex. Teachers' decisions need to take into account what is known about the foreign language learning process. Norbert Pachler (see 1999a: 97) identifies four broad stages of learning grammar:

- Noticing:
  The identification that language forms patterns and the labelling, in the learners' own words, of these patterns.
- Integrating:
  The process of identifying and labelling through personal rule formation needs to be related to existing grammatical knowledge.
- Internalising:
  Learners need to apply their own rules in order to manipulate language forms for their own purposes. This completes the process of committing the form to the long-term memory.
- Proceduralising:
  Use of the structure becomes 'automatic' through regular usage in a range of contexts.

From this follow important pedagogic questions, such as: to what extent should these processes be made explicit to learners? And, how can they be taught?

THE INPUT STAGE

Two main approaches to providing input can be distinguished: an *inductive* approach, where linguistic structures are introduced through examples from which to develop (personal) rules, and a *deductive* approach, where the pupil is provided with a grammatical rule or pattern followed by examples before putting it to use.

Both methods have a legitimate place in mfl teaching and learning. Grammar is highly conceptual, which appeals to some pupils more than others. Certain aspects of language are difficult to explain. Why, for instance is the word 'table' feminine in French and masculine in German and why has it no grammatical gender in English? To accept certain concepts as given and to apply some rules in a mechanical way without trying to understand them seems on occasion to be a sensible way forward. Nevertheless, having understood a grammatical concept, for instance gender, many pupils are able to work out a rule, such as for adjectival agreement, from a set of carefully constructed examples.

Some pupils can get a sense of security from understanding language patterns and rules. Ian Forth and John Naysmith (1995: 78) distinguish

- *'external' rules*: 'the kind of statements, diagrams, tables, etc., which we can find in coursebooks, grammar reference books or which we as teachers provide'; and
- *'internal' rules*: 'the learner's own intuitive, informal hunches of how elements of the language might work'.

Whilst they stress that there is 'no one, single approach to the presentation and use of grammar rules in the classroom' (Forth and Naysmith 1995: 80), they posit that learners should be encouraged to reflect on how they themselves use rules and what works for them. Teachers should encourage learners to challenge grammar rules, for instance, by:

- asking students to change or modify rules presented in their coursebooks so that they are clearer and more accessible;
- asking students to add their own examples;
- asking students to re-present rules in the form of classroom poster-displays perhaps with the addition of pictures or diagrams.

(Forth and Naysmith 1995: 80)

Input is concerned with the selection of material and of a suitable approach. One possible consideration is for items, which can be seen to be of future use and are therefore 'transferable', to be explicitly taught, especially in the early stages of learning. Such items need to be readily understood by all learners and the teacher needs to be sure that they are relatively simple to understand. Ellis (1997: 91), referring to research by Green and Hecht (1992) on what constitutes easy-to-learn rules, lists the following features:

- those that refer to easily recognisable categories;
- those which can be applied mechanically; and
- those that are not dependent on large contexts.

Reflection
Activity 7.1 Grammar rules

Write a rule for the English use of 'yet' and 'still' as in 'I've not been to London yet' and 'I've still not been to London'.
- How did you go about approaching this task?
- When is it useful to resort to a rule and when does it help to refer to examples?

The selection of grammatical items to be covered within units of work is not simple. Some topics lend themselves more easily to new grammatical input than others (e.g. the topic 'Around town' for the teaching of the imperative). However, the selection of grammar points to be covered requires the consideration of more complex questions, such as:

- which items need to be 're-cycled' from previous units covered?
- which items meaningfully build on existing knowledge?
- which items should not be explained in full at this stage, but will require revisiting at a later date?
- which items can be treated as lexical items at this stage?

The schemes of work produced by QCA (QCA 2000b; also available at *http://www.standards.dfee.gov.uk/schemes2/*) and coursebooks tend to include suggestions concerning grammar items to be covered. Where possible, account needs to be taken of prior learning and how certain grammatical concepts link with what has come before. Also, extension activities for more able learners are important in so far as the decision to treat certain grammatical structures as lexical items/phrases at a particular stage of learning may not be appropriate for all learners.

Learners need to be prepared for the demands of new language features. Also, they need to be trained to identify patterns, structures, exceptions to rules etc. and be able to learn from the teacher's corrections. Teachers need to be aware of possible misconceptions and difficulties pupils might have, which might impact upon their motivation.

Reflection
Activity 7.2 Examining the grammar content of the GCSE Criteria

Consider the grammatical items listed within the GCSE Criteria (QCA 2000a: 5–10) for your teaching language(s). Which items do you consider to be essential? How can the underpinning concepts be taught to mfl learners in the early stages of their learning experience?

Reflection
Activity 7.3 Grammar input

Figure 7.1 shows an outline of a unit of work used by one mfl department. The section on grammar has been left blank. In light of the language functions as well as the core and extension language listed, consider

- what should be included in the grammar section? and
- which of these grammatical points should not be explained but presented as lexical items?

Compare your answers with the way the coursebook(s) used by your placement school approach(es) the topics of personal detail and daily

Year 8	Personal details and daily routine		
Language functions			ATL
Be able to: 1. Exchange details about the family 2. Introduce people 3. Describe and understand appearance 4. Describe places and buildings 5. Talk about chores 6. Describe daily routine at home			AT1 L3&4 AT2 L2,3&4 AT3 L3&4 AT4 L3&4
Core language		Extension	
Names of members of immediate family Description: hair, eyes, height, weight Name of rooms Household chores Routines		Other relatives Description of personality Other accommodation More complex routines and chores	
Grammar			
Key activities			
Letter to penfriend Design ideal home Identikit pictures			

Figure 7.1   Grammar and the unit of work

Walter Grauberg (1997: 104) stresses the importance of the text on which introductory work is based. In his opinion it should:

- deal with a topic of interest to the learners;
- build on lexical and grammatical knowledge acquired earlier;
- at the same time have the attraction of novelty; and
- feature a context, which lends itself to varied and interesting practice where form and function are brought out clearly without distortion to normal use.

In our reading of Grauberg we interpret 'text' very broadly as any type of stimulus material, be it written or spoken.

Rutherford (1987) advocates a process of 'consciousness raising' focussing the learner's attention on features of the TL, which are deemed by the teacher to be significant at a given stage of learning. This might well involve a degree of comparison with the mother tongue, the breaking down of larger items into component parts etc. in order to sensitise the learner to the structure of the TL.

Eric Hawkins (1984) conceives of grammar learning as a voyage of discovery and argues against a prescriptive model. The recognition that different learners will respond to different approaches requires teachers to understand a wide range of techniques and to develop strategies to suit specific learner characteristics.

The discussion of the inductive and deductive methods below is intended to provide a framework within which a range of strategies for grammar teaching can be categories and consequently better understood.

The inductive approach: an example

Pupils need to be made aware of the concept of gender early on. In German, for instance, the awareness of this concept should precede the introduction of the case system. The teaching of the accusative case can be done meaningfully in the context of the topic of 'family and pets'. The assumption in this example is that the new vocabulary has already been introduced (see Chapter 3 for presenting new language and question-and-answer techniques) and that the teacher follows a policy of discussing new grammar items within the context of familiar vocabulary.

Pupils could be presented with a number of sentences such as those in Table 7.4.

The pupils are then asked to sort these sentences according to categories of their own choice. Some pupils will choose the categories according to whether the object is a person or an animal. Clearly from the examples given, pupils would not be wrong to apply such categories. The purpose of the inductive approach is for pupils to make up and apply rules of their own, which fit the examples provided. As the examples given in Table 7.4 are ambiguous and allow for different interpretation, the mfl teacher needs to provide further examples in a structured way, which lead the pupils to the intended focus. Eventually the majority of pupils should choose the categories: *'einen'*, *'ein'* or *'eine'*.

In groups, pupils are then asked to discuss (in English) the ways in which they have categorised the sentences and why and to attempt to generate a rule, which is subsequently discussed in a plenary. An example of one such rule could be: 'If you have something masculine you add '-en' to *'ein'*. If it's feminine stick with the normal *'eine'* and for neuter stick with *'ein'*.

At this stage it is sufficient for the mfl teacher to say that the inflections occur after *'haben'*. Once the concept is familiar a more formal explanation of the accusative case can be attempted. In this approach new metalanguage is not introduced until the learner has demonstrated understanding of the concept through use of language familiar to her at the point of input.

In another example the inductive approach can be used to teach the perfect tense in Spanish. Pupils are asked to read the penfriend letter in Figure 7.2 and underline or highlight any linguistic patterns they seem to notice. In this example it is the auxiliary *'haber'* in the present tense plus the respective past participle. The teacher then elicits pupil observations in the TL and collects them on the board/OHP. The grammatical

Table 7.4   The accusative case in German

Ich habe einen Bruder.	Ich habe ein Kaninchen.
Ich habe eine Schwester.	Ich habe eine Katze.
Ich habe ein Meerschweinchen.	Ich habe einen Wellensittich.

Albacete 7 de septiembre

Querida Alison:

¿cómo estás? He vuelto al colegio hace una semana y he empezado mis clases. Lo he pasado muy guay este verano ¿ y tú ? He viajado a la costa de Valencia con mi familia y he ido a la playa todos los dias por las mañanas donde me he bañado y donde antes del almuerzo hemos jugado mucho al balónvolea con amigos nuevos que he conocido allí.

Me he puesto muy morena. Mi hermana y yo hemos ido a la discoteca por las noches y hemos disfrutado mucho. Mis padres han ido al restaurante todas las noches y han comido comida típica de la región. También hemos visitado pueblos famosos como Elche y sus museos.

He recogido mis fotografias del laboratorio esta mañana y estoy muy contenta con el resultado. He seleccionado cuatro fotos para madarte para que puedas ver lo bonito que es la costa del este de España.

De momento nada más.

En tu carta háblame de tu verano, por ejemplo: ¿has estado de vacaciones? ¿has visitado a tus amigos? ¿has viajado?

Recuerdos a tu familia y espero recibir tu carta pronto.

Con cariño, tu amiga
Sonia

Figure 7.2   Introducing the Spanish perfect tense

Reflection
Activity 7.4 The inductive ap-

Try to think of another example for the inductive approach appropriate for your first foreign language and discuss it with your mentor or another teacher you regularly work with.

rule that infinitives ending in '-ar' form the past participle in '-ado', those ending in '-er' and '-ir' in '-ido' is subsequently explained in the TL by drawing parallels to the similarities and differences in the English language. In this way, appropriate use is made of English for comparing and contrasting with the mother tongue.

The deductive approach: an example

For many pupils the concept of grammatical gender is difficult to conceptualise. One possible way of introducing the definite article to pupils is by providing them with a table such as the one in Figure 7.3.

THE			
le = **m**asculine	**le** chat	=	**the** cat
la = **f**eminine	**la** souris	=	**the** mouse
les = **p**lural	**les** chiens	=	**the** dogs
l' = before a vowel			
(**a, e, i, o, u**)	**l'**araignée	=	**the** spider
or '**h**', '**y**'	**l'**hôtel	=	**the** hotel

Figure 7.3 The definite article in French

1............. cheval (m)	2. .... cahier... (pl)	3. .... tortue (f)
4............. lapin... (pl)	5. .... prénom (m)	6. .... soeur (f)
7............. hôpital (m)	8. .... stylo... (pl)	9. .... jour...(pl)
10............. anniversaire (m)	11. .... poubelle (f)	12. .... animal (m)
13............. frère... (pl)	14. .... éléphant (m)	15. .... femme (f)
16............. homme (m)	17. .... serpent... (pl)	18. .... table (f)

Figure 7.4 Practising the definite article in French

Pour formuler le **passé composé** vous avez besoin de:				
un sujet	**un verbe auxiliare**		**un participe passé**	
	avoir	*être*		
je	*ai*	*suis*		
tu	*as*	*es*		
il/elle	*a*	*est*	e	irregular
nous	*avons*	*sommes*	stem + i	
vous	*avez*	*êtes*	u	
ils/elles	*ont*	*sont*		

Alors, choisissez le verbe.	
Est-ce que c'est un verbe réfléchi?	
oui	non
• utilisez être comme auxiliare • n'oubliez pas le 'me/te/se/nous/vous' entre le sujet et le verbe	C'est un verbe MRS TRAVENDAMP RDR?

	oui	non
	utilisez 'être' comme auxiliare	utilisez 'avoir' comme auxiliare
ajoutez l'accord au participe passé: f. sg.: -e m. sg.: - f. pl.: -es m. pl. -s		n'ajoutez pas d'accord au participe passé

Figure 7.5 The perfect tense in French

Pupils are then asked to complete the exercise in Figure 7.4 by referring to the table in Figure 7.3.

The deductive approach to grammar teaching can, for instance, also be used in the context of the perfect tense in French. This can be a stumbling block for pupils and for them to devise a comprehensive rule can be too difficult. Pupils should be able to produce a series of rules, which the teacher might want to pull together. The flow chart in Figure 7.5 gives an example of such a structure, which can help pupils generate many sentences. Such an approach may be suitable for more able pupils preparing for their GCSE examination.

Although this chart is not all-encompassing – it does not take account of reflexive verbs with indirect reflexive pronouns, which require no agreement – it provides a useful point of reference assisting pupils in generating TL utterances and can be taught in stages. The columns allow coverage of *avoir* verbs in isolation from the *être* and reflexive verbs. The need for past participle agreement can be added to the column as learners progress.

One way to help pupils remember which verbs take *être* in the perfect tense is to present a mnemonic. The first letters of the following verbs spell out MRS TRAVENDAMP RDR: *monter, rester, sortir, tomber, revenir, arriver, venir, entrer, naitre, descendre, aller, mourir, partir, rentrer, devenir, retourner.*

Reflection
Activity 7.5 Inductive or deductive approach?

- Focussing on the scheme of work for one particular year group, make a list of three to five grammar points for each approach. You might find it useful to look at the grammar summary of the coursebook.
- In your opinion, which grammar points lend themselves to an inductive approach and which to a deductive one?

THE EXPLANATION STAGE

The high level of complexity of language can tempt mfl teachers to provide quite detailed explanations of grammatical concepts. The exploration of concepts might on occasion seem easier to achieve through the medium of English than that of the TL as the process of learning might be accelerated in this way by focussing pupils' attention on linguistic structures in a conscious manner. However,

> central to the language learning process must remain 'exposure, exposure and more exposure', that only through the constant engagement of receptive skills can learners begin to get a feel for a language, to sense nuances of meaning, to produce spontaneously.
>
> (Heafford 1990: 12)

Heafford also suggests (1990: 12) that 'we need to experiment with various forms of formal grammar teaching to see which approaches least compromise exposure to the target language and which most help accuracy'. Careful selection of TL forms used by the teacher as part of general classroom talk serves to reinforce rules and patterns taught in an explicit manner. Pachler (1999a: 102) notes that it is therefore incumbent upon teachers to provide rich and varied but carefully considered input, which can be exploited by:

- focussing pupils' attention on noticing new structure;
- providing activities to use new and old structures to formulate personal meaning; and
- assisting learners to reflect on learning and their own use of language.

For some strategies for teaching grammar in the TL see Chapter 5.

Use of metalanguage

The choice of whether or not to use metalanguage such as 'verb', 'noun', 'adjective' remains a question of professional judgement of individual teachers within a coherent departmental approach. The mfl trainee has to decide in line with the approach taken by the placement school to what extent to use metalanguage. The National Literacy Strategy, which features a number of grammatical concepts to be developed during Key Stages 1 and 2, might provide some guidance (see Table 7.5 based on DfEE 1998: 68).

The non-statutory schemes of work for Key Stage 3 (see QCA 2000b) and the GCSE Criteria for Modern Foreign Languages (QCA 2000a) also provide expectations for learners' exposure to and understanding of grammatical terminology. And Alan Cornell (1996: 28) suggests that by the time they study mfl as a subsidiary part of their degree programme, students should understand and use the following terms and concepts:

- the 'word classes' or 'parts of speech' (noun, verb, adjective, etc.)
- the main sentence constituents (subject, direct object, indirect object; clause)
- the concept of tense
- for German, the nomenclature of the case system
- miscellaneous terms which would include, for example, relative pronoun, reflexive

Table 7.5 Grammatical concepts covered in the National Literacy Strategy

Syntax	Superlative
Adjectives	Passive voice
Nouns	Adverb
Pronouns	Clauses
Verbs	Imperatives
Tenses	Prepositions
Comparative	Active voice

Reflection
Activity 7.6 Explicit knowledge of grammatical terms

With reference to the list of terms and concepts drawn up by the National Literacy Strategy (Table 7.5), the recommended schemes of work, the GCSE Criteria for Modern Foreign Languages and Cornell's list, consider which grammatical terms pupils should be able to explain (know explicitly):
• by the end of Key Stage 3 and
• by the end of Key Stage 4.

Reflection
Activity 7.7 Grammatical concepts

Table 7.6 shows some grammatical concepts in alphabetical order.
• In what order do you think they should be first introduced?
• Ask your mentor or another colleague you work with frequently to place them in an order. Do you both agree?

– pronoun/verb, subjunctive, imperative, modal verb, auxiliary verb, past participle, active/passive, but not that many more.

By introducing new linguistic structures through unfamiliar terminology mfl teachers run the risk of their pupils struggling with concepts at a level one step removed from the linguistic phenomenon itself. On the other hand, using 'pupil friendly' terms may deny pupils maximum use of reference material in support of their learning. The use of terminology like 'doing words' and 'describing words' has a place in the learning process and pupils should not necessarily be discouraged from using their own terms. Making some selective, carefully planned and well targeted use of the mother tongue when discussing and reflecting on grammar can help pupils develop personal terms and rules. Metalanguage can be introduced once a concept is understood by pupils.

Table 7.6 Sequencing grammatical concepts

Ranking	Concept
	adjectival agreement
	definite and indefinite articles
	expressions of quantity
	gender and number
	imperative
	negatives
	perfect tense
	present tense
	transitive and intransitive verbs

THE HABIT-FORMING STAGE

The role of the teacher does not end with the explanation of concepts contained in Table 7.6. Explanation is useful if learners are to proceed to using structures and to developing good language habits. Accurate use of the TL by pupils should be one of the aims of mfl teachers with the ultimate goal of pupils reaching a point when language forms 'sound' or 'feel' right or wrong. A first notion of an intuitive 'feel' can be worked towards by habitual use of the TL.

The process of developing a 'feel' for correct language forms requires a lot of practice and mfl activities need to serve a purpose beyond the generation of accurate language as an end in itself.

In a further example, the introduction of the perfect tense in Spanish in Figure 7.2 is followed up by the habit-forming activity in Figure 7.8. Pupils are given a combination table based on the language used in the penfriend letter. Their task is to generate as many grammatically correct sentences in the perfect tense as possible. Pupils have to use the correct form of the past participle. At the same time they have to find the correct complement to the verb. The use of an adverb(ial) of time can be made optional. Differentiation can, therefore, be built into this activity by outcome, i.e. the number of sentences pupils generate, or by task, i.e. the number of variables pupils are asked to combine. For a discussion of differentiation see Chapter 10.

Another example of a habit-forming activity is given in Table 7.8. German word order in the context of the perfect tense can be practised by writing a number of sentences on card, mixing the cards up and asking pupils (in pairs or groups) to reconstruct correct sentences.

Table 7.7   Practising the Spanish perfect tense

	comer	al baloncesto	a las ...... y media
	disfrutar	a la playa/la montaña	antes
he	empezar	a Málaga/Francia/América	antes del almuerzo
has	estar	de vacaciones	dos semanas
ha	ir	el museo/la discoteca	durante las vacaciones
hemos	jugar	estupendo/guay/muy bien	en el verano
habeis	(lo) pasar	fotografías	esta mañana
han	seleccionar	las clases	por las mañanas
	viajar	pueblos famosos	por las noches
	visitar	comida típica	de la costa

Table 7.8   The German word order

Ich	bin	mit Klara in die Stadt	gegangen.
Wir	sind	um 16 Uhr	angekommen.
Sie	hat	eine rote Hose	getragen.
Du	hast	Pommes Frites	gegessen.
Sie	haben	eine Tassee Tee	getrunken.
Ihr	habt	einen tollen Film	gesehen.
Er	ist	mit dem Bus	zurückgefahren.

As an extension to this activity, adverb(ial)s of time can be added such as: *gestern, vor zwei Tagen, am Abend, um 10 Uhr, letzte Woche, zu Mittag* or *am Vormittag*. This allows pupils to practise the positioning of adverb(ial)s of time including the inversion of subject and auxiliary verb. To differentiate the activity further, the sentences could add up to a story for pupils to recreate.

The application of rules is easier for some pupils than for others. There is a need to grade activities to cater for the different needs of pupils. In this way should one level prove too difficult, pupils can attempt the preceding one or pupils can quickly move on to the next level if they find one too easy. The levels can be set in a variety of different

Table 7.9   Practising present tense verb endings in German

	**Die Regel**
	ich	spiel	e	wir	spiel	en
	du	spiel	st	ihr	spiel	t
	er/sie/es	spiel	t	sie	spiel	en
	**Teil 1**
	*Schreibe den richtigen Satz!*
1.	Meine Schwester spiel	e / t / en	gern Fußball.			
2.	Mein Freund schwimm	st / t / e	im Hallenbad.			
3.	Mein Bruder und ich tanz	e / t / en	in der Disco.			
4.	Ich geh	st / en / e	oft in die Stadt.			
5	Sie schreib	e / st / t	viele Briefe.			
	**Teil 2**
	*Schreibe einen ganzen Satz!*
6.		Mein Vater (kochen) das Abendessen.			
7.		Wir (wollen) etwas trinken.			
8.		Ich (suchen) meine Kleidung.			
9.		Sie (spielen) gern Volleyball.			
10.		Ja natürlich, ich (schwimmen) besonders gern.			
	**Teil 3**
	*Was macht man, wenn ...? Erfinde eine Antwort.*
11.	colspan="3"	Was macht sie, wenn die Sonne scheint?	colspan="3"	Sie geht ins Schwimmbad, wenn die Sonne scheint.
12.	colspan="3"	Was machst du, wenn es regnet?	colspan="3"	...
13.	colspan="3"	Was machen wir, wenn es schneit?	colspan="3"	...
14.	colspan="3"	Was macht er, wenn das Wetter schlecht ist?	colspan="3"	...
15.	colspan="3"	Was macht ihr, wenn es sehr schön ist?	colspan="3"	...

ways. An example of this is given in Table 7.9, which shows one way of practising present tense verb endings in German in the context of 'hobbies, pastimes and weather' by referring to a 'rule' or paradigm, in this case a conjugated verb in the present tense.

The assumption is that pupils have been informed that the exercises are designed to enable them to conduct a survey of who does what and in which weather conditions. Firstly, pupils select the correct ending from a given list. Secondly, they apply the 'rule' in given examples and thirdly, they use the rule to generate language of their own.

Activities of this type bridge the use of grammatical 'rules' or paradigms and their communicative application by preparing pupils for a survey, e.g. of what pastimes pupils pursue in different weather conditions.

It is crucial that teachers consider the length of time required for pupils to master particular grammatical concepts. This will, of course, vary from pupil to pupil. Input and explanation stages may occur on several occasions as understanding develops. Opportunities for practice must be introduced on a regular basis and the revisiting of grammatical features needs to be well planned.

Reflection
Activity 7.8 The development of grammatical concepts

We suggested above that some topics lend themselves better to the introduction and practice of certain grammatical concepts than others. Consider which topics lend themselves particularly well to the teaching of certain grammatical concepts.
- Choose three to five grammatical concepts from Table 7.5 and consider through which topic they might meaningfully be introduced.
- Reflect on how long it will take learners to master the concepts and their application.
- Identify other topics in which practice of the structures could be included.

COMMUNICATIVE APPLICATION STAGE

A key feature of communicative language teaching is the emphasis on the message as opposed to the linguistic form, on conveying meaning rather than demonstrating knowledge about language. Whilst we deem the conveying of meaning to be central to mfl teaching at secondary level, we recognise the need for systematic coverage of the grammatical system linked to thematic progression. From pre-communicative language practice, including implicit and explicit manipulation of linguistic patterns and structures, pupils need to be moved on to communicative application.

Marking and error correction are important in the language learning process. Constructive feedback on pupils' TL production can reinforce accurate use and is an important tool in moving pupils from pre-communicative to communicative language use. Richard Beaton (1990: 42–3), for instance, suggests that '(when) errors are corrected, it goes without saying that revision of the correction is essential. ... there needs to be an incubation period in which the learner acquires a feel … .' Work featuring a considerable number of mistakes and errors is a clear sign that the pupil is not ready to progress to the stage of using language in 'authentic', communicative situations. Pupils' readiness to progress to communicative situations, therefore, needs to be carefully monitored. The mfl trainee needs to consider the nature of her feedback carefully. It is important to strike the right balance between providing constructive support and demotivating pupils through over-correction. For a more detailed discussion of marking and error correction see Chapter 9.

Once comfortable with certain structures, pupils should be given opportunities to apply these language forms meaningfully. The use of the TL for a perceived purpose and with success can lead to a sense of achievement. One example is the information-gap activity in Figure 7.15 focussing on the German perfect tense.

Another example of the communicative application stage is, for instance, an activity known as the 'alibi game', which is useful when reinforcing the perfect and imperfect tenses as well as question forms in any foreign language. (For other examples of the 'alibi game' see Langran and Purcell 1994: 24 or Miller 1995: 7.)

The teacher sets the scene in the respective TL: 'The crown jewels have been stolen from the Tower of London over the weekend. Two suspects have been arrested when they were seen in the vicinity around the time the theft has occurred.'

Table 7.10 *Was hast du am Wochenende gemacht?*

A	am Morgen	am Nachmittag	am Abend
Freitag	zur Schule _gehen_ mit dem Bus _fahren_ Erdkunde _haben_		Hausaufgabe _machen_ Kassetten _hören_ mit dem Computer _spielen_
Samstag		in die Stadt _fahren_ einkaufen _gehen_ neue Schuhe _kaufen_	
Sonntag	zur Kirche _gehen_ Großmutter _besuchen_ Kaffee _trinken_ und Kekse _essen_	zum Park _gehen_ Fußball _spielen_ angeln _gehen_	

B	am Morgen	am Nachmittag	am Abend
Freitag		in der Kantine _essen_ mit Freunden _plaudern_ Deutsch _haben_	
Samstag	im Bett _bleiben_ um 11 Uhr Frühstück _essen_ die Zeitung _lesen_		zu Hause _bleiben_ _fernsehen_ um 10 Uhr ins Bett _gehen_
Sonntag			Hausaufgaben _machen_ ein Buch _lesen_ Briefe _schreiben_

Two pupils are asked to play the role of the 'suspects'. Any number of paired pupils can act as 'suspects'. The 'suspects' have to prepare a story between them, which will serve as their alibi. The rest of the pupils are tasked with formulating questions, which they will ask the two 'suspects' in turn. The aim is to extract information, which shows that the two 'suspects' are making inconsistent statements. Once familiar with the format of activity, pupils can be asked to work in groups supported by the teacher and the foreign language assistant, who circulate from group to group so that pupils get a number of opportunities for language production.

Once an alibi has been thought of and questions have been devised, the first pupil is 'questioned' and peers note the responses. Afterwards the second pupil is 'questioned' and the questioners note the information provided. The questioners are required to use the information extracted to compile a report and a recommendation for 'prosecution'.

The activity requires pupils to extract and use information through the medium of the TL and allows for repetitive practice of a particular linguistic form. At the same time pupils are generating their own forms of language. Care should be taken when choosing the scenario for the alibi game: where possible scenarios should be embedded into the target culture.

SUMMARY

Grammar is an important aspect of the foreign language learning process and mfl teachers need to use their professional judgement and take on board theoretical considerations when deciding on their personal approach to grammar teaching.

Teachers and learners need to be aware that grammar is not assimilated instantly, nor can it be presented in an oversimplified, linear fashion. Learners need time to become accustomed to what they notice about the TL and transform it to personal use.

Grammar can be taught and learnt explicitly and implicitly. Either way, successful learning is, at least in part, dependent on the teacher's skill in planning, presenting and enabling practice as well as opportunity for personalisation of language forms. There are no hard and fast rules governing the teaching and learning of grammar, but a carefully structured and thought through approach can be seen to be helpful. In this chapter we presented a possible framework aimed at helping the mfl trainee develop a coherent approach to the teaching of grammar.

It is important to remember that, in the context of mfl teaching and learning in the secondary school, grammar should not be taught in isolation from communicative objectives. At the same time, pupils should not be left to assimilate and absorb information without the support and guidance of the mfl teacher.

8 Developing Cultural Awareness Inside and Outside the Modern Foreign Languages Classroom

The ability to understand the cultural context of foreign language use is a key aspect of effective communication in the target language (TL). The development of cultural awareness is an important and integral part of the National Curriculum (NC) modern foreign languages (mfl) Orders. Cultural awareness is more than simply the identification of different cultural characteristics or knowledge about the countries where the TL is spoken. It involves the understanding and appreciation of different ways of life. The Programme of Study (PoS) suggests a particular approach to the teaching of cultural awareness, which is based around ethnographic methods, i.e. the use of 'authentic' materials and contact with native speakers. It aims to enable pupils to identify with, recognise and draw comparisons between the cultures of their own country and the countries where the TL is spoken. Whilst a lot can be achieved in the mfl classroom, cultural awareness is often more meaningfully developed outside. Importantly, the pupil's point of view and her experiences should be taken as a starting point and not necessarily specific aspects of the target culture (see Pachler 1999b: 84).

In this chapter we discuss possible approaches to cultural awareness at 11 to 16 and describe activities that require and enable pupils to use the TL inside (including internet and e-mail projects and working with a foreign language assistant) and outside (educational visits, exchanges and work experience abroad) the classroom.

In order to enhance their value, activities involving TL use and the development of cultural awareness outside the mfl classroom should relate to, build on and extend work carried out in mfl lessons. Importantly, they need to be planned carefully and pupils need to be prepared well for them.

Whilst trainee teachers will not necessarily always have the opportunity to be involved in activities such as visits abroad, they should, wherever possible, try to become involved in preparing any pupils at their placement schools engaging in such activities. The ability of mfl teachers to provide opportunities for pupils to develop the use of the TL and their awareness of the target culture(s) beyond the mfl classroom, is often considered a distinct advantage by schools when looking for new members of staff.

OBJECTIVES

By the end of this chapter you should:

- understand the rationale for and some important issues of the development of cultural awareness in mfl teaching;
- be aware of possible approaches to and strategies of developing cultural awareness in pupils through mfl teaching including internet and e-mail projects;
- recognise the value of educational activities outside the mfl classroom; and
- understand what is involved in organising a range of learning opportunities outside the mfl classroom.

DEVELOPING CULTURAL AWARENESS: WHY?

The target culture can be seen as inextricably linked to the TL. In order to understand language and its use fully, an awareness and knowledge of culture are important (see Pachler 1999c: 78). Whilst it is possible to teach the culture(s) of a country in a way which is divorced from its language(s) – and in the past coursebooks have tended to provide English accounts of aspects of the way of life of the target culture(s) such as cultural facts, figures and habits – we do not believe this is necessarily appropriate in the context of the NC as it

- ignores the inter-relationship of 'language-and-culture' (Byram, Morgan et al. 1994);
- adds a level of abstraction; and
- requires pupils to imagine the potential rather than experiencing real use of the TL.

To place language learning within a cultural context is to make both the TL and the target culture(s) more accessible and understandable. The task for the teacher is to some extent to re-create and simulate the cultural environment and to create a purpose for realistic language use within that environment whilst ensuring that learning activities are not contrived.

A further important reason for developing pupils' cultural awareness is to learn to empathise with speakers of other languages, to understand that there are other ways of life and to tackle (negative) stereotypes. Stereotypes can be seen as a strategy to simplify perceptions of other peoples (see Byram 1989: 70). There is a danger that, by exaggerating the typical in the target culture(s), the perception pupils have of the ways of living and communicating in the target cultures(s) become distorted (see Byram 1989: 16). Mfl teachers, therefore, need to guard against use of negative stereotypes as well as engage in awareness raising about the use of (negative) stereotypes (see also Pachler with Reimann 1999).

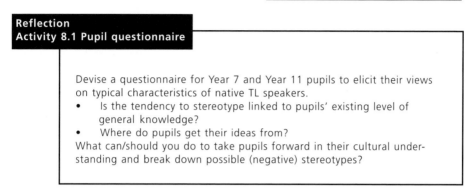

Reflection
Activity 8.1 Pupil questionnaire

Devise a questionnaire for Year 7 and Year 11 pupils to elicit their views on typical characteristics of native TL speakers.
- Is the tendency to stereotype linked to pupils' existing level of general knowledge?
- Where do pupils get their ideas from?

What can/should you do to take pupils forward in their cultural understanding and break down possible (negative) stereotypes?

Coursebooks can vary enormously in the representation of the cultures of the countries where the TL is spoken. Many coursebooks provide a multi-cultural picture. But, coursebooks tend to date quickly. This ephemeral nature of presenting culture in print requires teachers to use supplementary up-to-date authentic materials, such as articles and pictures from magazines and newspapers or audio and video recordings of programmes concerned with current issues. The internet offers ample opportunity in this respect and is discussed in Chapter 12.

Amongst many other criteria (for details see Chapter 11), coursebooks can be evaluated against a number of culture-related criteria (see e.g. Meijer with Jenkins 1998); they include:

- functionality, e.g. does the coursebook concentrate on facts and knowledge about the target culture?
- target audience, e.g. are materials selected in accordance with the likely interests of the target audience?
- diversity, e.g. does the coursebook take account of intracultural differences?
- realism, e.g. is the representation of culture in the coursebook authentic? Are (negative) stereotypes in evidence?
- intercultural approach, e.g. are attempts made to make comparisons between home and target countries? or
- choice, e.g. do learners have the possibility to choose culture-related topics they are particularly interested in?

Reflection
Activity 8.2 Evaluating the culture content of a coursebook

Evaluate one of the coursebooks in use in your partnership school against some of the above criteria. How well is the target culture presented?

Then, carry out an internet search for relevant supplementary materials to supplement an aspect the coursebook in your opinion doesn't cover very well.

For guidance on internet use in teaching and learning, see e.g. Pachler 1999e.

DEVELOPING CULTURAL AWARENESS: H.D. BROWN'S FOUR STAGES OF ACCULTURATION

H.D. Brown's four broad stages of acculturation (see Brown 1986: 36) are used here are as one possible way of conceptualising the development of cultural awareness (see Figure 8.1). Each of these stages cannot be separated from the natural process of maturation and not all need necessarily occur. In all of them the (trainee) teacher can play an important role in guiding and encouraging pupils. The four stages do not imply a linear progression. Slipping back and leaping forward are characteristics of the development not only of linguistic but also of cultural awareness.

For a range of other possible approaches to the teaching about the target culture(s) see Pachler 1999b: 83–90.

Excitement

For many young pupils the learning of mfl is exciting. Year 7 will often offer pupils their first encounter with mfl, only some will have been introduced to mfl earlier. An introduction to a new culture offers a range of interesting learning opportunities. Continental Europe is not completely alien. The study of the target culture(s) from the security of the classroom offers some shelter from the challenge of 'the foreign' or 'the other'. The behaviour and the way of life of others from an outsider's perspective can be stimulating and fun.

The challenge to the mfl teacher, therefore, is to provide ample opportunities for pupils to engage in activities related to the target culture(s). This can be done in a number of ways.

The use of anecdotes involving the mfl teacher's personal experiences, supported by realia and photographs, can provide a personal context for the presentation of the target culture(s). A story by the mfl teacher about participation in a 'Faschingszug', for example, can demonstrate that experiencing a foreign culture can be very enjoyable.

The internet provides an effective way of accessing relevant authentic material and to carry out research into the target cultures. For some useful links see the website accompanying this book at *http://www.ioe.ac.uk/lie/pgce/*. Sample replicable modules on target culture teaching, which were developed through a LINGUA A project part-funded by the European Commission, can be accessed at *http://ict.ioe.ac.uk/culture/*. The Goethe-Institut has put together a series of webpages called *'Kaleidoskop: Alltag in Deutsch-land'* available at *http://www.goethe.de/z/50/alltag/deindex.htm*. Inter-Nationes offers some relevant links for the teaching of cultural awareness at *http://www.inter-nationes.de/d/frames/*

Table 8.1 Four broad stages of developing cultural awareness

No.	Stage
1	excitement
2	alienation
3	recovery
4	acceptance

schulen/laku/landkuninfo-t.html. Useful French materials called *'Civilisation française'* are available at *http://www.cortland.edu/flteach/civ/*. And an interesting cross-cultural initiative entitled CULTURA can be accesses at *http://web.mid.edu/french/cultura* (see also Furstenberg et al. 2000).

A fundamental methodological consideration is whether to stress cultural similarities or differences at an early stage. Research suggests that attention should initially be given to similarities as 'doing so can undermine the human tendency to exaggerate and generalise differences' (Pachler 1999b: 85).

Similarities between the pupils' own way of life and that prevailing in the countries where the TL is spoken can be accentuated, for example, at a very early stage by a display of 'foreign' foods available in the local supermarket.

The simulation of cultural practices in the classroom allows pupils to demonstrate their knowledge. Setting up a French café or organising a meal are very popular activities. To provide such culinary delights in a restaurant situation for 'customers' other than fellow pupils is even more rewarding. Parents, colleagues, even adult mfl learners can act as customers for the pupils.

Mfl (trainee) teachers should explore the cross-curricular dimension of cultural awareness. Aspects of the target culture(s) might be taught in other subject areas such as Geography, usually but by no means always in English, which can be built on in the

---

Reflection
Activity 8.3 Stressing cultural similarities

What ways of stressing the similarities, rather than the differences, between home and target cultures at an early stage of mfl teaching and learning can you think of?

Reflection
Activity 8.4 Cross-curricular links

Examine the statutory requirements, e.g. for Geography. These can be accessed on the internet at *http://www.nc.uk.net/*.
- Find out what aspects of the target culture(s) can be found and where links are possible.
- Through discussion with teachers of Geography find out more about when and how these aspects are taught.
- Make up a quiz, drawing on knowledge of the target culture(s) incorporating details from the NC Geography Orders. Use the results of the quiz as a basis for cross-curricular and cultural discussion. You may want to invite colleagues from other subjects to one of your lessons to demonstrate the full value of cultural awareness.

mfl classroom. In Geography, for instance, pupils often study a European country other than the UK with a focus on geographical questions such as 'What/where is it?', 'What is it like?', 'How did it get like this?', 'How and why is it changing?' 'What are the implications?' The study of a European country other than the UK provides opportunities for the mfl teacher to feed into other subject areas.

The project 'Science across Europe', part of 'Science across the World' organised by the Association for Science Education available online at *http://www.scienceacross.org*, allows pupils to compare their work on scientific topics with peers across Europe and the wider world. There are a range of resource units in a wide range of languages providing stimulus material on topics such as acid rain, using energy at home, renewable energy, drinking water, food, global warming or domestic waste. Databases of participating schools are also available. Work on these units can meaningfully combine learning objectives relating to Science as well as mfl. Figure 8.2 shows an adapted sample activity from the pack 'What did you eat …?'.

Alienation

The greater the personal involvement with another culture, the more differences become apparent. Dealing with alternative ways of life can be threatening and challenging. Goal-oriented and purposeful personal contact with TL speakers as well as appropriate activities, such as educational visits to the target culture(s), can help to understand

---

Compare the information from a school in a country where the TL is spoken with that from your class.

1. Compare:
   a. the pattern of daily life: when other pupils get up, start school, etc.,
   b. who chooses and prepares the food,
   c. what is eaten for breakfast,
   d. snacks and sweets eaten,
   e. arrangements for meals during the school day.
2. Do pupils in the target country think that eating a good breakfast is important?
3. What do you think is responsible for the similarities and differences in the foods eaten by pupils in the target country?
4. Did you learn about any traditional beliefs about foods? Can they be explained by science?
5. Are eating habits in both countries changing? If so, how?
6. Do you think that most pupils eat a balanced diet?
7. Are pupils concerned about the links between diet and disease? If so, do their concerns differ in the two countries?
8. Compare food labels from the two countries. How is the nutritional value of food shown? Do the same foods contain the same ingredients?
9. What suggestions can you make for improving the diet of your class?

Figure 8.1 Eating habits: a comparison

**Reflection
Activity 8.5 Eating habits:
a comparison**

- Consider how these tasks could be linked to your mfl department's unit(s) of work on food and drink and illness.
- By talking to your mentor or an interested class teacher as well as a teacher from the Science department, explore which of these activities could be carried out in mfl lessons and which in the Science lesson.
- How could they be translated into the TL and how can the contents be covered in the TL?

**Reflection
Activity 8.6 Personal awareness
raising**

This activity provides you with an opportunity for self-reflection.
- In Table 8.2 list ten items you would choose to represent the culture of your home country and ten items you would choose as representative of the culture of a country where the TL is spoken. What influenced your choice?
- What differences are there between your two lists and what do they tell you about the cultural differences between the two countries or your own perceptions about these differences?
- In Table 8.3 list how each of these differences could be addressed in the mfl curriculum: by display work, classroom activities, project/enquiry work or visits abroad?

Table 8.2   Choosing items representing culture

	'Home' country	'Target' country
1		
2		
3		
4		
5		
6		
7		
8		
9		
10		

Table 8.3 Accounting for cultural differences in mfl teaching

Display work	Classroom activities	Project/enquiry work	Visits abroad

certain differences in context and reduce the potential threat by engaging pupils in reflecting on and discussing perceived differences between cultures.

Many schools organise day visits abroad, which can be used to encourage pupils to investigate familiarities and differences of their own and the target culture. The relationship between language learnt and its potential use should be highlighted by the provision of structured activities when abroad.

Table 8.4 illustrates how pupils might be given an opportunity to reflect on cultural differences around the topic of 'bullfighting'. Work on this activity can be meaningfully extended through letters or e-mail messages with partner schools or display work as described above.

Recovery

A positive response to discussions about perceived differences can be a sign of recovery. First-hand experience of the target culture(s), the productive use of personal knowledge, skills and understanding through displays or presentations for the benefit of others can lead to a familiarisation with the target culture(s). Recovery can be worked towards, for instance, by engaging pupils in 'experimentation' with the target culture(s) and comparison with their own culture. At this stage of developing cultural awareness cultural similarities might once again be accentuated.

A useful activity (adapted from Jones 1995: 27–34) comparing two cultures is to ask pupils to put into a shoe box ten items they feel represent their own culture. The scenario is that this will be buried for future generations to find. A brief written or taped explanation should accompany the artefacts. A similar exercise is then undertaken only this time the 'time capsule' should contain ten articles representing the culture of a country where the TL is spoken. The selection of artefacts should stimulate meaningful discussion about the TL culture in question, particularly in relation to the perceived 'home' culture.

Gerhard Neuner and Hans Hunfeld suggest the use of what they call 'universal experiences of life' as a basis for intercultural comparison. They list a number of such experiences loosely translated from German here (see Neuner and Hunfeld 1993: 112–13):

- fundamental experiences, e.g. birth, death, living;
- personal identity, e.g. personal characteristics;
- social identity, e.g. private self, family; neighbourhood, local community, nation;
- partnership, e.g. friendship, love;

LAS CORRIDAS DE TOROS

Torear es considerado como un arte y no un deporte. La tradición de las corridas de toros se remonta a más de trescientos años. La crianza de toros salvajes adecuados para llevar a las plazas de toros es normalmente llevada por ciertas familias que viven del mundo del toro y de las corridas. Torear y criar toros salvajes se pasa de padre a hijo.

Hay toreros que desde que son niños estan en las plazas y torean a vaquillas (toros pequeños). Ellos ven y viven el mundo de los toros desde muy pequeños en casa y así, cuando pueden, ellos van a torear también.

No sólo hombres pero también mujeres y niños torean en las plazas.

Hay *corridas de toros* y *novilladas:* las corridas de toros consisten en torear seis grandes toros de entre seiscientos y setecientos kilos de peso. En las novilladas se torean a toros pequeños de trescientos a cuatrocientos kilos de peso. Toreros jóvenes empiezan con novilladas y luego pasan a torear toros grandes.

Otro tipo de toreo es el *Rejoneo* que es torear y matar al toro montado a caballo; estos se llaman *rejoneadores* y son magníficos jinetes.

Los toreros visten *el traje de luces* que es muy especial y de un color favorito del torero. Lleva una *montera* sobre la cabeza y una *coleta* de pelo detrás. Cuando el torero se jubila, se corta la *coleta* y así pues esto es una expresión española. Por ejemplo cuando una deportista abandona el deporte se puede decir: ella *'se corta la coleta'* !

Los toreros son muy religiosos y antes de cada corrida se toman unos minutos para meditar y rezar.

También son muy superticiosos y llevan algun detalle para tener buena suerte.

Todas las personas conectadas con los toros como toreros, rejoneadores, criaderos y otros hablan de su respeto y amor a los toros. Ellos admiran a un animal tan bravo y valiente. En las corridas, los toreros se enfrentan al toro para arriesgar su vida y jugar con la idea de la muerte. El toro va a morir y el torero puede morir también!

Si un toro es muy valiente, el torero puede perdonar su vida reconociendo así su valor.

El torear es una tradición muy española y es un espectáculo muy popular con españoles y extranjeros.

En Portugal, sur de Francia y en algunos países de Sudamérica también hay corridas de toros pero no matan al toro. En España matan a los seis toros de cada corrida todas las tardes de la temporada taurina.

Reflection
Activity 8.7 Cultural comparison

- Examine the scheme of work at your placement school and try to match the 'universal experiences of life' listed in this chapter to particular topics.
- Then, devise a number of activities comparing pupils' own culture with the target culture(s) for a particular class you teach for one of these areas. For guidance you might want to have a look at how available coursebooks approach the topic of 'education' and how they compare 'school life' in England to the target culture(s).

Table 8.4   Las corridas de toros

Vocabulario			
la crianza de toros	the breeding bulls	montado a caballo	on horse back
se remonta	it has existed since	matar al toro	to kill the bull
las plazas de toros	bullrings	jinetes	horse riders
toros salvajes	wild bulls	traje de luces	bullfighter's costume
vaquillas	young bulls	montera	bullfighter's head wear
novilladas	bullfights with young bulls	coleta	bullfighter's hair worn as a pony tail
morir	to die	'se corta la coleta'	s/he retires
rejoneo	bullfighting on horse back	temporada taurina	bullfighting season

Tareas		
Ejercicio 1: ¿verdad? o ¿mentira?		
	¿verdad?	¿mentira?
1. Torear es un deporte.		
2. Todos los toreros son hombres.		
3. 'Se corta la coleta' significa empezar una profesión.		
4. Rejoneo es torear montado a caballo.		
5. Las corridas de toros son un espectáculo reciente.		
6. Los toreros son muy religiosos y superticiosos.		

Ejercicio 2: Encuesta					
Pregúntale a cinco compañeros de clase:	1	2	3	4	5
1. ¿Crees que la tradición es importante?					
2. ¿Crees que las corridas son un espectáculo emocionante?					
3. ¿Te gustaría ver una corrida de toros?					
4. ¿Opinas que las corridas son crueles para el toro?					
5. ¿Te parece que las corridas se deben abolir?					
6. ¿Crees que las corridas sin matar al toro son acceptables?					

Ejercicio 3: ¿a favor? o ¿en contra?

¿Cuántas personas están a favor?   ....% están a favor de las corridas

¿Cuántas personas están en contra?   ....% están en contra de las corridas

- environment, e.g. house and home; local area, nature, civilisation;
- work, e.g. making a living;
- education;
- subsistence, e.g. food, clothing;
- mobility, e.g. traffic;
- leisure and art;
- communication, e.g. media;
- health care, e.g. health, illness, hygiene;
- ethics, e.g. morals, values, religion;
- events, e.g. past, present, future;
- spirituality, creativity, imagination, emotions, memory; etc.

Acceptance

Acceptance is more than tolerance. Some, particularly more advanced, learners can be seen to embrace certain aspects of the new culture. Participation in and interaction with the target culture(s) through communication in the TL can help to develop the ability to analyse and critically appraise 'otherness'.

For pupils of appropriate maturity taking part in an exchange can present an invaluable experience. Preparation for and follow-up to an exchange is important. Pupils could present an account of their stay – individually or collaboratively – for the benefit of parents and other interested parties. The identification of positive experiences and the public appreciation of the specific TL culture can not only be a motivating factor for the pupils themselves, but also a source of reassurance for other pupils less advanced in the process of acculturation.

> **Reflection**
> **Activity 8.8 Encouraging acceptance of the target culture(s)**
>
> Look through the departmental scheme of work and note classroom activities requiring use of the TL to collect information, for instance surveys.
> - Consider how such activities could be extended to include communication with a parallel class in the partner school abroad.
> - Through discussion with your mentor or another interested class teacher, investigate the possibility of setting up such a project.

INTERNET AND E-MAIL PROJECTS

Most schools have links, sometimes even established partnerships, with educational institutions abroad and many encourage penfriend and e-mail links. A useful online resource developed by the Goethe-Institut for teachers of German as a Foreign Language is called '*Internet-Kl@ssenpartnerschaften*' and can be found at *http://www.goethe.de/z/ekp/deindex.htm*. The website provides useful guidance on how to establish e-mail links and some interesting case studies on which this section draws. A UK-based case study and guidelines on how to find e-mail partners can be found in Chapter 12. E-mail projects can provide useful opportunities for realistic and meaningful communication. For example, survey work carried out in the classroom or the local community can be extended through an e-mail project to which a series of lessons is dedicated. Pupils can share, compare and analyse their findings with (those of) pupils in a partner school.

When considering the use of e-mail or the internet in mfl teaching it is important to ensure they are properly embedded in the scheme of work. Experience suggests that personal contact with a colleague tends to be an important factor in ensuring the success of work involving partner schools abroad. Successful projects tend to have very clear aims and objectives and a clearly defined thematic structure and time-frame. It is advisable to divide classes into smaller groups who in turn communicate with small groups in a partner school. This way the teacher can ensure all pupils can get actively involved and flexibility in the development of topics is allowed for.

Project work might comprise the following phases:

Preparation:	Coordination between teachers in both schools
Phase 1:	Pupils introduce themselves, their schools, their environment in writing and pictures
Phase 2:	Questions and answers, exchange of information
Phase 3:	Exchange of detailed answers based on research; follow-up questions
Phase 4:	Analysis and comparison of results
Phase 5:	(Joint) presentation of results (e.g. compilation of a display, brochure, newspaper, video/audio recording or webpages), summary of learning outcomes, project evaluation, good-bye letters

Each group should be required to keep a log or learner diary in which they reflect on their work, note new vocabulary and structures etc. From time to time group work needs to be supplemented by plenaries during which the teacher provides necessary input – for example on strategies for working independently – and revises previous learning outcomes relevant to the project, and during which pupils are required to report on the progress they have made. This way the teacher can ensure that pupils stay on task. The teacher also needs to be available throughout to clarify any difficulties, questions and misconceptions pupils might have. Decisions will need to be taken, for instance, whether pupils' messages have to be checked by the teacher before they are sent and to what extent redrafting by the teacher is required. Alternatively, pupils in the partner school could be asked to provide diagnostic feedback for each other. A further important consideration concerns the use of the TL. Where possible pupils should be encouraged to use the TL during group work to communicate with each other and with peers in the partner school. Experience suggests, though, that the mixing of languages might at times be required and necessary to ensure maximum outcomes (see e.g. Butler and Kelly 1999).

Projects can meaningfully be linked to controversial topics about which pupils have an opinion that they are keen to communicate, as well as to real-life experiences of pupils, such as their reading, listening and viewing habits, school-life, hobbies and pastimes, family life etc.

Reflection
Activity 8.9 Planning an internet or e-mail project

Drawing on the guidance given above and in Chapter 12, develop an internet/e-mail project in conjunction with your mentor or an interested class teacher, which relates to a relevant topic in your placement school's scheme of work. Look at the projects suggested by the Goethe-Institut at *http://www.goethe.de/z/ekp/deindex.htm* for guidance. You might want to use the following framework when planning your project:
- preparation required
- age-range
- objectives (linguistic and cultural)
- activities and time-scale
- useful links and resources
- methodological considerations.

To share your ideas and experience with the readership of this book, send them as an e-mail attachment to *norbert@languages.zzn.com*. The most interesting case studies will be published on the website accompanying this book at *http://www.ioe.ac.uk/lie/pgce/*.

EDUCATIONAL VISITS, EXCHANGES AND WORK EXPERIENCE ABROAD

Curiosity about the culture(s) of the countries where the TL is spoken can be a form of intrinsic motivation for some pupils. Many mfl departments are eager to provide opportunities for pupils to visit countries where the TL is spoken. Pupils who have (had) such an opportunity can have an increased interest in the subject and the TL as a means of finding out more about the respective countries and cultures. In some cases first-hand experience of the target culture(s) can lead to acculturation in later life. Some pupils, however, can get frustrated and demotivated as the result of a 'culture shock'. Negative experience might lead to estrangement, anger and hostility (see Brown 1986: 35). Teachers involved in visits and exchanges should, therefore, not take anything for granted. Some pupils will have experience of travelling, others may never have stayed away from their own homes. Some pupils will have a good general knowledge base, whereas others may even be unaware of the geographical location of the country in question. School visits should be accompanied by meaningful linguistic and cultural awareness tasks, which can be of a cross-curricular nature.

Mfl departments in many secondary schools offer their pupils visits to a country where the TL is spoken. Three main types of activities are distinguished here: visits, exchanges and work experience placements. The type of visit undertaken by pupils tends to reflect their linguistic, social and cultural development. Whilst, on visits, the exposure to the target culture and the TL tends to be tightly structured and controlled and the pupils tend to remain in close contact with their English-speaking peer group throughout their stay abroad, the amount of opportunities to interact with native speakers and their way of life increases on exchanges. These are in the main organised around the pupils' stay with exchange partners, whom they may know already from previous visits, letters and/or e-mail links and whose families tend to act as an interface between the 'otherness' of life in the foreign culture and the 'universal' features of life at home. Work experience placements abroad often present the greatest challenge to pupils and tend to depend on adequately developed personal, social and linguistic skills in pupils who need to cope, frequently independently, with the vocational and occupational demands made by TL interactions in the 'world of work'.

If the opportunity arises, trainee teachers should try to observe the various tasks involved in preparing and planning visits and exchanges at their placement schools. Many valuable lessons can be learnt from teachers with relevant experience.

We would strongly recommend newly qualified teachers (NQTs) to work in tandem with experienced mfl teachers on planning visits and exchanges and to take on responsibility for some of the tasks involved only gradually.

Visits and exchanges can help to make both the TL as well as the target culture(s) more accessible to pupils and can be motivating. They provide valuable opportunities to find out more about the target culture(s) and can help to illustrate that the TL can be used effectively for communication. Also, visits and exchanges can enrich pupils' general knowledge base by giving them an opportunity to experience first hand the excitement of travelling, meeting new people and finding out about their way of life.

One key element of successful visits and exchanges is having *clearly delineated aims and objectives*. Both staff and pupils need to be aware what the benefits and reasons for carrying out such an activity are.

When organising exchanges, finding a suitable partner is another essential pre-requisite. Often, personal contacts with teachers abroad are most effective. To establish good channels of communication is equally important. Preparatory visits can provide useful information. The Central Bureau offers assistance in finding a partner school as well as useful guidance through publications such as *Making the most of your partner school abroad* (Central Bureau 1991).

Linda Fisher and Michael Evans (2000: 16) make the following practical suggestions based on their research study into the effects of school exchange visits on attitudes and proficiency in language learning:

- prepare pupils for the kind of language they will need when staying in the family; for example, including a range of expressions of social convention in the scheme of work and continuing to focus on the sometimes neglected area of pronunciation
- offer guidance to parents about the value of linguistic support for the exchange pupil staying with their family and offer suggestions as to the amount and nature of the correction and encouragement they give
- offer guidance to parents on ways of helping pupils settle in: for example, using photographs as a prompt
- consider arranging the exchange schedule to include a weekend with the family straightaway
- seek to develop pupils' cultural awareness before visiting the country, with an emphasis on 'the acquisition of ways of investigating and observing' (Snow and Byram 1997: 31) to prepare pupils better for their stay
- discuss 'language gathering' strategies, encouraging pupils, for example, to keep diaries or log-books of all new language they use

Reflection
Activity 8.10 Aims and objectives
of visits and exchanges

Where possible, find out what the aims and objectives of the visits and exchanges organised by your placement school are, for instance, by asking appropriate members of the mfl department.

- be encouraged to look for evidence of linguistic progress in the pupils on their return and to build on this in their subsequent teaching
- encourage pupils to maintain contact with their partner through correspondence and e-mail
- use the exchange experience to contribute to an overall ethos within the department of promoting language learning as part of a real communicative experience.

It is important to fully understand, cover and comply with all *legal responsibilities and requirements* and abide by school, LEA and/or any other regulations and guidelines. These cannot be covered in this chapter. They must be considered fully in the planning of any such activity. Activities beyond the classroom should not be taken on lightly! Useful guidance is *inter alia* available from the DfEE (1998b) entitled *Health and safety of pupils on educational visits.*

For instance, there needs to be consideration of insurance implications or issues such as seeking written agreement from parents/guardians consenting to their children taking part, informing the school of any medical or dietary needs of their children and agreeing to emergency medical treatment to be given to their children if necessary.

It is also important to ensure that unambiguous ground rules are established, which are communicated clearly to all pupils involved and, where appropriate, their parents/guardians. Pupils, for instance, need to agree that they will not accept any form of payment when on work experience.

Since 1992, the Package Travel, Package Holidays and Package Tours Regulations apply to travel packages sold by tour and travel operators. Obligations relating to bonding, insurance and compensation may also apply to teachers or schools if they organise a package as defined by these regulations. If a visit is organised as part of a course of education and no package in the normal sense is being sold the regulations might not apply. In any event, specialist advice must be sought.

Some of the important organisational issues, which need to be considered in planning visits or exchanges, are identified below. As has been noted already, legal requirements cannot be covered here and we can merely raise awareness of the sorts of issues involved. Specialist advice must be sought on all relevant legal requirements.

Being 'in loco parentis'

Persons supervising pupils during visits and exchanges are responsible for the well-being of all pupils in the group. They take on a supervisory role for the duration of the activity and, therefore, have to conduct themselves as a responsible and sensible parent would. Extreme care and attention to detail are required.

Supervision ratios

The level of supervision by adults, at least one of them a qualified teacher, must be appropriate to the age of pupils and the type of experience being undertaken. For educational visits in the UK the recommended ratio under 'normal conditions' for pupils up to the age of 16 is 1:15, for visits outside the UK 1:10. Parties of both sexes should be accompanied by at least one male and one female adult with a minimum of three adults accompanying mixed parties outside the UK. All supervisors need to be vetted for previous criminal offences.

Insurance

In order to safeguard pupils' welfare, teachers organising visits and/or exchanges need to ensure that they have considered the full range of requirements in advance and that appropriate insurance cover is arranged. As has been noted, parents'/guardians' written consent must be obtained before any pupil can take part in such activities. Completed consent forms need to be taken on the visit by the group leader. Parents/guardians should be sent written notification of all details of the venture and they should be encouraged to take out personal (travel) insurance for their children. The 'certificate of entitlement to benefits in kind during a stay in a member state', the E111 form, is one document all eligible pupils need to take for travel within the European Union (EU) as this can simplify the administration of medical assistance. Parents/guardians should be asked to complete an application form for an E111 prior to the visit, which may best be taken on the visit by the group leader.

Local Education Authorities (LEAs) tend to provide assistance with insurance arrangements for eligible schools. Teachers organising such an activity need to ensure that any activity or residential centres to be used are also insured against public liability etc. Those planning excursions involving instruction and support by other trained adults need to check the qualifications of instructors carefully in order that all insurance cover is valid.

Passports

All pupils need to have the necessary travel documents on the day of departure. Although for some (EU) countries identity cards may suffice for day visits, it is strongly recommended that all pupils and accompanying adults hold a valid passport. In order to avoid unpleasant delays or complications it is important to ensure that all pupils have the required documentation (including visas and any other documents in the case of non-British passport holders) well in advance of departure. A clear record of all relevant details must be compiled and retained by the party leader. A group passport may be an option. On (exchange) visits to France pupils need an identity card if they are travelling on a collective passport, for which passport photographs for all pupils are required. Requirements need to be checked with the local immigration and/or passport office at least six weeks in advance.

Transport

Accompanying teachers are expected to travel on the same vehicle as the pupils for the entire journey. If teachers use their own transport to carry pupils, it is essential that they are in possession of an adequate insurance policy endorsed for this purpose.

Customs

Accompanying teachers need to take adequate precautions that no party member (even inadvertently) violates customs regulations. A list of allowances and regulations should be obtained and pupils need to be informed of these regulations prior to the visit as penalties are being levied on individuals who fail to declare goods on which duty should be paid. It is recommended that pupils are not allowed to transport alcohol or tobacco as presents for parents, even when presented with them by host families.

Emergency procedures

All schools should have an appropriate policy and procedures covering emergencies and any accidents. A checklist is a valuable resource to group leaders. It should, as a minimum, include the following considerations:

- ✓ procedures ensuring receipt of accurate information concerning pupils' health;
- ✓ identification of key personnel as well as 'first aiders';
- ✓ a system enabling (emergency) communication with parents/guardians;
- ✓ contingency plans to allow for the supervision and transportation of hospitalised pupils; and
- ✓ details and contact numbers of emergency services and British officials in the foreign country.

First aid

When planning off-site activities, pre-planning and risk assessment of all activities needs to be carried out including the evaluation of hazards of all activities to be undertaken, the location of the site and the levels of skills available by trainers or leaders at the site in order to indicate the levels of first aid required. It is recommended that group leaders are trained in basic first aid. First aiders should record all cases they treat, including the name of the patient, date, place, time and circumstances of the incident. Details of the injury sustained and treatment given needs to be kept and be readily available. Teachers must be properly qualified to administer any medicines.

Charging

The charging for school visits and exchanges is an important and complicated issue. Important points of reference are the respective school policy as well as DES Circular 2/89 (1989) entitled *Charges for school activities*. Rules vary according to the nature of the activity. As a general rule of thumb it might be said that organisers can levy a charge for any visit that comprises less than 50 per cent of school time. If the majority of the activity takes place on what would otherwise be ordinary school days, the organiser cannot insist on payment. Voluntary contributions from parents may be asked for but no child should be excluded from participating for financial reasons. Parents/guardians should not be asked to subsidise the participation of another child. Schools operate different policies and often it is made clear that if the contributions requested do not add up to the sum required to fund the visit, the visit may have to be cancelled. Relevant policies need to be checked when planning any visit.

Payment in the form of voluntary contributions is often best spread over a period of time, enabling parents/guardians to pay by instalments. Group leaders should keep detailed accounts including a record of who pays by cash/cheque etc. Receipts should be issued to parents/guardians for any sums received.

Many group leaders insist on taking a 'contingency fund' on any visit to cover any emergency costs. Any such moneys left over after the event should be returned to parents/guardians. Once again all details of expenditure, including receipts, should be noted and retained. It should be remembered that, as part of the activity, there may be a cost implication of hosting pupils from partner schools. Group leaders need to plan and publish expected costs in terms of visits and excursions, social gatherings and travel arrangements for the period of time the visitors are hosted.

Another issue is the advice given to pupils and parents/guardians regarding 'spending money'. Some teachers are happy to leave this to the discretion of parents/guardians. Others recommend a minimum and maximum amount. Some allow pupils to organise their own budget throughout a visit, others choose to distribute moneys to pupils on a regular basis. Any decisions should involve discussions with parents/guardians in order that all parties are aware of the procedures.

Reflection
Activity 8.11 Advertising an event

Imagine your placement school is organising an exchange programme with a school in Oyonnax (between Lyon and Geneva). Write a letter to parents advertising the ten-day exchange (outgoing in February and receiving in July) to the parents of pupils in Year 10. Pupils are hosted in families, spend two to three days in school and go on excursions, e.g. Geneva, Lyon, a *parc ornothologique*, a long walk/ski in the Jura mountains. Usually the party flies to Geneva and is met at the airport by a French coach.

You may wish to use a different scenario, such as one based on an exchange run by your placement school.

Imagine your school is in the process of organising a visit with the aim of maximising the development of pupils' mfl skills and cultural awareness. Here is a possible scenario but you may wish to use an alternative one, maybe one based on a visit organised by your placement school.

Thirty Year-8 pupils have applied to go on a visit to Normandy.

Hostel accommodation has been booked at Cabourg, a seaside town with shops and beach within walking distance. Full board is available, picnic lunches on request. There is a games room. You will be the only group staying at the centre.

The coach will take you from your school to the centre and is available for excursions.

You will arrive at the centre at 1800 hours on July 14. You need to vacate the hostel in the morning of July 18 to catch the ferry later that day.

Possible excursions include: Mont St. Michel, Bayeux (and tapestry), Arromanche and the Normandy landing beaches, Falaise (William the Conqueror's birth place), war cemeteries and Deauville/Trouville.

The coach driver will need one full day off.

Work out an itinerary for your stay to achieve your aims.

- Draft a letter to parents outlining the *aims* and *purpose of* as well as the *programme* for the visit.

  Also, include the following information:

  - pocket money: how much do you recommend? Will you distribute the money or will the pupils handle their own?
  - grouping of pupils and bed-time etc.: the hostel has bedrooms accommodating groups of four;
  - contact with home: what contact can parents expect, e.g. post-card, telephone calls?
  - shopping: pupils will want to buy souvenirs and presents.

- Where possible, compare your outline programme and letter to parents with the one used by your placement school and discuss it with your mentor or the member of staff responsible for visits and exchanges at your placement department.

Reflection
**Activity 8.13 Visits and ex-
changes – organisation and**

Table 8.5 provides a list of tasks often associated with organising a visit abroad. Please note that the list does not necessarily include all the required tasks. The tasks are not in the correct order.

Put them into a logical sequence indicating an approximate time scale in relation to the departure date.

Then discuss your sequence with the colleague in your placement department with the most experience of organising visits and exchanges.

Table 8.5 Some tasks for the preparation of visits and exchanges

Tasks	Sequencing	Timing
Advertise visit to parents in writing outlining details		
Complete form for group passport and send off		
Develop materials and activities for the visit		
Collect second payment		
Change contingency fund into foreign currency		
Carry out preparatory visit: location, duration, cost, travel arrangements		
Double check coach company		
Investigate educational potential of visit: mfl and cross-curricular		
Issue activity pack to pupils		
Explain system of payment by instalments to parents		
Collect E111 forms		
Collect deposit		
Issue important telephone numbers		
Check school calendar		
Collect 'repeat prescription' and put First Aid kit together		
Inform head and governing body of proposals, including itinerary		
Pay deposit to travel company		
Collect final payment		
Check you and the deputy leader have a full valid passport		
Issue E111 application forms		
Arrange initial information exchange meeting with parents		
Count pupils onto coach		
Organise staffing: ratio, gender, skills, nominate a deputy leader		
Final meeting with parents		
Collect pupils' personal and medical details		
Advise on spending money		
Report to headteacher and governors in writing		
Collect deposit/first payment		
Arrange for insurance cover		

Property

If any personal property is lost by a group member this needs to be reported to the police. In the event of insurance claims a police statement tends to be required as evidence of the loss. If any item entrusted to an accompanying adult is lost, the adult is responsible for it.

Task 1: School environment survey
Look at the survey items below:

- add three or four more items about a school and its environment;
- translate all items into the target language (use your dictionary and/or ask your partner and host family for help);
- complete this survey about your partner school.

	Score	
quiet		noisy
attractive		unattractive
varied		all the same
like		dislike
clean		dirty
welcoming		hostile/not welcoming
well looked after		not looked after at all
uncrowded		crowded
historic		modern
interesting		boring
...		...

Score: +3   +2   +1   0   −1   −2   −3
         very good   very bad

Task 2: General information about Hamburg
Find out as much as you can about the following:

	Topic	Answer
1	Climate	
2	Geographical location	
3	Geographical makeup of the area (mountains, rivers etc.)	
4	Natural resources	
5	Industry (incl. reasons for industrial location)	
6	Public transport	
7	Population	
8	Occupations / employment	
9	Average weekly wage	
10	Private transport	

Task 3: Comparison between life in Whitton and Hamburg
Compare your life with that of your German partner; here are some suggested topics:

No.	Topic	Whitton	Hamburg
1	Housing		
2	Family life		
3	Food		
4	Shopping (choice, prices etc.)		
5	Finances (income, pocket money etc.)		
6	School/education		
7	Leisure and entertainment facilities		
8	Attractions in town		
9	Transport (public and private)		
10	Environment (cleanliness, recycling etc.)		
11	...		

Figure 8.2 Geography curriculum-related tasks for pupils on a school visit abroad

Reflection
Activity 8.14 Geography-related mfl tasks

Put the relevant sections of Tasks 1–3 in Figure 8.2 into a mfl of your choice: translate the instructions for Task 1 and, for Tasks 2 and 3, devise questions for the items in the column 'topics' to make the gathering of information easier for pupils, e.g. instead of 'climate' write 'What is the climate like in Hamburg?' in the TL. Use language appropriate for Year-10 pupils.

Figure 8.2 shows how educational visits abroad can be meaningfully accompanied by a structured programme of activities, in this example relating to both the scheme of work for mfl and Geography. It shows some sample tasks developed by Roswitha Guest in conjunction with a colleague from the Geography department of her school to be completed by pupils during their school visit to Hamburg, Germany. Given the personal nature of some of the information required for these tasks, colleagues from the partner school should be briefed to alert hosting parents about the fact that pupils are being asked to find out certain information.

Hosting exchange partners

The hosting of exchange partners is not as simple as it may at first appear.

Before the visitors arrive the teacher in charge of the exchange has to ensure that visitors and hosts are appropriately matched. For this purpose a proforma could be devised. The following information, provided by parents and the pupils themselves, might be useful: name, sex, age, a passport photograph, number of brothers and sisters and their ages, pets, personality, hobbies, whether they would prefer a boy or girl with similar or different characteristics to themselves.

The teacher with responsibility for exchange visits might want to try to help the visiting members of staff, for instance, by organising excursions to local places of interest. Planned excursions for visitors and hosts can provide useful opportunities for the TL

Reflection
Activity 8.15 Matching pupils

You have been asked by your head of department to match up the Spanish and English participants on the annual Spanish exchange.
- Design a checklist including all the relevant details and information you will need to know about individual pupils to enable you to match them.
- How does your list compare with the criteria used by your placement school?

to be used in authentic situations. Many schools insist that during such journeys pupils have to sit next to their own exchange partners. This can avoid divisions by nationality and create opportunities for interaction. It is well worth considering visits to places familiar to the British pupils and to provide activities, which necessitate – through collaboration – communication and explanations between the visitors and the hosts.

In order to give the exchange a suitable profile it is important to involve the senior management of the host school. A formal welcome in an assembly serves at least two purposes: first it demonstrates courtesy and second it introduces the exchange partners to the unique experience of school assemblies and the ethos of the school as a whole. A reception or welcome party is often an integral part of a successful exchange visit. At such an occasion host families could be introduced to visiting pupils, and visitors and hosts can get to know each other in an informal atmosphere.

There are also arrangements to be made for when the foreign pupils visit and take part in life at the British school. Once there, visiting pupils can shadow host pupils and accompany them to lessons. Clearly, colleagues have to be asked if they are happy to have in some of their lessons visiting pupils who could, for instance, be used for cross-curricular work.

Parents might wish to become involved in the exchange by providing 'family' days where they put on further excursions on free days at weekends. It might be useful to provide a list of possible venues and activities to support parents in arranging days out for their visitors. Often parents are happy to organise social events during the exchange at their own homes.

It is quite common that host institutions put on a farewell disco.

There is always the risk of some pupils feeling homesick. Providing a list of telephone numbers of all participating families can allay some concerns and allow visiting pupils and their hosts to network amongst each other if necessary. Approval to distribute telephone numbers in such a way needs to be sought from all concerned.

It might be appropriate to remind parents that whilst visiting pupils are in their homes they – the parents – are responsible for them which includes, for instance, determining meal and bed times.

Work experience placements abroad

Work experience should not be a 'one off' but the culmination of work on mfl skills as well as the understanding of the requirements of 'the world of work'!

Work experience placements abroad, like visits and exchanges, clearly require extremely careful preparation. Many of the issues discussed in the context of visits and exchanges above apply equally. In addition there is the need, for instance, to find suitable work placements for pupils/students, to ensure that employers are covered by adequate public liability insurance or that respective employment legislation is adhered to.

The best way to develop work experience schemes is probably through existing links with partner schools. A partner school may be able to assist in finding and vetting placements, for instance by finding out who in the company will be responsible for the pupil(s)/student(s), that they will be adequately supervised or that appropriate health and safety procedures are in place.

The need to prepare pupils/students linguistically as well as for their specific placements and associated responsibilities is very important. Linguistic preparation across topics such as jobs and future careers, work environment, daily work routine, reading and writing business letters, fax messages or e-mails, making appointments, conducting telephone conversations, dealing with answerphone messages and videoconferencing or comprehending advertisements can meaningfully link the mfl work of the classroom with its application in real situations.

Where possible, planning for work experience placements abroad should take into account pupils'/students' preferences regarding the type of placement as this will help them to gain as much as possible from the experience. Care and attention must be given to pupils'/students' accommodation needs, travel and transport and the hours and conditions of work. Regulations governing youth employment and insurance at work do differ from country to country. It is essential to comply with regulations and conventions. For young people the whole experience can be hugely motivating, yet at the same time daunting and stressful.

Pupils/students need to be aware of the (inter)personal and linguistic skills a work placement abroad will require of them. Pupils/students should be involved as much as possible in the planning process, for instance by helping to make the travel arrangements. They can also be asked to research the specific linguistic demands of their type of placement.

Advice from the Central Bureau (Molyneux, no date: 4) includes a list of skills which pupils/students should develop in advance of the work placement. These are:

- linguistic skills
- social skills
- assertiveness training
- problem solving skills
- personal effectiveness
- the development of a work culture.

A lot can be learnt from schools and mfl teachers who have experience in organising work experience placements abroad. We strongly recommend expert advice is sought when, as a qualified teacher, organising work experience placements abroad. Working in tandem with experienced mfl teachers can provide an excellent opportunity for continuing professional development. For a case study see *http://www.ioe.ac.uk/lie/pgce/ewe/* and for useful information see e.g. EWEP 1989; Griffiths, Miller and Peffers 1992; Molyneux (no date); Brown and Barren 1991; Griffiths and Romain 1995.

In order to ensure that mfl-related work outside the classroom offers maximum learning opportunities for pupils relating to classroom-based learning objectives, it is very important to accompany it with a *structured programme of activities,* which need to be carefully prepared in advance.

In Figure 8.3 is an outline of a programme of work prepared for Key Stage 4 pupils for their one-week work experience in France. It could equally be used for pupils going on visits or exchanges. These tasks link the aims and objectives of the stay abroad to the scheme of work by covering a range of GCSE topics. The tasks are included here in English to make them accessible to mfl trainees of all languages. Each of these tasks can be further developed, differentiated and supported by handouts or worksheets with

Finding out about Fontainebleau
by Naomi Fletcher

1. In the High Street
a)   What is the distribution of shops/services?
b)   Give the name of a stationers', book shop, shoe shop, haberdashers' and hardware store as well as their opening and closing times.
c)   Check prices of key items.
d)   Pick up free leaflets, price lists etc.

2. Leisure activities
a)   What opportunities are there for 'active' leisure activities (e.g. sports centre, swimming pool, tennis courts, riding, golf etc.)?
b)   What opportunities are there for 'passive' leisure activities (e.g. cinema, theatre etc.)?
c)   What can be done in the way of cultural activities (e.g. libraries, art galleries, museums, concert hall etc.)?

3. Communications
a)   How easy is it to travel from Fontainebleau a. to Paris b. to other parts of France?
b)   Check road, railway and underground, coach and bus, airports facilities etc.

4. Cost of living
     How much does it cost for a young person (15/16/17 years old) to:
a)   go to the cinema, swimming pool etc.
b)   travel to Paris by train (make notes of any special offers)
c)   travel to Paris by bus (make notes of any special offers)
d)   have a snack (specify which)
e)   buy a coke/bar of chocolate/bag of crisps
f)   buy tapes/videos
g)   buy a pair of trainers/jeans/T-shirt

5. Parking
     Check on parking meters/car parks:
a)   what does it cost to park in the town centre for half an hour?
b)   when/where is there free parking?

6. Housing
     Find an estate agent.
a)   What is it called?
b)   List a few properties for sale in Fontainebleau and surrounding area (detached houses, flats)
c)   How are properties for sale/to let advertised?
d)   What is the proportion of properties for sale compared to those to let?
e)   Pick up any free leaflets/publicity material

7. Travel and tourism
a)   Find a travel agency. What is its name?
b)   How much does it cost for one person/family of four to have a two week package holiday to Spain/the UK/the USA?
c)   What is the cost of a return flight from Paris to London?
d)   What is/are the name(s) of the airport(s) in Paris?
e)   Where can you hire a bike?
f)   How much does it cost per day?

8. Interviews
a)   Design a number of interview questions asking local people for information about themselves and their town
b)   Ask these questions to three different people
c)   Write a paragraph introducing each of these people

Figure 8.3   Finding out about Fontainebleau   (continued...)

---

9. Cross-curricular links (history/geography/business studies)
a) What can you find out about France and Fontainebleau during World War II?
b) Why did Fontainebleau develop on this site?
c) Are there any large businesses/factories in Fontainebleau? If so, what are they?

10. Cross-curricular themes: careers education
a) Ask five young people what they hope to do when they leave school. Do they think it will be easy to find a job after completing their education?
b) Get a local newspaper and note any jobs that are advertised. Do advertisements specify the age or sex of the person wanted?
c) Is there an employment agency in Fontainebleau? Who is it for: professional people, young people etc.?

11. I-spy in Fontainebleau
a) What is the Town Hall plaque for?
b) What is the specialist name for an ice-cream shop?
c) To whom is the plaque on the police station?
d) What is the name of the market?
e) What is the market used for on non-market days?
f) In the market list five kinds of fish, fruit, cheese and meat
g) Name one or more banks and find out their opening times
h) Buskers: what are they doing?
d) Name the church in the market place
e) What is the name of the local newspaper and how much does it cost?

Figure 8.3   Finding out about Fontainebleau (*continued*)

Reflection
Activity 8.16 Finding out about Fontainebleau

- Translate the task sheet in Figure 8.3 into a TL of your choice and adapt it to suit the destination of the visit(s) undertaken by your placement school. Use language that is appropriate for pupils in Year 10.
- Then choose one of the sections of the programme of work in Figure 8.3 and develop it further by designing differentiated, self-contained worksheet(s) including activities as well as the necessary support for pupils who will not have access to many reference sources whilst on the visit.

---

explanations and linguistic structures to suit the ability level of pupils in a particular group. Help and support in formulating questions might need to be given to individual pupils by the teacher. Pointers about where to find relevant information will also be useful to them. Pupil responses should then be collected and discussed on a task-by-task basis in follow-up classroom work.

Working through these activities requires pupils, for instance, to read authentic material, familiarise themselves with the 'foreign' environment, talk to native speakers, use interpersonal and 'life skills'.

THE FOREIGN LANGUAGE ASSISTANT (FLA) AS A CULTURAL RESOURCE

Working with FLAs can present a very valuable opportunity to enhance mfl work across all stages of cultural awareness. Therefore, if the support of an FLA is available, this should be maximised. Useful guidance on how to work with the FLA is, for instance, available from the National Association for Language Advisers (NALA) and the Central Bureau (see e.g. Central Bureau 1993; Channel Four Schools 1995; NALA/Central Bureau 1992, Page 1997 or Rowles et al. 1998). There might be occasions when mfl trainee teachers have the opportunity to work with FLAs during their training. In any event, trainees need to be aware of the potential of working with FLAs and how to maximise this resource in preparation for their work as qualified mfl teachers.

FLAs are, in the main, used by departments to allow pupils to come into contact with native speakers of the modern foreign language(s) they study, to provide a direct link to the culture(s) associated with the TL as well as more specifically to provide opportunities for pupils to speak and to prepare them for their oral examinations.

One of the advantages of FLAs is the fact that they tend not to be that much older than the pupils themselves and potentially, therefore, constitute a resource regarding the particular areas of their interests.

The NALA/Central Bureau guide on working with FLAs (1992: 11–12) provides a range of valuable ideas and suggests a number of different ways in which the cultural dimension can be portrayed with the help of the FLA:

- straightforward – and probably simple and concise – presentations by the FLA on an aspect of their background, followed or preceded by questions from the pupils;
- role-play, whereby the FLA portrays national figures, professions, members of society within their country;
- establishing differences and similarities by questioning pupils closely about their own culture and encouraging them to articulate their views on what they understand to be characteristic of other countries;
- data collection and project preparation with the FLA working with particular groups on specific cultural dimensions, e.g. music, sport, leisure, the media;
- working on European awareness projects with other departments within the school;
- collecting newspapers and magazines throughout the year and keeping an ongoing survey of, for example, sport results, major events, local incidents, political happenings, leisure and arts activities;
- joint FLA/pupil compilation of 'A day in the life of a pupil/commuter/ shop-keeper/lorry driver, etc.' as perceived in both countries;
- using maps and historical viewpoints from the FLA's own country to obtain comparative viewpoints;
- using magazines and the press for cultural updates but also for predictability exercises where issues are ongoing;
- discussing not only habits and customs but also attitudes (e.g. towards racism, class, religion, poverty, leisure).

Reflection
Activity 8.17 Working with the FLA

- Through observation, note what classroom activities have been made possible by the presence of an FLA.
- Scrutinise a number of lesson plans of your own and identify opportunities which would enhance pupils' learning if an FLA were avail-

SUMMARY

Pupils need to develop cultural awareness as an integral part of their mfl learning, for example, for linguistic and educational reasons. The mfl teacher plays an important part in facilitating the development of cultural awareness, as relevant activities require in-depth knowledge and understanding of the target culture(s) as well as very careful planning and structuring.

In this chapter we presented a possible framework for developing cultural awareness making use of a range of learning opportunities inside and outside the mfl classroom, including first-hand experience of the target culture: for example, by way of contact with FLAs, internet/e-mail projects or visits, exchanges and work experience abroad.

In developing cultural awareness, particularly outside the mfl classroom, thorough preparation is vital in order to safeguard the welfare of pupils and to ensure success. It is imperative that teachers give due consideration to relevant legislation, regulations and guidelines.

9 Pupil Differences and Differentiation in Modern Foreign Languages Teaching and Learning

It is fundamentally important for modern foreign languages (mfl) trainee teachers to recognise that pupils are individuals with different needs. No group of pupils is ever homogenous. Differences in areas such as gender, interest, self-concept, self-esteem, social class, ethnic background or creativity can, for instance, determine pupils' degree of progress, achievement or participation in mfl work.

In any given class there is normally a combination of factors pertaining to individual differences, which is one of the reasons why teaching is a highly complex process. In order to minimise differences in classes, some schools operate a setting policy, where some departments – usually including mfl – group pupils according to certain criteria but particularly their ability. In a school where setting takes place pupils can be in different (ability) sets in certain subjects like mfl, maths and English. Other schools adopt a streaming policy. On entry they place pupils into (ability) groupings across the whole curriculum with pupils being taught in the same group in all or most subjects of the curriculum. This happens often on the basis of test scores in English and Maths and/or information passed on from the pupils' primary schools. Nevertheless, mfl classes, be they setted, streamed or mixed-ability, invariably contain pupils, for example, with different ability levels, interests and backgrounds. For a discussion of mixed-ability grouping in mfl teaching see Redondo 2000.

Mfl trainee teachers need to ensure that all pupils can participate, become involved in lessons and have learning experiences of equal worth. Individual differences should be catered for by building classroom practice on the notion of equality of opportunities in education, that is helping all pupils to realise their full potential or to maximise their aspirations. To achieve this, three issues are of particular importance: setting suitable learning challenges, responding to pupils' diverse learning needs and overcoming potential barriers to learning and assessment for individuals and groups of pupils (see DfEE/QCA 1999: 20–3). The notion that pupils respond consciously or unconsciously to the expectations of the teacher, be they explicitly stated or implied, is generally accepted. From this follows that high expectations in terms of achievement and behaviour of pupils by the mfl trainee teacher can help pupils fulfil their potential. Differentiation, which is discussed in detail in this chapter, aims at maximising the potential of pupils by building on their prior learning and taking into account their individual differences.

Catering for the full range of differences in and individual needs of pupils and helping all pupils maximise their potential is very challenging. It requires the recognition of pupils' individual differences and needs, familiarisation with their backgrounds and the identification of appropriate teaching strategies and activities (see also Turner 2000: 134–50).

The National Curriculum (NC) documentation includes a section on inclusion for all subjects. Inclusion is defined implicitly as 'providing effective learning opportunities for all pupils' (DfEE/QCA 1999: 20). It is in the spirit of the NC for all pupils to study a modern foreign language between the ages of eleven and sixteen. Booth et al. (2000) provide explicit guidance at all levels of provision (see in particular Section C1 entitled 'Orchestrating learning', pp. 75–88). They encourage teachers to audit their own practices in terms of the following: whether

- lessons are responsive to pupil ability;
- lessons are made accessible to all pupils;
- lessons develop an understanding of difference;
- pupils are actively involved in their learning;
- pupils learn collaboratively;
- assessment encourages the achievements of all pupils;
- classroom discipline is based on mutual respect;
- teachers plan, teach and review in partnership;
- teachers are concerned to support the learning and participation of all pupils;
- learning support assistants are concerned to support the learning and participation of all pupils; and
- homework contributes to the learning of all.

We believe in the entitlement of all pupils to study a modern foreign language in some form and this chapter is intended to provide guidance for trainee teachers on how to make available support to pupils who experience possible barriers to foreign language learning.

OBJECTIVES

By the end of this chapter you should:

- appreciate the importance of getting to know your pupils as individuals with a view to catering for their different needs; and
- consider strategies for addressing these needs.

ENTITLEMENT

Mfl trainee teachers need to ensure that they make the full programme of work defined by the statutory framework accessible to all pupils, as 'the right to share the curriculum

... does not automatically ensure access to it, nor progress within it' (NCC 1989: 1). In order to achieve this, individual differences in pupils need to be identified and pupils' individual needs assessed. Only then can the process of addressing pupils' individual needs begin in order to maximise the rate of progress and to enhance the degree of participation.

Four important principles of equality of opportunity in making the full programme of work available to pupils are *entitlement*, *accessibility*, *integration* and *integrity* (see DES/ Welsh Office 1991: 56–7). According to these principles:

- all pupils have a right to participate in the study of mfl;
- the mfl trainee teacher needs to ensure that activities are planned and delivered in a way that allows all pupils to become involved in the mfl learning experience and that the individual needs of pupils are catered for;
- pupils with special educational needs (SEN) should participate in mfl activities alongside pupils without SEN, where possible without alteration of the programme of work or where necessary with modifications to it; and
- activities need to be of equal worth and not patronising or tokenistic to the pupils concerned.

Certain aspects of recent policy statements, in particular the NC published in 2000, are of concern to those who believe that mfl learning should be an entitlement for all pupils and that it is an essential element of a broad and balanced curriculum. As we have noted in the Introduction, disapplication from the study of mfl is now possible. It is important for trainee teachers to be aware of this, particularly if and when the need arises to defend their subject in specific situations.

Reflection
Activity 9.1 Mfl for all?

Consider the reasons for disapplication outlined in the Introduction.
   Do you believe that foreign languages should be taught to all pupils, particularly in Key Stage 4? If so, list arguments in support of mfl for all in the curriculum. If not, outline your reasons against.
   In your opinion, what are the implications of 'languages for all' for mfl teachers? And, what impact would disapplication have?

DIFFERENTIATION

The notion of 'differentiation' is a key strategy in catering for differences in a group of learners. It is based on the principle of helping individual pupils achieve to the best of their ability by planning learning experiences that take into account their individual characteristics, particularly in terms of ability and interest, as well as their prior learning.

Differentiation requires careful and thoughtful planning. Mfl trainees need to adapt the ways in which the subject matter is presented at the input/presentation stage, for instance by using a range of visual aids and by varying the presentation of new lexical items and structures. At the practice and exploitation/production stages mfl trainee teachers need to offer pupils opportunities to interact with the subject matter at different levels and in different ways. Allowing pupils to talk/write about themselves in the course of mfl work and enabling them to relate their own experiences to the way of life of people in the target culture(s) can make the study of mfl relevant to pupils and the target language (TL) a vehicle for self-expression. In this way, pupils can draw on their different experiences for the purposes of mfl learning.

Apart from an awareness of pupils' individual differences, mfl trainees need to anticipate what difficulties might arise from the subject matter and skills to be taught, for instance whether the pronunciation, orthographic conventions, linguistic structures or semiotic boundaries are different to those in the mother tongue(s) of pupils and, therefore, need particular attention or whether the types of activities, material or inter-action modes might pose certain difficulties. In preparing a lesson or unit of work, mfl trainees need to consider strategies to provide reinforcing support for some pupils whilst stretching others.

Reflection
Activity 9.2 Pupil perceptions
of a unit of work

Following the completion of a unit of work, issue the pupils with a brief questionnaire asking them to identify what they found easy, difficult and/ or enjoyable within the unit. You will need to remind pupils of the tasks and activities undertaken in the unit of work. How can this information be used to inform future planning and the differentiation of work?

Discuss the findings with your mentor or a class teacher you work with closely.

In its non-statutory guidance to mfl teachers, the National Curriculum Council suggests the differentiation of mfl work according to three categories (see NCC 1992: E3):

- *core:* language items and structures as well as tasks, which all pupils are expected to master;
- *reinforcement:* tasks for those pupils who need more practice in order to achieve the planned core outcomes; and
- *extension:* language items and structures as well as tasks for those pupils capable of carrying out more advanced and complex work than their peers.

Table 9.1 shows an example of how these three categories can be applied to the planning of a unit of work in order to cater for the needs of all pupils in the class. It follows the approach to planning suggested in Chapter 4. On the basis of differentiated learning objectives the unit of work 'In the restaurant' identifies a range of activities building on what pupils already know and covers a number of learning opportunities at various levels in order for the full ability range to be challenged.

In a unit of work the various activities are normally cross-referenced to the specific coursebook, worksheets or OHTs available to, or used by, the department to make

Table 9.1 Sample unit of work plan

Im Restaurant		
Year: 9	Number and length of lessons: 5×70mins	
Learning objectives		
Core	Extension	
• to be able to read and understand a menu • to be able to order food from a menu in a restaurant • to be able to understand the waiter/waitress • to be able to pay the bill	• to be able to ask for clarification of what items on a menu are • to be able to complain about the quality of food provided • to be able to question the bill • to be able to ask to pay by cash or Visa	
Main language items/structures		
Core	Extension	
common items of food and meals common restaurant phrases and structures	Kann ich mit ... bezahlen? Es gibt ein Probelm. Mein Essen ist kalt/nicht gut et.c	
Main materials and resources		
visual aids (flashcards, OHTs), authentic menus, tapes of short dialogues, transcripts of tapes		
Main activities	**PoS**	**ATL**
Core		
• visual aids to present items of food	1a 2a 2b	AT2L1
• categorise food into starters, main courses and desserts		
	2f 2l 2j 3a	AT3L3
• listening comprehension extracting details of food ordered	3b 5h	
• structured pair work: ordering food	2i 3b 5e 5g	AT1L3
• open-ended role play in a restaurant	5a 5h	
• reading exercise from menus with unfamiliar foods, matching with descriptions	4a 5h 5i	AT2L3
	2i 3d 4a 4c	AT2L4
• writing descriptions of types of food/meals	2j 3b 3c	AT3L4
	3e	AT4L4
Reinforcement		
• compile vocabulary list of basic foods	2k	AT4L1
• categorise dishes contained on samples of menus	2f 3a	AT4L1
• decipher taped dialogues from jumbled transcripts	4a	AT3L2
• use gapped text of taped conversations as a prompt for pair work	1g 2l	AT1L2
• prepare open-ended role play in pairs/groups	2a 2f	AT2L2
• use reference material and drill exercises to practice	1d 2o	AT2L3
• match items of unfamiliar foods with descriptions	1d 1h 2n 3g	AT3L3
	3i 4a	AT4L2
Extension		
• provide additional vocabulary to learn	3d 3e 5c	AT2L1
• devise own menu to cater for full range	5h 5l	AT3L4
• rework taped dialogues from details extracted from tape		
• conduct pair work without scripts but with visual prompts; insist that 'extension' vocabulary and phrases are incorporated	2e 2f	AT1L4
	1b 2e 3e 5c 5l	AT2L4
• prepare open-ended role play but in groups which will perform together; ask all the waiters and all the customers to prepare together; pupils will not know exactly what peers will say	2c 2d 2f 3d	
	3e 5d 5l	AT2L5
	4a 4b 4c 4d	
• research and describe traditional English dishes in the TL		AT3L5
		AT4L4

(continued...)

Table 9.1 Sample unit of work plan (*continued*)

Homework		
• note and learn vocabulary • complete drill exercises reinforcing common vocabulary and phrases • write the scripts of dialogues • produce a full menu in German • prepare for end of unit goal	as above	as above
Assessment opportunities		
Continuous		
• peer assessment of pair work • take in marks for listening • mark drill exercises, menu, transcripts • one-to-one assessment of role plays	as above	as above
Summative		
• in mixed-ability groups write and act out a short play to be video-taped: a family is celebrating exam success, but all goes wrong in the restaurant • end-of-unit test covering listening, reading and writing	as above	as above

Table 9.2 Some types of differentiation

Differentiation type	Description
Text	level of difficulty and type of stimulus material
Task	level of difficulty of what learners are asked to do with the stimulus material; number of tasks
Outcome	quantity and quality of performance attainment expected from pupils
Support	amount of teacher time/access to reference material etc. available to pupils
Interest	opportunity for pupils to choose tasks, stimulus material, medium etc.

individual lesson planning easier. This is not possible here but needs to be done in any planning carried out by mfl trainee teachers.

In this unit of work all pupils are expected to complete the core activities. At appropriate times in the unit some pupils are set reinforcement activities consolidating core learning objectives whilst others will be able to work on extension activities in order to gain a deeper knowledge and understanding and develop additional skills. As Table 9.2, adapted from Convery and Coyle 1993: 3–5, illustrates, this can be done in a number of ways.

Those pupils who complete the core tasks more quickly can be set additional extension activities allowing pupils who need it more time to complete the task. For instance, the core task of writing descriptions of types of food/meals can be followed by the extension task of researching and describing traditional English dishes in the TL.

Pupils can be given the same task(s) but different stimulus material, for instance to extract meaning (categorise food into starters, main courses and desserts) from authentic texts (from different menus). This is an example of differentiation by text.

Alternatively, pupils can be given the same stimulus material but differentiated tasks to complete. Pupils can, for instance, be asked to listen to a dialogue in a restaurant.

Some pupils can focus on word recognition by choosing items of food/dishes they have heard from a list whilst others write down additional items they hear, which are not included in the list.

Differentiation can also come via open-ended tasks, for instance, producing a menu. This is differentiation by outcome. It allows for differences in quantity as well as linguistic difficulty of work produced, such as the use of core vocabulary by some pupils and extension vocabulary by others. It also allows pupils to bring their own interest to the task, for instance by including their favourite dishes.

Different levels of support constitute another possibility. The amount of time the teacher spends with individual, pairs or groups of pupils or the access to reference material can vary. Pupils can be asked to perform a role play in a restaurant by producing a script with the help of a gapped text, from visual clues, by working simply from a scenario or by making use of help from the foreign language assistant (FLA).

When differentiating by interest the teacher might allow pupils to choose from a range of stimulus material or activities, for instance pupils could choose one of a number of menus or select from a range of scenarios for pair or group work. They might assume different roles in pair or group work, for instance play the waiter or the client, or invent things that may go wrong to add spontaneity to dialogues, such as the waiter bringing the wrong order or there being a hair in the soup, which necessitates the inclusion of language associated with complaints.

**Reflection
Activity 9.3 Differentiated
lesson planning**

Following the guidelines for lesson planning given in Chapter 4, plan a number of lessons for a Key Stage 3 class you have already worked with/ observed. You may wish to use the unit of work in Figure 9.1 as a point of reference.

- For every key activity consider what form of support you can provide for pupils. How can you cater for pupils' different needs? And, how can support be phased out?
- Consider means by which a task can be presented to pupils of different abilities. Will the inclusion of illustrations help? How many examples will you provide? What size print will you use on a worksheet/acetate?
- Devise follow-on activities, which enable pupils who finish sooner than others to extend their knowledge, skills and understanding within the given topic area. How will you reward the completion of this supplementary work?
- Also devise reinforcement activities for those pupils who are not (yet) ready to carry out extension work.
- Discuss these lesson plans with your mentor or the respective class teacher.
- Ask if you can teach the lessons you have planned with the respective teacher observing and providing feedback on what worked well, what did not work so well and how you could improve (in) these areas.

When differentiating programmes of work, mfl trainees need to ensure that reinforcement and extension activities are of equal worth and that pupils who are working on reinforcements activities do not feel belittled in their capability.

In the remainder of this chapter we discuss a number of pupil differences and identify a range of different teaching strategies to cater for them. The differences discussed are:

- gender differences;
- bilingual pupils;
- pupils with SEN;
- exceptionally able pupils; and
- pupils with motivational difficulties.

The various teaching strategies identified in this chapter need to be seen in the context of differentiation.

GENDER DIFFERENCES

It is important for mfl trainees to be aware of gender differences. Inspection reports by the Office for Standards in Education (OfSTED), for example, frequently draw attention to the fact that girls tend to do better than boys in a range of school subjects, but particularly in mfl. A look at Figure 9.3 confirms this.

Many schools and mfl departments are looking at what they can do to tackle this issue.

The realisation that there are certain differences between boys and girls is clearly important. Ann Clark and John Trafford (1996) report a range of research findings on the basis of which mfl trainee teachers might be able to take pre-emptive or remedial action. These are shown in Figure 9.4.

It is important for mfl trainees to consider and use effective strategies to address these research findings and thereby cater for gender differences in mfl. Field (2000) warns against a simplistic approach to gender differences and suggests that teachers need to bear in mind gender-related matters, which include maturational rates,

Table 9.3 GCSE results 2000

Percentage of 15-year-old pupils who obtained Grades A*–C			
	Boys	Girls	Difference
French	37.2	54.3	17.2
German	44.0	58.9	15.0
All subjects	48.1	57.9	9.8

Differences between boys and girls at GCSE in terms of percentage of 15-year-old pupils who obtained Grades A*–C			
	French	German	All subjects
1999	17.2	14.8	10.6
1998	16.8	15.3	9.5
1997	15.8	16.1	9.3
1996	15.8	16.2	9.4

Source: OfSTED 2000: C3

Table 9.4 Gender differences

Research findings	Pre-emptive/remedial action
Differences in the perception of usefulness, enjoyment and difficulty of mfl between girls and boys.	When planning programmes of work, are the perceived interests of boys and girls taken into account, e.g. in the choice of types of sports to be taught in the context of the topic 'hobbies'?
Boys tend to have a less conscientious approach towards their work and mature later than girls.	Are accuracy and communication being encouraged equally?
Boys tend to do better than girls at problem-solving whereas girls tend to be better at verbal reasoning.	When planning programmes of work, are different learning styles being catered for, e.g. are various types of activities being used?
Boys tend to be more demanding of time and attention from the teacher than girls.	Are boys and girls given the same amount of teacher attention? Is there a gender balance in who is asked to answer questions in class?
The presentation of girls' work can be 'seductively' better than that of boys.	Is presentation but one of a number of assessment criteria such as effort and accuracy?
Girls tend to be less obviously disruptive than boys, less confident about speaking than boys but more concerned about 'getting it right'.	Are boys and girls equally encouraged to carry out oral work and perform role plays in front of the whole class?
Boys tend to give less attention to lesson and course work and more to revision and examination work.	Are both formative/continuous and summative assessment used? Are learning and revision strategies being taught explicitly?

motivational factors, teaching and learning styles, parental support and attitudes, concentration spans and behavioural matters. Trainees should guard against adopting 'boy friendly' and 'girl friendly' approaches to redress any perceived imbalances, but instead to draw on a broad understanding of gender-related issues to inform planning and delivery methods.

BILINGUAL PUPILS

The term bilingual is used here

> as a shorthand to describe pupils who come from homes or communities where languages other than English are spoken, and who in consequence have developed competence in those languages. The term does not necessarily imply a high level of proficiency in both languages.
>
> (DES/Welsh Office 1990: 83)

The term 'home language' has been described as

> the language which the bilingual pupil is able to use in addition to English. It is nearly always the language used in the pupil's home; but it is not necessarily

Reflection
Activity 9.4 Gender differences

Observe a number of mfl lessons focussing on the participation rate of boys and girls, both during whole-class activities and pair/group work.

Devise (a) tally sheet(s), which help(s) you in recording, for instance, how often boys and girls put up their hands or make a contribution to a lesson. Also note which strategies the teacher uses to encourage equal participation by boys and girls, such as targeting questions to specific pupils.

Then discuss with your mentor or a relevant class teacher possible strategies for ensuring equal participation of girls and boys.

the only home language. Also it may not be the language used most frequently by the pupil, which will often be English. … When the home language of a number of bilingual pupils in a school is being discussed as a modern language option, the term community language is also used.

(DES/Welsh Office 1990: 83)

The challenge for mfl trainees is to take into account and build on the linguistic and cultural understanding, skills and knowledge pupils bring to the classroom.

In the mfl classroom with the TL as the main means of instruction, interaction and assessment, weaknesses some pupils may experience in their command of English need not necessarily be a disadvantage. Linguistic skills in languages other than English can offer a basis for comparative and contrastive language work for the whole class.

Some schools (have) run language awareness programmes with aims such as '(to bridge) the 'space between' the different aspects of language education (English/foreign language/ethnic minority mother tongues/English as a second language/Latin)' (Hawkins 1987: 4). Such programmes might, for instance, include an examination of which languages are spoken in (particular parts of) the world, what families of languages there are and how languages are 'related' to one another. This might help pupils in the application of language learning strategies such as the use of cognates. Also, work might be carried out on an awareness of the diachronistic dimension of language development through the comparison of, say, the TL and English on the basis of a few words or phrases. Pupils could be shown how particular words have changed in form or meaning over a period of time. This might help them appreciate that form and function of language are determined by their use and that language evolves over time. From this pupils might gain an appreciation that certain features of the TL, such as different grammatical genders, which they might perceive as 'idiosyncratic', were at one time also characteristic of the English language. An invaluable resource in developing such programmes is David Crystal's encyclopaedia of language (see Crystal 1997). Another important point of reference is, of course, the National Literacy Strategy (NLS) (DfEE 1998). For a brief discussion of the NLS see the Introduction. Language awareness programmes should build on the understanding pupils are developing during their time in primary school, in particular work on metalinguistic understanding and writing frames.

Mfl departments can be seen to have a key role to play in the development of a whole school language policy. Mother tongue and mfl teachers might work collaboratively and follow a clear and consistent policy to assist pupils in their language development (see e.g. Kingman 1988: 69).

Mfl learning can be beneficial for pupils in terms of developing general language skills including summarising, redrafting and varying language to suit context, audience and purpose. Beyond functional aspects of foreign language teaching and learning there is also the need to become familiar with the structure of the TL. All these activities can be seen to reinforce work carried out in English and be beneficial in terms of the development of pupils' understanding of and ability to use language. The skills of paying attention to detail and of producing accurate spoken or written utterances are transferable from one language to another. In the TL sounds or patterns can normally not be taken for granted because they are, in the main, unfamiliar. Pupils have to pay attention to every letter and sound, which can be easier in the TL because the amount of input tends to be finite/limited. This attention to detail can be a valuable skill for pupils with difficulties in writing and listening to their mother tongue/English.

Reflection
Activity 9.5 Literacy and foreign language work

Familiarise yourself with the National Literacy Strategy and the National Curriculum Orders for English.
   Drawing on your reading as well as your observations of English lessons and teaching in a primary school, what specific examples of literacy-related foreign language work can you think of?

PUPILS WITH SEN

Many classes include pupils who have learning difficulties significantly greater than those of the majority of children of the same age. They are referred to as pupils with SEN. The Warnock Report (1978) came to the conclusion 'that services should be planned on the basis of one child in five requiring some form of special educational provision at some stage' (HMI 1993: 1). This led to the recognition by the 1981 Education Act of the value of the integration of pupils with SEN into mainstream schools where possible.

The following categories of learning difficulties have been identified:

- a physical disability
- a problem with sight, hearing or speech
- a mental disability
- emotional or behavioural problems
- a medical or health problem
- difficulties with reading, writing, speaking or mathematics work.

(DfE/Welsh Office 1994: 6)

The publication of the SEN Code of Practice – for details about the most recent version of the Code of practice and other SEN-related resources see the DfEE's online Centre for SEN available at *http: //www.dfee.gov.uk/sen/* – has important implications for the work of all teachers, including modern linguists. Subject teachers have an important role to play in the identification and support of pupils with SEN. Where a so-called individual education plan (IEP) is drawn up, subject teachers need to familiarise themselves with its content. IEPs are supposed to set out the following:

- the short-term targets set for the pupil
- the teaching strategies to be used
- the provision to be put in place
- when the plan is to be reviewed
- the outcome of the action taken.

(DfEE 2000b: *http: //www.dfee.gov.uk/sen/*)

According to the 2000 revised draft of the Code of Practice the IEP should focus on three to four targets, which relate to the areas of communication, literacy, numeracy and behaviour and social skill. It should be discussed with the pupil and parents and reviewed at least twice a year. Subject specialists need to liaise closely with the school's special educational needs coordinator (SENCO) as well as, on the basis of knowledge of the nature of a pupil's learning difficulties, help to achieve the specified targets or learning objectives in class.

> **Reflection**
> **Activity 9.6 Identifying pupils**
> **with SEN**
>
> During your work at your first placement school, enquire about the procedures in place in the mfl department concerning the identification of pupils with SEN. Compare them with those of the mfl department at your second placement school or discuss similarities and differences with the procedures identified by a fellow trainee placed in a different school.

A Centre for Information on Language Teaching and Research (CILT)/National Curriculum Council (NCC) project supports the view that pupils with SEN can have positive experiences when learning a modern foreign language and considers the exposure of pupils with SEN to mfl to be beneficial (see NCC 1993: 1). The report notes that pupils with SEN can benefit in three main aspects of mfl work, i.e. in terms of:

- linguistic development;
- social development; and
- cultural awareness.

The findings of this project clearly underline the principle of entitlement to the study of an mfl for all.

For details about working with pupils with SEN see also the website of the National Association for Special Educational Needs available at *http://www.nasen.org.uk/* and Edwards 1998.

Some teaching strategies

Mfl teachers use a wide range of strategies in order to cater for pupils' individual differences. There is no specific methodology for teaching pupils with SEN. The strategies described here tend to be considered to constitute good practice in mfl teaching generally. They do not only pertain to pupils with SEN. Since we feel that they can be particularly useful when teaching pupils with SEN, they are discussed at this point.

Consistency in approach

Teachers of mfl often aim for consistency in approach in their teaching because familiarity with the format of material, types of tasks used and with classroom routines can increase the accessibility of the content of work for pupils.

As was noted in Chapter 5, using certain 'stock' types of activities can be reassuring to pupils. It can help minimise the amount of TL instruction needed and allows pupils to carry out their language work without apprehension about not knowing what to do.

Greeting pupils in the TL on entry to the classroom and expecting pupils to make a TL utterance in response or when calling the register can serve to reinforce a sense of purpose of TL use for pupils. It also provides a regular opportunity to reinforce key linguistic items and structures.

Planning in terms of small, achievable steps

In the tradition of the graded objectives movement, reducing the content of work to a manageable size and breaking it down into small, achievable steps, are also often used. Memorising new words and phrases is an important skill in mfl learning. Manageability of the number of new lexical items the mfl teacher introduces at any one time or the number of items pupils have to remember in order to complete a task successfully can be particularly useful for pupils with SEN. This can help them gain a sense of security and achievement as well as break down possible affectional barriers towards the TL. It is important to recognise that

> pupils with special educational needs can and do make significant progress in terms of their capabilities ... . although the steps of progress may be small compared to those of other pupils, they often represent huge progress for individual children.
>
> (Dearing 1993: 54)

Using praise

Praise for effort and/or achievement is one form of feedback as are constructive comments when marking pupils' work. For marking and error correction see Chapter 10.

> Feedback from teachers to children, in the process of formative assessment, is a prime requirement for progress in learning. Formative assessment is that

process of appraising, judging or evaluating students' work or performance and using this to shape and improve their competence.

(Tunstall and Gipps 1996: 389)

Many teachers have adopted systems of praise and encouragement, which are attractive to pupils and make them want to achieve. Mfl trainee teachers need to remember that 'although the steps of progress *(of pupils with SEN)* may be small compared to those of other pupils, they often represent huge progress for individual children' (Dearing 1993: 54). 'Small' steps of progress made by pupils with SEN deserve equal praise as the 'bigger' steps of progress made by pupils without SEN.

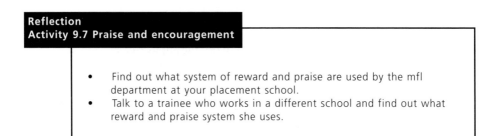

Reflection
Activity 9.7 Praise and encouragement

- Find out what system of reward and praise are used by the mfl department at your placement school.
- Talk to a trainee who works in a different school and find out what reward and praise system she uses.

Planning in terms of multi-dimensional progression

The NCC non-statutory guidance suggests that progression should be built into mfl work in a number of ways (see Table 9.5).

Table 9.5 has clear implications for unit of work and lesson planning, which can be explored in Activities 9.8 and 9.9. For multi-dimensional learning objectives see also Chapter 4.

Creating a non-threatening learning environment

For pupils who are not so confident in speaking, opportunities should be created to practise in pairs or small groups with the teacher or the foreign language assistant (FLA) rather than in front of the whole class. This can avoid feelings of insecurity about

Table 9.5   Multi-dimensional progression

From		To
concrete	ideas	abstract
simple	aspects	complex
specific	themes	general
factual	topics	non-factual
classroom	experiences	wider
familiar	contexts	unfamiliar
less	controversial aspects	more

Source: adapted from NCC 1992: D2

Reflection
Activity 9.8 Planning for
progression in mfl teaching I

Look at the scheme of work for Key Stages 3 and 4 of the mfl department at your placement school.
- Make a note of how many times certain topics, for instance free time or holidays, are taught across Key Stages 3 and 4.
- Discuss with your mentor or a class teacher with whom you work closely what is taken for granted when a given unit of work, e.g. free time or holidays, is re-visited at Key Stage 4 and how much revision of material covered at Key Stage 3 is necessary.
- Now try to relate the different approaches in how topics are covered in Key Stages 3 and 4 to the continuum in Figure 9.5. How is progression from concrete to abstract, from simple to complex, from specific to general, from the classroom to the wider world or from the familiar to the unfamiliar etc built in?

Reflection
Activity 9.9 Planning for
progression in mfl teaching II

Look at the scheme of work of the mfl department at your placement school.
- Note how two consecutive units of work build on existing knowledge and skills.
- Discuss with your mentor or a class teacher with whom you work closely what is taken for granted at the beginning of the new unit of work and how much revision of linguistic items and/or structures covered in previous units is necessary.
Your findings for this activity are likely to vary considerably according to which units of work you choose and at what stage of the linguistic development of pupils they come. Therefore, carry out this activity with a number of different units across different stages of the learning process.

incorrect TL production. Extended periods of practice of a small amount of TL can also help pupils in this respect.

The NCC/CILT project report referred to earlier suggests the use of 'language squares', i.e. an area of the classroom where only the TL may be spoken, but which pupils can leave, or 'the right to remain silent' as strategies to reduce stress levels in pupils in using the TL (see NCC 1993: 5).

Clarity of presentation and using clear instructions

For pupils with difficulties in reading, worksheets and writing on the board/acetates need to be clearly legible and sufficiently big. Visual support as well as uncluttered presentation of material are also important. The board and/or OHP screen should be visible from all angles of the classroom. All of this can be particularly important for pupils with difficulties with sight.

Pupils with difficulties with hearing should be encouraged to sit in a position that allows them to lip-read if necessary.

Instructions in the TL should be clear and precise and, where possible, be accompanied by visual support, e.g. the word 'listen' in the TL can be used together with a symbol of a tape or a mime, i.e. the teacher pointing to her ear. Symbols and instructions used by the coursebook should be the same as those used on worksheets as well as assessment material in order to avoid confusion. Familiarity with 'stock' types of tasks can also help to keep instructions manageable (see also Chapter 5).

Presenting new language with the help of visual support

As can be seen in Chapter 6, new language forms can be presented through reading and listening activities. Pupils with SEN are more likely to have difficulties with the highly conceptual nature of mfl learning. Visual support in the form of pictures and flashcards as well as real objects such as, for instance, fruit can make non-abstract language more imminent and accessible. The visual support material can subsequently be used effectively as stimulus material for language practice and production.

Creating opportunities for non-verbal responses

Equally, the opportunity for pupils to respond physically to stimuli for instance by miming, making gestures, ticking boxes can help them overcome difficulties in speaking and writing. By agreeing physical responses with a class, for instance what mime to use for *'juego al tenis'* ('I play tennis'), pupils are given an opportunity to contribute to the lesson content. Pupils could be asked to stand up, put up their hand or hold up a word card when they identify a specific word or phrase in a listening text.

Planning in terms of tangible and practical outcomes

Tangible and practical outcomes and 'products' of the learning process, such as a project booklet produced with the help of the word-processor or a desk-top publishing package building on drafting and re-drafting, a collage for display purposes or the focus on the process of learning, such as carrying out simulation tasks, can help pupils in breaking down real and perceived difficulties with the linguistic content. The NCC non-statutory guidance offers many suggestions concerning 'concrete goals' and considers them as essential elements in the planning of units of work (see NCC 1992: G1–13).

Reflection
Activity 9.10 Production of a
study guide for a unit of work

In a collaborative teaching situation, work alongside pupils who have difficulties with mfl.

- Make a note of the particular difficulties experienced by them. These may include bringing the right equipment, using reference material, maintaining concentration, recalling key vocabulary, understanding instructions and other aspects identified in this chapter.
- As a result of your findings produce a short 'study guide' for a future unit of work. This guide may include an equipment check, activities such as puzzles and games to reinforce key vocabulary, guidance on how and where to find reference material, a 'skills' profile ('can-do' checklist) and help on what to do if objectives prove too difficult. To assist you with this task, refer to the unit of work plan. The guide might also include guidance on established TL routines.
- On completion, discuss the guide with your mentor or a class teacher with whom you work with closely.

Assume that the pupils will be able to work with a support teacher.

Recycling small amounts of language

Because of the importance of the ability to memorise linguistic items and recall them, which pupils with SEN are more likely to have difficulties with, the key to successful mfl learning for pupils would appear to lie in presenting new language in different guises, 'recycling' small amounts of language in many different ways, yet in familiar types of tasks, to engage pupils in the process of carrying out activities without being aware that they are repeatedly practising the same language content.

EXCEPTIONALLY ABLE PUPILS

There are some pupils whose individual differences relate to their exceptional ability and who have the potential for exceptional achievement, often in a range of subjects. Another widely used term for these pupils is 'gifted children'. For a discussion of working with very able pupils see also Jones (2000).

Clearly a key consideration in working with pupils of exceptional ability is their identification in order to avoid underachievement and to be able to take remedial action. Early identification of exceptionally able pupils is particularly important as they may display symptoms similar to those shown by pupils with motivational difficulties: they may appear inattentive or exhibit attention-seeking behaviour and underachieve. David George (1993: 3) distinguished three types of gifted underachievers:

- low self-esteem;
- academic avoidance behaviour;
- poor study skills, poor peer acceptance and lack of concentration.

George lists a number of ways of identifying exceptionally able pupils, among them teacher observation, checklists, intelligence tests and achievement test batteries.

Cliff Denton and Keith Postlethwaite (1995: 31–2) suggest a non-subject-specific checklist as possible means of identification of very able children:

Gifted Pupils:
1.   Possess superior powers of reasoning, of dealing with abstractions, of generalizing from specific facts, of understanding meaning, and of seeing into relationships.
2.   Have great intellectual curiosity.
3.   Learn easily and readily.
4.   Have a wide range of interests.
5.   Have a broad attention-span that enables them to concentrate on and persevere in solving problems and pursuing interests.
6.   Are superior in the quantity and quality of vocabulary as compared with children their own age.
7.   Have ability to do effective work independently.
8.   Have learned to read early (often well before school age).
9.   Exhibit keen powers of observation.
10. Show initiative and originality in intellectual work.
11. Show alertness and quick response to new ides.
12. Are able to memorize quickly.
13. Have great interest in the nature of man and the universe (problems of origins and destiny, etc).
14. Possess unusual imagination.
15. Follow complex directions easily.
16. Are rapid readers.
17. Have several hobbies.
18. Have reading interests which cover a wide range of subjects.
19. Make frequent and effective use of the library.
20. Are superior in mathematics, particularly in problem solving.

Reflection
Activity 9.11 Identifying exceptionally able pupils

What mfl-specific knowledge, skills and understanding characterise exceptionally able pupils? Draw up a list of indicators which in your opinion signal exceptional ability in mfl learning and discuss them with your mentor or a class teacher you work with closely.

A number of checklists of this nature can be found in specialist literature. These can serve as *aide-mémoires* in identifying exceptionally able pupils. For details about identifying gifted children also see the National Association for Gifted Children (NAGC) website at *http://www.nagcbritain.org.uk*.

The particular challenge for teachers working with exceptionally able pupils is always to provide work that stretches them and to have high expectations (see HMI 1992: vii).

Some teaching strategies

When working with exceptionally able pupils mfl teachers need to look out for the characteristics described above. Tasks, activities and exercises need to be challenging and stimulating for all pupils, including pupils with exceptional ability. There is, once again, no distinctive methodology for working with very able pupils or pupils with exceptional ability. The inclusion of extension work into a programme of study building on differentiated learning objectives is a strategy used by mfl departments to cater for more able and exceptionally able learners in a class. Often it is not so much the quantity of work set than its nature that is important. Below are some suggestions, which represent good practice in mfl teaching generally but which may appeal to more able and exceptionally able learners in particular:

Using creativity and problem solving

The language prescribed in GCSE examination specifications tends to be functional and can be perceived as narrow. Therefore, trainees need to ensure, through careful planning, that there is room for 'risk taking' and 'experimenting' with language as this can benefit more able pupils in particular. Working with language can take the form of manipulation. Pupils capable of higher level work in particular can gain a lot from exploring and articulating thoughts and ideas.

Conundrums and puzzles allow for the use of language by appealing to pupils' imagination. Also, open-ended tasks in the respective TL can present pupils with a challenge, allowing them to use their imagination and to solve a problem in a creative way. One example is known as 'Le jeu des poubelles'. The teacher places a collection of authentic materials and realia in a bag. These might include menus, bus tickets, food wrappers, receipts, magazines, newspaper articles, personal letters or audio recordings. The aim of the activity is for pupils to adopt the role of a detective. This involves scrutinising the materials and (re-)creating a story featuring an imaginary or real person, who has (supposedly) collected the materials during a period of time in the target country. Outcomes can range from creative prose writing to role plays. Activities like this allow for the use of pupils' imagination. They draw on lexis from various topics and require pupils to make use of reference material.

The development of learning activities for peers on their own or in pairs or groups can also offer a challenge to more able pupils in particular.

Going beyond understanding detail

GCSE specifications (formerly syllabuses) tend not to go much beyond the identification of details within TL texts. Responding to texts by adapting the meaning of poems and songs or drawing out themes and images portrayed in texts are all higher-level skills. To 'experiment' with language extends beyond the manipulation of grammatical forms and can include the expression of meaning through a range of literary techniques.

Fostering independence

Learner independence is important. More able and exceptionally able pupils are often effective independent learners. Mfl trainee teachers can try to build on this by encouraging more able and exceptionally able pupils to reflect on how they learn, practise and exploit new language. They can then devise activities and provide some input for peers: for instance, from time to time become involved in 'teaching' other pupils. Keeping a 'learning diary' is one way to encourage reflection. Work by Leni Dam (1990 and 1995) demonstrates the value of self-evaluation in the TL, both in terms of the ability to manipulate the language learnt and in motivating pupils. Striving towards independent language learning and language use is also a feature of teaching and learning mfl at A and A/S level. For a detailed discussion see Pachler and Field 1999.

Focussing on accuracy and nuances of language use

To help them improve accuracy, pupils can be encouraged to carry out language analysis tasks such as the comparison of different language styles and registers. To contrast the language forms used in two newspaper articles covering the same story can, for instance, be a very productive way of addressing how language is used beyond conveying essential facts. Again, some strategies recommended for students of A and A/S level may be appropriate for older 'able' pupils (see e.g. Powell 1999 and Field 1999).

Conceptualising

In Chapter 7 we argue that grammar requires conceptual thinking. Invariably, this challenge will appeal to some pupils more than others. To provide pupils with texts and examples and ask them to draw conclusions about the structure of the TL can be a demanding task. Given the opportunity, some pupils might be able to produce explanations, which can be used by the mfl trainee for teaching certain grammar points to the whole class.

Developing extended cultural awareness

To research particular cultural issues with the help, for instance, of articles from the press, reference material or the internet can appeal to pupils. The focus is on learner independence and the extension of pupils' general knowledge. It can also help pupils to place mfl learning into a wider cultural context. For a discussion of authentic material see Chapters 3 and 11, for the use of the internet see Chapter 12.

**Reflection
Activity 9.12 Working with
exceptionally able pupils**

- Examine activities in an existing unit of work. Consider which of the
  following, or any other, challenging activity types could be added to
  stretch exceptionally able pupils:
    - research skills;
    - creative writing;
    - extended reading;
    - translation;
    - conundrums;
    - grammar exercises; or
    - preparing a presentation.
- Develop relevant materials and, in collaboration with your mentor or
  a relevant class teacher, plan how to work with (an) exceptionally
  able pupil(s) on extension tasks throughout the unit of work.
- When evaluating the project, consider the impact of your work on
  the attainment and motivation of the pupil(s).

To provide texts such as short stories, poetry and prose to complement topics covered in a scheme of work with extended reading/reading for pleasure is a possible strategy. Work carried out by pupils on such supplementary material needs to be carefully monitored and time must be made available for feedback and discussion. The outcomes can be rewarding for both the teacher and the learner. Monitoring of progress might be achieved by the pupil recording her efforts in a learner diary. Mfl teachers often build into lesson plans and/or their non-contact time, for instance at break or lunchtime, opportunities to discuss progress with pupils. This way a record of the work carried out is kept and the pupils themselves are involved in building up a profile of their achievements.

PUPILS WITH MOTIVATIONAL DIFFICULTIES

One particular challenge for mfl teachers are pupils who display behaviour patterns that are disruptive to the delivery of lessons or those who are indifferent to the tasks planned. Pupils in these categories tend to be insufficiently motivated towards their study of mfl. For a detailed discussion of motivation see Chambers 1999.

Internal as well as external motivation facilitate learning (see Child 1993: 47–51). Internal or intrinsic reasons for wanting to learn could, for instance, be the wish of pupils to tell a pen-friend about themselves, the desire to complete a challenging task or to win in a competitive situation. External or extrinsic reasons for wanting to learn could be the need to pass an examination at the end of compulsory schooling as a means of entry into post-16 education. Research would suggest that the more imminent the reasons for wanting to learn and the more they can be determined by the learner, the more influential they are.

Gary Chambers carried out some research into what makes pupils learn/want to learn mfl. From the answers received when questioning Year 9 pupils, Chambers (1993: 15) distilled the following messages from the learners:

1. We do take notice of the learning environment. The foreign language room should be special and immediately recognisable by its realia and posters.

2. We are conscious of the problems caused by class-size. We don't like big groups either.

3. We haven't a preference when it comes to teacher-centred or pupil-centred approach. Variety is the spice of life.

4. We are less likely to give you a hard time if you make your instructions clear, start from a basis of what we know and progress at an appropriate pace.

5. Some of us like practising speaking most of all. Some of us dread speaking because we find it embarrassing. Please bear this in mind.

6. Please prepare your listening tasks very carefully. It is soul destroying to decipher a muffled, crackly recording on a little, clapped-out cassette-recorder. Try to get one with a pause button so that long, fast texts can be broken up a bit.

7. Reading – we don't do a lot of that. It just might be nice, for a bit of a change. Some of us read aloud around the class. It's murder having to listen to our pals reading! It wouldn't be so bad if we understood the text!

8. Writing – sometimes this is a nice change from speaking and listening, especially if we are writing to our penpals. We all look forward to getting the replies. Just copying with no purpose that we can see, is no fun at all.

9. Not all of us find learning a foreign language easy. We don't like being shouted at. We don't like being ignored, just because we are not very good. Some of us just need a little bit of help and encouragement to boost our confidence.

10. If we do not write neatly, the teachers criticise us. But have you seen some of their worksheets?

**Reflection
Activity 9.13 The use of explicit objectives**

- Examine the coursebook used by your placement school for one particular year group from the point of view of whether and how unit objectives are made explicit. Also, observe how the mfl teachers, whose lessons you observe, communicate lesson objectives.
- Devise an end-of-unit goal for a specific unit of work. Engage pupils in a discussion about what is required to achieve this goal. Make a note of the pupils' comments and then translate these into meaningful learning objectives. This will allow you to measure the value of each planned learning activity by relating it to the agreed objectives.

To make lesson objectives explicit and occasionally even to negotiate them with pupils can be motivating. Making objectives explicit is widely considered to be good practice as it enables the learners to set targets. Many coursebooks feature unit objectives in the form of a preamble or as a 'can-do' self-check list. The differentiation of objectives and the avoidance of unrealistic objectives are particularly important when working with pupils with motivational difficulties. This is effectively demonstrated by Michèle Deane's diagram (see Figure 9.1), which illustrates that to have unrealistic objectives can lead to a 'downward spiral'.

Some teaching strategies

Below are some additional teaching strategies, which – as the ones already introduced earlier in this chapter – apply to mfl teaching generally but might prove to be particularly useful in the context of working with learners with motivational difficulties:

Target setting

One of the challenges faced by mfl teachers in secondary schools is the fact that the (externally) accredited assessment of pupils' proficiency tends to take place in the main, particularly in non-modular specifications, only at the very end of pupils' period of mfl study. Only a limited amount of coursework is permitted. Because many learners find it difficult to derive motivation from this long-term objective, the content required by the examination specification needs to be broken down into achievable steps and pupils'

Figure 9.1 Michèle Deane's downward spiral
Source: (Deane 1992: 44)

progress monitored through continuous/formative assessment. This way pupils can aim at achieving short-term targets.

Personalised language and purposeful activities

In her book on working with reluctant learners, Jenifer Alison points out the importance of ensuring that the language pupils are exposed to is *'their own language* and that they see a *valid purpose* in learning it' (Alison 1995: 20) This is a notion frequently echoed by mfl teachers. For the presentation stage Alison identifies the strategies of letting pupils find out for themselves what they need to learn and to give them opportunities to show what they already know whilst for the practice stage she lists strategies/activities involving speculation, remembering, timing, guessing, the manipulation of objects, competition and the inclusion of pupils' ideas in the lesson.

Emphasis on enjoyment and creativity

Peter Shaw makes a similar suggestion in an account of his experience with reluctant learners suggesting that pupils should be involved in the production of language where the emphasis is on enjoyment and creativity. He describes a task that is based on the use of stimulus material from authentic sources, for instance pictures, short texts or adverts from newspapers or magazines, in English or the TL, as a basis for language production. Pupils are allowed to mix the TL with English. As examples of pupils' work Shaw quotes, for instance: *'uno, dos, tres* – I know Shaw's address', 'A man in a dress? Is he *inglés?'* or 'Monumental cities: Vivo *en* Birkenhead' (Shaw 1994: 39).

The pacing of lessons and the use of a variety of tasks and material

The pacing of lessons and the use of a variety of tasks and material, which is an important consideration in planning mfl lessons in general, can be seen to be particularly important for pupils with motivational difficulties.

Susan Halliwell suggests that there needs to be a balance of 'peace and quiet' as well as 'stimulation and excitement'. In support of this she proposes an important concept for the planning of interactive mfl lessons, namely the balance of 'settling' and 'stirring' activities (see Halliwell 1991: 25–6). Mfl teachers, she argues, should and do carefully consider whether an activity is 'stirring' – such as oral work, competitions or games – increasing pupils' engagement or whether it is 'settling' – such as copying, labelling or listening – helping to calm pupils and, as a consequence, lessons down (see Halliwell 1991: 3–4).

Variety in the use of teaching strategies, whole-class work, group work, pair work, independent study, as well as the use of a range of teaching aids such as the tape recorder, listening stations, the overhead projector, the concept keyboard, language games and software or CD-ROM packages/the internet can help to motivate pupils.

Use of competition

Often, the introduction of a competitive element, which focuses on pooling the strengths of individual pupils in a team or allows pupils to compete against their previous performance or their own targets – rather than on identifying their individual weaknesses for the benefit of a small number of 'winners' for whom the competition serves as motivation – also work well.

The use of vocational contexts

Vocational settings can provide useful contexts for mfl learning. Combining work-related activities with language learning can provide useful contexts for mfl work and can have a beneficial motivational impact. Pupils working through scenarios taken from the world of work, such as those suggested in the context of the GNVQ Language Units at Key Stage 4, are considered to be of motivational value because they are perceived to be relevant to pupils:

> … teaching might be based on simulated work experience as assistant to a conference organiser in a hotel which caters for multilingual training conferences. Students could undertake activities such as: responding to initial enquiries by telephone, fax, e-mail or letter; preparing a plan of the hotel and its conference facilities; making up a written, audio or video guide to local amenities and to places or events of local interest.
>
> (RSA 1996: 5)

For a detailed discussion of vocational contexts in mfl teaching and learning see Pachler 1997.

**Reflection
Activity 9.14 The use of teaching strategies**

With reference to table in Table 9.6, observe a number of mfl lessons focussing on what strategies mfl teachers in your placement school use in working with pupils in order to overcome some difficulties commonly experienced by them. Following your observations discuss with your mentor how you can include these and other suitable strategies in your own teaching.

WORKING WITH SUPPORT TEACHERS

An important aspect in catering for the different needs of pupils in the mfl classroom is working with support teachers. These might be (peripatetic) SEN specialists, staff specialising in English as an additional language assigned to individual or groups of

Table 9.6   Catering for individual needs of pupils

Pupil difficulty	Strategies observed	Additional strategies identified in discussion with colleagues
Short concentration span		
Poor organisational skills		
Lack of confidence		
Untidy writing		
Weak first language skills		
Isolation from other pupils		
Weak spelling		
Physical/sensory impairments		
Bad memory skills		
Lack of interest		
Poor general knowledge and cultural awareness		

pupils or colleagues from within the mfl department providing support with specific groups.

Working in tandem with other adults in the classroom is not always easy for many mfl teachers as it raises a number of important issues such as who is responsible for what aspect of the lesson. Of particular relevance for mfl contexts is the question of what mfl skills a support teacher has. In order to maximise the impact of 'another pair of hands' in the classroom on pupil learning, careful planning of lessons by the mfl specialist together with the support teacher is essential.

As support teachers work very closely with particular pupils they tend to be intimately familiar with pupils' needs. This expertise can be invaluable, for example, when designing worksheets and other teaching material. Support teachers are often willing to act as a 'model learner' to demonstrate role plays, pair work, games and puzzles. Organising 'carousel' lessons and group work can become easier with help from a support teacher, who can supervise a particularly demanding activity and/or circulate around the classroom.

**Reflection
Activity 9.15 Working with
support teachers I**

During your work at the placement school, enquire about the nature of support mfl teachers receive by talking to mfl staff as well as some support teachers. What do they consider to be best practice in collaborative work?

Reflection Activity 9.16 Working with support teachers II

When working with a support teacher, where possible:

- design a list of key TL phrases. This will allow the support teacher to help pupils with their productive mfl skills if she is not an mfl specialist;
- discuss the presentation of material in advance of lessons and adapt existing worksheets. What are the key features and underpinning principles of the changes?
- consider which support activities the support teacher could use with pupils when a given activity designed for the whole class proves too difficult. A set of very basic activities on numbers, days, dates, personal details, gender rules and other core linguistic items can support her work on the reinforcement of pupils' key linguistic skills.

Reflection Activity 9.17 Planning a lesson taught with a support teacher

Refer to the sample lesson plan in Chapter 4, Table 4.2. Modify this lesson plan by building in the use of a support teacher.

SUMMARY

It is very important to recognise that pupils are individuals with different needs – for instance, due to their ability, gender, interests, motivation, social class, self-concept, self-esteem, ethnic background or creativity – and that, therefore, no teaching group is homogenous.

A big challenge for the mfl trainee teacher is to identify individual differences and needs in pupils and to devise strategies to cater for the needs of all pupils in a class.

10 Assessment, Marking, Recording and Reporting

Assessment is a central aspect of modern foreign languages (mfl) teaching and learning in the secondary school. It plays a prominent role in the statutory framework and it has been subject to a lively educational and public debate in recent years.

In this chapter we:

- discuss general principles and purposes of assessment;
- outline the assessment process;
- discuss the main types of mfl assessment in the secondary school; and
- give examples of mfl assessment activities, tasks and exercises.

Our discussion of assessment of mfl needs to be seen in the wider context of a 'paradigm shift' over recent years, of a change in pattern

> from psychometrics to a broader model of educational assessment, from a testing and examination culture to an assessment culture. There is a wider range of assessment in use now than there was twenty-five years ago: teacher assessment, standard tasks, coursework, records of achievement as well as practical and oral assessment, written examinations and standardized tests. There is criterion-referenced assessment, formative assessment and performance-based assessment, as well as norm-referenced testing. In addition, assessment has taken on a high profile and is required to achieve a wide range of purposes: it has to support teaching and learning, provide information about pupils, teachers and schools, act as a selection and certificating device, as an accountability procedure, and drive curriculum and teaching.
>
> (Gipps 1994: 1)

Whilst we contextualise our discussion in this chapter by way of the statutory requirements for England, i.e. the National Curriculum (NC) and the GCSE criteria published by the DfEE/QCA, much of what is said about assessment issues is generic and, therefore, equally relevant to readers working in Wales, Scotland, Northern Ireland and beyond.

OBJECTIVES

By the end of this chapter you should:

- understand the key principles and some important purposes of assessing mfl learners;
- be familiar with key assessment terminology;
- understand the various stages of the assessment process;
- be aware of important issues of and a range of activities for mfl assessment; and
- have an appreciation of internal and external assessment, including teacher assessment, pupil peer- or self-assessment and the GCSE examination.

DEFINITION OF TERMS

By way of an introduction to the theory and practice of mfl assessment, Table 10.1 provides a glossary defining and explaining some important terminology.

PRINCIPLES, PURPOSES AND THE PROCESS OF ASSESSMENT

The assessment process requires mfl trainees to ask themselves three important questions: why, what and how to assess.

The purposes of assessment, i.e. the reasons why to assess, are manifold. For instance, assessment is a tool:

- to generate information for pupils about their learning;
- to ensure that learning objectives have been reached;
- to motivate pupils;
- to gather data for reporting what pupils know, understand and/or can do;
- to select pupils (e.g. for groupings in school or for opportunities in later life);
- to identify strengths and weaknesses in pupils;
- to provide certification;
- to fulfil statutory requirements; or
- to measure standards and hold teachers accountable.

This list of reasons why to assess pupils clearly shows that assessment is inextricably linked to teaching and learning. Assessment opportunities need to reflect learning objectives, which in turn reflect the statutory framework and examination specifications (formerly syllabuses) and not be a 'bolt-on'. The answer to the question what to assess is, therefore, to be found in lesson, unit of work and scheme-of-work plans. Planning needs to take place with assessment in mind.

When considering how to assess mfl learning, a number of general principles can be identified assessment should:

Table 10.1 Glossary of mfl assessment terminology

Term	Definition
achievement	progress made by pupils in relation to past performance
attainment	progress made by pupils in relation to the statutory framework
criterion-referencing	the relating of a pupil's progress to clearly defined performance indicators
diagnostic	assessment opportunities aimed at identifying weaknesses and providing pointers for future work
external assessment	assessment opportunities designed by outside agencies such as Awarding Bodies; the standardised GCSE
fitness for purpose	the extent to which an assessment opportunity reflects the reasons for carrying out the assessment
formative/continuous assessment	assessment opportunities, which are ongoing and an integral part of teaching
internal assessment	assessment opportunities carried out by the teacher (teacher assessment) or pupils (self- and/or peer-assessment); designed by the teacher or course book writers
norm-referencing	The relating of a pupil's progress to that of other pupils
proficiency	level of linguistic skill and knowledge in relation to external criteria
reliability	the accuracy with which an assessment opportunity measures progress, attainment, achievement, proficiency etc.
standardised assessment	assessment opportunities devised by outside agencies, such as Awarding Bodies or the National Foundation for Educational Research (NFER)
summative assessment	assessment opportunities coming at the end of a unit of work, term, year or course
validity	the extent to which an assessment opportunity measures what has been taught and what pupils should have learnt

- be an integral part of teaching and learning and follow from curricular objectives;
- inform future teaching and learning;
- provide useful information about the progress, achievement and attainment of pupils to relevant parties;
- involve the learner in the process;
- come at regular intervals to provide a critical mass of data to validate judgements and to motivate the learner;
- consist of a variety of methods to make data more reliable; and
- be manageable.

Mfl trainees need to plan the assessment of pupils' learning on the basis of the principles identified above as well as in recognition of its purposes. Table 10.2 offers a summary of what assessment of pupils' learning means in the context of mfl trainees' work in schools.

Reflection
Activity 10.1 Personal assessment experience

- Think about a number of different ways in which your mfl learning has been assessed in the past. What were the purpose and the nature of the assessments?
- Then, consider if the assessments were fit for purpose. List the strengths and weaknesses of the various assessments you undertook.

Table 10.2   Nine stages of the assessment process

No.	Stage
1	Decide on what learning objectives are to be assessed, *e.g. for pupils to show that they are able to order a meal in a restaurant or for pupils to have an understanding of how to formulate and when to use the imperfect tense.*
2	Decide on the type of assessment, *e.g. whether to use continuous or summative teacher assessment or pupil self- or peer assessment.*
3	Define the criteria to be used in relation to the planned learning outcomes/ objectives.
4	Select tasks from the teaching material suitable for assessment purposes and/or design tasks reflecting the types of teaching material used.
5	Collect evidence, *i.e. carry out the assessment.*
6	Pass judgement, *i.e. mark pupils' work.*
7	Record the data, *e.g. note results in the mark book.*
8	Report the data, *i.e. feed back the results to relevant parties as verbal comments (in writing or orally), grades, percentages, levels etc.*
9	Review and evaluate the assessment process and outcomes: *was the assessment valid and reliable? What diagnostic information did it yield to inform future teaching and learning? What, if anything, needs to be re-taught or re-explained on the basis of the evidence gathered? Might a different approach yield better results?*

ASSESSMENT TASKS

In covering the statutory requirements pupils need to be given opportunities to experience a range of learning opportunities. The choice of assessment tasks needs to reflect this variety. Therefore, the mfl trainee needs to use different types of assessment activities, which accurately measure what has been taught and should have been learnt (validity) and which can easily be replicated and are dependable, i.e. yield similar results if carried out at a different time or by a different teacher (reliability). Assessment tasks should be chosen on the basis of their usefulness as learning tasks. Activities, which allow pupils to show what they *can* do, understand and/or know rather than focus on their weaknesses, are potentially motivating. There are many different learning activities, which can yield useful evidence, be it oral, written, graphic or even product-based. Examples of useful evidence are: role plays, simulations, questioning, interviews, poems, descriptions, short written answers to questions, notes, printouts, games or flyers/leaflets.

The inception of assessment and testing in the target language (TL) was accompanied by a redefinition of types of activities to be used for external, standardised assessment. These activities increasingly appear to be chosen with a view to accommodating assessment and testing in the TL and do not necessarily cover the full range of tasks traditionally used by mfl teachers and coursebook writers:

> Our feeling is that it is far better to restrict the range of test-types used in public examinations. The degree of task complexity should not be such that requires extensive scene setting or detailed instructions.
>
> (Powell et al. 1996: 17)

In order to prepare pupils well for external examinations, this change in pattern needs to be given consideration by mfl trainees. Throughout their teaching at Key Stages 3 and 4 they need to use types of tasks that will prepare pupils for what external examinations require. For example, mfl trainees will have to ensure that the rubrics and visual clues/symbols they use for/to support TL instructions and scene setting on their worksheets and continuous assessment tasks, coincide with those included in the examination papers. For listening and reading activities the GCSE criteria published in 2000 (see QCA 2000: 3) require responses to be in the TL, except where the use of another language is a necessary part of the task. A maximum of 10 per cent of the total marks for a subject may be awarded for answers in English (Welsh or Irish). This allows for the inclusion of interpretation exercises, although no more than half of this allocation may be assigned to any particular assessment objective, i.e. skill.

In Tables 10.3 to 10.5 a range of assessment activities, which do not involve the use of English, are discussed and evaluated in terms of their advantages and disadvantages as well as the resulting implications for mfl trainees. The categories of 'features' and 'implications for teachers' overlap to some extent. We feel, nevertheless, that this distinction makes the description of some features of assessment tasks more transparent. This description of types of activities is intended to familiarise mfl trainees with commonly used types of activities. It is also intended to guide their choice of assessment activities and to clarify, which type lends itself best to which aspect of mfl learning.

The description of these activities is guided by the work of Neather et al. 1995, and Powell et al. 1996 on TL testing. Neither the lists of tasks nor their descriptions purport to be exhaustive. This typology aims to serve as a starting point for designing formative and/or summative teacher assessment opportunities.

GENERAL TYPES OF MFL ASSESSMENT USED IN SECONDARY SCHOOLS

This section discusses three general types of internal and external assessment associated with mfl teaching and learning in secondary school:

- teacher assessment (continuous and/or summative);
- pupil self- and/or peer assessment; and
- national tests and/or tasks.

We have already noted that mfl assessment needs to be related to the specific statutory requirements as well as to the learning objectives of units of work and particular lessons.

Table 10.3   Receptive language skills: listening and reading

No.	Activity	Features	Implications for teachers
1	multiple choice, e.g. true/false, ticking correct answers	a carefully designed test focussing on specific aspects can distinguish between pupils who understand, know and/or can do and those who cannot/do not; analysis of results can identify areas of weakness; the system does not allow for an understanding of why pupils fail; reliability is high but validity is low; there is the danger of pupils guessing	in order to allow for remedial action, analysis needs to take place on an individual basis
2	gap filling	there is a danger that pupils know/understand what is required but are unable to show it due to deficiencies in productive language skills; the method is easily manageable and marking allows for simple indication of right or wrong	the activity lends itself well to end-of-unit tests; the integrative nature of the task makes it difficult to identify and act upon problems
3	labelling in the TL	easy to administer but little more than a vocabulary test; content rather than application of knowledge is tested	the teacher needs to select appropriate moments to use such tests; use early in a unit of work allows shortages in knowledge to be addressed
4	selecting the correct answer from a range	allows pupils to demonstrate their receptive skills (listening, reading) without having to rely on their productive ones (speaking, writing); allows for guessing	there is a need to analyse results to identify the reasons for the answers given; teachers should ensure that pupils, apart from demonstrating the final outcome, are able to reason the process so that purposeful feedback can be given
5	matching language to symbols/images	the method is reliable if all the symbols are recognisable; it is manageable but does allow for guessing; it provides little useful information for future teaching	the activity is mainly suited to end-of-unit tests; marking, on the basis of the identification of right and wrong, is simple; self- and peer-marking can be used
6	note taking	integrative nature; careful categorisation is required in order to identify pupils' strengths and weaknesses	grading needs be based on broad and comprehensive indicators in order to take full account of the evidence generated
7	recognising false statements relating to a passage	the understanding of gist can be identified through simply marking right/wrong; there is a risk of alternative interpretations of the text by pupils	pupils can mark their contributions themselves although a detailed teacher-led feedback session can be useful
8	answering comprehension questions in the TL	pupils must be aware of the need to answer in the TL; it needs to be clear whether comprehension or the ability to respond accurately in the TL is being assessed	the teacher needs to mark the work herself to ensure consistency; qualitative feedback (written comments), as opposed to grades, should reward accurate expression
9	sequencing and re-assembling texts	the reasons for pupils' choices should be more important than the final product; the process is not reliable, but it is valid and manageable	opportunities to discuss the process should be provided rather than simply grades awarded; feedback could be given through peer discussion
10	summaries	pupils' development can be monitored if the focus is on the process; the risk is that productive skills are assessed instead of comprehension; validity is high, despite the low level of reliability	pupils' plans, application and knowledge should be assessed separately and qualitative comments be attached to any grades; grades should be allocated to the different skills displayed

Table 10.4 Productive language skills: speaking

No.	Activity	Features	Implications for teachers
1	whole class question and answer	pupils may lack the confidence to contribute despite being able to do so; the general tone and enthusiasm of the class are subjective indicators for achievement	the teacher needs to structure and target questions carefully in order to acquire a general picture of the entire group's achievement
2	structured role play	the amount of time needed constrains manageability; assessment criteria are particularly important and the content needs to be defined; there is a need to distinguish between memory skills and the ability to build language independently	marking needs to be focussed on particular criteria; instructions must be very clear; communicative competence should be the focus
3	open-ended role play	allows pupils to produce language independently; future learning needs can be identified; it can be difficult to relate criteria to individuals' competence	as marking can be subjective, clear criteria need to be identified; one outcome could be the identification of personal objectives and targets for future development
4	information gap in pairs/groups	the ability to communicate the message is important; reliability is low as the reaction of the partner is unpredictable; the direct experience is authentic but lacking in objectivity	the teacher is the observer; pupil self-assessment is a feature of this activity
5	oral presentation	explicit criteria are particularly important and the content needs to be clearly defined	pupils need to be briefed in advance of the presentation; there is potential for peer assessment to support the teacher's judgements
6	oral essay responding to stimuli	pupils need to be familiar with the task type and the content; there might be tensions between the open-ended nature of the task and the invariably limited linguistic means of pupils	performance requires rehearsals; peer assessment is possible if all are aware of the criteria; grading should be based on broad indicators
7	conversation/ interview	realistic conversations require an integration of speaking and listening skills; the authenticity of such a direct assessment reduces validity and reliability	the teacher should allow pupils to lead the conversation and react to the unexpected; qualitative comments should be reflected in the grades awarded

Teacher assessment

Teachers' professional judgement is essential in the assessment process. Assessment and testing need to arise naturally out of the teaching context. In the course of initial teacher education (ITE) the mfl trainee needs to learn to make valid and reliable judgements about pupils' progress in terms of the statutory requirements and/or the examination specifications as well as in relation to lesson and unit of work objectives. Mfl teachers in England are currently required to report on pupils' attainment in terms of NC levels across the four skills of listening, speaking, reading and writing. Familiarity with the mfl department's and placement school's assessment policies is another prerequisite for developing competence in assessing pupils' achievement and attainment. A typical departmental policy on assessment might cover, for instance:

Table 10.5 Productive language skills: writing

No.	Activity	Features	Implications for teachers
1	labelling, listing and vocabulary tests	these 'low level' activities reflect knowledge of the TL but demonstrate no application skills	useful as interim assessments; self-assessment is possible
2	writing messages	the ability to communicate the message is important; tasks can be differentiated	the teacher needs to reward successful communication; over-correction can be inhibiting
3	repetitive drill exercises	tasks are not authentic but have diagnostic value	such exercises serve as useful interim assessments; their content should not be divorced from the communicative context
4	essays and free expression	the integrative nature of the task means that poor knowledge can hide an ability to write and vice versa; successful application of process skills can be shown through clarity of expression; essay writing is not authentic but pupils tend to consider it to be a valid assessment task	the teacher should separate grades for knowledge and process skills

Reflection
Activity 10.2 Analysing end-of-unit assessment tasks

Choose a unit of work devised by the mfl department at your placement school.
- Make a list of the types of activities featured in the unit of work. Compare this list with the types of activities of the unit assessment. What other types of activities listed in Tables 10.3 to 10.5 could be used?
- List the purposes, strengths and weaknesses of the individual assessment tasks.
- With reference to Table 10.2, consider how similar or different these assessment activities are to the way in which your own mfl work has been assessed in the past?
- Discuss the findings with your mentor or a class teacher with whom you work closely. Also, discuss the reasons for using particular assessment tasks for particular purposes.

- agreement trialling, that is marking and grading pupils' work and matching it to the statutory framework and/or grade descriptions as a team;
- the nature of a departmental portfolio including samples of levelled and annotated pupils' work (pieces of pupils' work, which are cross-referenced to the statutory requirements and have teacher comments attached explaining, for instance, how the work was completed) in order to reach a shared understanding and interpretation of the statutory requirements;
- the overt use of assessment criteria clearly linked to teaching and learning objectives;

**Reflection
Activity 10.3 Identifying
assessment criteria**

> The activities in Tables 10.3 to 10.5 are presented outside the context of
> the unit of work they would have been designed for.
>   Hypothesise about the learning objectives, which might be associated
> with these activities, and draw up a list of criteria against which pupils
> could be assessed when carrying out work related to these activities.

- a mixture of both continuous and summative assessment activities covering all four Attainment Targets (ATs) across a range of different contexts/topics including a range of different task types;
- the use of effective, multi-skill language activities for assessment;
- the use of the TL for instructions and feedback on assessment tasks;
- the systems to be used for marking/grading pupils' work; and
- the use of dictionaries.

In order to help mfl teachers make secure judgements about pupils' attainment in terms of NC level descriptions, SCAA/ACCAC (1996) published a useful booklet entitled *Consistency in teacher assessment: exemplification of standards. Modern foreign languages: Key Stage 3*. The examples in the booklet are related to the 1995 NC Orders but at the time of writing the Qualifications and Curriculum Authority (QCA), the successor of SCAA, is planning to bring the exemplification of standards in line with the NC document published additional on the internet. The booklet remains a very useful resource for agreement trialling for mfl trainees. Departments and individual teachers must make accurate assessments of pupils' level of performance. At Key Stage 3 in England the levels of performance are specified by the level descriptions of the NC. Collective judgements through a process of agreement trialling and levelling as a team help to ensure greater accuracy and objectivity.

As could be seen, mfl trainees can reach their judgement on pupils' level of attainment/ achievement through continuous/formative assessment, using normal teaching activities to yield assessment evidence, or through specifically designed summative assessment, for instance end of unit tests.

Below are some examples of assessment activities, which could – depending on the professional judgement of the mfl teacher – be part of continuous or summative teacher assessment, i.e. assessed in the course of teaching or as part of an end-of-unit test. They are: a German reading comprehension activity in Figure 10.1 and a French writing activity in Figure 10.2. Figure 10.3 shows a multi-skill continuous assessment task covering the topic of personal information. This activity, which exemplifies how certain assessment tasks could be cross-referenced to the statutory framework in terms of coverage of the PoS and ATs, is suitable for pupils about to complete their first term of study of a modern foreign language.

The purpose of these activities can be to diagnose pupils' learning needs, to describe their progress and motivate them or to measure learning outcomes.

F: Guten Tag, Wie Heißt du ?

K: Ich bin's, der Felix! Du kennst mich doch schon!

F: Ja, aber wir machen ein Interview. Also, bitte, beantwrote die Fragen!

K: Sinf die Fragen einfach?

F: Ja, ja, die Fragen sind sehr einfach.

K: Na gut, los!

F: Also, erste Frage: Wie heißt du?

K: Ich heiße Felix Kaninchen.

F: Und wie alt bist du?

K: Ich bin sieben Jahre alt.

F: Wann hast du Geburtstag?

K: Mein Geburtstag ist am dritten Oktober.

F: Wo wohnst du?

K: Ich wohne in einer kleinen Wohnung in einem großen Bau in einem Garten nebem dem
        Rhein in Bonn. Und wo wohnst du?

F: Nein, nein, ich stelle die Fragen!

K: Warum?

F: Dummkopf! Ich bin der Interviewer!

K: Oh! und was bin ich?

F: Du bist ein Kaninchen.

K: Oh ja, das stimmt! Sind wir mit dem Interview fertig?

F: Nein, wir sind noch nicht fertig. Setz' dich!

K: Oh, es tut mir leid, Fritz.

F: Also, hast du Geschwister?

K: Ja, ich habe zwei Schwestern und drei Brüder.

F: Hast du Haustiere?

K: Ja, ich habe fünf Spinnen, elf Mäuse und einen Tausendfüßler!

F: Und was sind deine Hobbys?

K: Ich mag Karotten fressen!

F: Vielen Dank, Felix. Auf Wiedersehen.

K: Sind wir jetzt fertig?

F: Ja, ja, das ist alles.

K: Prima! Tschüß dann!

Figure 10.1 *Ein Interview*

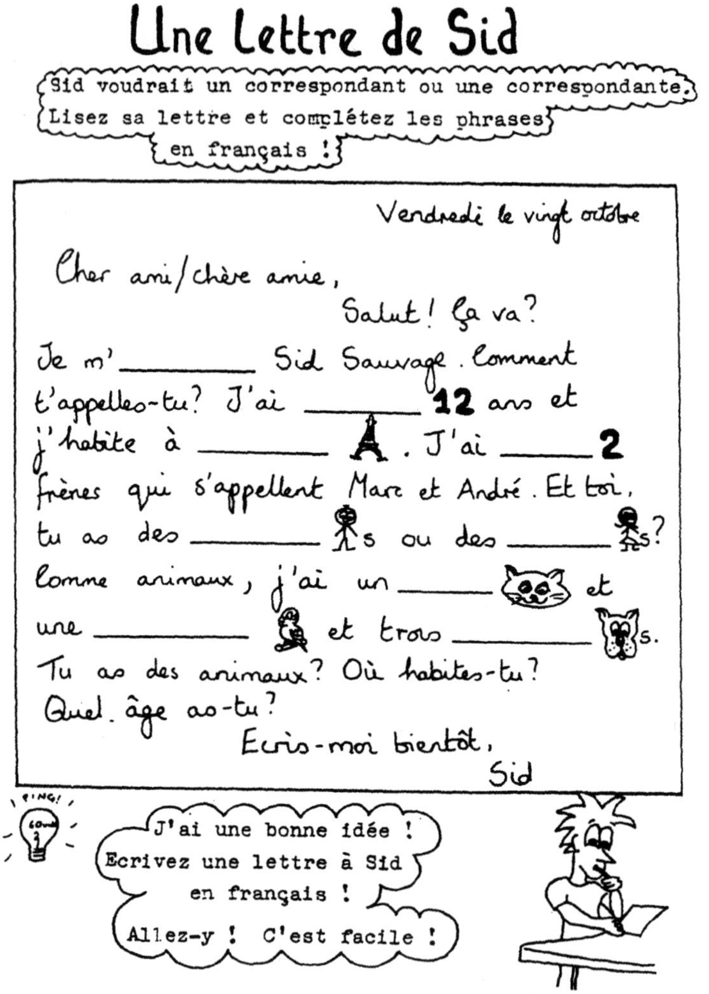

Une Lettre de Sid

Sid voudrait un correspondant ou une correspondante.
Lisez sa lettre et complétez les phrases
en français !

Vendredi le vingt octobre

Cher ami/chère amie,
                    Salut ! Ça va?
Je m'_____ Sid Sauvage. Comment
t'appelles-tu? J'ai _____ **12** ans et
j'habite à _____ **A**. J'ai _____**2**
frères qui s'appellent Marc et André. Et toi,
tu as des _____s ou des _____s?
Comme animaux, j'ai un _____ et
une _____ et trois _____s.
Tu as des animaux? Où habites-tu?
Quel âge as-tu?
            Ecris-moi bientôt,
                        Sid

J'ai une bonne idée !
Ecrivez une lettre à Sid
en français !

Allez-y ! C'est facile !

Figure 10.2 *Une lettre de Sid*

Increasingly, teacher assessment is linked to **target setting** with pupil performance targets being seen as a yardstick against which to measure pupil progress. Since September 1998 schools are required to set challenging targets for improved pupil performance in relation to NC assessments and public examinations. In order to be successful, targets need to be SMART: specific, measurable, achievable, realistic and time-related. For details on target setting, see the Pupil Performance Area on the DfEE Standards Site at *http://www.standards.dfee.gov.uk/performance/*.

Marking, recording and reporting

An integral part of teacher assessment is the marking and correction of errors in pupils' oral language production and written work, such as homework, exercise books or course-

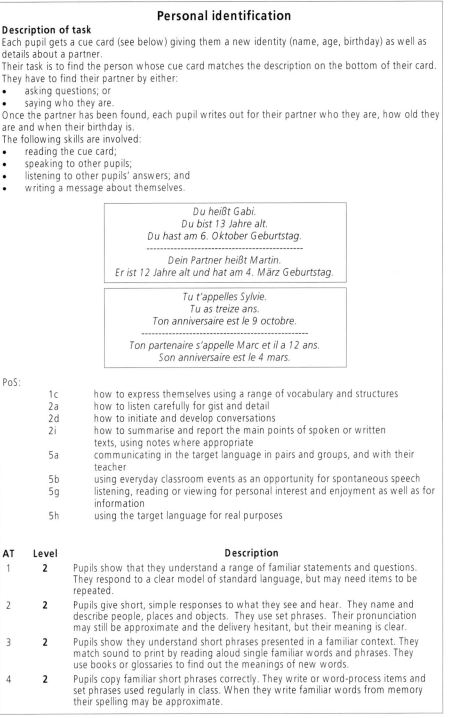

Personal identification

Description of task

Each pupil gets a cue card (see below) giving them a new identity (name, age, birthday) as well as details about a partner.

Their task is to find the person whose cue card matches the description on the bottom of their card. They have to find their partner by either:

- asking questions; or
- saying who they are.

Once the partner has been found, each pupil writes out for their partner who they are, how old they are and when their birthday is.

The following skills are involved:

- reading the cue card;
- speaking to other pupils;
- listening to other pupils' answers; and
- writing a message about themselves.

> *Du heißt Gabi.*
> *Du bist 13 Jahre alt.*
> *Du hast am 6. Oktober Geburtstag.*
> --
> *Dein Partner heißt Martin.*
> *Er ist 12 Jahre alt und hat am 4. März Geburtstag.*

> *Tu t'appelles Sylvie.*
> *Tu as treize ans.*
> *Ton anniversaire est le 9 octobre.*
> --
> *Ton partenaire s'appelle Marc et il a 12 ans.*
> *Son anniversaire est le 4 mars.*

PoS:

1c	how to express themselves using a range of vocabulary and structures
2a	how to listen carefully for gist and detail
2d	how to initiate and develop conversations
2i	how to summarise and report the main points of spoken or written texts, using notes where appropriate
5a	communicating in the target language in pairs and groups, and with their teacher
5b	using everyday classroom events as an opportunity for spontaneous speech
5g	listening, reading or viewing for personal interest and enjoyment as well as for information
5h	using the target language for real purposes

AT	Level	Description
1	2	Pupils show that they understand a range of familiar statements and questions. They respond to a clear model of standard language, but may need items to be repeated.
2	2	Pupils give short, simple responses to what they see and hear. They name and describe people, places and objects. They use set phrases. Their pronunciation may still be approximate and the delivery hesitant, but their meaning is clear.
3	2	Pupils show they understand short phrases presented in a familiar context. They match sound to print by reading aloud single familiar words and phrases. They use books or glossaries to find out the meanings of new words.
4	2	Pupils copy familiar short phrases correctly. They write or word-process items and set phrases used regularly in class. When they write familiar words from memory their spelling may be approximate.

Figure 10.3 Personal identification
Source: Adapted from Pachler 1994: 37–9

Reflection
Activity 10.4 Agreement trialling

- Listen to various examples of recordings of pupils' oral language production and look at some examples of pupils' written work. Try to match the pupils' work to the statutory framework or other relevant assessment criteria. For instance, what statements of the Programme of Study (PoS) or levels do the pieces of work cover?
- Where possible, study the mfl department's portfolio of pupils' work. In addition, look at the samples of pupils' work featured in the SCAA/ ACAC exemplification booklet. Do you agree with the judgements about levels and/or learning opportunities made (bearing in mind they refer to the 1995 NC document)?

Reflection
Activity 10.5 Devising summative teacher assessment

- Devise an end-of-unit test for a class you are currently teaching. Clearly relate it to the unit objectives, base it on the principle of TL use, cover all four skill areas and match individual tasks to the statutory framework.
- Discuss your test with your mentor or the relevant class teacher and ask if you can administer the test to pupils. Then, mark the scripts. Note any queries, problems, insecurities, observations etc. you have as a basis for a follow-up discussion with your mentor or the class teacher.
- Also, interview a couple of pupils immediately after they have taken the test. Ask them if they feel that the test allowed them to demonstrate what they think they *can do*, *understand* and *know*. Find out what they *liked* and *disliked* about the unit and the end-of-unit test.

work. Marking and error correction are means of providing diagnostic feedback to learners about their progress, achievement, attainment and/or performance.

For mfl trainees the departmental handbook is a useful point of reference as it usually features a policy statement on marking. Marking policies should be in line with the overall school policy ensuring consistency across members of a department but also across school subjects for the benefit of the various 'audiences' of assessment such as pupils, parents, inspectors and the wider public. The departmental policy on marking might, for instance, give guidance on how criteria for assessment or the terminology of the statutory framework can be made available in a language that is readily understood by pupils. It might include guidance on when and how to use grades, ticks and/or verbal comments. There might be reference to the use of the TL, that is when to use the TL and when to comment in English. If the departmental policy contains a list of phrases or a bank of comments in the TL to provide feedback on pupils' written work it should be used by trainees.

There is a range of different types of errors such as (see Beaton 1990: 42–4):

- *grammatical errors*, for instance in the formation and structure of words (morpho-logical), in the meaning of words (semantic), in the building of sentences (syntactic) or in spelling (orthographic) and punctuation;
- *failures in 'sociolinguistic competence'*: the inappropriate use of language in relation to the social context, e.g. use of the informal *'du'* form in a formal situation;
- *failures in 'strategic competence'*: e.g. lack of 'repair' strategies in the case of a break-down in communication and lack of availability of alternative means of expression; or
- *errors in the instrumental function of language*: lack of success in transactional terms for a variety of reasons such as bad pronunciation.

The following three hypothetical pupil questions posed by Brian Page are very impor-tant when discussing marking and error correction. They might be addressed in the departmental documentation and mfl trainees should seek advice on departmental practices in these respects:

1. What do you mean, it's wrong?
2. What do I have to do to make it better?
3. Why should I get it right anyway?

The first question requires the teacher to define what a defective performance is and the second what action is to be taken in order to improve it. …

If communicative competence is the objective why do the adjectives have to agree anyway since, in the main, mistakes in agreement do not affect communication?

(Page 1990: i–ii)

It is important to recognise that there are no definite answers to the questions identi-fied by Page above. Answers will vary according to (see Beaton 1990: 40–1):

- *the level of the pupils*: for instance, insecurities in the formulation of the future tense will be approached differently when made by a Year 8 pupil who has just been introduced to the concept as opposed to a Year 11 pupil preparing for public examination;
- *the objectives associated with the task*: for instance, in a gap-filling exercise designed to assess how well pupils have understood the concept of difference in gender, respective mistakes are less likely to be tolerated than in a piece of creative writing; and
- *the interaction mode between teacher and pupil*: for instance, whether mistakes occur in a written or oral utterance, in whole-class or pair or group work situations.

The mfl trainee needs to be clear what constitutes mistakes or unacceptable deviations from the expected norm and feed back to the pupil what can be done to remedy mistakes.

In order to help pupils learn from their mistakes and for them to build on diagnostic feedback, pupils should be encouraged to re-examine marked pieces of work and correct certain mistakes. Mfl trainees need to avoid inappropriate feedback to pupils. Pupils' work full of teacher comments in red ink or grades or symbols without explanations might prove demotivating to pupils. To avoid overcorrection, mfl trainees might focus on mistakes relating to the learning objectives in their marking. Mfl trainees should try to give constructive, measured and intelligible feedback, where possible in the TL. Some generic examples are: *'Gute Arbeit'* (Good work), *'Eine deutliche Verbesserung'* (A big improvement), *'Schreib ganze Sätze, bitte.'* (whole sentences, please), *'Komm nach der Stunde zu mir.'* (See me after the lesson), *'Das kannst du (viel) besser!'* (You can do that [much] better), or *'Unvollständige Arbeit. Bitte, mach das noch einmal.'* (Incomplete work, please do it again). To personalise marking, the pupil can be addressed directly: *'Das hast du gut gemacht, Ahmed.'* (Well done, Ahmed).

Reflection
Activity 10.6 Departmental marking policy

- Study the marking policy of the mfl department at your placement school.
- Ask your mentor or a class teacher with whom you work closely if you can have a look at a set of books/some pieces of work she has marked to help you with the implementation of the departmental policy. Some mfl departments have statement banks with relevant comments, which will help you in marking.
- Ask your mentor or the class teacher for an opportunity to mark a set of books following the recommended procedures. Make a note of any queries, problems, insecurities or observations you have. Then, discuss your queries with your mentor or the class teacher and ask for her advice.

Once assessment evidence has been generated, mfl trainees have to record it systematically with a view to reporting it to relevant parties, such as pupils or parents. At the time of writing, parents in England are entitled to one written report on their child's progress per academic year and a report in terms of NC levels per AT at the end of Key Stage 3. Some schools operate a policy that requires teachers to report in terms of levels for each academic year.

In order to be able to identify pupils' progress in terms of individual skills, many mfl teachers subdivide their mark books into sections. See Table 10.6 for an example how this might be done.

The section on the TL allows the mfl trainee to record, for example, spontaneous use of the TL in role-play situations or pupils making a particular effort in using the TL in pupil–teacher and pupil–pupil interactions. In assessing pupils' spoken language, mfl trainees offer encouragement to pupils who make contributions to lessons. To record these in the mark book might provide an incentive to some pupils. Also, to accept approximations might be a useful strategy to encourage oral TL production by pupils.

Within each skill area there are sub-divisions enabling the teacher to provide a mark or percentage in relation to certain criteria for each assessment opportunity. The criteria are normally drawn from the level descriptions and the PoS. A benchmark should also be identified, which is the number of marks or the percentage at which – in the professional judgement of the teacher – a pupil has completed a task successfully. For example,

Table 10.6 Sample mark book page

Name	TL use	Listening		Speaking		Reading		Writing		Homework	
		level/ mark incl. bench -mark	...								
Date											
1.											
2.											
...											
Nature of activity											

a pupil might need to get fifteen out of twenty to satisfy the teacher that she has reached the criteria associated with that particular task. If she tends to score below the benchmark a pupil will probably be deemed to be working towards the NC level associated with the task rather than having achieved it. If the pupil regularly scores top marks, she is likely to be working towards the next higher level. In this way, the teacher can norm-reference, i.e. compare pupils with each other, whilst using a criterion-referencing approach, i.e. relating pupils' progress against the ATs of the NC or another set of criteria.

The grading systems used to record mfl marks will vary from school to school with some departments, for instance, awarding numbers out of 10, others using a system based on letters. Whichever system is used, there should be consistency between teachers.

In addition to recording marks, many departments award effort grades as well, indicating how hard individual pupils have tried in relation to particular assessment opportunities.

**Reflection
Activity 10.7 Recording assessments in the mark book**

- Discuss with your mentor the departmental approach to recording marks in the markbook. Agree with her how you should record marks of assessments you are undertaking.
- Then, record assessments you have carried out on the basis of the guidelines given to you. Discuss your progress and any difficulties with your mentor.

Pupil self- and/or peer assessment

The importance of the involvement of pupils in the assessment process is widely recognised:

> **Reflection**
> **Activity 10.8 Writing a report**
>
> - Find out about the school's policy for report writing and ask your mentor for some specimen report proformas and sample reports. On the basis of your own records, your 'professional' opinion and the sample reports, write a report on a number of pupils of different abilities of a class you teach. Choose pupils your mentor also knows well.
> - Discuss the reports you have written with your mentor. Do they reflect what she thinks of the pupils? Did you have enough evidence to formulate objective judgements?

> Pupils need to be actively involved in their learning in order to develop the skills highlighted in the programme of study … . This will involve pupils in planning, understanding learning objectives, making action plans to achieve individual goals, organising tasks and understanding the criteria for assessment. Pupils should be made aware of how and why they are being assessed. Discussions between teachers and pupils about which pieces of work provide the best evidence … can be especially helpful.
>
> Opportunities for pupils to review their work should be built into normal classroom activities in order to check that goals are being achieved and ensure that information gained through assessment is used to set further goals and help pupils to progress.
>
> When pupils are involved in reviewing their work in this way they are more able to see and understand their progress in the subject.
>
> (SEAC 1992: 3–4)

Assessment can offer pupils an opportunity for real communication. To discuss and reflect on their own performance, even in the mother tongue, can assist pupils in clarifying concepts and can contribute to learning. Self- and peer assessment foster this process, the outcomes of which are often recorded in profiles and records of achievement. Mfl trainees need to remember, though, that in order to be successful, pupil-self assessment has to be introduced systematically in line with the departmental assessment policy.

End-of-unit profiles or 'can-do' checklists allow pupils to evaluate themselves and set targets. These are increasingly included in coursebooks as 'Lernzielkontrollen' or 'bilans'. The use of the TL by pupils and teachers needs to be given particular attention when carrying out such activities. Individual or small-group support from the foreign language assistant (FLA) is one strategy to maximise the use of the TL when working with 'can-do' checklists.

In the example in Table 10.7 the level descriptions of the NC are broadly applied to 'holidays and leisure activities'.

Pupils assess their attainment by marking the relevant boxes with a diagonal line when a task is attempted, followed by a second diagonal line forming a cross when the task is successfully completed. When the teacher has assessed the task the box can be

Table 10.7 Pupil self-assessment sheet 'Holidays and leisure activities'

Level	AT1 Listening	AT2 Speaking	AT3 Reading	AT4 Writing
5	To be able to understand when someone explains about a possible date, e.g. cinema, disco etc. ☐	To be able to respond to a suggested date, making suggestions and negotiating a meeting place and time. ☐	To be able to extract details of tourist amenities from authentic brochures. To be able to revise an itinerary from details available with a set budget and constraints. ☐	To be able to seek details from a tourist information office in preparation for a future holiday; friends recommended the area and you would like more details. ☐
6	To be able to understand details of tourist spots when described by the attendant at the tourist office. To be able to recognise recommendations as well as details of prices, times, costs etc. ☐	To be able to give an oral account of activities when on holiday abroad. To be able to ask a friend about details of his/her holiday. ☐	From a range of texts, to be able to comment upon the events related to someone's holiday. To be able to plan a holiday in a different location for particular people from details of previous holidays. ☐	To be able to complete a diary for a holiday at a given location; write postcards to friends to provide more detail of the events portrayed in the diary. ☐
7	To be able to follow and understand advertisements about holiday locations from a TV or audio broadcast. ☐	To be able to provide a critical narrative of local amenities for tourists from notes - but not from a script. ☐	To be able to understand relevant details from an official proposal for a holiday theme park planned for the locality. ☐	To be able to produce a leaflet supporting/ protesting against the proposed holiday theme park planned for the locality. ☐

coloured in. Cross-referencing learning outcomes, against the statutory framework and/or examination specification, allows pupils to become aware of what is required to improve and progress as well as of the different levels of difficulty of certain tasks and activities. Whilst evidence from such pupil self-assessment tasks serves a real purpose in that it helps to diagnose learning needs and to describe progress, it cannot be equated with formal attainment at the given level. However, this approach allows pupils to become involved in the assessment process and take responsibility for part of it. With advanced/higher ability learners this approach might even be attempted in the TL with guidance from the FLA.

The example in Figure 10.4 is intended to encourage pupils to think about the requirements of a speaking task and to discuss these with peers. It illustrates that if pupils are aware of the criteria for assessment, they can comment upon peer performance.

ROLE PLAY ASSESSMENT SHEET

1. Est-ce que chaque partenaire emploie des mots suivants? Cochez les bonnes cases.

Client(e)   **Réceptionniste**

	une chambre	
	pour une/deux personne/s	
	avec douche	
	avec salle de bain	
	une/deux/trois nuits	
	un bar	
	un restaurant	
	un parking	

2. Cochez la bonne boîte si chaque partenaire utilise ces phrases.

Client(e)	**Réceptionniste**
Bonjour	Bonjour
Je voudrais	Qu'y a-t-il pour votre service
Avez-vous	Que désirez-vous
Est-ce qu'il y a	Je regrette
Y a-t-il	Certainement
Où se trouve	Au premier/deuxième étage
Merci	Il y a
Au revoir	à + time
A quelle heure	

3. Est-ce que chaque partenaire...

Client(e)	**Réceptionniste**
answers questions without pausing?	asks questions clearly?
speaks with a good accent?	speaks with a good accent?
speaks fluently?	speaks fluently?

Figure 10.4   Role play 'assessment' sheet

Instead of placing pupils in pairs for a role play, the teacher can group them in threes. The scenario for this role play is 'at the hotel reception desk'. Pupil A plays the role of the customer. Pupil B is the receptionist. Pupil C is given the 'assessment' sheet in Figure 10.4, which is not shown to A or B. As A and B carry out the task, C completes the sheet noting if key vocabulary and structures are being used and commenting on the perceived pronunciation, fluency and independence of each speaker. After the role play has been completed, pupils discuss the outcome. A pupil may, for example, acknowledge that she has not used one particular vocabulary item, but may suggest the alternative used by her was equally effective. The completed sheet is not really as accurate a record of pupils' performance as teacher assessment. However, provided pupils are prepared for working on activities such as this they can all learn from it in terms of their productive language skills and/or about what constitutes successful communication. If not prepared adequately, there is the danger that feedback from the assessor can be negative rather than constructive.

National tests and/or tasks

At the time of writing there are no statutory tests for mfl at Key Stage 3 in England as there are for the core subjects. Instead, the School Curriculum and Assessment Authority (SCAA), the predecessor of QCA, and the Curriculum and Assessment Authority for Wales (ACCAC) published assessment tasks to be used by mfl teachers as they see fit. These are optional, are tasks rather than tests and are internally administered and marked. The accompanying teacher's notes encourage mfl departments to integrate the tasks into existing schemes of work as appropriate and to adapt them according to their needs. Provided the necessary adjustments are made to compensate for changes in the PoS and ATs in the NC published in 1999, these optional tasks will continue to provide useful guidance for mfl teachers concerning teacher assessment (see SCAA/ACCAC 1996 and 1997). Also, at the time of writing QCA is due to publish updated material on the internet.

At Key Stage 4 there is no statutory requirement for teacher assessment and, in certain circumstances, it is possible to disapply some pupils from the study, and by implication the assessment, of a modern foreign language at Key Stage 4. A range of different assessment opportunities does exist at Key Stage 4. There are:

- GCSE Full or Short Courses;
- the GCSE Short Course General National Vocational Qualifications (GNVQ) language units; and
- approved qualifications for pupils attaining below NC level 3.

Care needs to be taken that the qualifications chosen by a school at the end of Key Stage 4 are approved by the DfEE/QCA. A list of approved qualifications, which is regularly updated, is available in the form of a DfEE circular. Readers should also consult the DfEE's *Qualifications Website* available at *http://www.dfee.gov.uk/qualifications/* for qualification matters in general.

Where pupils follow a GCSE Full Course (approximately 10 per cent of curriculum time) the examination specification will specify topic areas, which must be consistent with the requirements of the NC. GCSE Short Course specifications (approximately 5 per cent of curriculum time) feature a more restricted range of topics. The GCSE Short Course, which was first introduced in September 1996 and can be completed in one or two year(s), was intended to 'allow those pupils who wish to apply their language skills in a more vocational context to gain recognised accreditation in one or more of the four skills' (SCAA 1994: iv). To allow for this, the Short Course GNVQ Language

Units were introduced, which are one accreditation route for the GCSE Short Course and meet the requirements of the NC but are at the same time, as the name suggests, linked to the GNVQ system. The Short Course has received a cautious response from commentators and schools. Whilst it potentially offers increased choice for more able pupils, who want to gain accreditation for taking an additional language without having to do a Full GCSE, it is difficult to see that less able learners can develop the required linguistic competence in a rather limited amount of curriculum time (see also Pachler 1997).

The General Certificate of Secondary Education (GCSE)

The GCSE examination is externally set and administered by so-called Awarding Bodies. Specifications must adhere to the GCSE criteria laid down by the Qualifications and Curriculum Authority (see QCA 2000a; see also *http://www.qca.org.uk*). At the time of writing, schools can choose from the following Awarding Bodies: the Assessment and Qualifications Alliance (AQA available at *http://www.aqa.org.uk/*), the Edexcel Foundation (available at *http://www.edexcel.org.uk/*) and Oxford, Cambridge and RSA Examinations (OCR available at *http://www.ocr.org.uk/*).

The distinctive features of GCSE examinations are expressed in the aims of the GCSE criteria for modern foreign languages (QCA 2000a: 1), which state that pupils must be given opportunities to:

i.   develop understanding of the spoken and written forms of the modern foreign language in a range of contexts

ii. develop the ability to communicate effectively in the modern foreign language, through both the spoken and written word, using a range of vocabulary and structures

iii. develop knowledge and understanding of the grammar of the modern foreign language, and the ability to apply it

iv. apply their knowledge and understanding in a variety of relevant contexts which reflect their previous learning and maturity

v.   develop knowledge and understanding of countries and communities where the modern foreign language is spoken

vi. develop positive attitudes to modern foreign language learning

vii. provide a suitable foundation for further study and/or practical use of the modern foreign language.

At the time of writing, the GCSE comprises separate assessment components for all four ATs. The skills of listening, speaking, reading and writing are weighted equally at 25 per cent each. There is a 'foundation' (grades G–C) and a 'higher' tier (grades A⋆– D) and pupils can be entered for either tier for each skill. This makes accurate teacher assessment at Key Stage 4 very important as, unless the teacher has reliable assessment data about a pupil, the pupil might be entered incorrectly and thus not be able to maximise her potential. In the tiering system pupils sit graded examination papers, which feature a certain overlap of activities characteristic of Grade C. In practice this means that unless a suitably able pupil is entered for the higher tiers, she will not be able to gain beyond Grade C. Conversely, if a pupil is entered for the higher tier, who is not able to complete tasks at that level of difficulty, she, too, might not be able to maximise her potential. There is, however, the proviso for her to gain Grade E, if she is able to demonstrate ability to work at that level. If not, she will be reported as 'Unclassified'.

Also, at the time of writing, continuous assessment, i.e. coursework, is permitted as a component and can count up to 30 per cent. Schemes of assessment must, however, include a terminal examination with a minimal weighting of 70 per cent in end-of-course assessment schemes and 50 per cent in staged assessment schemes.

Continuous or periodic assessment, such as coursework, has the advantage of spreading assessment over a period of time rather than grouping it all at the end. The coursework option tends to be used by many schools for the assessment of pupils' written work. Some Awarding Bodies publish useful guidance on the coursework option of their specifications and mfl trainees are advised to study those carefully. Awarding Bodies also tend to offer free training in the use of their specifications and we strongly recommend the attendance of such training for the specific GCSE specification used by the school, particularly as a newly qualified teacher (NQT) or in the first year of taking an examination class.

One important and controversial difference to the previous criteria is that the use of dictionaries is not permitted in any external assessment in the GCSE criteria published in 2000. Whilst there clearly are problems associated with incorrect use, including overuse, of dictionaries in examinations, the ban on dictionaries in examinations can be seen to be questionable as far as the development in pupils of desirable foreign language learning skills is concerned. Also, it sits ill-at-ease with requirement 3d of the PoS NC, which states that pupils should be taught 'how to use dictionaries and other reference materials appropriately and effectively' (DfEE/QCA 1999: 16).

Reflection
Activity 10.9 GCSE specifications

Ask your mentor or the relevant colleague at your placement school for a copy of the GCSE specification used and familiarise yourself with its specific requirements. What do you perceive to be the strengths and weaknesses? What implications can you discern for your work with Key Stage 4 classes?

In addition to the emphasis on grammar brought in by the 2000 GCSE criteria, there is also now an expectation that GCSE specifications should provide opportunities for developing and generating evidence for assessing the Key Skills of:

- application of number
- communication
- information technology
- improving own learning and performance
- problem solving
- working with others.

Reflection
Activity 10.10 Key skills

Re-read the GCSE specifications used at your placement school and summarise how the Key Skills requirement is met.

The GCSE is not without problems and critics. Lack of space does not allow for a detailed analysis here but a few points are, nevertheless, worth enumerating:

- Despite the 30 per cent coursework option, the GCSE is ostensibly a terminal examination, testing the outcomes of five years of study, rather than an assessment of the learning process; it thereby militates against 'assessment motivation' (see e.g. Adams 2000: 207) and places a lot of emphasis on memorisation;
- The fitness for purpose of the examination is questionable: to what extent does it test what pupils should be taught in the context of the NC? For example, how well are pupils' cultural awareness or their ability to use reference material examined?
- The examination appears to have a considerable backwash effect on teaching and learning at Key Stage 4, often leading to the PoS of the NC being relegated in favour of 'teaching to the test'. This can result in a narrow rote-learning approach and has led to considerable emphasis being placed by many departments on the teaching of examination techniques and examination practice, for example in the form of so-called mock exams. See also Barnes 1999 and the Childline factsheet entitled *Exam stress and how to beat it* available at *http:// www.childline.org.uk/factsheets/exam1.htm*;
- The policy of testing in the TL (i.e. the requirement for test questions and answers to be in the TL) together with a skills-based approach (i.e. separate papers for listening, speaking, reading and writing) raises certain questions about the reliability and validity of the examination. Also, how authentic are the tasks pupils are asked to perform, i.e. to what extent do they mirror real-life TL use? For example, to what extent are spontaneity and unpredictability of real-time language use reflected in the examination?

Pachler (2000a: 30) posits that the methodology underpinning the GCSE is characterised by:

a narrow transactional-functional orientation in which pupils are prepared for the linguistic (and non-linguistic) needs of tourists, such as making travel arrangements, going to bars, restaurants, museums, booking into hotels, buying petrol for the car etc, with the emphasis on 'getting by'. On the one hand this approach is characterised by a heavy emphasis on recall of often random lexical items and phrases derived from narrowly defined, idealised interactions and exchanges at the cost of transfer of knowledge and skills across topics. On the other hand, it tends to ignore the teenage learner's communicative needs and does not allow her to engage in meaningful and realistic interaction, both supposedly central tenets of communicative methodology.

This view is supported by research into examination performance by cognitive psychologists, who found that IQ had no impact on GCSE examination performance. Instead, general memory ability was found to account for up to 20 per cent of variance in examination results, which suggests that the GCSE relies more on memory than on understanding. According to the report,

> (for) all candidates above a basic intelligence threshold, GCSE favoured those who could reproduce memorised material rather than those who were capable of devising original solutions.
>
> (Cassidy 1999)

The report also suggests that factors such as motivation, application, study methods and home background were significant factors of GCSE performance.

At the time of writing it remains to be seen whether recent changes to the NC, such as the deletion of the Areas of Experience and of topics, as well as the GCSE criteria, such as the increased emphasis on language understanding, are sufficient to address the weaknesses identified above.

> We still appear to be operating in a environment where the link between assessment and learning is that assessment determines the curriculum – decisions of how a subject is to be tested are made before content and teaching methods are decided.
>
> (Adams 2000: 208)

SUMMARY

Assessment should be integral to mfl teaching and learning and not 'bolt-on'. It is multi-faceted and serves many purposes.

Teacher assessment, aimed at providing constructive guidance and information on the teaching and learning process, is governed by the professional judgement of the teacher based on her knowledge of specific groups of pupils.

Pupil peer and self-assessment should be used in order to allow pupils to feel ownership of and take responsibility for their learning.

Mfl teachers are required to work within the respective national statutory assessment framework. It is one of their responsibilities to prepare pupils for external assessment at the end of secondary schooling. Familiarity with the statutory requirements for internal and external assessment is, therefore, imperative.

For a very useful in-depth discussion of assessment issues see Lambert and Lines 2000.

11 Managing Resources and Learners in the Modern Foreign Language Classroom

Modern foreign languages (mfl) teachers have a whole range of material and resources at their disposal. The nature of the subject requires a variety of methods and material and a regular change of focus. The restricted range of linguistic means available to pupils to express themselves and the need to cover the language skills of listening, speaking, reading and writing equally are determinant factors. Some resources are used with great regularity, others are deployed from time to time to enhance and enrich learning experiences. This chapter covers the most commonly used resources, namely those which find application in almost every lesson.

The use of material and resources in the classroom is inevitably related to teaching and learning activities discussed in Chapter 6. Engaging pupils in a wide range of activity types demands highly developed classroom management skills. Pupils need to be guided and instructed how to use learning material effectively.

Effective classroom management cannot be separated from other aspects of teaching. Indeed, DfEE Circular 4/98, the standards for newly qualified teachers, groups classroom management with planning and teaching. There are generic issues and strategies, which are discussed in many useful publications, e.g. Neill 1993 or Watkins 1999. In this chapter we discuss this major concern of trainee teachers (first) embarking upon classroom teaching in the context of foreign languages and in relation to the use of specific resources and material.

The effective use of resources and material is an essential component of effective teaching and learning. Pupils needs to know the purpose of activities and the value of resources in relation to lesson objectives. Establishing positive attitudes to activities aids transition and makes the relevance of learning activities understood. To stimulate the use of the target language (TL) in the classroom requires careful planning and the encouragement of pupil involvement. Pupil participation depends upon pupils being interested, motivated, challenged and capable of full engagement. None of these can be taken for granted.

The mfl teacher should not be a slave to the resources available. As could be seen in Chapter 4, learning objectives in units of work and lesson plans determine the process of learning. Course and supplementary material should be selected in line with the learning objectives and the coursebook.

The development of linguistic skills and cultural awareness is best achieved through a variety of means. The writers and publishers of course material tend to be acutely aware of this notion. For many years now course material have included audio material, visual aids, worksheets and, more recently, video recordings and computer software. But it is very difficult for one single coursebook and its ancillary material to cover all aspects at the same depth and with the same quality.

The various versions of the National Curriculum (NC) stimulated the publication of many new course material. Due to the confines of this book, let alone this chapter, as well as rapid changes in this field, a detailed evaluation of available resources for different mfl is not feasible. There are, however, professional organisations and bodies such as the Centre for Information on Language Teaching and Research (CILT available at *http://www.cilt.org.uk*) and the Association for Language Learning (ALL available at *http://www.languagelearn.co.uk*), which provide useful mfl-specific publications and opportunities for teachers to acquaint themselves with specific course material.

Learners must take part in different types of activities ranging from whole class work, small-group work, pair work to individual work – all covering the skills of listening, speaking, reading and writing. This 'four-by-four' approach generates a multitude of variables, all of which the teacher must bear in mind when selecting and using resources and material. The teacher needs to plan and organise activities which maximise learning opportunities. In this way, effective lesson management can be seen as an outcome of careful planning and positive teacher/pupil relationships. It is crucial that the teacher commands respect and authority and conveys high standards.

This chapter also provides a framework enabling a personal evaluation of course material to be undertaken and indicates effective and potential uses of the range of resources and material available. Mfl teachers invariably have to select, adapt and generate material irrespective of whether or not a coursebook and its ancillary material are used. This requires a certain level of competence and confidence in the handling of resources and the recognition of the relevance and appropriateness of the material.

Trainee teachers tend to be very anxious about pupil misbehaviour. Positive attitudes to teaching and learning activities can be established through the conveyance of high standards. It would be naïve to suggest that all misbehaviour can be pre-empted, but awareness of what characterises successful lessons is a useful starting point. The Elton Report (DES 1989), amongst others, identifies the following features of successful lessons: good planning, rewards for pupil effort, variety and interest, availability of resources and alertness on the part of the teacher. Adherence to clear whole school policies and procedures and a willingness to share responsibility for the management of learners also help to foster an atmosphere of stability and security.

Nevertheless an awareness of the types of misbehaviour likely to occur assists the trainee teacher when considering pre-emptive measures. The Elton Report (DES 1989) acknowledges that most forms of misbehaviour are, in fact, minor misdemeanours. An alert teacher can plan to pre-empt, even be aware of impending opportunities for misbehaviour – too much classroom talk, excessive noise, not getting on with work set, interfering with other pupils and excessive movement. When starting their practical teaching, trainee teachers will soon realise that some resources and activity types can more easily lead to pupil misbehaviour than others. Focussed observation of lessons taught by experienced colleagues, careful planning, clear guidance and instructions, organisation and monitoring are necessary skills to ensure that learning rather than work avoidance takes place.

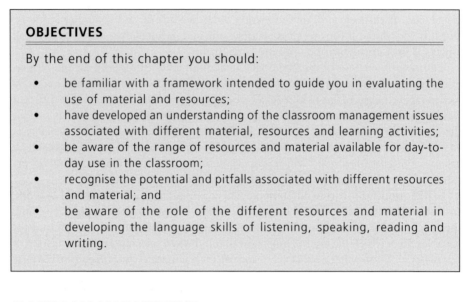

OBJECTIVES

By the end of this chapter you should:

- be familiar with a framework intended to guide you in evaluating the use of material and resources;
- have developed an understanding of the classroom management issues associated with different material, resources and learning activities;
- be aware of the range of resources and material available for day-to-day use in the classroom;
- recognise the potential and pitfalls associated with different resources and material; and
- be aware of the role of the different resources and material in developing the language skills of listening, speaking, reading and writing.

CLASSROOM MANAGEMENT

Although use of particular types of material and resources is determined to some extent by methodological considerations, teachers must ensure the effectiveness of their use. For David Nunan, communicative language teaching requires the teacher to use materials which encourage communicative language use through task-based learning (see Nunan 1989: 195). In our view good practice in mfl teaching in the secondary school is characterised by a balanced and purposeful use of and the avoidance of over-concentration on particular types of material and resources. Each of the various types of material and resources has the potential to enhance, support and structure learning. Variety can help the mfl teacher to appeal to pupils' wide range of learning styles and interests.

In order to deploy a range of material and resources to provide the variety of activities required to maintain pupils' interests, teachers do need to establish an agreed code of conduct.

Use of the TL for classroom management purposes demands careful consideration. Ted Wragg (1984: 67) lists the eleven most common rules used by teachers (see Activity 11.1) and trainees should consider how they can be operationalised in the TL.

Establishing and maintaining a code of conduct through rules, routines and procedures demands that mfl teachers draw on a wide range of presentation and communication skills. All pupils must understand the code and recognise its value as well as the need for sanctions when it is breached. At times classroom management will require the teacher to use non-verbal communication as pupils may find a TL explanation

Reflection
Activity 11.1 Types of classroom rules

To what extent are the following types of rules listed by Wragg relevant to the mfl classroom?
- no talking when the teacher is talking
- no disruptive noises
- rules for entering, leaving and moving around the classroom
- no interference in the work of others
- work must be completed in a specified way
- pupils must raise hand – not shout out
- pupils must make a positive effort in their work
- pupils must not challenge the authority of the teacher
- respect must be shown for property and equipment
- rules to do with safety
- pupils must ask if they do not understand

Consider how these classroom rules might be adapted and presented to pupils through use of the TL. This may include displays with symbols and pictures, role-plays and teacher-led presentations. How can these be reinforced through regular use? What rewards and sanctions could be linked to the code?

difficult to follow and may even feign non-comprehension as a work avoidance strategy. Trainee mfl teachers must take care to be aware of gestures and postures, which signal different messages in different cultures. Not only do teachers need to develop and use these skills, they also need to be able to read the body language of pupils to gauge levels of interest, motivation and involvement. Robertson (1989) identifies some aspects of body language which facilitate communication and contribute to the development of positive relationships.

Body orientation

The position of a teacher in relation to pupils helps to determine role definition. Whilst face-to-face on a one-to-one basis can be perceived to be confrontational, sitting side-by-side can lead to higher levels of cooperation. This is relevant for teacher–pupil (helping individuals) and pupil–pupil (e.g. pair work) interaction.

Bodily posture

Standing straight with the chin held high tends to indicate a wish to dominate (whole class work). Leaning towards someone with a warm smile can indicate encouragement (question-and-answer activities).

Head movements

Nodding is important as it signals permission to speak as well as agreement. Reticent speakers can be encouraged in this way (question-and-answer work).

Eye contact

Eye contact can be seen as a sign of mutual respect. The higher the interest level in a person/topic, the greater the amount of eye contact tends to be (whole class teaching).

Use of voice

Volume, pitch, tone, speed, expressiveness and articulation can convey messages associated with mood, e.g. anger, calm, frustration, control, interest or boredom. For mfl teachers it is essential to exaggerate features like these to accentuate the precise meaning of what is being said.

Hands and feet

Open postures (hands and feet pointing slightly outwards) convey a sense of welcome and calm. 'Inward pointing' represents insecurity.

Reflection
Activity 11.2 Giving basic instructions

Conduct a brief microteaching session on the theme of giving classroom instructions. As the teacher, mime all instructions (coats off, bags on the floor, pens out, books on the table, listen, repeat, copy etc.). Once peers have mastered the messages you are conveying, list each instruction and add the simplest form of the TL to the mimes.

Facial expressions

Exaggerated expressions, e.g. smiles, frowns, inquisitive looks, agreement and pleasure, should all be part of a mfl teacher's repertoire.

Effective lesson management should be more concerned with the promotion of good behaviour and attitudes than the use of sanctions in response to misbehaviour. Rewards, praise and encouragement must be placed in the context of the TL. Many mfl departments will have developed standardised approaches through the use of agreed phrases. For a detailed discussion of TL use see Chapter 5.

Selection and use of material and resources need to be determined by the intended learning outcomes. Effective use of certain material and resources requires particular types of activities and pupil response and the use of certain material and resources in turn affects classroom layout and seating arrangements. The characteristics of each classroom and each group, established practice, the age of pupils and the types of planned activities will affect the decisions made about room layout. The use of particular resources will require focussed individual work, the use of reference material, interaction with others through group and pair work or movement around the classroom to support communication (e.g. surveys). Trainee teachers need to carefully consider the seating arrangements which best facilitate different activity types. Trainees should experiment with different classroom layouts. However, they should not do so without consultation with and agreement of the mentor and/or the respective class teacher.

Essentially, four types of classroom layout can be distinguished.

Rows

The advantages of seating pupils in rows are that they are less able to copy from each other and disrupt through inappropriate talk. Sitting in a row assists with concentration and disruptive pupils can be isolated from others in the class. The disadvantages are that the arrangement hinders collaborative and cooperative work. Pupils are unable to see each others' faces to assist them in the communicative process. Also, the sharing of resources and material can be problematic.

The horse shoe

The teacher can stand or sit in the centre and thereby have ready access to all pupils. Pupils are able to see each other and pair work is relatively simple to organise. However, movement to the corners of the classroom can be difficult. The teacher is almost always face-to-face with pupils, even when assisting individuals during independent work.

Groups of desks

Not all pupils are facing the teacher for whole class work. Due to the proximity to each other, pupils might be tempted to interfere with each other's equipment. However, interaction between pupils is greatly facilitated for both group and pair work. Movement around the classroom can be eased by careful placement of desks.

Desks placed around the edge of the room

Many computer rooms, for example, require pupils to face the wall, which can prevent distraction by other pupils. Often this provides a large space in the middle of a room, where teachers can work with groups of pupils who require support or extension. This arrangement can also be useful for carrousel lessons. However, pupil collaboration for pupils seated around the edge of the room can be difficult, particularly where there is insufficient space between work stations or where there are no swivel chairs. Whole class explanations require pupils to move their positions.

Different teaching styles, different activities and different groups require different layouts. Teachers need to remain flexible and be prepared to adapt according to the particular demands and needs.

This discussion of classroom management is not intended to be provide hard and fast rules. It merely raises some issues which warrant consideration at the planning stage. The examination of different types of resources also contains guidance on classroom management issues specific to each resource. They are not intended to relate simply to the use of one particular resource.

THE COURSEBOOK

Potential and purpose

For many pupils the coursebook is their first point of contact with the TL and its culture(s). It can offer a form of security in that it organises the language content and conveys messages about the values, attitudes and culture(s) of TL speakers, albeit from the point of view of its writer(s). Of this the user needs to beware.

> One of the functions of coursebooks is to present the language in such a way that it is learned as effectively and quickly as possible. This implies that the coursebook writers have a view on how language is learned and how it is best taught. Although the coursebook may not seek to impose a rigid methodology on learners and teachers, nevertheless the way it organises its material and the kind of activities it promotes can have a profound influence on what happens in the classroom.
>
> (Cunningsworth 1995: 97)

Recent coursebooks tend to be structured and tailored to suit NC requirements and GCSE examination specifications (formerly syllabuses) and methodological imperatives such as the use of the TL for instructions and explanations. Many course and teacher's books cross-reference activities and tasks to the NC in order to help teachers in their planning. Frequently, use of colourful photographs is made and (quasi) authentic texts are used to provide cultural detail in an attempt to open up pupils' minds. It could be argued that coursebooks are a window to the life and culture(s) of native speakers.

Coursebooks can contain brief summaries of the content in terms of vocabulary, structures and even grammatical rules, which are linked to particular exercises. Some provide examination practice. The coursebook can help teachers in sequencing activities to bridge the gap between the known and the new and provide graded exercises allowing for steady progression and lead towards independent study. It can function as a resource for presenting new language, contain reference sections on grammar and vocabulary, stimuli for classroom activities and self-directed study as well as support for less experienced teachers (see Cunningsworth 1995: 7).

The coursebook is primarily a resource and learning tool for pupils. It is a resource that enables pupils to work independently from the teacher. This, in turn, allows teachers to work with individual pupils. When using a coursebook, the teacher needs to bear in mind common causes of misbehaviour identified by Davison (2000: 122): 'boredom; an inability to do the work a teacher has set; and effort demanded for too long a period without a break'. Trainees, therefore, need to ensure that instructions are clear and understood by all pupils. Comprehension checks are essential and they can take different forms. First, TL instructions can be translated by a pupil for the whole class. Teachers can use question-and-answer techniques to ensure comprehension. Visual displays of instructions, particularly when there is more than one exercise to be completed, and demonstrations of the activity by way of an example prior to pupils commencing are useful. Second, independent work should not be set until whole class work has enabled the practice of specific language skills and has established a confidence in pupils to undertake the task. Lastly, the teacher should set clear time limits for activities, enabling learners to pace themselves. This should, of course, be done in the TL. Such an approach helps to establish a routine as well as a secure working environment.

Davison (2000: 126) also points out that a teacher should be 'on hand to give academic help'. Once again it is crucial to establish routines: raising one's hand before talking or using reference material before asking the teacher are widely used strategies. Pupils should be made aware of the need to wait their turn, to ask courteously, where possible in the TL, and not to waste time waiting for assistance whilst the teacher attends to other pupils but to attempt another aspect of the activity in the meantime.

It would be erroneous to assume that careful plans never go wrong. In particular during pair, group and/or independent work it is difficult for the teacher to be sure that all pupils are on task and fully engaged all the time. There will sometimes be a need to reprimand some pupils. Kyriacou (1991: 92–6) advises that reprimands should be targeted correctly and that teachers should avoid expressing anger. The behaviour not the pupil should be criticised and 'quiet words' are often more helpful than whole class reprimands. Very often careful positioning by the teacher in the location of potential miscreants, stares, the use of body language and gestures can re-focus pupils without creating a hostile and confrontational atmosphere. More serious misbehaviour may require more serious action. Kyriacou (1986: 161) points out that teachers must not respond without consideration:

> What must be borne in mind is that when taking action, the teacher needs to take account of its effect on the individual pupil, its effect on the class, its relationship to school policy, and its short term and long term consequences.

During individual work teachers need to circulate to assist pupils with difficulties and also to monitor the activity. American research (see Taylor 1994: 162) indicates that quick teacher feedback and the close monitoring of individual performance increases the quality of pupils' work. While pupils are working individually using the coursebook teachers should monitor the class by looking and walking around the room. When assisting individuals it is sensible to place oneself in a way that the majority of the rest of the class can be seen. Turning one's back to the majority of the class can be an invitation to pupils to display off-task behaviour.

Kyriacou (1991: 53) calls qualities like the ones described above 'withitness' and suggests that these skills improve with experience. Activity 11.3 sets out a step-by-step approach to developing 'withitness'.

Reflection
Activity 11.3 Withitness

- Observe an experienced colleague engaging pupils in independent and individual work. Try to identify signs of misbehaviour
- Relate the signs of misbehaviour to possible causes.
- Identify strategies deployed by experienced teachers, which create the belief that they have eyes in the back of their heads.

Pitfalls and possible problems

No coursebook is perfect. In some the presentation of new language and structures can appear cluttered. Because of a focus on the introduction and practice of new language in a wide range of topics, there rarely are extended passages. The cultural aspect of a coursebook can quickly date, which can lead to a false impression of the culture of the countries where the TL is spoken. To introduce cartoons and fictional characters in a bid to achieve greater durability by being less susceptible to changes in fashions and trends runs the risk of presenting a stereotyped view of life in the target countries. Language is underpinned by the cultural and social context of its use. For commercial reasons coursebooks tend to be designed for as large an audience as possible. They are, therefore, invariably impersonal and pupils will associate them more with life in the classroom than life in the countries where the TL is spoken. The extent to which coursebooks allow for the 'personalisation' of language through the solving of realistic problems through authentic communication tends to be limited.

Understandably, coursebooks reflect the writers' own preferred methodology. Grammar, for example, can be presented inductively or deductively but there often tends not to be much of a choice of methods within one coursebook. When using the coursebook as a guide to unit of work and lesson planning, the mfl teacher, therefore, needs to exercise professional judgement according to the learning needs of pupils and make deliberate choices and select those materials best suited to achieving the learning objectives identified for a particular class.

Obviously, too, the coursebook is limited in its coverage of the examination specification. According to Cunningsworth, syllabuses tend to contain the following (see Cunningsworth 1995: 55):

- forms: structures and grammar;
- functions: communicative purpose;
- situations: context of language use; and
- topics.

A coursebook contains a finite set of activities and exercises to cover these four aspects, which can be adequate but may also be either insufficient or ample in number. This means the teacher needs to be either selective or to supplement according to the needs of pupils and the time available. Often, and importantly, the teacher also needs to grade and sequence the activities in a coursebook to take account of the needs of a particular class.

Unlike in some Continental European education systems, coursebooks do not have to be vetted by the respective Department for Education for suitability. Mfl departments in UK secondary schools are free to choose coursebooks from competing publishers. Mfl teachers need to judge the suitability of coursebooks for themselves. Many questions need to be asked about a coursebook.

- Does the coursebook lend itself to extending an active knowledge of vocabulary and does it stimulate oral work in a variety of contexts?
- Is the accompanying listening material appropriate?
- Does the coursebook develop reading strategies through a variety of types of text, encouraging the use of a range of reading skills and providing information of real interest?
- Does it serve as a model of accurate writing in appropriate styles?
- Is grammar presented as well as recycled in an attractive and meaningful way?
- Is an accurate cultural impression presented free of stereotyping in terms of class, gender, race, ethnicity, social relationships and personal feelings?

The coursebook is a teaching and learning tool and should be used and adapted to fit a specific learning context rather than simply be followed. Cunningsworth (1995: 137) suggests a useful method to decide whether to adapt an exercise or change it altogether. This method is shown in a slightly modified form in Figure 11.1.

VISUAL AIDS

Most coursebooks now provide a wealth of visual aids in the form of overhead transparencies, flashcards, cue cards and video material. Teachers often supplement these with similar aids designed by themselves and also with posters, diagrams and display work. All have their place in the learning process and provide useful foci for pupils' work.

Is the objective of the activity/topic suitable?

YES — Is the method appropriate?
NO — omit or replace

YES — Is the content suitable?
NO — change or replace

YES — use it as it is
NO — keep method and objective but change content

Figure 11.1 Flow-chart for evaluating teaching activities in coursebooks
Source: Adapted from Cunningsworth (1995: 137)

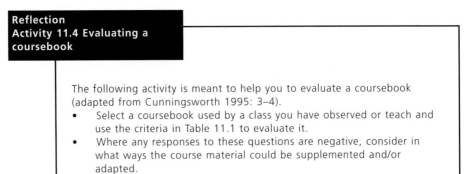

Reflection
Activity 11.4 Evaluating a coursebook

The following activity is meant to help you to evaluate a coursebook (adapted from Cunningsworth 1995: 3–4).
- Select a coursebook used by a class you have observed or teach and use the criteria in Table 11.1 to evaluate it.
- Where any responses to these questions are negative, consider in what ways the course material could be supplemented and/or adapted.

Table 11.1 Criteria for choosing a coursebook

No.	Criteria	Evaluation
A	**Aims and objectives**	
1	Do the aims of the coursebook correspond to aims and objectives expressed in units of work?	
2	Does the coursebook allow for different teaching and learning styles?	
3	Is the coursebook comprehensive in its coverage of topics?	
B	**Design and organisation**	
1	What components make up the total course?	
2	How is the content organised? (structures, functions, topics, skills)	
3	Are the grading of exercises and progression suitable for all learners?	
4	Is there adequate recycling and revision?	
5	Are there reference sections? (grammar, vocabulary etc.)	
C	**Language content**	
1	Does the course book provide material and activities to allow for vocabulary and grammar learning?	
2	Does the material include opportunities for pronunciation work?	
3	Are style and appropriacy accounted for?	
4	Are there examples of language use in a range of contexts?	
D	**Skills**	
1	Is equal emphasis placed on the development of all four skills?	
2	Are there opportunities for the integration of skills?	
3	Is the content of extended reading passages suitable for learners' interests and the level of the majority?	
4	Are listening materials authentic and accompanied by background information? Are exercises graded?	
5	Are speaking activities designed to equip learners for real-life interactions?	
6	Do writing activities allow for a suitable range of styles?	

(continued...)

Table 11.1   Criteria for choosing a coursebook *(continued)*

E	Topics	
1	Is there enough variety and a range of topics?	
2	Will the topics help to expand learners' cultural awareness?	
3	Are women portrayed and represented equally to men?	
4	Are people represented with reference to ethnic origin, occupation, disability etc.?	
F	**Methodology**	
1	Is the methodology underpinning the coursebook suitable for the learning environment?	
2	What level of learner involvement is expected?	
3	How broad is the range of activities for presenting new language?	
4	Is communicative competence developed?	
5	Does the coursebook contain advice to learners on study skills and learning strategies?	
G	**Teacher's book**	
1	Is there adequate guidance for teachers on the use of the coursebook and accompanying material?	
2	Do accompanying materials adequately cover teaching techniques for language items such as grammar and culturally specific information?	
H	**Practical considerations**	
1	What is the total cost of the coursebook and associated material?	
2	Are the books strong and long lasting?	
3	Is the material attractive?	
4	Does any of the material require particular equipment and if so are these available in the department?	
5	Can the course be used without particular material?	
6	What can and cannot be copied?	

Reflection
Activity 11.5 The coursebook and the statutory framework

Analyse one unit of work of your choice for Key Stage 3 and one for Key Stage 4 in a coursebook used by your placement school and describe to what extent the Programme of Study (PoS) statements of the National Curriculum (NC) are met. Table 11.2 shows a sample recording sheet for the PoS for England.

Discuss the findings with your mentor or a class teacher you work with frequently.

Table 11.2 Matching NC PoS statements to mfl coursebook activities

No.	Statement	Comment
5.h	Use language for real purposes ...	
2.e	How to develop their independence in learning and using the target language	
2.f	How to adapt language they already know for different contexts	
5.g	Listening, reading or viewing for personal interest, as well as for information	
4.a	Working with authentic materials in the target language, including some from ICT-based sources (e.g. handwritten texts, newspapers, magazines, books, video, satellite television, texts from the internet)	
2.d	How to initiate and develop conversations	
2.j	How to redraft their writing to improve its accuracy and presentation, including the use of ICT	
2.e	How to vary the target language to suit context, audience and purpose;	
3.a	Techniques for memorising words, phrases and short extracts	
3.d	Use of dictionaries and other reference materials appropriately and effectively	
4.d	Considering their own culture and comparing it with the cultures of the countries and communities where the target language is spoken, considering the experiences and perspectives of people in these countries and communities	

Potential and purpose

Visual aids are often used to present new language forms and to promote the practice of the language skills of listening, speaking, reading and writing. They provide a non-verbal link between the actual language used and the idea or concept expressed. David Nunan notes that the use of realia and/or symbolic representation is close to the 'natural approach' (see Nunan 1989: 195). As the link between words and concepts represented by visual aids is in the main arbitrary – with possibly the exception of onomatopoetic words – they can be used to avoid translation. Translation could be considered an obstacle at this early stage of learning as it can slow down and lengthen the process of skill development. An overemphasis on word-for-word translation can be considered as a hindrance.

In order to facilitate the learning process, visual aids should be clear and instantly recognisable. The teacher needs to help the learner progress beyond simple one-word utterances. Visual aids should, therefore, also represent a series of words and phrases rather than just single items. It should be recognisable by all pupils, irrespective, for instance, of their ethnic background, but at the same time it should represent the cultural context of the TL. The use of bold colours and simple pictorial representations tend to ensure easy recognition by pupils.

The use of flashcards is usually associated with whole class work. It requires high levels of pupil concentration and participation. Ground rules need to be clear. Chapter 6 provides suggestions for activities, some of which require pupils to put hands up, others to shout out. Teachers need to make the conditions clear and to establish routines for different activity types. Pupils are required to speak publicly, which demands a non-threatening and supportive atmosphere. Kyriacou (1991: 66) asserts the need for the teacher to appear calm and controlled. Placing flashcards in order, not dropping them on the floor, effectively targeting and sequencing of questions all contribute to this aura. Trainee teachers may well wish to script questions on the reverse side of flashcards to ensure pace and flow.

Flashcards should be made visible to all pupils. The layout of the classroom is important. A horseshoe layout lends itself well to flashcard work, enabling equal access for all pupils and allowing teachers to approach individuals as a means of securing their attention and targeting questions.

Trainee teachers need to make it a priority to get to know and use pupils' names to be able to target questions. Individual pupils should be asked questions they can answer, to encourage participation. For some this will involve simple repetition and for others the answering of open questions. Praise and encouragement should be used freely. Pupils failing to respond should be asked (a) similar question(s) again at a later stage to demonstrate care and concern for their progress. This helps the teacher to demonstrate that she makes good use of pupil responses and that learning outcomes are ensured for all pupils in the class (see Kyriacou 1986: 105).

A further teaching skill identified by Chris Kyriacou (1986) in whole class teaching activities is the maintenance of pace and flow. Chapter 6 illustrates several activities which can be undertaken with flashcards and/or overhead transparencies. Maintaining pace means adjusting activities as pupils seem ready, not necessarily changing resources. Very often activities to follow the use of flashcards are slower in pace and calming. Susan Halliwell (1991: 3–4) suggests the notion of 'stirrers' and 'settlers', which can help to maximise pupil participation and prevents the risk of over-excitement.

Whole class activities such as the use of flashcards and other visual aids require the teacher to deploy effective strategies to maintain good class control. These include use of gestures, eye contact, movement around the room and effectively targeted questions. Such activities are meant to engage the whole class. Interruptions and disruption on the part of individual pupils are therefore very undesirable. Breaches of the code of conduct can be dealt with by referring to assertive discipline techniques (see e.g. Rogers 1982). Rather than breaking the flow of a lesson, miscreants' names can be noted on the board and appropriate action taken later. This avoids disruption of the activity in hand, prevents the potential for confrontation and enables private rather than public admonishment.

An important purpose of using visual aids is to illustrate the meaning of new lexical items and to enable the learner to discriminate between key sounds and peripheral detail. Visual aids can motivate pupils to speak by providing non-verbal clues and by creating a context for communication. They can also be used to encourage interaction through pupil involvement. Once pupils are able to discriminate sounds, words and phrases, flashcards can be distributed amongst pupils and games be played. Learners can give instructions for the movement of objects and overlays on the overhead projector. A picture or story can be built up step by step as transparencies are placed in or out of sequence on the screen. The teacher need not direct activities herself but pupils can be asked to come to the OHP or handle the flashcards. Information introduced in this way can offer a recognisable, colourful and attractive context for writing. Pictorial representations can be used to decorate texts and provide clues for gist comprehension as well as the extraction of detail in reading exercises. Similarly, cue cards can be used to focus pupils' attention when carrying out listening comprehension work.

In his discussion of the use of images and pictures in foreign language teaching and learning, Douglas Allford (2000) usefully distinguishes 'convergent' and 'divergent' exploitation tasks. He posits that divergent, i.e. open-ended tasks, should be used where possible to maximise opportunities for spontaneous and meaningful productive language use. Allford stresses that convergent, i.e. closed, and often inauthentic tasks can limit the potential value of images and pictures in the foreign language learning process. In the use of pictorial images the distinction between learning new language, which may entail a focus on form, and language use, which is suited to practice of already familiar language, should not be overlooked.

Pitfalls and possible problems

The use of visual aids can be exciting and stimulating. Visual aids can be very effective tools to encourage repetition and the reproduction of language forms. Therefore, mfl teachers need to develop the necessary skills for using them effectively.

However, the need for pupils to progress needs to be borne in mind. Audiovisual course material used in the late 1960s and 1970s followed a set format: learners listened to 'texts' and watched film strips. For each and every unit, they listened, repeated and responded to simple questions. The film strip prompted reactions from the learner. The content of each unit of work remained distinct and separate from the previous units. Consequently, learners found it difficult to transfer known language to and use it in this new context. Trainees need to be aware that they run the same risk when using visual aids. This is not to belittle the value of visual aids in the language learning process, though.

Over-use of one set of visual aids can be stultifying. Given the limited range within any particular topic, activities need to be changed regularly to maintain pupils' interest. Teachers need to provide ample opportunity for practice, re-using the same language forms within different contexts.

One phrase should be represented by one visual symbol. Consistency is important: to introduce new images for familiar language can be seen to be as ineffective as to introduce new language with known images.

Visual aids tend to be used by mfl teachers as a strategy to achieve a number of different purposes such as to increase comprehension, facilitate interaction, avoid translation or increase cultural awareness.

Once able to respond comfortably to visual aids in a teacher-centred activity, pupils can be asked to use small cards depicting similar images for a variety of activities. For instance, a game of 'pairs' can be played, providing pupils with opportunities to practise new language. Pupils put the cards upside down on the desk and have to remember where matching pairs can be found.

'Happy families' requires pupils to communicate information to each other. Accurate communication is rewarded by obtaining a card from a peer. Pupils need to complete a set of four to win. For instance, cards depicting four goods which can be bought from four different shops can be made into playing cards. The entire pack of sixteen is shuffled and distributed to four players. Player one turns to her left and asks player two in the TL for a particular item: '¿*Tienes el queso?*' ('Have you got the cheese?') or the name of the shop where they can purchase certain types of goods ¿*Tienes algo de la carnicería?* ('Have you got anything from the butcher's?'). If player two has the card depicting the item in question or a relevant card she must pass it to player one. Player one will give player two a card of her choice (which she does not feel she needs) in return. If player two does not have a relevant card she will reply: '*Lo siento, no tengo.*' ('I'm sorry, I haven't got it'). Player two then turns to player three and requests a card. The conversations continue around in this way until one player has a full set and wins the game.

In this example visual aids in the form of cue cards clearly stimulate real communication. Yet the range of language is restricted to suit the language abilities of the players.

Reflection
Activity 11.6 Visual aids

Which visual aids are used by mfl teachers at your placement school?
* With reference to the table in Table 11.3, and through discussions with mfl teachers, find out the purposes for using the aids. Which visual aids fulfil which of the stated purposes?
* Does the use of visual aids require specific classroom management strategies?
* Use visual aids in a collaborative teaching situation for a particular purpose, which you should agree on with your mentor or the relevant class teacher.

Table 11.3 Purposes of the use of visual aids

Purpose	Flashcards	Cue cards	OHP	Realia	Displays
To encourage oral presentation					
To aid comprehension					
To present new language					
To increase cultural awareness					
To provide a context for language use					
To enable communication and interaction					
To avoid translation					
Other – specify					

PAIR WORK

Pair work needs careful management. Kagan (1988, quoted in Bennett and Dunne 1994: 166) points out that cooperative learning must be accompanied by effective classroom management, which includes attention being paid to pupil behaviour and the structure and sequence of activities in a lesson. Bennett and Dunne (1994: 171) also quote the findings of the National Oracy Project suggesting that pair work is a helpful preparation for group work and that younger pupils respond more positively to the smaller grouping.

Deciding on pairs is important. Quick practice is often best undertaken by friendship pairs or two pupils positioned side by side. This reduces unnecessary movement. Instructions need to be clear and noise is an important issue. Denscombe (1980, quoted in Kyriacou 1991: 62) suggests that loudness does not necessarily equate to a loss of control. If instructions are clear, teachers should allow acceptable levels of noise.

The sequence and structure of a lesson is crucial. Pair work requires careful preparation and demonstration. The length of an activity needs to be spelt out clearly. During pair work the teacher should circulate around the class, listening to pupils' oral work, making informal and formative assessments. This way pupils know that an activity is important. To avoid the indignity of trying to shout louder than a classroom full of pupils speaking at once, the teacher can circulate giving advance warning that a pair work activity is due to end imminently. Pupils also need time to quieten down. Once warned that an activity is coming to an end, an effective strategy to achieve silence is to count backwards from ten to zero in the TL, encouraging pupils to join in the 'countdown'. Such a routine, once established, can be very effective. Another is to write 'silence' on the board slowly in the TL until all pupils fall quiet. Following pair work activities, good work can be rewarded by asking some pairs to demonstrate to the class. Transitions from one activity to another are always problematic for teachers. Pair work, which can be hectic and exciting, is a relatively high-risk activity in this respect. Trainee teachers need to develop a bank of strategies to end 'stirrers' effectively and to continue with 'settlers'.

Reflection Activity 11.7 Ending lively activities

Observe experienced teachers, including those in other subject areas such as music and drama, and note:
- the ways lively activities are brought to a close; and
- the types of activities which follow lively activities.

GROUP WORK

In principle managing group work is not so different to pair work. Group work, however, often takes longer and pupils perform different roles within the small group. Group work rarely requires only a single instruction. Projects demand discussion, negotiation, planning, re-drafting and presentation. Pupils can be allocated tasks to fit these demands – scribe, researcher, presenter, actor, editor etc. Teachers should decide in advance the roles which best serve the learning needs of individual pupils. Clear instructions and briefing sheets in the TL are helpful. Pupils need to be aware of the need for teamwork and how they can interact with peers to inform their own contributions. This involves careful consideration of groupings – mixed ability, gender mix, ability groups, friendships, learning needs etc. As Bennett and Dunne (1994: 167) note, the structure of lessons, where cooperative work takes place, is complex and pupils must be prepared to assume different roles from traditional teacher-led situations.

Research into the optimum size of groups (see Kagan 1988) has come to no firm conclusions, but teachers should nevertheless be aware of some of the findings. Teams of four are suggested as the ideal, teams of three often result in two teaming up together and excluding the third. Teams of five can lead to cliques (a two and a three). On the other hand, the larger the number of pupils in a group, the greater the possible lines of communication. A final issue is the number of roles required by the task set. Trainee teachers should bear these issues in mind when planning for group work.

Pupils can be prepared for group tasks from the start of a lesson. As they enter the classroom, the teacher should determine seating arrangements. Coloured or numbered cards can be placed on tables. As each pupil enters the room she can be given coloured or numbered slips of paper indicating at which table she should sit. This prevents unnecessary movement during the lesson and also demonstrates that the teacher is in control. The mechanics of grouping pupils are relatively simple. However, the reasons for placing pupils in defined groups are often complex and requires the teacher's professional judgement.

AUTHENTIC MATERIAL

When asked at interview how to make the learning of a modern foreign language interesting, many prospective mfl trainees reply that they would appeal to pupils' interests. Authentic materials offer teachers the opportunity to expose pupils to material produced for 'real', out-of-classroom contexts and for specific purposes.

Potential and purpose

Authentic materials are one effective resource for teachers. If used sensibly and sensitively they can motivate pupils. Such materials are up to date and reflect the current context and culture(s) of the TL. Their use fits well within the aims and objectives underpinning communicative language teaching.

Authentic texts, either for listening, reading or viewing, are produced not with didactic-pedagogical objectives in mind but with the general intention of conveying information and/or ideas. The focus is on the message, and tools other than language are used to help to communicate this message. The format and design, the style and, indeed, the content are moulded to suit a particular audience or readership. As a consequence, authentic material contains cultural information and overt clues to meaning. The level of language need not, therefore, be the sole determining factor for suitability.

Learners can draw on their existing general knowledge to predict meaning.

In their book on learning mfl from authentic texts, David Little, Sean Devitt and David Singleton (1989: 29–67) discuss a number of exercise types for working with authentic texts, such as the use of comprehension questions, information extraction techniques, predictive activities, vocabulary organisation, productive exercise chains, rewriting texts or letter writing.

Use of authentic material serves several purposes. Simple props such as labels, packets, menus, timetables and advertisements can provide the bridge between the classroom and the real world. This bridge can reinforce the teacher's aim of demonstrating that what is taught and learnt in the classroom is actually of real use. The very fact that the material is recognisably designed to fulfil a social function can be motivating.

Undoubtedly, material must be selected with care. Pupils need to be able to understand and interact with the content and this is clearly not through word-for-word translation. Apart from drawing on existing skills and knowledge, pupils can develop particular strategies for comprehension. Focussing on headlines and titles, relating pictures to key phrases and understanding captions all contribute to gist understanding, which pupils need to develop.

Little, Devitt and Singleton also suggest a widely used technique for reading comprehension, which is based on the use of question words for content categorisation as a basis for language production (see Figure 11.5).

Many authentic material lend themselves to particular topics and many mfl teachers are very creative in their use. Prices on posters and publicity sheets for supermarkets can support the reinforcement of numbers. Even the use of telephone directories can achieve this. The benefits in terms of developing pupils' cultural awareness are obvious. Menus, town plans and tourist guides contain language relevant to examination specifications but also to the realistic needs of pupils when visiting countries where the TL is spoken.

Authentic material also provide excellent models for language production by pupils. Advertisements in particular can stimulate creative language use and can provide an appropriate context.

When used sensitively, authentic material offer much to the mfl teacher. Bernard Kavanagh and Lynne Upton draw attention to four important considerations, which are adapted here (see Kavanagh and Upton 1994: 12):

- the material must be interesting for pupils; the same text will probably not be of interest to all pupils in a class;

Table 11.4 Working with authentic texts

Qui? Wer? ¿Quién?	Quoi? Was? ¿Qué?	Où? Wo? ¿Dónde?	Quand? Wann? ¿Cuándo?	Comment? Wie? ¿Cómo?

Source: Adapted from Little, Devitt and Singleton (1989: 99–101)

- the content must be accessible and objectives clearly defined and understood; this can guard against pupils feeling that they have to understand the meaning and grammatical function of every word;
- the task itself must appeal and *authentic material* should involve *authentic tasks*; also
- the nature of the task should be varied and relevant to the original purpose of the text.

Pitfalls and possible problems

Above we considered it to be an advantage that authentic material are not designed for use in the classroom. This can, however, also be a pitfall. No allowance is made for the learners' lack of knowledge of vocabulary, nor is the grammar used designed to support a particular stage of learning. Passages need to be placed in context. To expose a learner to authentic texts without prior preparation can be demotivating. Consequently, efforts should be made to introduce the topic, present key phrases and even ideas expressed in the text in advance. The length of many passages is daunting. Pupils need to feel comfortable with a text before embarking on reading or listening to it. Tasks designed for particular texts can be graded. Activities involving the highlighting of key vocabulary, such as times, dates, addresses and prices, do not require a detailed understanding. The identification of particular details can be achieved through non-verbal responses.

Iain Mitchell and Ann Swarbrick stress the need to 'exploit pre-knowledge' (Mitchell and Swarbrick 1994: 2) to pre-empt learner alienation when faced with a lengthy authentic text. In Chapter 6 examples of such preparatory activities, such as identifying known vocabulary or inferring meaning on the basis of headlines, are discussed.

Another benefit of using authentic material can also lead to problems: the material are *not* designed for the reader to focus on the *language* used *but* more to understand the *message*. The tasks designed for a text need to match this aim.

Working in groups with authentic material can be problematic. Often pupils may be distracted by the material being used by other groups. Access to reference material inevitably involves movement to other areas of the classroom. Pupils do not always work at the required pace and pupil absence can inhibit the work of others in a group.

Kyriacou (1991: 61) advises that teachers establish ground rules in advance:

- pupils should move from their seats for specified reasons only;
- only a pre-specified number of pupils should be out of their seats at any given time;
- pupils should be presented tasks in stages, with time limits on each stage; and
- pupils should demonstrate completion of a stage to the teacher.

Marilyn Leask (2000: 78) notes that it is crucial that teachers establish routines and procedures in advance for the movement of pupils, the management of relationships, attitudes and expectations and for gaining attention. Group work accentuates the need for these to be met.

Exemplification

The range of material available varies enormously. The activity described here is designed to familiarise pupils with the format and content of newspapers without requiring an in-depth knowledge of the vocabulary of and background to particular articles.

Pupils are issued with newspapers. They are asked to cut out five articles which depict a happy event and five which depict a sad event. They then separate the headlines and pictures from each story. From the text they extract five key sentences which serve as a summary of the events. The headlines, pictures and summary are exchanged with another group, whose task it is to reproduce the story. For support a pupil from each group may read the entire story in private but she is only allowed to report back to her group without reference to the text.

In order to relate the content of lessons to pupils' 'real' needs and interests the material selected could relate to a planned visit abroad. Pupils can be presented with brochures of all the places they are likely to visit. In groups they are asked to extract from the brochures details of opening times, cost of entries or accessibility and to draw up an itinerary. In the event of the visit being to a partner school abroad, pupils from the partner institution could be approached to provide details of possible excursions. Taped interviews and written surveys are useful this context. This way authentic material can be used to develop effective communication for real purposes.

Reflection
Activity 11.8 Authentic material

- Examine whether the use of authentic material is built into a unit of work currently in use in your placement school.
- Devise an exercise appropriate for a Year 9 class you are currently teaching or observing around some authentic material. Then, with the same material, devise an activity for a Year 11 class you are currently teaching or observing. Do any principles for the use of authentic material with pupils of different levels of linguistic skill emerge?
- Seek out some authentic material and devise activities which will support the learning objectives of a unit of work of a specific class. Discuss the material and tasks with your mentor or a relevant class teacher; then adapt them as necessary. Ask your mentor or the class teacher if you can teach the activity.

THE CASSETTE PLAYER

Potential and purpose

Apart from representing a welcome change from the sound of the teacher's voice, the cassette player provides faithful recordings of authentic speech and examples of relevant vocabulary and grammatical items in quasi-authentic situations. Listening to recorded texts can obviously improve comprehension but it can also stimulate language production. In terms of comprehension it is important to exploit the fact that recordings can be replayed. The recordings are 'faithful' in that each time a passage is replayed it remains the same. The speakers' intonation, pronunciation and accent as well as the accompanying background noise are constant. This allows for the development of comprehension in stages (see Dakin 1976: 167–8). Learners need to have the opportunity to decipher the sound system independently of the information processing required, to orientate themselves, to pick out relevant detail and then to confirm that they have constructed correct forms of meaning when listening.

The cassette player allows teachers to structure language production and use repetition. Using the cassette player allows learners to note that different speakers share a phonology despite varying local accents. Indeed, learners need to be aware of the range of regional accents in order to be prepared for future language use.

The cassette player is also a valuable resource as a stimulus for more independent language use. Activities requiring non-verbal responses to record details expressed in passages allow pupils to rebuild 'texts'. Coursebooks nearly always provide transcripts for the passages contained on the accompanying audio tapes. These allow for the skills of reading and writing to be integrated with listening and for work to focus on the particular language forms used.

Pitfalls and possible problems

Audio cassettes lack the glamour of video recordings, and comprehension of the spoken word can be very demanding without access to the accompanying paralinguistic support of gestures, expressions and visual background/contextualisation. Julian Dakin comments on the dangers of using taped material purely for drill purposes. The benefits are limited when learners use language as if there is 'an absence of meaning' (Dakin 1976: 57). In order to be realistic, listening must take place in a context, so that the listener can place the language heard into a perceived situation, helping her to understand what the speaker means. The placing of a passage into a communicative context may well be a preliminary task, yet it is essential to do so in order to convey relevance and meaning of a passage. For a detailed discussion of the teaching of listening skills see Chapter 6.

Cassette players can be effective tools in developing good linguistic habits. There is a place for repetition and drill exercises, for instance, through listening to songs and rhymes. Pronunciation can be focussed on without necessarily fully comprehending the words. To attempt to place such an activity in a communicative context is worthy but may well lead to frustration. Pupils may opt out and resort to the 'tum te tum' effect described by Dakin, when pupils imitate the sounds without distinguishing the words (see Dakin 1976: 55).

It is difficult to separate listening comprehension skills from memorising. Many pupils may need to hear a passage several times. It is crucial that use is made of the 'counter' on the cassette player so that the tape can be wound and rewound to the appropriate place with ease.

Many teachers view listening activities as 'settlers'. Use of the cassette player in whole class situations requires silence, which the teacher needs to ensure before the listening activity commences. Frequently pupils disrupt listening activities with questions which could have been answered in advance. Clear instructions often include a statement on how many times a passage will be heard, that pupils need to sit quietly throughout, that answers required are verbal or non-verbal, that answers are expected in the TL/English or in note form/full sentences and that questions do/don't follow the structure of the text.

As a whole class activity the cassette player should be strategically placed in order that the passage can be heard by all and that loose trailing wires do not represent a health and safety hazard. Standing centre stage and needing to respond to pupils appearing to lose concentration, without making a noise, is demanding of mfl teachers. It is during such activities that body language, gestures, eye contact and classroom scanning are essential. Pupils should be aware that any form of misbehaviour impinges on the quality of learning of others and that misdemeanours will be noticed and dealt with afterwards. The teacher should avoid disturbing the whole class for the sake of one miscreant, but must not allow this to prevent action being taken. An essential part of Kyriacou's concept of 'withitness' (see above) is the readiness on the part of the teacher to take action.

It is clear that the use of the cassette player is invaluable. However, trainees need to be confident in using it and selective in their choice of listening material. An awareness of what makes a passage difficult beyond the actual content facilitates the selection of 'texts'. Length of passage, speed of speech, local accents, background noise, number of speakers all contribute to the difficulty of a text. Activities need to be carefully structured to suit the learning process and the level of difficulty of tasks needs to be increased gradually. Support for less able listeners, for instance in the form of differentiated listening tasks, is crucial. Visual aids in the form of clues and prompts can be used to provide such support. Pupils need to know the purpose of listening activities and, in order to prevent constant interruption, pupils should be informed in advance of how many times they will hear the passage.

Reflection
Activity 11.9 Using taped material

Listen to a range of taped material from a variety of courses.
- What do you notice about the different approaches?
- Which type of passage lends itself to repetition, gist understanding, extraction of detail, rebuilding of language or stimulates language production?

SUMMARY

Some resources and materials are used very regularly by mfl teachers.

Each resource serves a particular purpose in the mfl teaching and learning process and it is important to devise appropriate activities to maximise the effectiveness of individual resources.

In order to ensure maximum effectiveness of teaching and use of resources, good classroom management skills are important.

There is a temptation to 'follow the book', yet trainees should recognise that course-books are only one of many 'tools of the trade'. Learning is enhanced by a variety of approaches and certain resources appear to be more suited to particular situations than others. Good mfl teaching is based on the identification of desirable learning outcomes followed by the selection of appropriate methods and strategies to achieve these.

In using the material and resources it is important to remember that lesson plans and units of work should contain variety as well as progression. The range of activities should not be narrow even if certain activity types appear to be more favoured than others by particular groups of pupils.

Within any class there will be a range of abilities as well as preferred learning styles. Mfl trainees need to be able to vary teaching styles and use of resources to suit pupils' needs.

12 The Use of Information Communications Technology in Modern Foreign Languages Teaching and Learning

For many years now, computer-assisted language learning (CALL) software has had a useful contribution to make to modern foreign languages (mfl) teaching and learning. It has been used to enrich pupils' language learning experience and has allowed learners to practise language skills independently according to need. Early computer programs tended to follow a behaviourist, drill-practice paradigm. Simple text manipulation programs such as 'Fun with Texts' remain a very popular option for mfl teachers.

OBJECTIVES

By the end of this chapter you should:

- understand the rationale behind the use of ICT in mfl teaching and learning and how ICT can contribute to achieving mfl learning objectives;
- understand how ICT use in mfl can contribute to the development of IT capability in pupils;
- be able to make decisions about when, when not and how to use ICT in your mfl teaching;
- understand the requirements of Annex B of DfEE Circular 4/98, the Initial Teacher Training National Curriculum for the use of ICT in subject teaching;
- understand the potential and characteristics of new technologies and how to exploit them;
- be able to evaluate ICT applications; and
- be able to evaluate the contribution of ICT applications to mfl teaching and learning.

Developments in multimedia technology now allow for the combination of authentic spoken and written texts as well as culturally rich visual stimuli supporting the constructivist learning paradigm, which is based on the premise that learning is a process of discovery, information processing and expression. ICT gives learners access to a range of resources in the target language and enables them to find out about how people of target language (TL) communities speak and live. Proponents of a social-interactionist view of foreign language learning stress the importance of the computer as tool for communication. As a result, synchronous (real-time, e.g. videoconferencing or online chats) and asynchronous (delayed-time, e.g. e-mail) computer-mediated communication (CMC) are increasingly being used to communicate with TL speakers (see Pachler 1999e).

In addition to computer-based applications a number of other technological aids are being used regularly by mfl teachers, such as (satellite) television and video-recorders or camcorders. Also, a number of computer-peripherals, such as scanners, digital cameras, digital video cameras, data projection units or interactive whiteboards, increasingly find application in the context of mfl teaching and learning.

DEVELOPING PERSONAL AND PUPILS' ICT CAPABILITY

The potential for enhancing (mfl) teaching and learning with ICT is being recognised by practitioners and policy makers alike. As a consequence, all trainee teachers are required to develop relevant ICT skills as an integral and assessed part of their course. These are listed in Annex B of DfEE Circular 4/98, the ITT NC for the use of ICT in subject teaching.

Importantly, the recognition of the importance of ICT by policy makers is evident in the NC Orders, which set out pupils' entitlement to develop ICT capability in terms of general requirements applying across the curriculum:

1. Pupils should be given opportunities to apply and develop their ICT capability through the use of ICT tools to support their learning in all subjects … .
2. Pupils should be given opportunities to support their work by being taught to:

    a) find things out from a variety of sources, selecting and synthesising the information to meet their needs and developing an ability to question its accuracy, bias and plausibility
    b) develop their ideas using ICT tools to amend and refine their work and enhance its quality and accuracy
    c) exchange and share information, both directly and through electronic media
    d) review, modify and evaluate their work, reflecting critically on its quality, as it progresses.

(DfEE/QCA 1999: 41)

The NC also includes a range of subject-specific opportunities and requirements for ICT use in the Programme of Study (PoS). Whilst there are some explicit references to ICT in the PoS (2h, 2j, 4a, 5d, 5e, 5h), the potential for ICT use is implicit in most statements:

- understanding the principles and interrelationship of sound and writing (1a), e.g. by using text manipulation software and listening devices or dictation software;
- learning about the grammar of the target language (TL) and how to apply it (1b), e.g. by using grammar software packages or electronic grammar reference software;
- correcting pronunciation and intonation (2a), e.g. by using voice recognition software;
- listening carefully for gist and detail (2b), e.g. by using real-time audio and video;
- varying the TL to suit context, audience and purpose (2e), e.g. by using word processors and desk-top publishing software to draft and re-draft;
- techniques for skimming and scanning written texts for information (2h), e.g. by using the internet to access authentic texts and search facilities of word processors or concordancing packages to analyse them;
- redrafting writing to improve its accuracy and presentation (2j), e.g. by using word processors or presentation packages together with electronic images (digitised with a scanner, taken with a digital camera, retrieved from a clip art library/a CD-ROM/the internet);
- using dictionaries and other reference materials appropriately and effectively (3b), e.g. electronic encyclopaedias or dictionaries;
- working with authentic materials in the TL (4a), e.g. by using the internet to access weather forecasts, TV listings, tourist information etc. or online newspapers;
- communicating with native speakers (4b), e.g. by using e-mail, real-time communication programs or videoconferencing to contact pupils from a partner school;
- considering their own culture and comparing it with the cultures of the countries and communities where the TL is spoken (4c), e.g. by compiling and exchanging video recordings or webpages of the locality with a partner school;
- considering the experience and perspectives of people in these countries and communities (4d), e.g. by studying personal webpages of TL speakers or culture-specific online resources;
- producing and responding to different types of written and spoken language (5d), e.g. by writing letters, e-mails or postings for electronic bulletin boards; recording answer-phone messages, simulating telephone conversations, producing a commentary for a video recording or sending voice-mail;
- using a range of resources for accessing and communicating information (5e), e.g. by retrieving authentic information from the internet to produce a word-processed/desk-top published/web-based brochure or leaflet for a specific purpose and audience;
- using the TL creatively and imaginatively (5f), e.g. by producing interactive multimodal webpages or displays or by creating poems and short stories illustrated with images and accompanied by sound;
- using the TL for real purposes (5h), e.g. by sending and receiving e-mail or video-mail messages in the context of project work (see Chapter 8).

Reflection
Activity 12.1 Developing pupils'
ICT capability

- Talk to the ICT coordinator at your placement school. Find out what ICT skills pupils are expected to develop at Key Stages 3 and 4 and what might constitute evidence of ICT capability. See also the ICT NC Orders available at *http://www.nc.uk.net/*.
- How do the ICT skills relate to the scheme of work of the mfl department at your placement school and what evidence of ICT capability could pupils show through their mfl work?

Clearly, trainees' ability to use technological aids is a pre-requisite for the development of I(C)T capability in pupils. Due to the lack of space it is not possible to provide tutorial material in this chapter. However, an online tutorial complementing this chapter, aimed at helping trainees develop personal and professional capability to make effective use of ICT for accessing, presenting and managing information, is available from the ICT section of the homepage accompanying this book. See also the 'ICT for Language Teachers' website at *http://www.ict4lt.org/*.

THE ITT NC FOR THE USE OF ICT IN MFL TEACHING

Annex B of DfEE Circular 4/98 (see DfEE 1998: 17–31) sets out the standards of ICT use required by newly qualified teachers (NQTs). Trainees need to develop the knowledge, skills and understanding outlined in the circular by the end of their course in order to be awarded qualified teacher status (QTS). In many courses evidence is collected through an ICT portfolio. From 2001–2 trainees will also have to pass an ICT skills test (for details see the Teacher Training Agency website at *http://www.canteach.gov.uk/*).

Annex B is divided into two parts. Part A deals with effective teaching and learning, whereas Part B outlines trainees' knowledge and understanding of, and competence with, ICT. The Annex requires trainees to know when ICT is beneficial in achieving teaching objectives and when its use is less effective or even inappropriate on the basis of an understanding of the characteristics and the potential of ICT. Trainees, for example, need to develop competence in relation to the following four areas (source: TTA 1999):

1. Planning, e.g.:
   - understanding and considering the advantages and disadvantages of using ICT;
   - planning to use ICT so as to provide access to the curriculum for those pupils who might otherwise have difficulties because of their special educational needs;
   - preparing for lessons using ICT by selecting and preparing appropriate sources of information, relevant software and the appropriate technology, and deciding on the most effective organisation of the classroom and pupils.

2.   Teaching, e.g.:
*   extending pupils' mfl learning through the use of ICT;
*   intervening and posing questions to stimulate, direct, monitor and assess the learning of pupils who are using ICT;
*   employing the most appropriate technologies for working with whole classes;
*   combining the use of ICT with other resources and methods to achieve teaching objectives.

3.   Assessing and evaluating, e.g.:
*   enabling pupils to demonstrate their knowledge, understanding and skills in mfl while using ICT;
*   ensuring pupils' mfl learning is not masked by the technology being used;
*   judging how the use of ICT can alter expectations of pupils' attainment;
*   judging the effectiveness of using ICT in achieving teaching objectives.

4.   Personal and professional ICT use, e.g.:
*   using generic and/or subject-specific hardware and software, e.g. databases, internet, presentation tools, scanners, printers etc;
*   using ICT to aid record-keeping, analysis of data, target-setting, reporting, transfer of information etc.;
*   accessing and using relevant resources;
*   accessing research and inspection evidence.

Reflection
Activity 12.2 Self-evaluation
and target setting

Using the competencies for planning, teaching, assessing and evaluating and personal and professional ICT use outlined above, evaluate your own strengths and weaknesses and identify some personal professional development needs.

In our experience a personal ICT portfolio, addressing the following questions, can yield useful and relevant evidence:

*   What skills did I have at the start of the course?
*   What have I learnt about ICT and what ICT skills did I develop during the course?
*   How did I use ICT during my course, e.g. whole-class presentations, work on stand-alone machines, work in the computer room, production of (online) worksheets, creation of a website, record keeping etc?
*   How did my pupils (of all abilities) benefit?
*   How did I use ICT to support the coverage of the NC PoS?
*   What are the implications of ICT use for the teacher?

- When is it appropriate to use ICT, and when isn't it?
- How can ICT enhance mfl learning and teaching?

The following documents might be collected:

- personal webpages;
- lesson plans featuring ICT use and their evaluation;
- evaluations of TV and video resources, software and web-based material;
- personal ICT skills audit;
- logs of personal ICT activities, e.g. worksheets or diary;
- ICT-related reflection activities completed by trainees;
- handouts, leaflets, printouts, annotated background reading; and
- pupils' work.

A realistic assessment of the potential and benefits of ICT remains essential at all times. The overriding rationale for the use of ICT has to be determined by its effectiveness in helping teachers and learners meet mfl-related aims and learning objectives. ICT should not be viewed as an end in itself but as a means to an end. It should be used to support genuinely meaningful mfl learning activities.

PLANNING FOR AND MANAGING EFFECTIVE ICT USE IN MFL

In order to become competent users, pupils need to be given frequent opportunities to use ICT. ICT use needs to be well planned and integrated with mfl learning objectives. 'Decisions about when, when not and how to use ICT in lessons should be based on whether the use of ICT supports good practice in teaching (mfl). If it doesn't, it should not be used' (TTA 1999: 8). Therefore, one key principle of ICT use is: how can technology support genuinely meaningful mfl learning activities? TV and video recordings might be used to consolidate pupils' understanding of certain linguistic items, CALL software to practise specific vocabulary or structures, or authentic material from the internet to develop reading skills in the foreign language. Certain aspects of the mfl curriculum, such as the development of cultural awareness, lend themselves particularly well to extensive use of ICT. Examples are given in Chapter 8. Mfl departments often carry out specific project work around the use of ICT, for instance the production of a desk-top-published 'glossy' brochure or a video clip of the school, its pupils and the local area for visitors from a partner school in preparation of an exchange visit. For details on internet- and e-mail-based project work, see also Chapter 8.

Many case studies and examples of good practice have been published. References can be found in a regularly updated list of relevant further reading available on the website accompanying this book. These readings can serve as a useful starting point for ideas for work with ICT in the mfl classroom.

Effective planning for ICT use in mfl teaching requires the realisation that ICT use 'involve(s) different classroom organisation strategies from those of chalk and talk' and that technological aids 'can malfunction due to mechanical or human error and (that they) are capable of disrupting the entire class' (Gray 1996: 61). Undoubtedly, this is a challenge a number of experiences mfl teachers encounter, and not just trainees starting to use ICT in their teaching. Carol Gray (1996: 61) has the following piece of advice:

A modern languages teacher trained to face a class of unmotivated adolescents armed only with a set of home-made flashcards and a worksheet need not be scared of a piece of machinery. Pupils are often more competent in the use of computers than their teachers; perhaps this should be regarded sometimes as an advantage rather than a risk – the pupil who struggles at French may find satisfaction in the prospect of teaching his or her French teacher how to cope with a mechanical computing defect, and benefit from a greatly increased self-esteem which may help alleviate behaviour difficulties.

However, planning has to be careful and detailed to minimise the potential for disruption inherent in the introduction of a new variable into the mfl classroom. Trainees should be familiar with pupils' IT capability at various different stages when planning an ICT activity, e.g. have the pupils been taught how to use the word processor? Do they possess all relevant skills, e.g. how to generate accented characters? If not, these skills need to be taught to pupils before they can be expected to use the word processor effectively in mfl contexts. Trainees need to ask themselves as part of their planning, for instance, where the TV and video recorder are stored and how to get them to the classroom. How long in advance do equipment or computer-rooms have to be booked? Familiarisation with relevant hardware and software is equally important. Trainees should make sure they are familiar not only with the content of a resource but also with its functionality.

We strongly advise trainees to have an alternative lesson plan available in case technical difficulties, such the server going down, or other unforeseen circumstances make it impossible to proceed according to the original lesson plan.

Additional considerations concern classroom organisation. Is ICT to be used with the whole class, a group of pupils or are some pupils going to work independently using ICT? Trainees need to consider carefully which mode is best suited for specific activities. If several pupils work with a technological aid at any one time, are they allowed to choose who to work with and to negotiate their roles themselves or do groups and roles within them need to be assigned? Either way, trainees need to ensure that all pupils are actively (physically and cognitively) engaged, that collaboration takes place (see e.g. Pachler 1999d) and that the teacher intervenes and asks pupils to report back where appropriate. Trainees need to consider carefully when to use ICT, e.g. for

Reflection
Activity 12.3 Auditing hardware, software and pupils' IT capability

Carry out an audit of computer hardware and software (including audio and video tapes) available for use by the mfl department at your place-ment school. Make a list of hardware and compatible software. Ask colleagues in the department and the ICT coordinator and consult relevant literature noting any particular features of available applications.

Also, find out from the ICT coordinator what IT skills pupils develop in Year 7 to 11. What are the implications for ICT use in mfl teaching with different year groups?

presenting new material with the help of a data projection unit during the input stage, during the practice phase with pupils working hands-on in the computer room or during project work with pupils using ICT resources independently as and when they see fit etc. Trainees need to ensure that pupils have been taught relevant vocabulary and structures and that instructions are clear so they can use ICT effectively. Importantly also, trainees need to ensure that due consideration is given to health and safety issues during planning. Many useful insights can be gained through the observation of lessons across the curriculum in which use is made of ICT. For a detailed discussion of classroom management issues and ICT use see also Selinger 1999.

Strategies for classroom organisation in the context of ICT use both in the classroom and the computer room can be different from the regular techniques used by mfl

---

Reflection
Activity 12.4 Classroom organisation and ICT use

Carry out a number of mfl lesson observations focussing on the implications of ICT use on classroom organisation.
*   What preparation is necessary? Does the furniture have to be changed? When and how is the equipment set up? Where is it stored and how can it be booked? Do pupils have to be grouped and if so, how are they grouped?
*   What strategies work well? Can you observe any actual or potential problems? What are the implications for your own lesson planning?

Reflection
Activity 12.5 Teaching in the computer room

Ask to observe a number of lessons taking place in the computer room.
*   Take notes on the seating arrangements by drawing out a plan of the room.
*   Note the language forms used to:
    *   introduce the activity and set up the task;
    *   interrupt pupils to give explanations;
    *   set a time scale for an activity; or
    *   bring the activity to a close.
*   If the lessons observed are not mfl lessons taking place in the computer room but, for instance, ICT lessons, consider how these language forms could be translated appropriately into the TL and note what visual aids could be developed to facilitate pupils' comprehension.
*   Note what the teacher says to individual pupils when circulating. (How can this be translated into the appropriate TL?)
*   What do pupils say to each other? What strategies are being/could be

teachers. Invariably, the methods employed to manage pupil learning and behaviour depend upon the nature of the technological aids used and whether the lesson takes place in the classroom or the computer room. Just as in lessons, which do not feature ICT use, good pace, challenging activities and high teacher expectations are important.

The use of the target language (TL) is an important subject-specific classroom management issue in the context of ICT use in mfl teaching. Unsurprisingly many trainees, as well as experienced mfl teachers, have limited knowledge of specialist TL terminology. First of all, therefore, trainees need to familiarise themselves with requisite TL terminology. Useful glossaries can be found in the 'ICT resources' section of the homepage of the website accompanying this book. In a second step, trainees need to teach pupils relevant ICT-related TL terms in order to ensure the TL can be used as the medium for instruction and interaction in ICT-based mfl lessons (see also Chapter 5). As in all other mfl lessons, trainees should attempt to maximise their use of the TL where appropriate.

Reflection
Activity 12.6 ICT-related TL

On the basis of observation of teacher–pupil and pupil–pupil interactions in ICT-based lessons, develop some displays and flashcards to support the use of the TL when working with technological aids or in the computer room.

TECHNOLOGICAL AIDS

Below we discuss the following technological aids and give practical examples and case studies of their use:

- (satellite) TV and video recorder;
- camcorder; and
- computer-based aids: CALL software, word-processor, databases, the concept keyboard, multimedia applications/CD-ROMs/DVD, authoring- and text-manipulation packages, computer-mediated communication (e-mail, video-conferencing, internet-relay chats etc.) and the internet.

For useful guidance also see the BBC World Service pages entitled 'Teaching with Technology' at: *http://www.bbc.co.uk/worldservice/learningenglish/teachingwithtechnology/*.

(Satellite) TV and video recorder

Through the video recorder two different types of material can be accessed: off-air recordings in the TL produced for non-educational purposes and language programmes produced specifically for educational purposes, either stand-alone or accompanying/ accompanied by printed material. Both types are readily available from national, satellite and foreign television stations.

One of the reasons for using television in mfl teaching is that it is often intrinsically motivating to pupils. It offers a degree of familiarity and with it security.

As Brian Hill points out (see 1989: 3), off-air recordings in the TL provide examples of real life, which are potentially up-to-date and offer an intercultural perspective on life. Off-air recordings can bring the culture(s) of the target countries into the classroom.

As a teaching and learning resource, the television offers useful listening material. The visual support allows pupils to make use of paralinguistic information and also to contextualise language use. The use of video recordings provides mfl trainees with many options. Depending on the learning objectives and the language skills to be developed, sound can either be on or off, the picture can be on or off, frames can be frozen and passages fast-forwarded or rewound. Each of these uses can support a range of different learning processes.

Simply playing an excerpt with strong visual clues can lead to passive understanding. Hill (see 1989:8) argues that this passive understanding is a necessary pre-cursor to oral work and that '(there) is also considerable evidence to suggest that learners will begin to speak when they are ready ...' (Hill 1989: 19).

Eddie Williams (see 1982: 69) recommends what he calls the 'witness activity' to stimulate a higher level of engagement. Learners are required to listen and observe and are quizzed on their non-verbal observations. This is intended to focus the pupils' interest on the context.

As with any resource, the use of television has its challenges. Television is ephemeral and the topicality, although appealing, needs to be harnessed in order to produce (mfl) learning outcomes.

Jim Coleman (see 1990: 17) provides 'ten commandments' for the use of TV, which include advice relevant for all technological aids, such as to know and understand the equipment or to provide clear instructions for related activities. Other advice is more specific to TV and video, such as not to use more than three minutes of a programme within a one-hour lesson. Coleman also notes that there is a need to vary the type of programme shown and also the types of activity set for pupils.

Janet Swaffar and Andrea Vlatten (1997: 175) argue that 'identifying values implied by ... pictorial messages ... helps students recognize how pictorial messages are underscored and elaborated in a video's spoken language'. They also report research on children and adult foreign language learners which suggests that, 'when compared with students who have only print or auditory texts, learners supplied with video materials understand and remember more'.

There is some agreement between commentators that certain television programmes lend themselves more to mfl teaching and learning than others (see Hill 1991: 15ff.; Bevan 1982: 137–55).

News items have a short life span but a high level of topicality. Watching news bulletins allows for structured note taking and can serve as an excellent stimulus for discussions. Key words can, for instance, be matched with newspaper headlines and comparisons between the presentation of a story in different media are possible.

Advertisements, on the other hand, have a longer 'shelf-life'. They often represent, yet also distance, 'real life' through symbolism. Often little language is used and consequently the stimulus is essentially visual. The 'freeze-frame' is particularly useful, as is guessing the product by playing the sound-track only.

Drama, notably soap opera, offers a wealth of transactional language. Short sequences can be used as stimuli for role plays by pausing at key moments of narration, by fast-forwarding or by switching off the sound. Prediction of events to come and the recapping of past events allow pupils to manipulate tenses.

Soap operas lend themselves to speculation about future events, which can lead to short dramatic performances by pupils. For drama work at a more basic level, scenes watched on screen can be copied.

In addition to presenting brief segments of 30 seconds to 3 minutes of longer video 'text' or to choose shorter 'texts' such as commercials or newscast excerpts, Swaffar and Vlatten argue the case for real-life video 'texts' of longer duration (between 10 minutes and 1 hour) on the grounds that they require pupils to produce their own language to generalise about what they have seen, where shorter extracts focus pupils' attention on the precise language used in the video text (see 1997: 177). Shorter extracts, they argue, deprive pupils of redundant and contextual information such as story line.

Reflection
Activity 12.7 Using off-air video recordings

- With a particular unit of work and its learning objectives in mind, record snippets of different programmes, such as sports broadcasts, weather forecasts, news items, advertisements, drama etc. and devise a range of activities for each programme type.
- In what way can any of your recordings be used to enhance this unit of work? What preparatory work needs to be undertaken in order to use the recordings successfully? What viewing tasks could pupils undertake and how would you follow them up?

The benefits video recordings offer go beyond personal interest and individual involvement. By dividing the class into two or more groups the viewing of an excerpt can be targeted to certain pupils: some pupils watch an excerpt whilst others are asked to come up with questions in the TL in order to find out what happened. This type of information gap activity can be further refined into 'jigsaw viewing': different groups of pupils can watch different excerpts and the task is to decide the sequence of events by communicating snippets to each other.

Although Coleman warns against over-*use of transcripts* (see 1990: 17), Hill points out the possible links to written work (see 1989: 19). Dictation, particularly on short news items, producing summaries, note-taking and scripting additional scenes or advertisements, all lend themselves to TV work.

The development of *accompanying material* can be rather time-consuming for the teacher. As has been noted, off-air recordings are not necessarily designed for educational purposes and turning them into teaching material can demand considerable effort and imagination from the teacher. Increasingly, newscasts and other source material, including transcripts and sometimes even activities for exploitation, are available on CD-ROM (e.g. '*Tele con textos*', '*Télé-textes*' or '*TV und Texte*' see *http://www.oup.co.uk*) or the internet (see e.g. '*Tagesschau*' available at *http://www.tagesschau.de*).

Increasingly *supplementary video material* accompanies coursebooks and audio-cassettes. Often teachers' notes give guidance on classroom use. Short snippets of language used in authentic situations allow for identification and repetition of key phrases. Once the content of a unit/episode has been presented in isolation, language items tend to be incorporated into a sequence of scenes. The language content is often limited and the visual content directs the viewer to the action. The placing of language into the dramatic context allows for recognition with the help of pronounced gestures, expressions and all sorts of para-linguistic support. The plots are often easy to follow even without understanding all the language content. This makes it easier for pupils to script and enact playlets based on what they have seen. Another possible activity is to watch a scene without sound and predict or speculate about its language content.

For useful guidance on satellite TV see, for example, Hill 1999.

In order to be able to use TV and video material effectively to support the development of lesson objectives, it needs to be viewed and evaluated in advance. In evaluating the material, mfl trainees might ask themselves the following questions (Kerridge 1982: 109):

a) What does the material teach?
b) Is what it teaches relevant to my learners?
c) Can it be integrated into the course system?
d) What relevant ancillary activities can be devised?
e) Can it be broken down into sequences?
f) Can it be exploited with more than one target group of learners?
g) Will the material have a primary or supportive role in the course?

Reflection
Activity 12.8 Using (coursebook-based) video material

- If available at your placement school, analyse the coursebook-based video material accompanying the current unit of work of a class of your choice. Alternatively use some other suitable video material. The BBC and Channel 4 regularly transmit relevant programmes. For contact details see the 'Contacts' page of the website accompanying this book available at *http://www.ioe.ac.uk/lie/pgce/*. Is there any video material which could meaningfully support the development of the unit of work's learning objectives?
- If so, plan a lesson using this material. How long should the extract be? At what stage of the lesson should the viewing take place? What might be useful preparatory, accompanying and/or follow-up activities?
- Discuss your lesson plan with the class teacher or your tutor before implementing it and evaluate the use of video material after the lesson.

The camcorder

The camcorder offers opportunities for objective summative and formative *assessment*. Recordings can be made by the teacher or by pupils. Communicative performance can be more easily assessed when watching a recording of a pupil's performance because the teacher can pause the recording and draw attention to and provide feedback on erroneous language production without having to interrupt the performance. Diagnostic feedback on errors and misconceptions are an important part of learning. John Klapper (see 1991: 13) recommends that adequate practice and rehearsal should take place in advance of a recording being made, thereby minimising the potential for error.

The opportunity to play sequences over and over is an important asset of video recordings. The evaluation of a recorded performance should take into account the different components which comprise the performance. Jack Lonergan (see 1990: 3) suggests focussing on:

- pronunciation;
- the coherence of (the) message(s) being conveyed;
- the register and tone of language; and
- the relevance of the content with a social/cultural context.

If used for self-assessment, there is the danger that to see oneself performing on video can be an anticlimax for performers. Pupils, therefore, need to be briefed carefully how to assess and appraise themselves and each other.

Filming individuals and groups can be an excellent motivator. As a practical piece of advice John Pearson (1990: 70) notes that '(imposing) a deadline for filming to begin, as in a live transmission, can focus minds very effectively'.

Pupils use a wide range of skills to produce their own information-based, documentary-type video clip such as a tour of their school in the TL. This requires a script and research. The following case study is an example of such a project.

The imitation of game shows is also a very productive approach to the use of the camcorder. Pearson (1990: 71) reports great enthusiasm and fun producing a French version of 'Blind Date' to practise standard GCSE phrases related to the topic of personal details.

The production of weather forecasts allows for the use of familiar language within a familiar context.

Reflection
Activity 12.9 Using the camcorder

- Film a class of your choice when they carry out an activity that lends itself to video recording, such as making a presentation, performing a role play, giving a tour through the school/town or exchanging personal details, views and opinions.
- Then, play the recordings back and engage pupils in analysing their performance.
- Finally, evaluate the process and consider how you could improve on it the next time.

A CASE STUDY OF A PROJECT BASED AROUND THE USE OF THE CAMCORDER

by Roswitha Guest

The 'German School Project' arose out of a need to 'kick start' a highly motivated and enthusiastic small group of Year-10 pupils at Whitton School, who had chosen German as their second foreign language GCSE option, having had one lesson per week in Years 8 and 9.

The overall objective of this project was to capitalise on pupils' enthusiasm and motivation and to stretch them intellectually as well as linguistically despite the deficit in their language skills over a conventional first-foreign-language German Year-10 group.

The aims of the project were:

* to practise, consolidate and extend Key Stage 3 language;
* to provide pupils with an opportunity to take charge of their learning and to 'own' their project, resuming responsibility for planning, execution, outcome and evaluation;
* progression from Key Stage 3 language situations to those more appropriate to Key Stage 4 despite pupils' linguistic shortcomings; and
* to utilise the individual interests and special talents within the group, e.g. technical and IT skills.

An article in German about the German School in Richmond in the *Education Guardian* (see Kasten 1995) intrigued the pupils who, despite its proximity, had not been aware of the school's existence. This article provided the stimulus for the project.

The German School has approximately 600 German native-speaking pupils from the age of five to nineteen and a mixture of English and German staff. It is very much a German environment and the working language at the school is German.

Once the go-ahead for the project had been given by both schools, the pupils' first task was to agree on a realistic programme for their visit to the German School. After lengthy discussions they settled for the production and presentation of a video for peers at their own school of

* the school environment at the German School (buildings and grounds);
* two or three lessons in the lower school there;
* interviews with three of four pairs of Year-3 pupils;
* break time in the dining hall; and
* lunch in the dining hall.

The preparations involved

* all technical equipment (camcorder, cassette recorder, boom microphone, tripod, camera etc.) to be booked, checked, loaded etc.;
* writing a commentary for filmed items;
* writing cue-cards and link sequences between items; and
* interview question cards to be prepared using phrase books, dictionaries, coursebooks etc.

The preparation of the interview cards involved the pupils in the recycling of all language items from Key Stage 3, starting with the topic of 'personal identification' and moving on to many more as they became more adventurous with their questions. Because the interviews were designed for young pupils (aged 8–9 years) at the German School, Whitton pupils' limited linguistic competence was appropriate for the audience.

The cue cards and link sequences required a more descriptive type of language. Pupils gathered the information for these from brochures and articles about the German School.

On the day of the visit the pupils were excited but quite nervous about their project. They were particularly worried about having to speak German all day and about how the German pupils would react to their linguistic efforts. But the day went very well.

The filming of a German lesson (pupils composing a poem about the topic 'spring'), a handicraft lesson (German Easter decorations) and a PE lesson (a German ballgame) turned out remarkably well on film – and Whitton pupils enjoyed and understood the lessons.

The most valuable part of the project turned out to be the interviews with the German pupils. Each pair of Whitton pupils interviewed a German boy and girl. It was most impressive how Whitton pupils adapted their questions to suit the individual pupils displaying an impressive linguistic agility. At the end of the interviews the Whitton pupils 'pooled' their questions and interviewed an additional pair of German pupils using the questions that had worked best previously. This last interview consequently formed the basis of the follow-up work to the project.

The pupils found it challenging to produce items in the TL that were clearly spoken and easily understood. They also realised that there was a real difference between authentic language production and role plays and found that the most useful items turned out to be those that had been thoroughly discussed, carefully prepared and fully scripted.

Back at Whitton School, the pupils spent a considerable amount of their own time editing a final version of the videotape, having decided a running order and what to cut. The transcribing of the individual interviews was followed by the preparation of a worksheet for their peers in Year 7.

The next stage of the project was the presentation of the film and the worksheet to the Year-7 pupils.

The Year-10 pupils were surprised how much work was involved to turn their 'raw product' into something usable, but they rose to the challenge. After the project they were also much more appreciative of any language videos they watched.

In addition, they wrote many thank-you letters and faxes to various teachers and pupils at the German School and to Whitton's German assistant whose help was invaluable.

As an evaluation of their experience and the project, pupils wrote an account of the day in the past tense. They all wanted to repeat the activity and do everything much better!

The list of achievements – apart from the pupils' enjoyment of and pride in their work – is long and covers most of the NC PoS requirements, but particularly the sections on language skills, language learning skills and cultural awareness.

The photographs taken and other items of information material gathered at the German School were displayed in the languages corridor at Whitton and generated considerable interest from pupils, staff and parents.

Recordings of pupils are also a means of communicating with others. The exchange of personal details with pupils in partner schools abroad through a video recording is to many pupils more exciting than writing letters.

But fear of the camera can lead to over-rehearsal and a tendency to learn scripts by heart can prevail. This needs to be guarded against. Frequent use can help overcome apprehension about being filmed, as can simply having the camera in the classroom without even using it. When using video recording as evidence for pupils' attainment, pupils should not be allowed to script their dialogues. Instead, where necessary, pupils should use prompt sheets or visual aids.

Computer-based aids

In the confines of this chapter it is not possible to discuss the strengths and challenges of individual types of applications such as word processors, databases, spreadsheets, text-manipulation and authoring packages, the concept keyboard, electronic dictionaries, language games, e-mail, videoconferencing or the internet in great detail. Many useful publications are available that examine individual applications in some detail. References to relevant background reading can be found on the website accompanying this book. Nor, indeed, is it possible to review individual software or CD-ROM packages. However, a regularly updated information sheet on selected mfl software can be found in the 'ICT resources' section of the homepage. In addition, on the 'Contacts' page of the website accompanying this book available at *http://www.ioe.ac.uk/lie/pgce/* there is a section entitled 'Software', which features links to some relevant online resources.

Due to limited space, in this chapter we concentrate on the main principles characterising the vast potential of individual computer-based aids for mfl learning and teaching and give some practical examples of mfl-based of ICT use.

ICT-based, and in particular computer-based, resources have specific characteristics (see e.g. Pachler 1999d, 1999e and 2000), of which users need to be aware and which allow teachers and learners to do new things in new ways (see Noss and Pachler 1999). These are:

- interactivity, i.e. allowing users to create content, fill in and submit forms, receive feedback/scores etc, and communicative potential, i.e. to send and receive messages and attached files;
- non-linearity and provisionality of information, i.e. hypertext-based pages through which there is often no sequential path and which can disappear as easily as they can be published;
- distributed nature of information, i.e. information is not held in a central location, as well as
- multimodality, i.e. the combination of writing, the spoken word and images.

These characteristics allow ICT tools to perform a number of functions in mfl teaching and learning, eg:

- to access authentic material and real language used in context;
- to practise language skills;
- to communicate with TL speakers;

- to develop language learning skills; or
- to develop cultural awareness.

Apart from *computer-assisted language (CALL) software* packages helping learners to develop their grammatical awareness of the modern foreign language by practising by-and-large specific patterns, the *word processor* has – for good reasons – been one of the most widely used applications:

> The essential characteristic of all wordprocessors, however simple or complex, is the provisional nature of the text generated. It is this which differentiates wordprocessed text from traditionally written or spoken forms. There need never be a final version. ... The potential for making changes has considerable implications for foreign language learners, some of whom, in the past, have found that the development of writing skills in the target language has been a less than successful and happy experience. Text produced using a pen and paper becomes a fixed object which can be criticised but which can only be corrected, often piecemeal, by rubbing out, crossing out or rewriting. The activity is oriented towards failure from the outset since, in the students' eyes, errors, detected by the teacher, denote failure.
>
> (Hewer 1992: 3)

Search-and-replace or TL spell-checking facilities make the word processor a versatile tool for learners of all abilities. The word processor empowers pupils to produce high-quality end-products and/or allows them to become sensitive to structural aspects of the modern foreign language, for instance by having to choose the correct spelling from a number of choices when using the spell checker. The mere writing up or copying of text, however, often does not satisfy one of the key principles which should underpin ICT use, i.e. '(allowing) the teacher or the pupil to achieve something that could not be achieved without it; or allow the teacher to teach or the pupils to learn something more effectively and efficiently than they could otherwise; or both' (TTA 1999: 8). Therefore, purposeful use of word processing is essential.

Databases, Sue Hewer notes, 'give students authentic reasons for information gathering before coming to the keyboard' (1992: 5). They offer a meaningful incentive to mfl learners to carry out survey work in class, input the data collected and print it out in the form of graphs for a project booklet or display. In simulation of real-life (work-based) tasks, databases can also be used effectively as stimuli for oral role-play work such as booking hotel rooms, locating lost property or finding an appropriate partner.

The *concept keyboard* is particularly useful for work with pupils with learning difficulties and/or special educational needs as it allows input of information and the generation of texts by depressing variably sized pads representing words, phrases, sentences or even short paragraphs rather than small keys on a keyboard representing individual letters. This peripheral, therefore, allows pupils with writing or spelling difficulties to produce correct written representations of pictures and other visual stimuli. The raw text or sequences of words/phrases can then be edited and linked on the word processor. Individual 'overlays', pieces of paper containing stimuli such as pictorial representations of the writing, which are triggered by depressing a particular pad, can be easily produced and 'programmed' by the mfl teacher as well as exchanged for others.

The *advent of multimedia applications* and *speech recognition software*, which run on modern desk-top computers equipped with CD-ROM drives and sound cards, allows for computer-based aids to be used meaningfully for mfl work relating to the four skills of speaking, listening, reading and writing. Programs such as 'Tell me more Pro' (see *http://www.auralog.com*) allow learners, amongst other things, to listen to native speaker recordings by clicking an icon on the computer-screen with the mouse, and record their own voice practising their pronunciation by modelling themselves against an example. All this without having to rewind an audio-tape to the exact spot over and over again. CD-ROM applications, which are capable of holding large amounts of data including pictures and sound, such as, for instance, all editions of a foreign newspaper published in one year, offer easy access to a wide range of authentic reading material.

At the time of writing, the first foreign language learning DVDs are starting to emerge. DVDs, which require a DVD player or drive, add an additional level of interactivity. They have a high storage capacity and can hold lots of video clips. This allows learners, amongst other things, to view, listen to and replay high-quality video clips. Learners can also record their own voices and dubb scenes of films. Eurotalk (*http://www.eurotalk.co.uk*), for example, sell didactically prepared popular television programs in French (*Au coeur de la loi*), German (*Ein Fall für zwei*), Spanish (*Querido maestro*) and Italian (*Mio padre innocente*) on DVD for advanced foreign language learners. Episodes are enhanced by way of exploitation activities and scripts.

CD-ROMs also yield great potential for (creative) writing. Multilingual programs such as 'Young Writers' Workshop' (see *http://www.granada-learning.com*) allow pupils to compose stories comprising text, sound and images on the basis of stimulus material and save them as webpages, ready for publication on the school's intranet/local area network (LAN) or the world wide web (WWW). 'Stop Press', at the time of writing available free of charge from the Goethe-Institut, is another CD-ROM, which includes text, audio and video sources and allows users to create their own webpage (see *http://www.britcoun.de/stop/start.htm*). It is based on a simulation model, which invites the user to explore the culture, society and media of Germany and the UK through the completion of a number of assignments, the setting for which is electronic journalism. Users' research, reporting and editing skills are developed in the process of working through the source material provided with a view to presenting, and publishing, a web-based report on a given topic taken, for example, from education, the environment, the economy, politics, youth culture or pastimes.

Regular contact with a range of background material and authentic resources on CD-ROM can facilitate the development of pupils' understanding of academic work, such as how to refer to background reading or quote source text. Compared with the internet, CD-ROMs have the advantage of a stable content, e.g. many CD-ROMs can be networked, which allows for the same information to be made available to all workstations without the potential problems and costs involved in connecting to sources via the internet. On the downside, the content can date as easily as that of coursebooks and site licences can be expensive. Increasingly, publishers make updates available over the internet.

Three broad categories of CD-ROM products for language learning have been suggested: '(firstly), collections of resources or reference materials; secondly, courseware or tutorial materials and thirdly, enhanced stories which may be more or less 'interactive' in design' (Bourne 1996: 55). All three types have potential application in mfl teaching and learning.

On a rather cautious note the view has been put forward that there are no good CD-ROMs for teaching mfl,

> but (that) there are some which are reasonable for learning. A pedantic distinction perhaps, but it does point to the fact that they tend to be more useful in independent learning rather than in whole-class teaching.
>
> (Atkinson, quoted in Lewis 1996: 17)

This has obvious planning implications for mfl trainees using CD-ROMs, for instance in terms of where to locate the equipment, how to enable pupils' access to it or how to link independent computer-based activities to the mfl curriculum.

Another important consideration in the context of ICT use in the mfl classroom is the need for teachers to ensure that pupils using information obtained particularly via CD-ROM and/or the internet have actually understood the material and developed and/or consolidated linguistic skills, knowledge and understanding in the process of using this technology. Trainees need to be clear – and make it clear to pupils – how the use of ICT relates to given mfl learning objectives. Pupils need to be taught early on how 'to sift, reject and re-use for their own purposes from the mass of material' (Horsfall and Whitehead 1996: 26). One strategy Phil Horsfall and Maurice Whitehead suggest in this context is the frequent use of 'self-set vocabulary tests' where pupils select a number of useful TL words from a source text for homework, find a definition for them in a monolingual dictionary, learn the words and are tested on them at the beginning of the next lesson. This strategy encourages pupils to interact with the source material in terms of relevance and meaning.

There are also a number of so called *authoring* packages, such as 'Storyboard' and 'Gapmaster' (see *http://www.wida.co.uk*) or 'Hot Potatoes' (available at *http://web.uvic.ca/ hrd/halfbaked/*) and *text manipulation packages*, such as 'Fun with Texts' (see *http://ourworld. compuserve.com/homepages/grahamdavies1/*), allowing the teacher – or indeed learners – to create exercises and activities following a given framework without having to know anything about computer programming. This is particularly useful as vocabulary or grammatical structures of activities can be tailored to specific topics or units of work. Also specific difficulties of (individual) pupils can be catered for in this way.

Text manipulation software allows pupils to make changes to previously written text. Sue Hewer (1997: 2) distinguishes the following types of activities:

- sequencing words, sentences and/or paragraphs;
- replacing existing words;
- inserting additional words;
- gap filling, including cloze tests;
- unscrambling words or chunks of text;
- reconstructing a text in part or in its entirety.

She (1997: 12) deems text manipulation to have the potential to produce tasks which

- improve (pupils') knowledge of structure;
- improve their knowledge of form;
- apply and improve their knowledge of collocation;

- consolidate and improve their vocabulary;
- consolidate and improve their spelling and punctuation.

Presentation packages, such as 'PowerPoint', and authoring packages such as 'Hyper-studio' (see *http://www.hyperstudio.com*) can be used by teachers and pupils to create multimedia content, combining text, images (scanned in, taken with a digital camera or found on the internet/in a clip art library/on a CD-ROM) and sound recordings. A number of wordprocessing packages also allow the creation of multimedia content. 'RealProducer' available at *http://www.real.com* is a software package which allows users to record high-quality sound files requiring very little disc space.

For guidance on producing multimedia content see e.g. Bruntlett 1999.

There exist, of course, also a large number of often relatively cheap (*shareware*) or even free (*freeware*) language learning games etc, which can be motivating for pupils and often lend themselves well to work in language clubs (see e.g. *http://www. download.com*), such as cross-word programs or bingo card generators. Increasingly, internet-based tools, such as '*Übungen selbstgemacht*' (available at *http://www.goethe.de/z/ 50/uebungen/deindex.htm*) or '*Quia!*' (available at *http://www.quia.com*) are becoming available, which allow teachers and learners to create interactive (online) activities without having to possess any programming skills.

The *internet* offers great potential to mfl learners and teachers. A vast amount of up-to-date authentic material can be accessed. The internet lends itself particularly well to mfl work post-16 and for independent study or research, but is also very useful in Key Stages 3 and 4, where it can, for instance, be used effectively to develop cultural aware-ness. As with all other technological aids there are a number of important considerations for mfl trainees. They need to research relevant internet addresses in advance and plan activities around them. Using the internet merely to 'surf' authentic resources rarely leads to relevant learning outcomes! A key pedagogic skill in the context of internet use is the creation of web-based worksheets, which can be stored online or on the school's intranet and which contain links to relevant websites and exploitation activities. Relevant webpages can be saved onto local computers or the school's network thus limiting the potential of pupils' viewing irrelevant or unsuitable pages. For a more detailed discussion of internet use in mfl teaching see Pachler 1999e and Pachler with Reimann 1999.

Reflection
Activity 12.10 Using the internet for mfl teaching and learning

- Explore the internet sites available at *http://www.ioe.ac.uk/lie/pgce/* and assess the potential of individual sites for your use in mfl teaching or for independent study.
- Create your own webpages and try them out in your teaching. How successful were they? Were the intended learning outcomes achieved? What modifications did you have to make? Send an e-mail to *norbert@languages.zzn.com* with details of your webpages and the lesson, or series of lessons, in which they were used for possible posting on the website accompanying this book.

Useful internet-based tools also include translation services and dictionaries. For details, see the 'Contacts' page of the website accompanying this book at *http://www.ioe.ac.uk/lie/pgce/*. See this website also for a regularly updated list of relevant internet links and teaching resources for French, German, Italian and Spanish. Guidelines for internet use in the teaching of German as a Foreign Language developed by the Goethe-Institut can be found at *http://www.goethe.de/ne/hel/destip1.htm*.

A particular benefit of ICT for mfl teachers and learners is the ability to communicate with TL speakers. ICT allows both real-time (synchronous) and delayed-time (asynchronous) *computer-mediated communication*. In real time teachers and pupils can communicate with TL speakers through online chats/one-to-one communication programmes such as 'MSN Messenger' available at *http://messenger.msn.com/*, 'MIRC' available at *http://www.mirc.co.uk* or 'ICQ' available at *http://web.icq.com* as well as *video-conferencing* and carry out joint projects. These chats tend to be text-based, whilst videoconferencing combines text and picture. For a detailed mfl case study on video conferencing, see Butler and Kelly 1999. Other very useful information on video conferencing is available online at *http://www.en.eun.org/news/vidconf-directory.html* (European Schoolnet) and *http://www.savie.com/* (Savie Videoconferencing Atlas). For more detailed discussions of CMC including characteristics of the language used see e.g. Pachler 1999e, Peterson 1997 or Warschauer 1997.

Electronic mail (e-mail) is increasingly seen as powerful tool in mfl learning and teaching. E-mail enables learners to send and receive messages including pictures, text files and graphs in the TL around the world in seconds via a modem and the telephone or a network card and connection without having to make an international call and often at the cost of a local call only. The potential for project- and group-work with partner schools in the TL is great. For details see Chapter 8. The messages can be produced 'off-line', i.e. on the word processor or any other computer package, without being connected to the telephone, then uploaded and sent at a convenient time or during cheap rate to minimise cost. With the help of a digital video camera it is possible to send *video mail*, whereby pupils can send a message comprising spoken text and moving images per e-mail. In order to allow pupils regular contact with peers in the target culture(s), trainees should sign up to one or more of the e-mail networks and web-based partner-finding services available on the internet such as the 'ePals Classroom Exchange' (available at *http://www.epals.com*) or 'Windows on the World' (available at

---

Reflection
Activity 12.11 Using e-mail for mfl teaching and learning

- If you haven't got your own personal e-mail address yet, set one up, for example at *http://languages.zzn.com*. Then send an e-mail to norbert@languages.zzn.com, for instance with some feedback on this book or an example of your use of ICT in mfl teaching and learning.
- Think of an interesting project you might want to carry out with a partner school abroad. Then go to 'ePals Classroom Exchange' or 'Windows on the World' and register your project. Also have a look if any interesting projects are being proposed.

A CASE STUDY OF USING E-MAIL LINKS IN MFL

by Jonathan Day

At the Lord Grey School, we viewed our long-standing exchanges with partner schools in Germany, Spain and France as starting points for exploiting the use of e-mail. We started to work with our German and Spanish partners on various fronts, as a pilot in the first instance, with the aim of subsequently expanding good practice and including more staff and pupils/students.

We started by establishing a functional e-mail link with one teacher at our partner school in Spain.

We used this link to organise the school exchange, a traditional exchange where there are outward and return legs and where pupils are allocated partners with whom they stay when travelling abroad. We saved hugely on phone bills and were able to carry on a continuous dialogue through our almost daily e-mail contact.

Once the exchange had been set up administratively, the pupils were able to write to their partners in Spain in order to get to know each other before meeting face to face. A digital camera enabled us to send pictures down the phone line.

Having established working routines on a small scale, it was clear that we could now begin to use e-mail for correspondence between larger numbers of A-level students who, with the help of ICT, would be able to participate in an exchange without actually travelling abroad.

We piloted this system of correspondence with a dozen post-16 A-level students who we paired off with peers in the Spanish and German schools. The results of these e-mail links were pleasing: exchanges were immediate, real and motivating, with students clamouring for replies from their partners abroad.

Having worked firstly on a small scale, we were subsequently able to involve more classes and other colleagues in the project. Our aim is for every pupil/student in the school to have a penfriend in a country where the language she is studying is spoken.

Further exploitation has been made by pupils at Key Stage 4 and students at post-16 familiar with the system using it for their own research. For example, students sent questionnaires to Spanish classes on bullfighting and on tourism in Ibiza in order to collect information for A-level coursework.

We have also set up a triangular link by putting our partner schools in Germany and Spain in touch with each other.

Some of the guidelines we drew up for developing successful e-mail links

- keep a record of partners of each pupil;
- keep a record of who has sent/received mail and when;
- double up partners if somebody does not get a reply – it's important not to let people down, as they can feel left out/demotivated if their partner fails them for whatever reason (if pupils miss a session through absence, they will often be prepared to catch up at a lunch- or breaktime or bring in work done on disk at home);

- explain to your pupils/students the implications of not keeping to their schedule;
- agree with your colleague abroad who will send first and what your topics will be;
- allow some flexibility, but structure your topics and link activities to your scheme of work – otherwise people run out of things to say;
- take advantage of seasons/times of the year/festivals and traditions as topics for description/discussion;
- current affairs and the way they are perceived/portrayed are good topics for A-level students; and
- vary the language used (by arrangement with your colleagues abroad), sometimes writing in the TL, sometimes in English, so that your pupils/students both read and write their foreign TL.

Implications

It is clear that e-mail has enabled us to enhance and broaden the scope of the traditional school exchange involving more staff and students than may have been possible previously. We hope that there will be a greater uptake in numbers on exchange trips as a consequence.

Other curriculum areas have begun to show an interest in becoming involved too.

In our experience, successful projects require:

- time to familiarise staff and pupils/students with the equipment and systems;
- access to computers!;
- personal contacts with our colleagues abroad and goodwill, which is particularly useful/necessary when there is a technical problem or delay when your mail has not got through when expected; and
- cheap phone time (we are lucky to have a very cheap system, but in any case, if you put all letters in a batch onto one file, then it takes next to no time to send the document).

Finally, some practical points

- pupils/students themselves can be immensely helpful in sorting out technical problems that are beyond you (I am an mfl teacher, not an ICT teacher!);
- this is an ideal opportunity to teach and use classroom ICT language: you do *not* need to lapse back into English as your main means of communication;
- don't rush to make your e-mail exchange frequency too high as 'normal' teaching must still go on; it all takes time, even if electronic communications are almost instantaneous! Once every three weeks is probably a realistic frequency for sending mail at first;
- keep backups of all files – it's not good to lose somebody's work!

Using e-mail definitely adds an extra dimension to our school exchanges!

http://www.wotw.org.uk). Further details on the use of e-mail in mfl teaching can be found in Townshend 1997. Readers who have not got a personal e-mail account can set up free web-based e-mail accounts for themselves and their pupils, for instance at *http://languages.zzn.com/*. Where possible, trainees should use a service which offers a target language interface, requiring learners to use TL commands for accessing and sending their e-mails.

The following case study describes an example of e-mail use.

EVALUATING ICT RESOURCES

The choice of which ICT resource to use or which software program to buy requires careful consideration, not least because of the considerable cost of many resources:

> The very nature of multimedia, vast, non-linear and readable only through the computer screen, means that it is difficult to assess the scope and quality of a title or source without spending considerable time on it. There is no equivalent to picking up and flicking through a book which will give an experienced teacher a clear view of its coverage and relevance.
>
> (McFarlane 1996: 4)

Research suggests that the choice of which resource to buy or use is often informed by the quality of support materials available helping the teacher with the classroom application such as activity sheets or suggestions for how the product fits into the curriculum (see Jones 1996:30).

Also, the creators of ICT-based resources make certain assumptions about the learning process, the teaching methodology and the knowledge, skills and understanding of the intended user group. Sometimes authors, particularly web-authors, are constraint by technical possibilities.

From this follows that the ability to evaluate ICT-based resources is an important skill for trainees.

The following questions should help trainees assess the value of a resource for mfl teaching (source: *http://www.ioe.ac.uk/lie/pgce/eval.html*):

- What assumptions are made about how pupils learn?
- What assumptions are made about pupils' cognitive abilities, i.e. what are the prerequisites for the use of this resource?
- Are the conceptual and linguistic/semantic assumptions clear and appropriate? Is the wording effective and appropriate?
- Are the scope and the aims of the resource explicit?
- Is the resource user-friendly and interactive?
- Does it have the potential for differentiated access?
- Has appropriate use been made of hypermedia: is the layout clear and consistent? Is the material well organised and nicely presented?
- Does the concept work and is functionality given, i.e. do all the 'buttons' work?
- Is the user able to pursue her own path through the material?
- Are examples of possible navigational structures available?
- Is there an 'About' page or a user guide?

- Is the authorship transparent and subject expertise given?
- Is the content accurate, reliable and up-to-date?
- Is the resource comparable with similar resources, e.g. what does it do a book doesn't /can't do?
- Is online help available and are error messages clear?
- Are there technical/compatibility problems?

In terms of how the resource can be integrated into mfl teaching and learning, trainees should ask themselves the following questions (source: *http://www.ioe.ac.uk/lie/pgce/eval.html*):

- Can links with existing learning objectives/schemes of work be easily established? Is there an appropriate indication as to the possible contexts of use?
- When do I use it? What aspects of the Programme of Study and the Attainment Targets of the National Curriculum does this resource cover?
- What skills/knowledge/understanding are being developed by using this resource?
- How do I use this resource? In what socio-cultural context is learning situated? What types of pupil–teacher, pupil–pupil and teacher–pupil interactions are facilitated? How flexible is it, i.e. does it stimulate individual work, pair work and/or group work?
- What are the implications for the role of the teacher?
- What specific TL do the learners need to be able to work with this resource?
- What ICT skills are prerequisite to the use of this resource?

These two lists of questions, whilst not comprehensive, are clearly too long to be given consideration in full for each resource. Trainees might well want to select two or three questions only per resource, which seem most relevant, and evaluate a specific resource against those questions in depth.

A page giving guidance on evaluating ICT-based resources can be found in the 'ICT resources' section of the homepage of the website accompanying this book. In addition to criteria and a useful grid, the page also contains a number of sample evaluations by

---

**Reflection
Activity 12.12 Evaluation of
ICT applications**

- Put the criteria above in order of your personal preference. What do you consider to be most important in ICT applications for mfl?
- Then use this checklist for the evaluation of an ICT application. Also, ask your pupils what they think. Compare your views with those of your pupils.
- If you are interested in having your evaluation published on the website accompanying this book, send it to *norbert@languages.zzn.com*. The most relevant and appropriate submissions might well be published after any necessary editorial changes have been made.

trainees on the Institute of Education Secondary PGCE in Modern Foreign Languages. Furthermore, the 'Software' section of the 'Contacts' page features a number of links to software evaluations.

SUMMARY

In this chapter we discussed the role of ICT in mfl teaching and learning. ICT should not be seen as a possible replacement or challenge to the importance of the mfl teacher. Indeed, the use of ICT makes the role of the teacher more important but ICT use requires new pedagogical skills from teachers, such as the ability to evaluate multimodal resources.

ICT can play a key role in the development of listening, speaking, reading and writing skills as well as transferable skills such as independent learning and the use of reference material and prepare pupils for their (working) lives in modern society.

ICT should be used on the basis of its appropriateness in achieving mfl-related learning objectives, as a means to a end and not as an end in itself.

ICT can be used effectively inside and outside the mfl classroom and has great motivational potential for learners. It can meaningfully enhance and enrich pupils' mfl learning experience.

Last, but by no means least, ICT yields considerable potential for continuous professional development and networking. This aspect of ICT use is covered in Chapter 13.

13 The First Appointment and Professional Development

One aspect uppermost in many modern foreign languages (mfl) trainee teachers' minds during the latter stages of initial teacher education (ITE) is finding a first post. Therefore, initially, this chapter looks at some of the issues concerning applying for jobs and going for interviews.

The recently reintroduced requirement for newly qualified teachers (NQTs) to complete a period of probation, the so-called induction year, is the focus of a subsequent section of this chapter. The role and nature of the statutory career entry profile (CEP) is also discussed.

OBJECTIVES

By the end of this chapter you should:

- understand the issues involved in finding your first teaching post, such as writing letters of application or preparing and going for interview;
- understand the issues involved in starting your first teaching post, such as going for a preparatory visit, building on your CEP, awareness of the induction standards, completing the induction year, team work with colleagues or interacting with parents;
- recognise the need for INSET and CPD throughout your teaching career including the role of ICT in this context;
- be aware of the importance of keeping a good record of evidence of your CPD; and
- be aware of mfl specific development and training opportunities with a particular emphasis on your first year of teaching as an NQT.

Furthermore we examine some issues concerning continuing professional development (CPD), including the role of Information and Communications Technology (ICT). CPD of already qualified mfl teachers is important because, as could be seen throughout this book, mfl teaching is a continually changing, highly complex and demanding occupation, requiring knowledge, skills and understanding as well as competence in a wide range of different areas. The need for ongoing development is clearly recognised by the teaching profession. The willingness to engage in in-service education and training (INSET) and CPD, which can be carried out 'in-house' or outside school, is one of many indicators for success in mfl teaching and can also be seen as a pre-requisite for promotion.

GETTING YOUR FIRST TEACHING POST

One considerable stress factor in the latter part of the ITE course tends to be the emotional upheaval associated with applying for jobs and preparing for as well as going to interviews. Securing a first teaching post tends to include the following steps.

Step 1. Finding out about vacancies

The national educational press – particularly the *Times Educational Supplement* (*TES*) on Fridays and the education section of the *Guardian* on Tuesdays – contains adverts of vacancies around the country. Both the *TES* and the *Education Guardian* maintain a searchable database of vacancies on the internet; they can be found at *http://www.tes.co.uk/* and *http://www.educationunlimited.co.uk/* respectively. Local education authorities (LEAs) also tend to publish bulletins of vacancies periodically. On request, schools send out particulars of vacancies and, where appropriate, an application form.

Finding the right (first) school has always been important but can be considered to be much more crucial since the introduction of the induction year. Identifying appropriate vacancies amongst the large number of adverts regularly featured in the *TES* and the *Education Guardian* is not easy. NQTs often benefit greatly in a supportive environment, in which they can consolidate and build on what they have learnt during their period of training.

There are a number of personal and professional considerations which govern the choice of school. They include:

- The characteristics and location of the school and the department: is it a boys', girls' or a co-educational school? What is the ethnic mix of the school? Is it a small or a large school? Where is it located: in a town or the country? Is it a community, comprehensive, foundation, grammar, independent school? Is it an 11–16 or an 11–18 school?
- The roles and responsibilities sought: are there opportunities to take part in cross- and extracurricular activities? Is there scope for promotion?
- The facilities available at the school and the local community: are the ICT facilities at the school and in the department good? Are there cinemas, theatres, sports facilities in the vicinity?

**Reflection
Activity 13.1 Choosing the
right school**

Consider the questions above in relation to a few vacancies you are
interested in. Do your answers help you narrow down your choice?

- The infrastructure: how easy is it to get to the school on foot, by public transport, by car?
- Proximity to friends and relatives: would you be able to keep in touch easily with your friends and family? or
- The affordability of housing: how much will it cost to rent or buy?

Step 2. Completing the application form and writing the covering letter

When applying for a vacancy, in the majority of cases, an application form needs to be completed and sent to the school together with a covering letter by a given deadline.

A successful application hinges on a well thought-out letter or supporting statement in which the personal philosophy and experience (of mfl teaching) of the applicant in relation to the job specifications and other details provided by the school are set out. There should be as much detail as possible about personal strengths, achievements and past experience in a covering letter related to what the school is actually looking for. The letter of application should attempt to address each of the items set out in the job specification directly. As different schools have different requirements and priorities, it is usually necessary to write a separate letter for each application rather than send out a 'standard' letter. Quality of use of English and presentation are two obvious criteria for judging letters of application. It is important to make sure the application form and the covering letter or supporting statement communicate strengths in a manner that is informative but without seeming arrogant.

Many schools will draw up a shortlist on the basis of the information applicants provide about themselves and the apparently most suitable applicants are invited for interview.

Step 3. Preparing and going for an interview

Where at one time the interview comprised meeting a small panel of people, schools appear to be moving towards employing more rigorous selection procedures including the teaching of sample lessons, the giving of presentations and the interviewing of candidates by pupils. Careful preparation for an interview, therefore, is essential.

Just as schools are eager to choose the right candidate to suit their needs, applicants should use the interview process as an opportunity to find out what working at a given

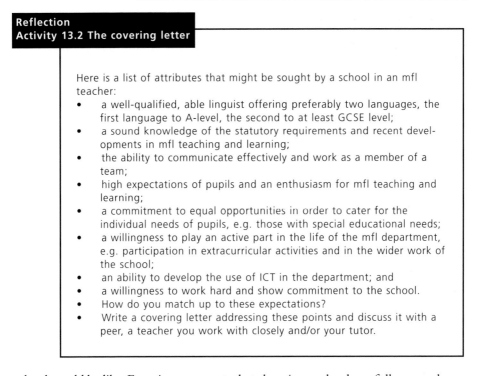

Reflection
Activity 13.2 The covering letter

Here is a list of attributes that might be sought by a school in an mfl teacher:

- a well-qualified, able linguist offering preferably two languages, the first language to A-level, the second to at least GCSE level;
- a sound knowledge of the statutory requirements and recent developments in mfl teaching and learning;
- the ability to communicate effectively and work as a member of a team;
- high expectations of pupils and an enthusiasm for mfl teaching and learning;
- a commitment to equal opportunities in order to cater for the individual needs of pupils, e.g. those with special educational needs;
- a willingness to play an active part in the life of the mfl department, e.g. participation in extracurricular activities and in the wider work of the school;
- an ability to develop the use of ICT in the department; and
- a willingness to work hard and show commitment to the school.
- How do you match up to these expectations?
- Write a covering letter addressing these points and discuss it with a peer, a teacher you work with closely and/or your tutor.

school would be like. Experience suggests that choosing a school carefully can make an important contribution to professional satisfaction. Candidates might, for example, access the latest OfSTED report on the school at *http://www.ofsted.gov.uk* to read up on inspection findings. In so doing, they need to bear in mind the purpose of and rationale behind the inspection process as well as the nature of the framework used and the validity and reliability of the judgements made. Areas identified in inspection reports might provide professional opportunities for NQTs and allow them to make a useful contribution to a department and/or school.

It is very important to be perceptive to the ethos and policies of the school and the mfl department on the interview day. At the end of that day, and often without an opportunity for any deliberation, the successful applicant is required to make a decision about accepting the post. Only very rarely will she be able to consider a job offer overnight.

In order to make this important decision easier, try to obtain as much relevant information during the day as possible. During the tour of the school on the interview day find out about the facilities available by observing, for instance, whether:

- there is a dedicated suite of mfl rooms which is decorated with stimulating and relevant displays;
- the department has an office to store resources, equipment and files, to work during non-contact time and to meet with colleagues;
- there are a cassette recorder and overhead projector in each classroom/for each member of staff in the department;
- the mfl department has easy access to a TV and video recorder;

- there is access to a satellite receiver and the internet;
- there is a departmental handbook with schemes of work;
- the department has its own computers with relevant software; or
- the school has an induction programme in place.

Also, try to find out:

- about possible teaching rooms;
- if pupils are issued with coursebooks they can take home with them;
- whether the department has a range of resources supplementary to coursebooks;
- about recent inspection recommendations;
- what extracurricular activities are offered; and
- how your personal approach to mfl teaching compares to that prevalent in the department.

This information can offer a useful insight into what mfl teaching at the school might be like for an NQT.

In our experience an atmosphere of mutual support and good working relationships with colleagues are not only desirable but essential. For this reason schools often provide an opportunity during the interview day for members of the mfl department to meet candidates. Although often informal, these occasions tend to be used by members of staff at the school to assess whether candidates are likely to fit into the department.

As part of one's interview preparation it is advisable to think of answers for questions the interview panel is likely to ask. These might include:

- Why did you want to become an mfl teacher?
- Please describe an mfl lesson you taught during your teaching experience which you feel was particularly successful and say why.
- Can you please briefly describe your personal approach to mfl teaching.
- What, in your opinion, makes mfl teaching and learning stimulating for pupils?
- Can you describe some strategies for teaching in the target language (TL)?
- What first-hand experience of ICT use have you been able to gain in your mfl teaching so far?
- Which resources do you consider essential for your teaching?
- What are the particular areas of interest and/or strengths you can offer to the mfl department and/or school?
- How important do you consider the role of the form tutor to be and what contribution do you feel you can make to the pastoral system of the school?

Reflection
Activity 13.3 Preparing for an interview

- How would you answer the possible interview questions above?
- Discuss your answers with a peer, a teacher you work with closely and/or your tutor.

- What do you consider to be the most important aspects of the National Curriculum (NC) mfl Orders/mfl teaching in the NC?
- What do you perceive to be areas in need of development in your teaching? What strategies might you consider to address them?
- Where do you see yourself in five years' time?

Useful information and support in matters relating to interviews and the writing of applications tends to be available from careers advisers (see e.g. Humphrys 1995). For further information on getting your first post see also Tolley, Biddulph and Fisher 1996.

On the day of an interview it is important to make sure all open questions, including the starting salary, have been answered before accepting a job, even orally. Useful guidance on finding a job, including up-to-date information on pay, is available from teaching unions.

STARTING AS AN MFL TEACHER

Finding a teaching post and gaining qualified teacher status (QTS) signals the start of the CPD process. In the initial stages of the career of an mfl teacher, but particularly during the NQT year, the priorities for professional development invariably focus on getting to know the school, its policies, procedures and curriculum as well as the many new colleagues who work there with responsibilities for the various aspects of school life. Most immediately there is, of course, the need to get to know the various groups of pupils and to become comfortable in the teaching situation. Only over time will the focus widen.

Preparatory visit

Newly appointed members of staff, and in particular NQTs, are often invited to spend a day or even a number of days at the new school before taking up their post. This

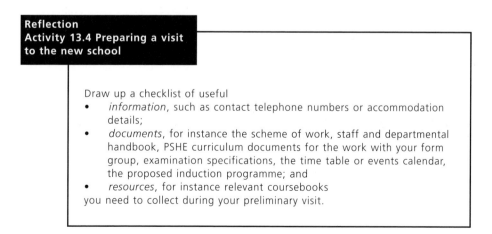

Reflection
Activity 13.4 Preparing a visit to the new school

Draw up a checklist of useful
- *information*, such as contact telephone numbers or accommodation details;
- *documents*, for instance the scheme of work, staff and departmental handbook, PSHE curriculum documents for the work with your form group, examination specifications, the time table or events calendar, the proposed induction programme; and
- *resources*, for instance relevant coursebooks

you need to collect during your preliminary visit.

enables them to get to know key colleagues in- and outside the department, to find out about the school procedures, departmental documentation including schemes of work, copies of relevant coursebooks and examination specifications (formerly syllabuses) and their time table, meet the classes they are going to teach and/or to find answers to questions that have arisen since the interview. Experiencing the school 'at work' helps to prepare for the term ahead. In order to make the most of the preparatory visit it might be useful to make a checklist of the information or documents to be collected and the people to be met.

The Career Entry Profile

The Teacher Training Agency's (TTA's) CEP, available at *http://www.canteach.gov.uk/info/induction/index.htm*, plays an important role in the induction arrangements for NQTs.

NQTs leave their course of initial training with a CEP, which sets out the NQT's strengths and areas for further professional development in relation to the standards of DfEE Circular 4/98 (see Chapter 2). The CEP provides the starting point for planning one's professional development and should be used as the basis for setting objectives and developing an action plan for the induction period.

INDUCTION YEAR

In 1999 the government introduced a statutory induction period, which applies to all NQTs and will usually be one academic year in length, combining an individualised programme of monitoring and support, providing opportunities for NQTs to develop further their knowledge and skills, with an assessment of their performance. In order to complete the induction period satisfactorily, all NQTs must meet a set of induction standards (see Figure 13.1) as well as to continue to meet the standards for the award of QTS outlined in DfEE Circular 4/98 (DfEE 1999) on a consistent basis in an employment context. At the time of writing the arrangements are set out in DfEE Circular 5/99 available at *http://www.dfee.gov.uk/circulars/5_99.htm* and the TTA (1999a) has produced a set of induction support materials available on their website at *http://www.canteach.gov.uk/info/induction/support.htm*.

1. In order to recommend that an NQT has satisfactorily completed the induction period, the headteacher should be satisfied that the NQT has:
    a. continued to meet the Standards for the Award of QTS consistently in teaching at the school;
    b. met all the Induction Standards.

The Induction Standards

2. To meet the Induction Standards, the NQT should demonstrate that he or she:

Planning, Teaching and Class Management
    a. sets clear targets for improvement of pupils' achievement, monitors pupils' progress towards those targets and uses appropriate teaching

strategies in the light of this, including, where appropriate, in relation to literacy, numeracy and other school targets;

b. plans effectively to ensure that pupils have the opportunity to meet their potential, notwithstanding differences of race and gender, and taking account of the needs of pupils who are:

- underachieving;
- very able;
- not yet fluent in English;

making use of relevant information and specialist help where available;

c. secures a good standard of pupil behaviour in the classroom through establishing appropriate rules and high expectations of discipline which pupils respect, acting to pre-empt and deal with inappropriate behaviour in the context of the behaviour policy of the school;

d. plans effectively, where applicable, to meet the needs of pupils with special educational needs and, in collaboration with the SENCO, makes an appropriate contribution to the preparation, implementation, monitoring and review of individual education plans;

e. takes account of ethnic and cultural diversity to enrich the curriculum and raise achievement.

Monitoring, Assessment, Recording, Reporting and Accountability

f. recognises the level that a pupil is achieving and makes accurate assessments, independently, against attainment targets, where applicable, and performance levels associated with other tests or qualifications relevant to the subject(s) or phase(s) taught;

g. liaises effectively with pupils' parents/carers through informative oral and written reports on pupils' progress and achievements, discussing appropriate targets, and encouraging them to support their children's learning, behaviour and progress.

Other Professional Requirements

h. where applicable, deploys support staff and other adults effectively in the classroom, involving them, where appropriate, in the planning and management of pupils' learning;

i. takes responsibility for implementing school policies and practices, including those dealing with bullying and racial harassment;

j. takes responsibility for their own professional development, setting objectives for improvements, and taking action to keep up-to-date with research and developments in pedagogy and in the subject(s) they teach.

(http://www.dfee.gov.uk/circulars/5_99/page2.htm#ANNEX)

In addition, there is the requirement to have passed the national tests in numeracy, literacy and ICT.

These standards, whilst being liable to change over time, give a clear indication of progression from working as a trainee teacher to taking on the responsibilities of a qualified teacher.

The induction standards very much build on the standards for QTS and emphasise those aspects of mfl teaching that are difficult to develop during initial training due to, for example, the relative brevity of time spent in any one placement school and the reduced teaching load of trainees etc. They should not be viewed as a checklist but as a set of criteria against which to discuss progress and to set targets for further professional development beyond the induction year.

The induction tutor of a school oversees an NQT's induction period but it is the headteacher who completes the report at the end of the year recommending whether or not all the required standards have been met.

At the time of writing NQTs should have the following during the induction period:

- a slightly reduced time table of 90 per cent of normal average teaching time with the release time being used for a coherent and relevant induction programme;
- support from a designated induction tutor, e.g. their head of department;
- their teaching observed and receive feedback in follow-up discussions;
- their professional progress reviewed;
- the opportunity to observe experienced teachers; and
- access to other targeted professional development activities in- or outside the school, which should be based on the CEP and aimed to help them meet the required standards.

There will be three formal assessment meetings between the NQT and either the headteacher or the induction tutor, usually with the following pattern:

A. the first meeting will focus on the extent to which the NQT is consistently meeting the Standards for the Award of QTS in an employment context, and is beginning to meet the Induction Standards;
B. the second meeting will focus on the NQT's progress towards meeting the Induction Standards;
C. the final assessment meeting will be used to determine whether the NQT has met all of the requirements for the satisfactory completion of the induction period.

(*http://www.dfeegov.uk/circulars/5_99/page1.htm*)

As part of the formal assessment there should be written reports on at least two formally observed lessons and on two progress review meetings per term. Judgements should be evidence-based with evidence coming from, for instance, lesson plans and evaluations, assessment data and record keeping, information about liaison with others, e.g. colleagues and parents, self-assessment or a personal portfolio.

The assessment procedures, therefore, centre around a process of target setting and review similar to those commonly applied in the period of initial training. The NQT should not be left in any doubt as to the progress being made and the development targets to be addressed.

In the case of an NQT failing to complete the induction period satisfactorily, she is no longer eligible to be employed as a teacher in a maintained school. No NQT may serve more than one induction period.

As part of the induction year, NQTs normally also take part in the induction pro-gramme for all staff new to a school, including experienced teachers who have come from other schools. This induction programme often includes opportunities to get to know key colleagues and to become familiar with the organisation of life and work at the school as well as to share and discuss experiences and problems with settling in.

Off-site sessions, e.g. LEA-led programmes, provide an opportunity to meet other newly qualified mfl teachers with whom it might be possible 'to compare notes'. Meetings of this kind are useful for consolidating certain aspects of subject methodology as well as for networking with peers from different schools with different subject specialisms.

Secondary schools in England are required to identify on their calendar five days a year for staff development when only teachers attend and pupils stay at home. These are commonly known as 'Baker days'. Each school decides how to organise these and, therefore, the format may differ from school to school. Often outside speakers are invited to talk to staff on whole-school issues, such as for instance how to raise achievement, followed by departments being given time to discuss the subject specific implications, e.g. how can the department improve mfl GCSE results for boys? These INSET days can provide useful information about school procedures and relevant issues but also allow NQTs to get to know established members of staff from other departments.

Reflection
Activity 13.5 'Who is who' at the new school?

During your induction programme try to find out the names of the members of staff listed in Table 13.1. Introduce yourself to them and find out about their responsibilities.

Table 13.1 'Who is who' at the new school?

Job title	Name(s)	Responsibilities
professional tutor		
school secretary		
resource officer		
heads of year/house		
GNVQ coordinator		
school nurse		
caretaker		
deputy heads: pastoral and curriculum		
Head teacher		
assessment coordinator/ examinations officer		
cover co-ordinator		

WORKING IN A TEAM

It is likely that NQTs join a team of professionals, who have worked together for a number of years, who have clearly defined roles and responsibilities and who follow well-established policies and procedures.

On joining the school, NQTs will have to work towards establishing themselves and becoming accepted members of the body of staff as a whole as well as members of specific teams, for instance at departmental or pastoral level (see also Capel 1997).

NQTs will have to earn the respect of colleagues and pupils and prove themselves by making meaningful contributions to the work of the school. In the main, experienced mfl teachers are very receptive to new ideas and inspiration from NQTs who, nevertheless, need to be aware that this is a two-way process. If an NQT is seen as a 'know-it-all' she might find it hard to be accepted.

One possible approach is to start with the areas of priority of the departmental development plan. Building on existing personal strengths, NQTs might take responsibility for specific issues identified as being in need of development. For example:

- a department might be keen to develop links with partner institutions abroad. Personal contacts with a school in the target country made whilst working there as a foreign language assistant (FLA) could be utilised by the NQT to set up a pen-friend or e-pal link or to develop educational (internet-based) project work; or
- a department might be keen to extend links with the 'world of work'. An NQT who has come into the profession with relevant work experience in business or industry might agree to build on her contacts and develop work-related mfl activities.

Various roles need to be assumed in team work and different responsibilities accepted. In order for teams to function well all necessary roles and responsibilities need to be taken care of. It might, therefore, be useful for NQTs to find out what roles they are suited for at a particular stage. Self-perception inventories such as the one suggested by F. M. Belbin (1981) might be a useful starting point for finding out about personal strengths and weaknesses in relation to the roles required in a successful team.

INTERACTING WITH PARENTS

An important aspect of the work of an mfl teacher is interacting with parents. The term 'parents' is used here to include carers.

Often communications with parents are channelled through form tutors or heads of year/house. It is important as an NQT to become familiar with and follow the procedures in place at the school for contacting and interacting with parents.

Parents' evenings provide a fruitful opportunity to give direct feedback to parents. Because not all trainee teachers have the opportunity to gain first-hand experience of parents' evenings during their training, the first parents' evening as an NQT can be the source of some anxiety. In order to make meeting parents as beneficial as possible, it is important to be well prepared. The anticipation of possible issues and the rehearsal of certain answers are useful strategies to which an induction tutor can contribute significantly, for example:

- Check your appearance. ...
- Greet parents formally. ...
- Whatever the circumstances, do appear to be concerned for the child and pleased that the parents have come.
- Never adopt a casual, off-hand, or flippant attitude towards the proceedings. ...
- If you have timed appointments keep *strictly* to your schedule. ...
- Make it clear to the parents that you know what you are talking about. Have some facts about the child at your fingertips. ...
- Don't invite obvious criticism by being behind with your marking. ...
- Always have *something* constructive and positive to say, even if your remarks must necessarily be heavily qualified. ...
- Try to advise the parents of something *they* can do.

(Wootton 1994:6–7)

Reflection
Activity 13.6 Interacting with parents

One of your responsibilities as an NQT will be to report to parents on pupils' achievement and attainment, both in writing and orally at parents' evenings.

As a preparation for this responsibility, consider the following scenarios. How would you react to:

- a parent who wants to know how they might help their child progress in mfl?
- a supportive single parent whose child's academic performance (including mfl) suffers from the recent divorce of her parents?
- a parent who wants to be convinced why his 14-year-old son has to continue to study mfl?
- a parent who is concerned about her child having been put into the bottom set?
- a parent who is concerned about a lack of/too much/difficult home-work? or
- a parent who feels her child is being picked on by you and given unfair detentions?

Prepare a line of argument and discuss it with a teacher in your placement department.

PERSONAL PORTFOLIO

The introduction of the induction period as well as the development by the TTA of qualifications and standards for various stages of teaching, such as qualifications for headteachers or standards for subject leaders, clearly demonstrates that qualified teacher status (QTS) is increasingly being seen as a 'beginning' qualification only, i.e. successful completion of a period of initial training is only the start in the course of the challenging and rewarding work of a teacher.

Job descriptions can provide a useful tool in the process of defining roles and responsibilities within mfl teams on the basis of personal strengths. They can also serve as an aide-mémoire and as the foundation for work on a portfolio of personal achievements and CPD, collecting evidence and documenting achievement when working towards the induction standards and/or in preparation for the next career move.

The personal portfolio might include outstanding features of the teaching or course file or details of and handouts from INSET courses or conferences.

If stored systematically, such evidence can be useful and relevant at various stages in an mfl teacher's career such as when applying for jobs, when preparing for appraisal discussions or when applying for accreditation of prior learning (APL) as exemption from parts of a higher degree or professional qualification.

BEYOND THE IMMEDIATE NEEDS OF AN NQT

After the initial period of settling into a new post – becoming familiar with the policies and procedures of the department and the school and getting to know new classes – and after having established themselves and successfully completed the induction period, many mfl teachers want to take on additional responsibilities and undergo CPD. Performance management can play an important role in this process and help with the identification of personal development needs. In most schools CPD is linked to the school and departmental development plans, which in turn often reflect issues identified in OfSTED inspections.

PERFORMANCE MANAGEMENT

Performance management has come into force in September 2000 and replaces appraisal, which was first introduced in the early 1990s but which was not always consistently implemented by schools. Maintained schools are required to have an agreed performance management policy in place by February 2001 – to which staff should be able to contribute – requiring every teacher, apart from those in their induction year or on a contract of less than a year, to set and review objectives annually together with their line manager. The DfEE (2000a) offers a model policy and recommends between three to six targets. It gives some specific examples of targets, such as raising the percentage of pupils attaining grade A at GCSE by 5 per cent a year for three years. The purpose of performance management is the establishment of a shared commitment to high performance and it needs to be seen as inextricably linked to schools' target-setting and evaluation procedures. Performance management can also be seen as part of the government's attempt to increase teachers' accountability and be linked to the threshold arrangements for performance-related pay. The procedures will, in most cases, not be very different to those they replace, with teachers and their line managers setting targets, monitoring progress and reviewing performance. The targets focus on pupil progress as well as on developing and improving teachers' professional practice. Classroom observation and meetings are integral parts of the monitoring and review procedures, which culminate in an annual report. This report is supposed to recognise a teacher's strengths and take into account contributory factors outside her control. Teachers can add their own comments to the report, which is confidential and 'should not be used as the basis for competency or disciplinary actions' (Duffy 2000:30).

The process is not unlike that of the induction year and enables the teacher to some extent to take responsibility for identifying factors which have a positive and/or negative effect on her work and how the latter might be addressed.

The periodical review of objectives can be regarded as an important part of a teacher's career development process.

DEVELOPING A CAREER PLAN

Once the development needs relating to the induction standards have been met, mfl teachers can start to develop a career plan. Personal career development needs to be carefully planned on the basis of individual interests and strengths. It has already been noted that target setting during the induction year and in the context of appraisal can play a useful part in identifying possible avenues for CPD.

The teaching profession offers wide scope for career development: (mfl) teachers can, for instance, aspire to expertise in teaching skills, subject area management, curriculum development, pastoral responsibilities or work with pupils with special educational needs. It is up to individual mfl teachers to consider and look for opportunities to gather experience in relevant areas such as post-16 or vocational mfl teaching, working as a form tutor or taking on extracurricular responsibilities such as organising exchanges.

The study for a higher degree such as an MA/MEd or PhD/EdD in an mfl-related or educational field is another possible way of developing professionally. Many higher education institutions offer such courses on a part-time as well as a full-time basis. The nature of these courses can be quite distinct. It is, therefore, worthwhile to 'shop around' for a course that suits personal requirements and caters for particular specific areas of interest.

Participation in courses and conferences might be an effective way not only of improving and updating subject-specific knowledge, skills and understanding but also to network with other professionals. Keeping in contact with colleagues from your initial training course might also be helpful at a professional level.

Where they are in post, LEA advisers and advisory teachers are possible external points of reference for support on curriculum development work and may well be involved in the assessment process during the induction year.

OfSTED INSPECTIONS

Office for Standards in Education (OfSTED) inspection visits to schools aim at identifying strengths and weaknesses of the work of teachers in a whole-school context with a view to improving the quality of education provided to pupils and the raising of standards.

Amongst other things, OfSTED inspectors (OfSTED 1995:70) evaluate the work of individual teachers in the context of their subject department and make judgements about the quality of their teaching against the following criteria:

- have a secure knowledge and understanding of the subject or areas they teach;
- set high expectations so as to challenge pupils and deepen their knowledge and understanding;
- plan effectively;
- employ methods and organisational strategies which match curricular objectives and the needs of all pupils;
- manage pupils well and achieve high standards of discipline;
- use time and resources effectively;
- assess pupils' work thoroughly and constructively, and use assessments to inform teaching;
- use homework effectively to reinforce and/or extend what is learned in school.

The OfSTED process can be built on meaningfully by individual teachers and departments by using the framework for inspection as a set of performance indicators for continuous internal review and as a basis for professional development. Inspection findings should inform the mfl department's action planning as well as the classroom practice of individual mfl teachers. In addition to inspection reports of schools, the OfSTED website available at *http://www.ofsted.gov.uk/* also features a number of useful documents providing guidance on the inspection process, for instance *Inspecting subjects and aspects 11–18: Modern Foreign Languages* (OfSTED 1999). Other relevant publications drawing on inspection findings include Alan Dobson's *MFL inspected* (1998).

OfSTED inspectors are required to compile a confidential report to the headteacher on particularly good or poor teaching.

MFL-RELATED DEVELOPMENTS

One of the characteristics of teaching as a profession is the need for teachers to keep up-to-date with the developments in an ever-changing educational world and their implications for classroom practice. CPD can be motivated by a number of factors.

As 'living organisms', mfl and their related disciplines invariably undergo changes that require the constant updating of the skills base of mfl teachers. In the process of their use as communicative tools, mfl invariably change over time. The year of 1996, for instance, has witnessed an official change in aspects of German orthography.

Ongoing research continues to push back existing boundaries of subject specialist knowledge and the understanding of the teaching and learning processes challenges teachers to keep up with developments in these fields.

Rapid technological innovations over the last few decades have not only been influencing teaching methodology greatly but have also brought with them new linguistic conventions. Multimedia, internet-based and computer-assisted language learning material are increasingly used in the mfl classroom and for personal use.

NQTs tend to be seen by experienced teachers as 'experts' in ICT and other fields. Depending on how ready they feel, such opportunities could be seized upon by NQTs to become proactive and organise in-house training sessions for the rest of the department or provide input to departmental meetings. There is, however, a danger in taking on too many extra responsibilities too soon.

For those with particular interest in mfl-specific career development, membership of a professional organisation such as, for instance, the Association for Language Learning (ALL; available at *http://www.languagelearn.co.uk*) or participation in local, regional or national networks facilitated by the advisory services of LEAs, local branches of professional organisations, CILT's regional Comenius Centres or higher education institutions (HEIs) might provide useful avenues.

Contact details and website addresses for national bodies, organisations and associations that offer support to mfl teachers, run mfl specific courses and conferences and/or provide other useful services/information can be found on the 'Contacts' page of the website accompanying this book available at *http://www.ioe.ac.uk/lie/pgce*.

In addition, regular reading of the national educational press such as the *TES*, which publishes a section on mfl a number of times a year, or the *Education Guardian*, which regularly prints TL features suitable for A-level teaching, as well as the exploration of useful internet resources can help in this respect. For details see the section 'Educational news and jobs' on the 'Pedagogy' page of the website accompanying this book available at *http://www.ioe.ac.uk/lie/pgce/*.

Another very useful source for information and inspiration are specialist publications such as books, journals and occasional papers published by professional and other organisations such as the bi-annual *Language Learning Journal* (ALL) or the annual *Studies in Modern Languages Education* (University of Leeds). In addition to mfl-specific literature there is a wealth of literature on (Teaching) English as a Foreign Language (T/EFL), which can be useful (in terms of methodological considerations).

INTERNATIONAL DEVELOPMENTS

In addition to changes at a national level, there are continually developments at an international level. This makes it necessary for the aims and objectives of national educational policy and the intended learning outcomes associated with them to be reviewed from time to time. The implication for mfl teachers is to keep up-to-date with these developments.

The identification in 1988 of a European Dimension as an aim in the education of young people by the member states of the European Community (EC) is, for instance, one of the more recent changes at an international level impacting on the everyday work of mfl teachers. Ever since, there have been many opportunities for mfl teachers to take part in CPD and/or joint educational projects with financial support of 'action programmes' under LINGUA and later SOCRATES and COMENIUS. The Central Bureau for Educational Visits and Exchanges (*http://www.britishcouncil.org/cbiet/*), which is now part of the British Council, is the national agency dealing with the many action programmes for which funding is currently available to (mfl) teachers such as:

- school partnerships for European education projects;

- in-service training, seminars and courses; and
- joint educational projects for language learning.

Participation in teacher exchange programmes, which are also organised by the Central Bureau, is another of the opportunities currently available to (mfl) teachers to deepen and update their knowledge in an increasingly complex educational world as well as to update their language skills base (see Capel and Pachler 1997: 267–8).

USING THE INTERNET FOR CONTINUING PROFESSIONAL DEVELOPMENT (CPD) AND ONLINE NETWORKING

Access to the internet affords mfl teachers ample opportunity to develop professionally as well as to communicate with colleagues from near and far, nationally and internationally.

One interesting way of networking with mfl professionals is to subscribe to an e-mail (discussion) list where mfl teachers exchange information and views about their teaching via e-mail, such as the 'Foreign Language Teaching Forum' available at *http://www.cortland.edu/flteach/* or 'LinguaNet' at *http://www.linguanet.org.uk*.

In order to learn about how to maximise the use of new technologies for foreign language (FL) teaching and learning, trainees should make use of the numerous interesting FL-related online tutorials, such as the one accompanying this chapter available in the 'ICT resources' section at *http://www.ioe.ac.uk/lie/pgce/*, and articles in specialist online journals. One notable example is the journal *Language Learning & Technology* available at *http://llt.msu.edu/*

The internet does, of course, also allow users to keep up with developments in the target countries and gives easy access to (authentic) materials, which can help them improve their own subject knowledge. The website accompanying this book at *http://www.ioe.ac.uk/lie/pgce/* offers a number of language-specific links under the headings of culture, education, language, literature, media and teaching.

Reflection
Activity 13.7 Using the internet for CPD

- Explore the internet sites available at *http://www.ioe.ac.uk/lie/pgce/*. Find one site that helps you improve your knowledge of language, one to deepen your knowledge of the target culture and one to develop your pedagogic skills.
- Set up a(n) (web-based) e-mail account, for instance using the multilingual service at *http://languages.zzn.com*, and subscribe to an e-mail discussion forum. Check your account from time to time and read the messages you receive. What new insights are you gaining?
- For your next assignment, look through some of the online journals listed on the "Pedagogy' page of the website accompanying this book available at *http://www.ioe.ac.uk/lie/pgce/* or carry out an internet search for relevant background reading. Can you find any relevant articles and sources?

THE FOREIGN LANGUAGE TEACHING FORUM

The Foreign Language Teaching Forum, FLTeach, at *http://www.cortland.edu/flteach/* is an academic discussion list. It is run by the State University of New York College at Cortland and moderated by Jean LeLoup and Bob Ponterio. The discussion list focuses on methods of foreign language teaching, the training of mfl teachers, classroom
activities as well as curriculum and syllabus design. Trainee teachers, experienced and less experienced mfl teachers, administrators and other professionals interested in any aspect of foreign language teaching are all able to participate.

At the time of writing you can join FLTeach free of charge by simply sending an e-mail to *LISTSERV@listserv.acsu.buffalo.edu* with the message 'SUBSCRIBE FLTEACH firstname lastname'. You will get a welcome message with instructions on how to use FLTEACH by return e-mail.

Once you have joined in this way, you can set your options. For instance, you can determine whether you want to receive individual messages or a digest, i.e. one single message containing all messages sent to the list during any one day. We strongly recommend you set up the digest option in order to control the volume of incoming mail. Don't forget to turn off FLTeach temporarily when you go on holiday. This is necessary because FLTeach is a very lively discussion forum. Otherwise you might find your inbox clogged with messages upon your return. The FLTeach website gives detailed instructions on how to set your options.

FLTeach membership is drawn from widely different institutions across the United States and around the world. Whilst you will find a certain bias towards US issues in discussions, in our experience a lot of interesting information is nevertheless to be gleaned through membership of FLTeach or similar discussion forums. FLTeach allows users to initiate discussions, seek information, resolve problems and share ideas, outlines, handouts and other teaching materials, syllabuses or suggestions for further reading. In essence, a discussion forum is a self-help group and participants can expect to get as much out of their membership as they are prepared to put in. It goes without saying that the tone of contributions should be supportive and in line with basic rules of netiquette. For guidance on netiquette, see the relevant page of the tutorial accompanying this
chapter available in the 'ICT resources' section of the homepage of the website accompanying this book.

In order to find out about the sorts of issues which are being discussed on UK-based e-mail discussion groups, have a look at the archives of the 'lingu@net-forum' available at *http://www.mailbase.ac.uk/lists/linguanet-forum/*. To actively contribute to the debate about mfl teaching in Britain, join the list.

SUMMARY

Obtaining a first teaching post cannot be left to chance. Various steps are involved. This chapter has shown that care in filling out application forms and in writing letters of application is needed to increase the likelihood of being shortlisted for a teaching post. It has also shown that preparatory work for the interview should enhance the chances of being successful on the day.

NQTs are required to successfully complete a period of induction and this chapter has briefly outlined what this involves.

In an ever-changing educational world the ongoing updating of personal skills, understanding and knowledge is important and can be seen as the professional responsibility of a qualified mfl teacher. It is up to the individual mfl teacher to seek opportunities for development. In this chapter we have identified various opportunities and sources for CPD, including those making use if ICT.

Epilogue: Modern Foreign Languages Teaching and Learning at 16 to 19

Modern foreign languages (mfl) teachers have faced numerous challenges over the last decade pertaining to changes to their clientele, teaching methods and assessment processes.

The Subject Criteria for mfl at GCE Advanced (A) and Advanced Subsidiary (AS), the guidelines used to draw up examination specifications (formerly syllabuses), have changed frequently in the last few years, most significantly at the beginning of 1997 and again in 1999 (see QCA, ACCAC and CCEA 1999). (For a detailed discussion of the 1999 criteria, see Pachler 1999c.)

These changes came about at least partly in response to Ron Dearing completing his review of qualifications for 16- to 19-year-olds in 1996, which resulted in the development of a new-style AS-level qualification to be taken by students at the end of Year 12 leading to the A-level at the end of the Year 13. The 1990s have also seen the advent of the National Language Standards (NLS) drawn up by the Languages National Training Organisation (LNTO, formerly Languages Lead Body [LLB]), which form the framework for vocational and professional accreditation at post-16 (see LNTO 2000).

OBJECTIVES

By the end of this Epilogue you should:

- have an appreciation of the general requirements of GCE A/AS-level compared to GCSE examinations;
- be aware of the main differences between GCSE and A/AS-levels from the point of view of both mfl teachers and learners; and
- know about the main features of vocational mfl accreditation at post-16.

As noted in the preface to this book, issues raised in this Epilogue are covered in detail in an accompanying volume entitled *Teaching and learning modern foreign languages at advanced level* (see Pachler 1999). Here we offer a summary and overview of pertinent questions with the main focus being on A and AS-level examination specifications with some references also being made to alternative, vocational routes.

GCE A- AND AS-LEVEL EXAMINATIONS

Recent trends in mfl education at 16 to 19

As could be seen in Chapter 1, Figures 1.1 and 1.2, the number of pupils entering GCSE examinations in mfl has increased significantly since the inception of the GCSE in 1988. The percentage of those achieving higher grades has also grown.

However, the success at meeting the demands of GCSE specifications does not always translate into a perception of success at preparing pupils for A/AS-level study. Indeed, John Thorogood and Lid King (1991: 2) comment:

> Today's complaint is that there is a 'gap' between the GCSE and the demands of A-level courses in modern languages. Somehow, somewhere along the line, GCSE has 'failed to prepare' the learner for the next stage up.

The explanation for the perceived lack of preparation of mfl study pre-16 for the requirements of A/AS-level courses therefore seems to lie in the difference in demands made on learners by GCSE and A/AS-level examinations. Statistics suggest that the positive trend concerning uptake and success rates at GCSE pre-16 was also prevalent at A/AS-level post-16 in the early 1990s. However, figures from 1993 onwards suggest a worrying decline in terms of uptake at post 16 in mfl (see Table E.1).

The decline in A-level uptake is due to a considerable decrease in the number of students choosing French – by far the largest group of mfl A-level learners – by 29.51 per cent between 1993 to 1999, with numbers for German holding up reasonably well, declining 'only' by 10.70 per cent. For Spanish, on the other hand, a noticeable increase of 23.17 per cent for the same period can be discerned.

Students who have opted to follow A/AS-level courses have become more diverse in ability and interests (see e.g. Coleman 1995 and Field and Lawes 1999). Their motivation and reasons for studying mfl have become more wide-ranging. Students taking A/AS-levels will not necessarily go on to study a modern foreign language at degree level. For many the mfl may be an additional A/AS-level, supporting other scientific, technological or commercial subjects.

Differences in demands of GCSE and A/AS-level examinations: an overview

Pupils following GCSE courses are, in the main, required to operate at a transactional level within (quasi-)communicative contexts in relation to defined content, i.e. clear

Table E.1 Number and results of GCE A-level candidates in modern languages

Number of GCE A-level candidates in French, German, Spanish and Italian (16, 17 and 18 year olds)

	French	German	Spanish	Italian
1992–93	25,215	9,548	3,767	429
1993–94	24,169	9,531	3,640	425
1994–95	22,909	9,218	3,595	443
1995–96	22,805	9,358	4,114	511
1996–97	21,326	8,970	4,318	548
1997–98	19,629	8,903	4,499	556
1998–99	17,775	8,527	4,640	556

Number of GCE A-level candidates in French, German, Spanish and Italian gaining grades A–C

	French	German	Spanish	Italian
1992–93	13,719 (54.41%)	5,483 (57.43%)	2,201 (58.43%)	295 (68.76%)
1993–94	13,373 (55.33%)	5,475 (57.44%)	2,300 (63.19%)	290 (68.24%)
1994–95	13,026 (56.86%)	5,386 (58.43%)	2,201 (61.22%)	332 (74.94%)
1995–96	13,265 (58.17%)	5,563 (59.45%)	2,583 (62.79%)	381 (74.56%)
1996–97	12,817 (60.10%)	5,445 (60.70%)	2,764 (64.01%)	425 (77.55%)
1997–98	12,229 (62.30%)	5,849 (65.70%)	3,050 (67.80%)	450 (80.94%)
1998–99	11,387 (64.06%)	5,600 (65.67%)	3,165 (68.21%)	467 (83.99%)

Number of GCE A-level candidates in French, German, Spanish and Italian gaining grades A–E

	French	German	Spanish	Italian
1992–93	21,811 (86.50%)	8,248 (86.38%)	3,282 (87.13%)	394 (91.84%)
1993–94	20,893 (86.45%)	8,384 (87.97%)	3,207 (88.10%)	402 (94.59%)
1994–95	20,125 (87.85%)	8,121 (88.10%)	3,161 (87.93%)	423 (95.48%)
1995–96	20,093 (88.11%)	8,337 (89.09%)	3,658 (88.92%)	480 (93.93%)
1996–97	19,065 (89.40%)	8,100 (90.30%)	3,908 (90.50%)	518 (94.52%)
1997–98	17,961 (91.50%)	8,217 (92.30%)	4,148 (92.20%)	533 (95.86%)
1998–99	16,372 (92.11%)	7,885 (92.47%)	4,323 (93.17%)	547 (98.38%)

Source: HEFCE 1999

parameters concerning the range of topics and structures as well as, at Foundation Tier, vocabulary to be used. Pupils are encouraged to work collaboratively through pair and group work, focussing on language use, which has communicative application.

A number of months elapse between sitting the GCSE examination and the start of the post-16 course. This break represents a discontinuity, which some departments try to overcome by setting preparatory work for prospective post-16 students. It also makes revision of GCSE work at the beginning of Year 12 very important.

At A/AS-level there are considerably more demands on students in terms of language generation and productive skills, such as essay writing and oral presentations, as well as receptive skills, such as reading extensively, which demand much greater implicit and explicit knowledge of grammar as well as knowledge about register and vocabulary. Students are expected to produce discursive texts on social, political and economic topics related to the target culture(s) as well as general knowledge. There are also considerably more demands in terms of students' ability to work independently and autonomously. The need to reflect upon teaching and learning and to understand the extent to which the learning processes help to meet the demands of developing key skills also adds to the demands for teachers and learners. Furthermore, there is the requirement of building opportunities to develop four of the key skills into schemes of work, namely communication, IT, improving own learning as well as performance and working with others.

Students are expected to know the relevant vocabulary associated with chosen topics, although this lexis is not actually defined. It can be difficult for students to prioritise which items of vocabulary they need to know, be it actively or passively.

Reflection
Activity E.1 Observing A/AS-level classes

Observe some A/AS-level classes.
- What differences in teaching methods can you observe in comparison to pre-16 classes?
- What knowledge, skills and understanding are required from students?
- What types of activities are students asked to carry out? How do they differ from those at Key Stages 3 and 4?

Reflection
Activity E.2 Discussion with A/AS-level students

Talk to a group of A/AS-level students in Year 12.
- Ask them what they have found difficult in the transition from GCSE to A/AS-level.
- What aspects of the course did they feel well prepared for?
What implication does this information have on the planning of the initial phase of A/AS-level courses?

Approaches to the study of mfl at A/AS-level are much less teacher-centred and demand a higher level of motivation from the student. The transition from dependence on the teacher to independence is a big challenge for students and mfl teachers alike (see Pachler and Field 1999).

The availability of documentary support

The transition from GCSE to A/AS-level can be just as challenging for the mfl teacher as for students.

Up to GCSE level, the mfl teacher is supported by the statutory framework and non-statutory guidance as well as, at Key Stage 4, by detailed examination specifications and past papers. Sample schemes of work for Key Stage 3 are available on the Internet, which inter alia provide guidance on the presentation and practice of grammatical structures. There are requirements/guidelines on what needs to be taught, why and to a degree, also how (see Chapter 10).

At A/AS-level there is noticeably less documentary support. Nevertheless, mfl teachers do have access to the subject criteria (QCA, ACCAC and CCEA 1999). They include aims and generic content for both AS and A-level as well as grade descriptions for each of the four assessment objectives of:

- understand and respond, in speech and writing, to spoken language;
- understand and respond, in speech and writing, to written language;
- show knowledge of and apply accurately the grammar and syntax prescribed in the specification; and
- demonstrate knowledge and understanding of aspects of the chosen society.

The subject criteria also include lists detailing the aspects of grammar expected at A and AS-level.

There are also examination specifications issued by awarding bodies, which inter alia prescribe grammatical structures in line with the guidelines of the 1999 subject criteria. These specifications identify a wide range of broad topics without specifying the lexis to be covered and there tends to be only a brief indicative content for some topics across cultural study and/or literature work.

In addition, mfl teachers can, of course, use past papers in preparing students and familiarising them with task types used in examinations.

Some awarding bodies have also drawn up guidance for the conduct of speaking exams.

Bridging the gap from GCSE to A/AS-level

Many mfl teachers are keen to teach at A/AS-level and often students embark upon their post-16 study with great enthusiasm. In order to avoid possible demotivation an awareness of the difficulties inherent in the transition from pre-16 to post-16 is important.

Given the differences in GCSE and A/AS-level, mfl teachers are often dedicating a considerable amount of time to bridging the gap between GCSE and A/AS-level. Figures E.2 and E.3 give an overview of the differences in GCSE and A/AS-level examinations in terms of functions and topics. Figures E.2 – E.4 have been drawn up on the basis of personal teaching experience and build on information extrapolated from the GCSE criteria, the A/AS-level Subject Criteria and various examination specifications. The information contained in these Figures does not purport to be exhaustive but is intended as a framework for devising a programme of work aimed at bridging the gap between GCSE and A/AS-level.

Reflection
Activity E.3 Bridging the gap to post-16: functions

Table E.2 details the language functions generally required for GCSE and A-level.
   Complete the centre column in a way that bridges the gap between GCSE and A-level requirements. Some examples have been provided for you.

Reflection
Activity E.4 Bridging the gap to post-16: topics and issues

The table in Table E.3 shows the progression from topics at GCSE to general issues at A-level. In order to help students broaden their range of understanding you need to provide a focus for study. Complete the centre column in such a way that there is manageable progression. Some examples have been provided for you.

Reflection
Activity E.5 A/AS-level topics

- Scrutinise a copy of the A/AS-level examination specification used at your placement school. Alternatively, look at Table E.3. How well prepared do you feel in terms of subject knowledge to teach the various topics?
- Discuss the programme of work students cover across Years 12 and 13 with the relevant mfl teacher(s) at your placement school. Which topics do the students cover? Do all students study the same topics? Are students allowed to choose some topics?

Table E.2 Bridging the gap to post-16: functions

GCSE	Progression	A level
Listening Understand specific details. Extract relevant information. Identify themes for points of view. Draw conclusions and relate ideas expressed by others. Follow instructions.	*State a personal reaction to a specific series of events.*	Recognition of the mood and emotions being expressed. Understand and participate in personal conversations, group discussions and debates. To extract key information to enable summary and oral and written responses.
Speaking Respond to closed and structured questions. Elicit information. Convey factual information. Respond to visual stimuli. Elicit and convey agreement and disagreement. Request basic services and products.	*Report on an event to more than one audience.*	To express full meaning by conveying facts, mood and emotion. To respond to other speakers in an appropriate register and tone. To initiate and sustain extended conversations and discussions. To elicit further detail by focused questioning. To express and justify opinions.
Reading Understand instructions. Extract relevant information from authentic texts. Identify themes or points of view. Draw conclusions. Relate ideas and themes contained within a text.	*Summarise the main arguments within a text, with support and guidance.*	Recognition of mood, emotions and appropriate register. To understand and respond critically to extended fictional and non-fictional texts. To recognise and react to themes, arguments, images and ideas expressed within authentic texts. To analyse and respond to arguments and points of view.
Writing Respond to given stimuli. Convey information. Express simple feelings and opinions. Report on real events.	*Respond by countering arguments presented in a short, authentic text.*	To summarise information and to expand upon detail. To translate and transcribe. To express ideas in a creative way. To generate and manipulate original language forms to develop coherent arguments and creative texts. To handle grammar and syntax implicit in all of the above.

Table E.3 Bridging the gap to post-16: topics and issues

GCSE	Progression	A level
personal identification and the family	*relationships with parents*	the generation gap and youth culture
house and home		economic and social conditions
geographical surroundings and weather	*local problems and issues*	urbanism, ecology and the Third World, environment, geographical topic
travel and transport		communications (infrastructure and the media) and the energy crisis
holidays		cultural diversity, festivals and customs
accommodation		living conditions
food and drink		consumerism, commercialism
shopping and services		consumerism, environment
health and welfare		health promotion, addictions
free time	*life styles of famous people*	leisure provision and opportunities
education and future career		professional life, responsibilities and education systems, minority groups
money		economic and political systems

Because topics do not, on the whole, feature in examination specifications as a finite, prescribed list with clearly defined lexis, coverage of content at A/AS-level is very complex. Departments need to judge carefully, for instance:

- how much time they ought to spend on any given topic;
- how many topics to cover in class and to what detail;
- whether to allow students to choose (some) topics according to personal interests;
- whether to prescribe topics according to the strengths of mfl teachers or the resources available;
- how much material to prescribe to students; or
- how much to rely on the research and self-study skills of students.

The focus on contemporary, up-to-date issues and stimulus material limits the amount of advance planning possible.

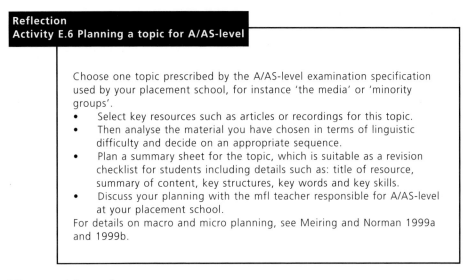

Reflection
Activity E.6 Planning a topic for A/AS-level

Choose one topic prescribed by the A/AS-level examination specification used by your placement school, for instance 'the media' or 'minority groups'.
- Select key resources such as articles or recordings for this topic.
- Then analyse the material you have chosen in terms of linguistic difficulty and decide on an appropriate sequence.
- Plan a summary sheet for the topic, which is suitable as a revision checklist for students including details such as: title of resource, summary of content, key structures, key words and key skills.
- Discuss your planning with the mfl teacher responsible for A/AS-level at your placement school.

For details on macro and micro planning, see Meiring and Norman 1999a and 1999b.

The teaching of grammar

Students' grammatical proficiency has emerged as a focal point for discussion. In recent years, some higher education tutors have expressed concern about the lack of grammatical awareness of their new undergraduate students (see e.g. Sheppard 1993 and McCulloch 1995 and 1996). There are also GCE examiners' reports that express concern about A/AS-level students' ability to generate grammatically correct language (see e.g. Metcalfe et al. 1995). In response it has been noted that the approaches to mfl teaching at degree level do not always reflect and build on the strengths of A/AS-level mfl students and that this might distort the perception of their level of preparedness (see Saunders et al. 1994: 10).

John Klapper argues that the apparent conflict stems from a misinterpretation of communicative language teaching. He puts forward the view that true communication denotes a high level of development predicated on a solid grasp of structure and lexis (see Klapper 1997: 27).

The fact that grammatical requirements have been made explicit in the Subject Criteria for mfl makes planning for grammatical progression and coverage of specification requirements much easier and this prescription of grammatical content sits more comfortably with the new GCSE criteria (see QCA 2000a) as well as the non-statutory schemes of work for Key Stage 3 (QCA 2000b), all of which feature increased explicit reference to grammar (see also Chapter 7). However, the gap between GCSE and A/AS-level in terms of understanding and application of grammar remains particularly difficult. Teachers need to build on existing knowledge and understanding, but should not put to one side aspects and concepts that do not follow coursebook models of presentation.

Because of the apparent differences of complexity of grammar use it is very important for A/AS-level mfl teachers to build on the tenets of the GCSE examination, namely of providing enjoyment and stimulation to learners, promoting an ability to communicate and developing confidence and proficiency within a foreign cultural context.

Table E.4 Bridging the gap to post-16: grammar (French)

	GCSE	AS level	A level
Nouns	gender, number and irregular forms contained within defined vocabulary list	nouns, unspecified but related to general issues	nouns, unspecified but related to general issues
Articles	all forms of direct, indirect and partitive articles	all forms including irregularities	all forms including irregularities
Adjectives	regular formation and position; irregular forms within a defined vocabulary list; possessive adjectives and recognition of comparatives and superlatives as lexical items	active knowledge of comparatives and superlatives, indefinite adjectives and position and formation of adverbs	position and agreement of all adjectives including interrogative adjectives; superlatives in concessive clauses
Pronouns	subject pronouns, recognition of object pronouns as lexical items; emphatic pronouns as lexical items and the recognition of interrogative and relative pronouns	active use of object pronouns, including correct positioning; use of disjunctive and relative pronouns	accurate use of direct and indirect object pronouns with correct past participle agreement; 'en' as a pronoun; use of demonstrative, indefinite and relative pronouns
Verbs and tenses	present indicative, perfect and immediate future; recognition of future, imperfect; past participle agreement with reflexive and 'être' verbs; active use of the imperative and the negative form of 'ne...pas'; recognition of the government of verbs and the present participle	active knowledge of imperfect, future, conditional, pluperfect, present subjunctive after 'il faut que'; all past participle agreements, government of verbs and the use of modal verbs; all negative forms including negatives with infinitives; recognition of the present subjunctive with expressions of fear, wishing, possibility and doubt	active knowledge of all tenses; use of the subjunctive in all tenses; all verbal agreements and inflections; use of the present participle and gerund; accurate use of verbs governing the use of the infinitive and all negative forms
Quantity	cardinal and ordinal numbers, dates and the time; basic expressions of quantity	fractions and dimensions	
Other	use of 'depuis' and recognition of common structures	use of conjunctions and complicated structures	use of idiom and complicated structures; conjunctions requiring use of the subjunctive
	Much of the grammar at this level is taught as lexical items and is implicit. The focus is on recognition and there is scope for the learning of paradigms and set phrases.	*At A/S level most knowledge should be active and explicit; additional items are added to the GCSE repertoire.*	*At A level all knowledge is assumed to be active to enable the generation and manipulation of language forms.*

In the light of the prescription of grammatical content, a systematic approach to linguistic structures throughout Years 12 and 13 seems all the more important. A consolidation of GCSE grammar during the first term of Year 12 (see e.g. Bond 1993) can lead to a systematic coverage of the required linguistic structures. A carefully formulated approach, where the teacher progressively adds grammatical knowledge to ease the transition from transactional language use to spontaneous TL use with the aim of enabling students to express opinions and ideas, can be seen to be consistent with the view that the language selected for the purpose of learning must be seen by the students to fulfil explicit and relevant objectives. Many commentators agree that progression in the understanding and application of grammatical structures is not a linear process (see Pachler 1999a and Jones 2000), which adds to the complexity of planning. Also, because of the paramount importance of the context in which the TL is encountered by students, i.e. mainly through authentic material at A/AS-level, grammatical progression is difficult to plan for.

The table in Table E.4 gives an example how, for French, the 'grammar gap' between GCSE and A-level might be bridged.

Reflection
Activity E.7 Bridging the gap
to post-16: grammar

> Where possible, compile a chart similar to the one in Table E.4 for German or Spanish by drawing on examination specifications, schemes of work and the 1999 subject criteria for A/AS-level.

Cultural awareness and general knowledge

Knowledge about and understanding of the target culture(s) should not be seen as separate from work on the TL. The development of ideas and the ability to formulate opinions about the target culture(s) go hand-in-hand with the learners' linguistic development.

The development of cultural awareness in students can be difficult for two main reasons:

- On the one hand there is a lack of specificity concerning the aims and objectives as well as the knowledge, understanding and skills required. The subject criteria for modern foreign languages require students at AS-level to 'develop critical insights into, and contact with, the contemporary society, cultural background and heritage of countries or communities where the modern foreign language is spoken' (QCA, ACCAC and CCEA 1999: 1). In addition, there is the requirement to 'explore and develop understanding of the contemporary society, cultural background and heritage of one or more of the countries or communities whose language is being studied' (QCA, ACCAC and CCEA 1999: 2). At A-level, students are, in addition, required to show 'a higher level of critical awareness' (QCA, ACCAC and CCEA 1999: 3). No further amplification is provided.

- On the other hand students' level of general knowledge and their knowledge about the target culture(s) is often limited at the beginning of Year 12.

Therefore, mfl teachers need to assume responsibility, particularly early in the course, for the selection of activities aimed at developing a deeper insight into and understanding of the target culture(s). The selection of appropriate texts, authentic material and the choice of topics requires extremely detailed, yet at the same time broad, subject knowledge on the part of the mfl teacher.

'Universal experiences of life' can be used to trigger meaningful intercultural comparisons. For examples of some useful techniques for teaching culture see e.g. Chapter 8, Anderson 1996 and Pachler 1999b.

Independent learning

Contact time with mfl teachers is limited. A/AS-level study involves usually up to six hours of 'contact time' per week and the same amount of independent study. Groups are often shared between different mfl teachers who, together, cover the syllabus requirements. It is important to ensure cohesion, continuity and progression.

The students need to assume responsibility for their learning from the very start of the course, but mfl teachers should not take this ability for granted. Students have to develop new study skills such as time management, learning strategies, personal organisation, use of reference material or research skills. Despite the importance of learner independence, mfl teachers need to oversee choices and decisions made by pupils throughout the period of study, but particularly at the initial stages.

Students need to be prepared to carry out the required preparatory as well as follow-up work and be proactive in order to maximise learning outcomes. For this reason, many teachers and commentators recommend the use of a learner diary as a focus for individual tutorial work with the teacher (see e.g. Field 1999: 52 or Pachler and Field 1999: 72).

Many awarding bodies offer a coursework component. This requires students to carry out independent work under the guidance of the mfl teacher. The advantage of coursework is that students can spend ample time on individual pieces of work and can make full use of reference material. The inherent danger is that they spend too much time on coursework to the detriment of other aspects of the specification. Due to the requirement for at least 20 per cent of synoptic assessment, through which students are required to demonstrate generic and cross-skill competence without the use of a dictionary, teachers need to ensure that students do not spend too long on their coursework throughout the period of study. Appropriate guidance from the mfl teacher can help minimise that risk.

Because of low numbers of mfl students in some schools and colleges, sometimes students in Years 12 and 13 are taught together for part of their contact time. This can complicate planning considerably. Where students are taught in a consortium of neighbouring schools, regular information exchanges of all mfl teachers involved in course delivery is very important.

The discussion in this section has shown that there are certain tensions between mfl teaching pre-16 and post-16 in A/AS-level contexts and that there is a significant demands made on both the students as well as the mfl teacher at post-16.

OTHER POST-16 ROUTES

Academic A/AS-level qualifications are not a suitable and/or desirable pathway for all mfl students at post-16 who want to (continue to) study a modern foreign language. The main alternative to academic A/AS-level study of mfl post-16 comes in the form of language units based on the national language standards (NLS) developed by the LNTO. The 2000 NLS (see LNTO 2000) specify criteria for assessment of linguistic competence at five levels of difficulty reflecting the needs of business and industry. The focus is on the use of mfl in the workplace. These units can be seen as a progression route for those students at post-16 who are interested in continuing with their modern foreign language from Key Stage 4 outside the academic route. They are also suitable if students wish to begin to learn a new modern foreign language.

NLS units can be taken as stand-alone units as part of the National Vocational Qualification (NVQ) framework or as optional and/or additional units on a range of General National Vocational Qualification (GNVQ) and Vocational A-level courses, such as Business or Leisure and Tourism.

These courses are frequently offered by secondary schools at post-16, are intended to provide a wider focus at post-16 than occupation-specific NVQs or academic A/AS-level. They are intended to offer a broad vocational qualification, which can lead on to employment of higher education. NVQs are work-related qualifications and focus on the ability to do a specific job well. For a detailed discussion see Lucas, 1997 or Lawes 1999.

'The NLS are generic or linguistically neutral, in that they apply to performance in any foreign language' (LLB 1995: 1). If taken as part of a general vocational qualification, language units are broad, covering general language (not dissimilar to GCSE requirements) and general employment language (vocational and business terminology and concepts). If taken as part of an NVQ, the focus is on general language coupled with specific occupational language (specialist vocabulary, expressions and concepts) (see Pachler 1997).

The focus of these units, which are competence-based, tends to be on a continuation of transactional language use in a broader range of contexts than at GCSE. The NLS range from predictable, simple everyday tasks to highly specialised ones across the language skills of listening, speaking, reading and writing. The descriptor for level two, for instance, requires:

> Competence in a limited range of language tasks, performed in familiar work and social contexts. Repertoire is equal to most routine language tasks and the user has sufficient grasp of grammar to cope with some non-routine tasks.
>
> (LNTO 2000: 23)

A voactional unit post-16 could, for instance, be Spanish – Level 2 Speaking 'Speak effectively' to deal with routine and daily activities':

> 2S1.1   Ask for information to carry out routine and daily requirements
> 2S1.2   Provide information to carry out routine and daily requirements
> 2S1.3   Establish and maintain spoken contact with others for routine purposes
> 2S1.4   Express spoken opinions on familiar and routine work and social topics.
>
> (LNTO 2000: 55)

This brief introduction alludes to the fact that vocational and/or occupational language units require from the mfl teacher knowledge of work-related vocabulary and technical terminology, an understanding of the processes involved in a given field of work, occupation or industry as well as different teaching strategies to be able to devise and deliver an appropriate programme of study and relevant assessment opportunities.

Reflection
Activity E.8 Planning activities for G/NVQ language units

> With reference to the scenario of a simulated work experience as assistant to a conference organiser, think of a number of situations which allow learners to show competence in any of the four performance indicators (2S.1–2S.4) listed above.
>
> For instance, for 2S.1 and 2S.2 learners might show that they are able to respond to an initial telephone enquiry by a prospective client giving details about the conference facilities available.

SUMMARY

In this Epilogue we examined some of the issues of academic as well as, to a lesser extent, vocational mfl teaching and learning at post-16.

The study of mfl at post-16 in one form or another can be seen to be a viable choice for students in post-compulsory education.

We have shown that there are certain tensions concerning the transition from pre-16 to post-16 in the academic route caused by differences in course requirements at both levels. These require careful planning by and due attention from mfl teachers.

The discussion of the vocational route has shown that there are challenges associated with respective mfl provision at post-16 for mfl teachers such as the need to understand work-related terminology in the TL and to be knowledgeable about work-related processes in the target culture(s).

Appendix

Table A.1 Lesson observation proforma

Lesson observation sheet			
Class:	Time:	Date:	Teacher:
Observation foci:		Comments:	
Time	Description of action		Reflection

Table A.2 Lesson planning proforma

Lesson plan			
Class:	Time:	Date:	Language:
Learning objectives			
Core		Extension	
Previous learning outcomes			
		Lesson … out of … .	
Resources required			

Time	Activities	PoS ATL
	Teacher · **Pupils**	
	Objectives	
	Plenary/summing up	

ICT		

Homework				

Evaluation	
re pupil learning	re own teaching

Action to be taken for next lesson

Table A.3 Lesson evaluation proforma

No.	Question	Response
1	Were my objectives for the lesson clear to me and did I achieve them?	
2	Did pupils know what they were trying to achieve at any given moment?	
3	Were my instructions clear?	
4	Were the material and lesson contents appropriate for the group?	
5	Did I cater for the range of abilities in the group? How?	
6	Do I need to re-think the order and structure of my lesson?	
7	Did I cope effectively with disruptions?	
8	Did I use the target language appropriately?	
9	Did everyone get the opportunity to participate?	
10	Did I help the more reluctant and less able to join in?	
11	Did I ensure that everyone was on task consistently and monitor their work?	
12	Were pupils alert, confident, enthusiastic or apathetic, uncertain, obstructive?	
13	Do I know what individual pupils' strengths and weaknesses are?	
14	Did I diagnose and assess pupils' difficulties? Did I respond to them?	
15	Did I comment on work, praising effort, achievement and accuracy and give encouragement?	
16	Do I know if the pupils learnt anything?	
17	Did I include pair/group work?	
18	Did I make good use of resources?	
19	Do I know all the pupils' names?	
20	Did I cover cultural awareness adequately?	
21	Did the pupils and I enjoy the lesson?	

Table A.4   Unit of work planning proforma

Unit of work planning		
Year:	Number and length of lessons:	
End-of-unit goal		
Learning objectives		
Core	Extension	
Main language items/structures		
Core	Extension	
Main materials and resources		
Main activities		**PoS ATL**
Core:		
Reinforcement:		
Extension:		
Main homework		
Assessment opportunities		
Continuous:		
Summative:		

References

Adams, J. (2000) 'It all ended in tiers'. In Field, K. (ed.) *Issues in modern foreign languages teaching*. London: Routledge, pp. 194–211.

Alison, J. (1995) *Not bothered? Motivating reluctant language learners in Key Stage 4*. London: CILT.

Allford, D. (1999) 'Translation in the communicative classroom'. In Pachler, N. (ed.) *Teaching and learning modern foreign languages at advanced level*. London: Routledge, pp. 230–50.

Allford, D. (2000) 'Pictorial images, lexical phrases and culture'. In *Language Learning Journal* (22). Rugby: ALL, pp. 45-51.

Anderson, J. (1996) 'Communicating culture – approaches to teaching about German re-unification'. In Shaw, G. (ed.) *Aiming high. Approaches to teaching A level*. London: CILT, pp. 58–69.

Arthur, J., Davison, J. and Moss, J. (1998) *Subject mentoring*. London: Routledge.

Barker, S., Brooks, V., March, K. and Swatton, P. (1996) *Initial teacher education in secondary schools: a study of the tangible and intangible costs and benefits of initial teacher education in secondary schools*. London: Association of Teachers and Lecturers.

Barnes, A. (1999) 'Assessment'. In Pachler, N. (ed.) *Teaching modern foreign languages at advanced level*. London: Routledge, pp. 251–81.

Batstone, R. (1994) *Grammar*. Oxford: Oxford University Press.

Bauckham, I. (1995) 'A Vygotskyan perspective on foreign language teaching'. In *Languages Forum* (4). London: Institute of Education, pp. 29–31.

Beaton, R. (1990) 'The many sorts of error'. In Page, B. (ed.) *What do you mean it's wrong?* London: CILT, pp. 38–47.

Belbin, F. M. (1981) *Management teams: why they succeed or fail*. Oxford: Butterworth-Heinemann.

Bennett, N. (1993) 'Knowledge bases for learning to teach'. In Bennett, N. and Carré, C. (eds) *Learning to teach*. London: Routledge, pp. 1–17.

Bennett, N. and Dunne, E. (1994) 'Managing groupwork'. In Moon, B. and Shelton-Mayes, A (eds) *Teaching and learning in the secondary school*. Milton Keynes: Open University Press, pp. 166–72.

Berwick, G. and Horsfall, P. (1996) *Making effective use of the dictionary*. London: CILT.

Bevan, V. (1982) 'The self-instruction video module: a solution in ESP'. In Geddes, M. and Sturtridge, G. (eds) *Video in the language classroom*. London: Heinemann, pp. 134–60.

Bialystok, E. and Hakuta, K. (1995) *In other words: the science and psychology of second-language acquisition*. London: BasicBooks.

Bimmel, P. (1993) 'Lernstrategien im Deutschunterricht'. In *Fremdsprache Deutsch. Zeitschrift für die Praxis des Deutschunterrichts* (8/1). München: Klett Verlag & Goethe Institut, pp. 4–11.

Biott, C. (1984) *Getting on without the teacher.* Sunderland Polytechnic: Centre for Educational Research and Development.

Bond, J. (1993) Chapter 4. In Bond, J., Darby, J., Hyland, S., Stockdale, S. and Tebbutt, S. *Aus eigener Erfahrung: von GCSE bis 'A' level.* London: CILT and Goethe Institut, pp. 83–103.

Booth, T., Ainscow, M., Black-Hawkins, K., Vaughan, M. and Shaw, L. (2000) *Index for inclusion: developing learning and participation in schools.* Bristol: Centre for Studies on Inclusive Education in collaboration with the Centre for Educational Needs, University of Manchester and Centre for Educational Research, Canterbury Christ Church University College.

Bourne, R. (1996) 'CD-Rom for language learning'. In *Information technology in modern languages teaching.* Studies in Modern Languages Education (4). University of Leeds, pp. 50–62.

Brandi, M.-L. and Strauss, D. (1985) *Training des Leseverstehens mit Hilfe von Sachtexten.* München: Goethe Institut.

Bromidge, W. and Burch, J. (1993) *In focus: the languages classroom. Learning to communicate.* London: CILT.

Brown, A. and Barren, P. (1991) *Post-16 European work-based activities.* Ipswich: Suffolk Euro-Links.

Brown, H. D. (1986) 'Learning a second culture'. In Valdes, J. M. (ed.) *Culture bound: bridging the cultural gaps in language teaching.* Cambridge: Cambridge University Press, pp. 33–48.

Bruntlett, S. (1999) 'Selecting, using and producing classroom-based multimedia'. In Leask, M. and Pachler, N. (eds) *Learning to teach using ICT in the secondary school.* London: Routledge, pp. 71–94.

Buckby, M. (1980) *Action 1. Teacher's book.* Walton-on-Thames: Nelson.

Buckland, D. and Short, M. (1993) *Ideas and strategies for homework.* London: CILT

Butler, M. and Kelly, P. (1999) 'Videoconferencing'. In Leask, M. and Pachler, N. (eds) *Learning to teach using ICT in the secondary school.* London: Routledge, pp. 95–108.

Byram, M. (1989) *Cultural studies in foreign language education.* Clevedon: Multilingual Matters.

Byram, M. (1997) *Teaching and assessing intercultural communicative competence.* Clevedon: Multilingual Matters.

Byram, M., Morgan, C. et al. (1994) *Teaching-and-learning language-and-culture.* Clevedon: Multilingual Matters.

Cambridgeshire LEA (1994) *Discovering dictionaries. Ideas for modern languages teachers by teachers.* Cambridge: Cambridgeshire County Council.

Capel, S. (1997) 'Working as part of a team'. In Capel, S., Leask, M. and Turner, T. (eds) *Starting to teach in the secondary school. A companion for the newly qualified teacher.* London: Routledge, pp. 137–48.

Capel, S. and Pachler, N. (1997) 'Opportunities for continued professional development'. In Capel, S., Leask, M. and Turner, T. (eds) *Starting to teach in the secondary school. A companion for the newly qualified teacher.* London: Routledge, pp. 257–69.

Carter, R. (1997) *Investigating English discourse.* London: Routledge.

Cassidy, S. (1999) 'IQ 'has no impact' on exam success'. In *TES*, June 18.

Central Bureau (1991) *Making the most of your partner school abroad.* London: Central Bureau.

Central Bureau (1993) *European awareness. Development projects 1990/91. Report No 2.* London, p. 4.

Central Bureau (1993) *Working together: the foreign language assistant in the classroom.* London: Central Bureau.

Chambers, G. (1993) 'Taking the de- out of demotivation'. In *Language Learning Journal* (7). Rugby: Association for Language Learning, pp. 13–6.

Chambers, G. (1999) *Motivating language learners.* Clevedon: Multilingual Matters.

Channel Four Schools (1995) *Working together.* Teacher's guide and video: *The foreign language assistant in the classroom* and *Strategies for group work.* Warwick: Channel Four.

Child, D. (1993) *Psychology and the teacher.* Fifth edition. London: Cassell.

Clark, A. and Trafford, J. (1996) 'Return to gender: boys' and girls' attitudes and achievements'. In *Language Learning Journal* (14). Association for Language Learning, pp. 40–9.

Coleman, J. (1990) 'Starting with satellite: a basic guide to using off-air video recordings in the language classroom'. In *Language Learning Journal* (2), pp. 16–18.

Coleman, J. (1995) 'The evolution of language learner motivation in British Universities, with some international comparisons'. In Wakely, R. et al. (eds) *Language teaching and learning in higher education: issues and perspectives.* London: CILT, pp. 1–16.

Coleman, J. (1996) *Studying languages: a survey of British and European students. The proficiency, background, attitudes and motivations of students in the UK and Europe.* London: CILT.

Convery, A. and Coyle, D. (1993) *Differentiation: taking the initiative.* London: CILT.

Cornell, A. (1996) 'Grammar: grinding or grounding?' In *German Teaching* (13). Rugby: ALL, pp. 26–9.

Crystal, D. (1997) *The Cambridge Encyclopaedia of Language.* Second edition. Cambridge: Cambridge University Press.

Cunningsworth, A. (1995) *Choosing your coursebook.* Oxford: Heinemann.

Dahlhaus, B. (1994) *Fertigkeit Hören.* Berlin: Langenscheidt.

Dakin, J. (1976) *The language laboratory and language learning.* Harlow: Longman.

Dam, L. (1990) 'Learner autonomy in practice'. In Gathercole, I. (ed.) *Autonomy in language learning.* London: CILT, pp. 16–37.

Dam, L. (1995) *Autonomy: from theory to classroom practice.* Dublin: Authentik.

Davison, J. (2000) 'Managing classroom behaviour'. In Capel, S., Leask, M. and Turner, T. (eds) *Learning to teach in the secondary school.* Second edition. London: Routledge, pp. 120–32.

Deane, M. (1992) 'Teaching modern languages to pupils with special educational needs? With pleasure!' *Language Learning Journal* (6). Rugby: Association for Language Learning, pp. 43–7.

Dearing, R. (1993) *The National Curriculum and its assessment.* London: SCAA.

Dearing, R. (1996) *Review of qualifications for 16 to 19 year-olds.* London: SCAA.

Denscombe, M. (1980) 'Keeping 'em quiet: the significance of noise for the practical activity of teaching'. In Woods, P. (ed.) *Teacher strategies.* London: Croom Helm.

Denton, C. and Postlethwaite, K. (1985) *Able children: identifying them in the classroom.* Windsor: NFER-Nelson.

DES (1989) *Discipline in schools. Report of the Committee of Enquiry chaired by Lord Elton* (The Elton Report). London: HMSO.

DES/Welsh Office (1988) *Modern languages in the school curriculum: a statement of policy.* London: HMSO.

DES/Welsh Office (1990) *Modern foreign languages for ages 11–16.* London: HMSO.

DES/Welsh Office (1991) *Modern foreign languages in the National Curriculum.* London: HMSO.

DfE/Welsh Office (1994) *Code of practice on the identification and assessment of special educational needs.* London: HMSO.

DfEE (1998) *Teaching: high status, high standards. Requirements for courses of initial teacher training.* Circular Number 4/98. London: DfEE. Also available at *http: //www.dfee.gov.uk/circulars/4_98/summary.htm*

DfEE (1998a) *National Literacy Strategy. Framework for teaching.* London: DfEE.

DfEE (1998b) *Health and safety of pupils on educational visits.* Suffolk: DfEE Publications.

DfEE (1999) *Circular 5/99: the induction period for newly qualified teachers.* London: DfEE. Updated May 2000. Also available at *http://www.dfee.gov.uk/5_99.doc*.

DfEE (2000a) *Performance management – guidance for governors.* London: DfEE. Also available at *http://www.dfee.gov.uk/circulars/dfeepub/jun00/060600/* .

DfEE (2000b) *The SEN Code of Practice.* London: DfEE. See also *http://www.dfee.gov.uk/sen/*.

DfEE/QCA (1999) *Modern foreign languages. The National Curriculum for England.* London: DfEE and QCA. Also available at *http://www.nc.uk.net* .

DfEE/QCA (1999a) *The National Curriculum handbook for secondary teachers in England. Key Stages 3 and 4.* London: DfEE and QCA

Dickson, P. (1996) *Using the target language: a view from the classroom.* Slough: NFER.

Dobson, A. (1998) *Mfl inspected: reflections on inspection findings 1996–97.* London: CILT.

Duffy, M. (2000) *Just more hoops to jump through?* In *TES* Friday, June 2, pp. 29–30.

Dunne, E. (1993) 'Theory into practice'. In Bennett, N. and Carré, C. (eds) *Learning to teach.* London: Routledge, pp. 105–19.

Edwards, S. (1998) *Modern foreign languages for all. Success for pupils with SEN.* NASEN

Ellis, G. and Sinclair, B. (1989) *Learning to learn English. A course in learner training.* Cambridge: Cambridge University Press.

Ellis, R. (1997) *SLA research and language teaching.* Oxford: Oxford University Press.

European Work Experience Project (1989) *European work experience pack.* London: ORT Resources Centre.

Evans, M. (1996) 'Entry barrier perpetuates status quo in language'. In *TES*. February 02, p. 24.

Field, K. (1999) 'Developing productive language skills – speaking and writing'. In Pachler, N. (ed.) *Teaching modern foreign languages at advanced level*. London: Routledge, pp. 184–208.

Field, K. (1999) 'GCSE and A/AS level teaching and learning: similarities and differences'. In Pachler, N. (ed.) *Teaching modern foreign languages at advanced level*. London: Routledge, pp. 33–59.

Field, K. (2000) 'Why are girls better at modern foreign languages than boys?' In Field, K. (ed.) *Issues in the teaching of modern foreign languages*. London: Routledge, pp. 134–45.

Field, K. and Lawes, S. (1999) 'The relevance of A/AS level courses to post-16 learners'. In Pachler, N. (ed.) *Teaching modern foreign languages at advanced level*. London: Routledge, pp. 7–21.

Field, K., Holden, P. and Lawlor, H. (2000) *Effective subject leadership*. London: Routledge.

Fisher, L. and Evans, M. (2000) 'The school exchange visit: effects on attitudes and proficiency in language learning'. In *Language Learning Journal* (22), Rugby: ALL, pp. 11–16.

Forth, I. and Naysmith, J. (1995) '"The good the bad and the ugly": some problems with grammar rules'. In *Language Learning Journal* (11). Rugby: Association for Language Learning, pp. 78–81.

Furlong, J. and Maynard, T. (1995) *Mentoring student teachers. The growth of professional knowledge*. London: Routledge.

Furstenberg, G., Levet, S., English, K. and Maillet, K. (2001) 'Giving a virtual voice to the silent language of culture: the CULTURA project'. In *Language Learning and Technology* (5/1), pp.55–102. Available at *http://llt.msu.edu/vol5num1/furstenberg/default.html* .

Furlong, J., Whitty, G., Miles, S., Barton, L. and Barrett, E. (1996) 'From integration to partnership: Changing structures in initial teacher education'. In McBride, R. (ed.) *Teacher education policy: some ssues arising from research and practice*. London: Falmer Press, pp. 22–35.

Gardner, H. (1983) *Frames of mind*. New York: Basic Books.

George, D. (1993) 'Meeting the challenge of the able child'. In *Topic* (10). Windsor: NFER-Nelson.

Gipps, C. (1994) *Beyond testing. Towards a theory of educational assessment* London: The Falmer Press.

Goleman, D. (1996) *Emotional intelligence: why it can matter more than IQ*. London: Bloomsbury.

Graham, S. (1997) *Effective language learning: positive strategies for advanced level language teaching*. Clevedon: Multilingual Matters.

Grauberg, W. (1997) *The elements of foreign language teaching*. Clevedon: Multilingual Matters.

Gray, C. (1996) 'Will your NQT use IT?' In *Language Learning Journal* (13), pp. 58–61.

Green, P. and Hecht, K. (1992) 'Implicit and explicit grammar: an empirical study'. In *Applied Linguistics* (13), pp. 168–84.

Grell, J. and Grell, M. (1985) *Unterrichtsrezepte*. Weinheim and Basel: Beltz Verlag.

Grenfell, M. (1998) *Training teachers in practice*. Clevedon: Multilingual Matters.

Griffiths, T., Miller, A. and Peffers, J. (1992) *European work experience: principles and practice*. Coventry: SCIP/MESP/EWEP (University of Warwick: CEI).

Griffiths, T. and Romain, L. (1995) *A teacher's guide to insurance and European work experience*. University of Warwick: Centre for Education and Industry.

Halliday, M. (1975) *Learning how to mean: explorations in the development of language*. London: Edward Arnold.

Halliwell, S. (1991) *Yes – but will they behave? Managing the interactive classroom*. London: CILT.

Halliwell, S. (1993) *Grammar matters*. London: CILT.

Harris, D. (1994) 'Learning from experience'. In *Languages Forum* (2/3). London: Institute of Education, pp. 33–5.

Harris, V. (1997) *Teaching learners how to learn. Strategy training in the ML classroom*. London: CILT.

Hawkins, E. (1984) *Awareness of language*. Cambridge: Cambridge University Press.

Hawkins, E. (1987) *Modern languages in the curriculum*. Revised edition. Cambridge: Cambridge University Press.

Hawkins, E. (1994) 'Percept before precept'. In King, L. and Boaks, P. (eds) *Grammar! A conference report*. London: CILT, pp. 109–23.

Heafford, M. (1990) 'Teachers may teach, but do learners learn?' In *Language Learning Journal* (1). Rugby: Association for Language Learning, pp. 88–90.

HEFCE (1999) Letter to Vice-Chancellors. December 17.

Hewer, S. (1992) *Making the most of IT skills.* London: CILT.

Hewer, S. (1997) *Text manipulation. Computer-based activities to improve knowledge and use of the target language.* London: CILT.

Hill, B. (1989) *Making the most of video.* London: CILT.

Hill, B. (1991) *Making the most of satellites and interactive video.* London: CILT.

Hill, B. (1999) *Video in language learning.* London: CILT.

HMI (1992) *The education of very able children in maintained schools.* London: HMSO.

HMI (1993) *Special needs issues. A survey by HMI.* London: HMSO.

Hornsey, A. (1993) 'The written word in oral language teaching'. In *Languages Forum*, vol. 1, 2/3. London: Institute of Education, p. 15.

Hornsey, A. (1994) 'Authenticity in foreign language learning'. In *Languages Forum* (2/3). London: Institute of Education, pp. 6–7.

Horsfall, P. and Evans, M. (1995) *Dictionary skills: French/German/Spanish.* Leamington Spa: Language Centre Publications.

Horsfall, P. and Whitehead, M. (1996) 'Exploring the Internet for post-16 language teaching and learning'. In *Information technology in modern languages teaching. Studies in Modern Languages Education* (4). University of Leeds, pp. 11–32.

Humphrys, G. (1995) *Getting a teaching job 1996. A guide to finding your first teaching appointment.* University of Greenwich: Careers Centre.

Hurren, C. (1992) *Departmental planning and schemes of work.* London: CILT.

Johnstone, R. (1988) 'Communicative methodology. Second generation'. In Kingston, P. J. (ed.) *Languages breaking barriers.* London: Joint Council of Language Associations, pp. 12–21.

Jones, B. (1992) *Being creative.* London: CILT.

Jones, B. (1995) *Exploring otherness: An approach to cultural awareness.* London: CILT

Jones, J. (2000) 'Teaching grammar in the mfl classroom'. In Field, K. (ed.) *Issues in modern foreign language teaching.* London: Routledge, pp. 146–61.

Jones, J. (2000) 'Teaching and learning modern foreign languages and able pupils'. In Field, K. (ed.) *Issues in the teaching of modern foreign languages.* London: Routledge, pp. 105–21.

Jones, N. (1996) 'A great buy with a little help'. In *TES Computers Update.* June 28, p. 30.

Kagan, S. (1988) *Co-operative learning: resources for teachers.* Riverside: University of California.

Kasten, J. (1995) 'Eine Insel in der Hauptstadt'. In *Education Guardian.* March, 21, p. 15.

Kavanagh, B. and Upton, L. (1994) *Creative use of texts.* London: CILT.

Kay, J. (1978) *Un kilo de chansons.* Cheltenham: Mary Glasgow Publications.

Kenning, M.-M. (1993) 'Diversification of mfl provision'. In *Studies in Modern Languages Education* (1). Leeds, pp. 1–20.

Kerridge, D. (1982) 'The use of video films'. Geddes, M. and Sturtridge, G. (eds) *Video in the language classroom.* London: Heinemann, pp. 107–21.

King, L. (ed.) (1991) *Graded objectives and the National Curriculum.* GOML News 15. London: CILT.

Kingman, J. (1988) *Report on the Committee of Enquiry into the teaching of English Language.* London: HMSO.

Klapper, J. (1991) 'The role of the video camera in communicative language teaching and evaluation'. In *Language Learning Journal* (4), pp. 12–5.

Klapper, J. (1997) 'Language Learning at school and university: the great grammar debate continues'. In *Language Learning Journal* (16). Rugby: Association for Language Learning, pp. 22–7.

Kolb, D., Rubin, I. and McIntyre, J. (1974) *Organisational psychology: an experiential approach.* Hemel Hempstead: Prentice Hall.

Kyriacou, C. (1986) *Effective teaching in schools.* Hemel Hemstead: Basil Blackwell.

Kyriacou, C. (1991) *Essential teaching skills.* Hemel Hemstead: Basil Blackwell.

Langran, J. and Purcell, S. (1994) *Language games and activities* London: CILT.

Lawes, S. (1999) 'Vocational alternatives'. In Pachler, N. (ed.) *Teaching modern foreign languages at advanced level.* London: Routledge, pp. 298–321.

Lambert, D. and Lines, D. (2000) *Understanding assessment. Purposes, perceptions, practice.* London: RoutledgeFalmer.

Lawes, S. (2000) 'Curriculum 2000 and modern foreign languages. Little change or fundamental shift?' In *Links* (21). London: CILT, p. 18.

Leask, M. (2000) 'Taking responsibility for whole lessons'. In Capel, S., Leask, M. and Turner, T. (eds) *Learning to teach in the secondary school*. Second edition. London: Routledge, pp. 78–9.

Leask, M. and Davison, J. (2000) 'Schemes of work and lesson planning'. In Capel, S. Leask, M. and Turner, T. (eds) *Learning to teach in the secondary school*. Second edition. London Routledge, pp. 66–77.

Leask, M. and Pachler, N. (eds) (1999) *Learning to teach using ICT in the secondary school*. London: Routledge.

Lewis, P. (1996) 'Pathways from Babel'. In *TES Computers Update*, June 28, p. 17.

Lightbown, P. and Spada, N. (1993) *How languages are learnt*. Oxford: Oxford University Press.

Little, D., Devitt, S. and Singleton, D. (1989) *Learning foreign languages from authentic texts*. Dublin: Authentik.

Littlewood, W. (1981) *Communicative Language Teaching*. Cambridge: Cambridge University Press.

LLB (1995) *Implementing the national language standards. A way to best practice*. London: LLB.

LNTO (2000) *The National Language Standards*. London: LNTO.

Lonergan, J. (1990) *Making the most of your video camera*. London: CILT.

Lucas, N. (1997) 'The changing sixth form: the growth of pre-vocational education'. In Capel, S., Leask, M. and Turner, T. (eds) *Starting to teach in the secondary school*. London: Routledge, pp. 211–31.

Macaro, E. (1997) *Target language, collaborative learning and autonomy*. Clevedon: Multilingual Matters.

Macaro, E. (2000) 'Issues in target language teaching'. In Field, K. (ed.) *Issues in modern foreign language teaching*. London: Routledge, pp. 175–93.

Macdonald, C. (1993) *Using the target language*. Cheltenham: MGP/ALL.

McCulloch, D. (1995) 'Where has all the grammar gone? An "accusative" search'. In *German Teaching* (12). Rugby: Association for Language Learning, 13–8.

McCulloch, D. (1996) 'What follows the revolution?' In Shaw, G. and Myles, S. (eds) *German grammar teaching in crisis?* Occasional Papers (4). London: Association for Modern German Studies, pp. 13–7.

McFarlane, A. (1996) 'Blessings in disguise'. In *TES Computers Update*. June 28, p. 4.

McLagan, P. (ed.) (1996) *The TES/CILT modern languages survey of secondary schools in England and Wales, Scotland and Northern Ireland*. London: CILT.

Meijer, D. with Jenkins, E.-M. (1998) 'Landeskundliche Inhalte – die Qual der Wahl? Kriterienkatalog zur Beurteilung von Lehrwerken'. In *Fremdsprache Deustch* 18(1). Stuttgart: Klett Verlag, pp. 18–5.

Meiring, L. and Norman, N. (1999a) 'Planning a programme of work'. In Pachler, N. (ed.) *Teaching modern foreign languages at advanced level*. London: Routledge, pp. 119–38.

Meiring, L. and Norman, N. (1999b) 'Planning an integrated topic'. In Pachler, N. (ed.) *Teaching modern foreign languages at advanced level*. London: Routledge, pp. 139–59.

Metcalfe, P., Laurillard, D. and Gates, P. (1995) 'The decline of written accuracy in pupils' use of French verbs'. In *Language Learning Journal* (12). Rugby: Association for Language Learning, pp. 47–59.

Miller, A. (1995) *Creativity*. Cheltenham: Mary Glasgow Publications and Association for Language Learning.

Mitchell, I. and Swarbrick, A. (1994) *Developing skills for independent reading* London: CILT.

Mitchell, R. (1988) *Communicative language teaching in practice*. London: CILT.

Mitchell, R. (1994) 'The communicative approach to language teaching. An introduction'. In Swarbrick, A. (ed.) *Teaching modern languages*. London: Routledge, pp. 33–42.

Molyneux, C. (no date) *Organising work experience: notes for guidance*. London: Central Bureau.

NALA (1988) *Using the foreign language assistant. A guide for schools and local education authorities*. Stafford: NALA.

NALA and Central Bureau (1992) *The foreign language assistant: a guide to good practice*. London: Central Bureau.

NCC (1989) *Special educational needs in the National Curriculum*. York: Curriculum Guidance.

NCC (1992) *Modern foreign languages non-statutory guidance*. York: NCC.

NCC (1992a) *Target practice: developing pupils' use of the target language*. York: NCC.

NCC (1993) *Modern foreign languages and special educational needs: a new commitment*. York: NCC.

Neather, T., Woods, C., Rodrigues, I., Davis, M. and Dunne, E. (1995) *Target language testing in modern foreign languages. A report of a project on the testing of reading and listening without the use of English.* London: SCAA.

Neil, P. (1997) *Reflections on the target language.* London: CILT.

Neill, S. (1993) *Body language for competent teachers.* London: Routledge.

Neuner, G. and Hunfeld, H. (1993) *Methoden des fremdsprachlichen Deutschunterrichts. Eine Einführung.* Berlin: Langenscheidt.

Norman, N. (1995) 'Initial teacher education in France, Germany and England and Wales'. In *Links* (12). London: CILT, pp. 5–7.

Noss, R. and Pachler, N. (1999) 'The challenge of new technologies. Doing old things in a new way, or doing new things?' In Mortimore, P. (ed.) *Understanding pedagogy and its impact on learning.* London: Sage, pp. 195–211.

Nuffield Languages Inquiry (2000) *Languages: the next generation. Final report and recommendations.* London: The Nuffield Foundation.

Nunan, D. (1989) *Designing tasks for the communicative classroom.* Cambridge: Cambridge University Press.

Nunan, D. and Lamb, C. (1996) *The self-directed teacher. Managing the learning process.* Cambridge: Cambridge University Press.

Oliver, M. (1994) 'Question-and-answer revisited: introducing reflexive verbs in German'. In *Languages Forum* (2/3). London: Institute of Education, pp. 16–18.

OfSTED (1995) *Guidance on the inspection of secondary schools. The OfSTED Handbook.* London: HSMO.

OfSTED (1999) *Inspecting subjects and aspects 11–18: modern foreign languages.* London: OfSTED. Available at *http://www.ofsted.gov.uk/public/docs00/11-18/modlang.pdf* .

OfSTED (2000) *National summary data report for secondary schools (PICSI & PANDA Annex).* London: OfSTED. Available at *http:///www.ofsted.gov.uk/public/docs00/2000secondarynsdr.pdf* .

O'Malley, B. (1996) 'Drive on languages runs out of steam'. In *TES.* February 02, p. 10.

Oxford, R. (1987) *Language learning strategies. What every teacher should know.* Boston: Heinle and Heinle.

Pachler, N. (1994) 'Teacher assessment of modern foreign languages in the National Curriculum'. In *Studies in Modern Languages Education* (2). University of Leeds, pp. 27–42.

Pachler, N. (1997) 'Modern foreign languages and vocational contexts'. In *Studies in Modern Languages Education* (5). Leeds, pp. 1–37.

Pachler, N. (ed.) (1999) *Teaching modern foreign languages at advanced level.* London: Routledge.

Pachler, N. (1999a) 'Teaching and learning grammar'. In Pachler, N. (ed.) *Teaching modern foreign languages at advanced level.* London: Routledge, pp. 93–115.

Pachler, N. (1999b) 'Teaching and learning culture'. In Pachler, N. (ed.) *Teaching modern foreign languages at advanced level.* London: Routledge, pp. 76–92.

Pachler, N. (1999c) 'The new A/AS level'. In Pachler, N. (ed.) *Teaching modern foreign languages at advanced level.* London: Routledge, pp. 22–30.

Pachler, N. (1999d) 'Theories of learning and Information and Communications Technology'. In Leask, M. and Pachler, N. (eds) *Learning to teach using ICT in the secondary school.* London: Routledge, pp. 3–18.

Pachler, N. (1999e) 'Using the internet as a teaching and learning tool'. In Leask, M. and Pachler, N. (eds) *Learning to teach using ICT in the secondary school.* London: Routledge, pp. 51–70.

Pachler, N. (2000a) 'Re-examining communicative language teaching'. In Field, K. (ed.) *Issues in modern foreign language teaching.* London: Routledge, pp. 26–41; pp. 22–37.

Pachler, N. (2000b) 'Secondary education'. In Byram, M. (ed.) *Encyclopedia of language teaching and learning.* London: Routledge, pp. 534–9.

Pachler, N. (2001) 'Connecting schools and pupils: to what end? Issues related to the use of ICT in school-based learning'. In Leask, M. (ed.) *Using ICT in schools: key issues.* London: Routledge.

Pachler, N. and Field, K. (1999) 'Learner independence'. In Pachler, N. (ed.) *Teaching modern foreign languages at advanced level.* London: Routledge, pp. 60–75.

Pachler, N. and Field, K. (2001) 'From mentor to co-tutor: re-conceptualising secondary modern foreign languages initial teacher education'. In *Language Learning Journal* (23). Rugby: ALL; and *Studies in Modern Languages Education* (9), University of Leeds.

Pachler, N. with Bond, J. (1999) 'Teaching and learning grammar'. In Pachler, N. (ed.) *Teaching modern foreign languages at advanced level.* London: Routledge, pp. 93–115'

Pachler, N. with Reimann, T. (1999) 'Reaching beyond the classroom'. In Pachler, N. (ed.) *Teaching modern foreign languages at advanced level.* London: Routledge, pp. 282–97.

Page, B. (1989) 'Language learning – objectives and forms of assessment. GOML submission to the National Curriculum Working Group'. In King, L. (ed.) *Graded objectives and TVEI.* GOML News 14. London: CILT.

Page, B. (1990) 'Why do I have to get it right anyway?' In Page, B. (ed.) *What do you mean it's wrong?* London: CILT, pp. 102–6.

Page, B. (ed.) (1992) *Letting go – taking hold. A guide to independent language learning by teachers for teachers.* London: CILT.

Page, B. and Hewett, D. (1987) *Languages step by step. Graded objectives in the UK.* London: CILT.

Page, R. (1997) *Working with your foreign language assistant.* Cheltenham: Mary Glasgow Publications/ Association for Language Learning.

Parkinson, B. (1992) 'Observing foreign language lessons'. In *Language Learning Journal* (5). Rugby: Association for Language Learning, pp. 20–4.

Passmore, B. (1996) 'The English start late and drop out early'. In *TES.* February 02, p. 11.

Pearson, J. (1990) 'Putting pupils in the picture: using the video camera'. *In Language Learning Journal* (2), pp. 71–2.

Peterson, M. (1997) 'Language teaching and networking'. In *System* (25/1), pp. 29–37. Also available at: *http://www.jaist.ac.jp/~mark/articlenetworking.html*

Pillette, M. (1996) *Developing dictionary skills in French.* Glasgow: Collins Educational.

Powell, B. (1999) 'Developing receptive language skills – listening and reading'. In Pachler, N. (ed.) *Teaching modern foreign languages at advanced level.* London: Routledge, pp. 160–83.

Powell, B., Barnes, A. and Graham, S. (1996) *Using the target language to test modern foreign language skills. A report on research conducted in 12 secondary schools.* University of Warwick.

Pugh, N. and Murphy, B. (1993) *Steps towards achievement.* Colchester: Essex Development and Advisory Service.

QCA (2000a) *GCSE Criteria for modern foreign languages.* London: QCA.

QCA (2000b) *Schemes of work: secondary modern foreign languages.* London: QCA. Also available at: *http://www.standards.dfee.gov.uk/schemes/.*

QCA, ACCAC and CCEA (1999) *GCE advanced subsidiary and advanced level specifications subject criteria for modern foreign languages.* London: QCA, ACCAC and CCEA. Also available at *http://www.qca.org.uk/ nq/subjects/mfl.asp.*

Rampillon, U. (1989) *Lerntechniken im Fremdsprachenunterricht. Handbuch.* München: Hueber.

Rampillon, U. (1994) *Lerntechniken im Fremdsprachenunterricht.* Second edition. München: Hueber.

Redondo, A. (2000) 'Mixed ability grouping in modern foreign languages teaching'. In Field, K. (ed.) *Issues in modern foreign languages teaching.* London: Routledge, pp. 122–33.

Reeves, N. (1986) 'Why German?' In CILT (ed.) *German in the United Kingdom. Issues and opportunities.* London, pp. 1–12.

Richards, J. and Rodgers, T. (1986) *Approaches and methods in language teaching. A description and analysis.* Cambridge: Cambridge University Press.

Rivers, W. ([1975]1988) *Teaching French: a practical guide.* Illinois: National Textbook Company.

Roberts, J. (1998) *Language teacher education.* London: Arnold.

Roberts, T. (1992) *Towards a learning theory in modern languages.* Occasional Paper No. 2. London: Institute of Education.

Robertson, J. (1989) *Effective classroom control: understanding pupil/teacher relationships.* London: Hodder and Stoughton.

Rogers, C. (1982) *A social psychology of schooling: the expectancy process.* London: Routledge and Kegan Paul.

Rowles, D., Carty, M. and McLachlan, A. (1998) *The foreign language assistant. A guide to good practice.* London: CILT.

RSA (1996) *GNVQ language units approved for Key Stage 4. German Syllabus.* Coventry: RSA.

Rumley, G. and Sharpe, K. (1993) 'Generalisable game activities in modern language learning'. In *Language Learning Journal* (8). Rugby: Association for Language Learning, pp. 35–8.

Rutherford, W. (1987) *Second language grammar: learning and teaching.* London: Longman.

SCAA (1994) *Modern foreign languages in the National Curriculum. Draft proposals.* London.

SCAA/ACAC (1996 and 1997) *Consistency in teacher assessment: exemplification of standards. Modern foreign languages. Key Stage 3.* London: SCAA/ACAC.

SEAC (1992) *Modern Foreign Languages: teacher assessment at Key Stage 3.* London.

Selinger, M. (1999) 'ICT and classroom management'. In Leask, M. and Pachler, N. (eds) *Learning to teach using ICT in the secondary school.* London: Routledge, pp. 36–50.

Shaw, P. (1994) ' Reluctant learners: – you can do it!' In McLagan, P. (ed.) *Steps to learning. Modern languages for pupils with special educational needs.* London: CILT, pp. 35–9

Sheppard, R. (1993) 'Getting down to brass syntax: German teaching and the Great Standards Debate'. In *German Teaching* (8). Rugby: Association for Language Learning, pp. 2–9.

Snow, D. and Byram, M. (1997) *Crossing frontiers. The school study visit abroad.* London: CILT.

Swaffar, J. and Vlatten, A. (1997) 'A sequential model for video viewing in the foreign language curriculum'. In *The Modern Language Journal* (81/ii), pp. 175–84.

Tabberer, R. (1996) *Teachers make a difference.* Slough: NFER.

Taylor, W. (1994) 'Classroom variables'. In Moon, B. and Shelton-Mayes, A. (eds) *Teaching and learning in the secondary school.* Milton Keynes: Open University Press, pp. 161–5.

Thorogood, J. and King, L. (1991) *Bridging the gap: GCSE to A level.* London: CILT.

Tierney, D. and Humphreys, F. (1992) *Improve your image. The effective use of the OHP.* London: CILT.

Tolley, H., Biddulph, M. and Fisher, T. (1996) *Pre-entry to first teaching post.* Beginning teaching workbook 4. Cambridge: Chris Kington Publishing.

Townshend, K. (1997) *E-mail. Using electronic communications in foreign language teaching.* London: CILT.

TTA (1999) *The use of ICT in subject teaching. Identification of training needs: secondary modern foreign languages.* London: TTA.

TTA (1999a) *Supporting induction. Materials to support the implementation of national induction arrangements for newly qualified teachers.* London: TTA. Also available at *http://www.canteach.gov.uk/info/library/suppind1.pdf* .

Tunstall, P. and Gipps, C. (1996) 'Teacher feedback to young children in formative assessment: a typology'. In *British Educational Research Journal* (4/22). Abingdon: Carfax, pp. 389–404.

Turner, K. (1995) *Listening in a foreign language. A skill we take for granted?* London: CILT

Turner, K. (1996) 'The National Curriculum and syllabus design'. In *Language Learning Journal* (14). Rugby: Association for Language Learning, pp. 14–8.

Turner, T. (2000) 'Differentiation, progression and pupil grouping'. In Capel, S., Leask, M. and Turner, T. (eds) *Learning to teach in the secondary school: a companion to school experience.* London: Routledge, pp 134–50.

Turner, T. with Field, K. and Arthur, J. (1997) 'Working with your mentor'. In Capel, S., Leask, M. and Turner, T. (eds) *Starting to teach in the secondary school. A companion for the newly qualified teacher.* London: Routledge, pp. 26–39.

Wajnryb, R. (1992) *Classroom observation tasks: a resource book for language teachers and trainers.* Cambridge: Cambridge University Press.

Warnock, M. (1978) *Report on the Committee of Enquiry into the Education of Handicapped Children and Young People.* London: HMSO.

Warschauer, M. (1997) 'Computer-mediated collaborative learning: theory and practice'. In *The Modern Language Journal* (81/iv), pp.470–81. Also available at: *http://www.gse.uci.edu/markw/cmcl.html*

Watkins, C. (1999) *Managing classroom behaviour: from research to diagnosis.* London: Institute of Education in association with the Association of Teachers and Lecturers.

Watkins, C., Carnell, E., Lodge, C., Wagner, P. and Whalley, C. (2000) *Learning about learning. Resources for supporting effective learning.* London: RoutledgeFalmer.

Westgate, D., Batey, J. Brownlee, J. Butler, M. (1985) 'Some characteristics of interaction in foreign language classrooms'. In *British Educational Research Journal* (11/3), pp. 271–81.

Wilkins, D. (1976) *Notional syllabuses.* Oxford: Oxford University Press.

Wilkinson, J. (1994) 'Self-access learning by German for business students: what role the tutor?' In Myles, S. (ed.) *German for special purposes*. Studies Occasional Papers 2. London: Association for Modern German, pp. 12–26.

Williams, E. (1982) 'The 'witness' activity: group interaction through video'. In Geddes, M. and Sturtridge, G. (eds) *Video in the Language Classroom*. London: Heinemann, pp. 69–73.

Wootton, M. (1994) *Meeting parents. Practical advice for the new teacher.* Upmister: Nightingale Teaching Consultancy.

Wragg, T. (ed.) (1984) *Classroom teaching skills.* London: Croom Helm.

Wringe, C. (1994) 'Ineffective lessons: reasons and remedies. Jottings from the tutor's notepad'. In *Language Learning Journal* (10). Rugby: Association for Language Learning, pp. 11–4.

Wringe, C. (1989) *The effective teaching of modern languages.* London: Longman.

Yaxley, B. (1994) *Developing teachers' theories of teaching: a touchstone approach.* Brighton: Falmer Press.

Index